Nazis in Pre-War London
1930–1939

# Nazis in Pre-War London
# 1930–1939

*The Fate and Role of German Party Members
and British Sympathizers*

James J. Barnes and Patience P. Barnes

sussex
ACADEMIC
PRESS

BRIGHTON • PORTLAND

2 4 6 8 10 9 7 5 3 1

*First published 2005 in Great Britain by*
SUSSEX ACADEMIC PRESS
Box 2950
Brighton BN2 5SP

*and in the United States of America by*
SUSSEX ACADEMIC PRESS
920 NE 58th Ave          Suite 300
Portland, Oregon 97213-3786

*British Library Cataloguing in Publication Data*
A CIP catalogue record for this book is available from the British Library.

*Library of Congress Cataloging-in-Publication Data*
Barnes, James J.
    Nazis in pre-war London, 1930–1939 : the fate and role of German party
    members and British sympathizers / James J. Barnes and Patience P. Barnes.
        p. cm.
    Includes bibliographical references and index.
    ISBN 1-84519-053-X (hardcover : alk. paper)
    1. Germans—England—London—History—20th century. 2. Germany—
Foreign public opinion, British—History—20th century. 3. Espionage,
German—England—London—History—20th century. 4. London
(England)—Ethnic relations—History—20th century. 5. Public opinion—
England—London—History—20th century. 6. Deportation—Great
Britain—History—20th century. 7. Nazis—England—London—History—
20th century. 8. London (England)—History—1800–1950. 9. Great
Britain—Relations—Germany. 10. Germany—Relations—Great Britain.
    I. Barnes, Patience P.   II. Title.
DA676.9.G47B37   2005
942.1083′088′320533—dc22

                                                            2005005581

Typeset & Designed by G&G Editorial, Brighton & Eastbourne
Printed by TJ International, Padstow, Cornwall
This book is printed on acid-free paper.

# CONTENTS

# PREFACE

This book seeks to answer a number of questions concerning the activities of Nazi Germans in London prior to World War II. Who were they? What were they doing in London? How many of them were there, and how long did they stay? Were they mostly professional espionage agents, or simply Germans living and working in Britain? Once war broke out, were they interned or expelled?

These are merely some of the issues we explore in this volume. Our focus is on German citizens who were members of the NSDAP and, for whatever reasons, were in London before World War II. We take note of British Fascists, but mainly because of their contacts with Nazi Party Members. In other words, this is not just another book about Fascism in Britain, but rather a study of a particular segment of Nazis about whom virtually nothing has previously been written.

The saga begins in September 1930 when the Nazi Party newspaper, the *Völkischer Beobachter*, sent its first representative to London. This took place more than two years before Hitler became Chancellor, and testified to the growing strength of the Party in Germany following the electoral gains earlier that year. Not long afterwards some of the German residents in London established an *Ortsgruppe*, or local Nazi group, which provided Party members with a place to congregate with like-minded Germans and share their enthusiasm for the new movement. By 1933 more than 100 members of the German community in London had joined the London *Ortsgruppe*, drawn from churches, clubs, business, education, and the arts.

In 1935 the British Home Office became concerned about the many German journalists admitted into England, and ordered the expulsion of one of them who had come to London five years earlier. Their presence in London raised suspicions that a network of Nazis might possibly be organizing in the country. Eventually, they were the first targets for deportation.

British tourists were encouraged to visit Hitler's New Germany, while Nazi sympathizers came to the United Kingdom to deflect criticism of Germany and extol its virtues. German cultural exports abounded. There were public readings by German poets, theater productions, musical performances, and artists' exhibitions, all geared towards fostering an image of Germany as the cradle of European civilization.

Perhaps the Nazi's most significant task was to put pressure on Germans in London who were not yet members of the Party. The British authorities took a very dim view of this because they viewed it as harassment.

The Foreign Office and the Home Office disagreed as to how to deal with resident aliens whose allegiance was to the Nazi Party and the German Reich. Some felt that all Nazi organizations abroad should be banned, and that Party Members should not be allowed to enter the United Kingdom. Others, including MI5, argued that it would be easier to keep track of them if they were let alone; then, if war broke out, they could be rounded up more efficiently for internment. Most of the internal discussions between government departments dealing with these problems have, until now, not been published.

Also unknown until the captured German documents were released after the war, was the fate of the German diplomats, businessmen, journalists, teachers, and other professionals who were in England when war broke out on 3 September 1939. Some were permitted to return to Germany, while others came under arrest and were interned indefinitely in Britain.

The Appendix lists the names, addresses, birth dates, occupations, years spent in England, Party numbers, dates of joining the NSDAP, and whether they were interned, for the 400 Germans who lived in Britain before the war and were members of the NSDAP.

One theme echoes throughout this volume: nazification. Increasingly during the 1930s Hitler sought to control all Nazi Party members both at home and abroad. In the chapters that follow we see how this was accomplished under tight Party discipline, even without communicating directly with Germany or obviously involving themselves in local British politics. Instead, they were urged to take an active role in the larger German community in London by joining clubs, business groups, churches, social gatherings, and veterans' activities. Gradually they dominated all aspects of daily living to the detriment of non-Party Germans and refugees.

Nazification ultimately led the British authorities to deport leading members of the Party as well as others they considered subversive.

This book sets out to explore the many and complicated facets of this process as it affected British society.

# ACKNOWLEDGMENTS

Since beginning the research for this book, there have been countless individuals and many institutions advising and helping us. The following stand out as particularly crucial. To all, we owe hearty thanks.

Auswärtiges Amt, Bonn, and its Archivist, Dr. Maria Keipert, for continuing assistance over the years.

Public Record Office, Kew: for the unfailing cooperation of many members of the library and security staff.

National Archives, Washington, DC, and College Park, Maryland: for substantial help answering queries both in person and by post; and supplying reams of microfilm. Special thanks to Robert Wolfe and John Mendelsohn.

Berlin Document Center: for responding to our many enquiries and requests for photocopies, as well as guiding our research on those occasions when we were in Berlin. Special thanks to Herr Pix.

Libraries and Archives: among the many we consulted either by mail or in person, we are grateful to the Bundesarchiv, Koblenz; Bayerische Staatsbibliotek, Munich; Zentrales Staatsarchiv, Potsdam; Foreign and Commonwealth Office Library, London; the Home Office Library and John Lloyd; Library of the Frei Universität, Berlin; Institut für Zeitgeschichte, Munich.

Hoover Institution, Stanford, California, for graciously microfilming many documents in their collection.

Lilly Library of Wabash College, Crawfordsville, Indiana, whose staff has been unfailingly helpful, especially Deborah Polley, for securing countless items through inter-library loan, and Jeffrey Beck, the Reference Librarian, for patiently searching for answers to our numerous queries.

Wabash College Computer Services, for guiding us through the hazards of information technology, especially Michael Heinold and Jeana Rogers.

Wiener Library, London, for access to their most valuable collection of newspaper cuttings and pamphlets.

Neville G. Brown, for encouraging and facilitating the publication of this volume.

ACKNOWLEDGMENTS

Stefan Kreisher, for many years of reliable and effective assistance with German language documents.

Daniel R. Zajac, for accompanying us on research trips throughout Germany, as well as sorting and translating German language materials.

Donald Cameron Watt, for always taking a keen interest in our research.

Michael R. D. Foote, for his longstanding encouragement, and being ever ready to discuss all topics related to intelligence.

Gerhard Hirschfeld, for timely advice early in our research.

Robert Cecil, for valued information about Alfred Rosenberg.

Christel Converse, for her adept navigation through Nazi Party files at the National Archives, Washington, DC.

Bridgie B. Brelsford, for her longstanding friendship and masterly indexing and proof-reading of our work.

# ABBREVIATIONS

| | |
|---|---|
| BDC | Berlin Document Center, recently renamed Bundesarchiv III, Aussenstelle Berlin-Zehlendorf |
| BL | British Library, London |
| BLO | Bodleian Library, Oxford |
| BUF | British Union of Fascists |
| *CIP* | *Comité International Permanent* |
| *DAF* | *Deutsche Arbeitsfront* |
| *DNB* | *Deutsches Nachrichtenbüro* |
| *FIDAC* | *Fédération Interalliée des Anciens Cambattants* |
| FO | Foreign Office, London UK |
| HO | Home Office, London UK |
| MI5 | British military intelligence (domestic) |
| MI6 | British military intelligence (foreign); also known as SIS |
| NA | National Archives, Washington, DC, and College Park, Maryland |
| *NSDAP* | *Nationalsozialistische Deutsche Arbeiterpartei* |
| *NSKOV* | *Nationalsozialistische Kriegsopferversorgung* |
| PAB | Politisches Archiv des Auswärtiges Amt, Bonn |
| PRO | Public Record Office, Kew, UK |
| *SA* | *Sturmabteilung* |
| SIS | Secret Intelligence Service; *see* MI6 |
| *SS* | *Schutzstafel* |

# I

# A NAZI JOURNALIST COMES TO LONDON IN 1930

On 14 September 1930 the Nazis in the Reichstag increased their numbers from 12 to 107, making them the second largest political party, and they began to take a number of measures indicative of their new position. Hitherto they had gained support by concentrating almost exclusively on domestic German issues, and their tactics were often frowned upon. Now they wanted to improve their image and cultivate better foreign relations. To this end, the official Party newspaper, the *Völkischer Beobachter*, decided to send a full-time correspondent to London.

Hans Wilhelm Thost was chosen for the assignment and thus became the first officially-sponsored Party member of the *NSDAP* to go to Britain. His background made him eminently suitable for the job.[1] Born in Hanover on 19 April 1899, he was ten years younger than the Führer himself. His parents, Valentin Louis and Elisabeth Oelssner Thost, were middle class and financially comfortable. He had one sister. In his early years the family had an English governess, and he visited England several times during the uncomplicated years before the Great War. He said of those days:[2]

> I learned English in my childhood. I owe part of my education to a young, blonde Englishwoman who lived with us before the war as our governess and who was very much a part of our happy and harmonious household. She was quite successful in keeping us unruly children in order during the many trips abroad with our parents.

Thost was just old enough to serve in World War I on the Western Front, and was wounded in the leg in July 1918 while fighting in France. The rest of that summer he spent in a German military hospital at Boppard on the Rhine River. Like many other war veterans, he viewed his generation as unique and scoffed at the pretensions of the young who came afterwards as well as his Nazi comrades who had never known the experience of war firsthand. After his hospital confinement he went to the universities of Heidelberg and Hamburg, earning a Doctorate in Politics. In the mid-1920s he worked for his grandparents' import–export business, and then became a Berlin correspondent for several provincial newspapers.

In addition to being well-educated, proficient in English, and a wounded veteran, Thost possessed one other attribute which greatly enhanced his qualifications for being sent to London. He had joined the National Socialist German Workers Party in 1929, and was considered an *Alter Kämpfer* (old fighter) compared with the latecomers who flocked to the Party in the spring of 1933 after Hitler had become Chancellor.

Within a fortnight of the stunning Nazi electoral victory of 1930, Thost embarked from Bremerhaven for Southampton. It was a smooth crossing, which he took as a good omen for his task ahead. Anglo-German relations had improved considerably from what they had been a decade before, but he represented the German party which was most vociferous in demanding repudiation of the Versailles Treaty. "Germany was looking to the future to break her chains; England to the past, to prevent such a war from ever happening again."[3]

He understood that his mission was threefold: to tell German readers what was "really" going on in Britain; to promote peace between the two nations; and to secure justice for the Fatherland. Whether he could become a mediator between the two nations depended on the tone of his articles, and the way they were viewed by the British authorities and the Nazi leadership.

Thost spent his first night in England in a hotel in Southampton, and made his way to London the next day where he settled into a boarding house off the Bayswater Road. On 5 October, he cabled his first story to the *Völkischer Beobachter*. It described the British reaction to a crash in France of their R-101 dirigible en route to India. Forty-eight of the fifty-four passengers on board were killed, including the Secretary of Air, Lord Thomson.

On 14 October Count Bernstorff, the German Ambassador in London, reported to his Foreign Minister in Berlin that Hans Wilhelm Thost was now officially recognized as their correspondent at the *Völkischer Beobachter*.[4] No further comment seemed necessary, since the *NSDAP* at this time was merely another German political party, still a long way from acquiring enough votes to seize power.

In early 1931 Thost moved from his centrally-located London lodging to a large Victorian house in Wimbledon Park, feeling that he would never truly understand English politics and character if he remained in a neighborhood where it was easy to converse and socialize with other Germans. His new quarters overlooked a small garden and contained the barest essentials: a bed, two chairs, a wardrobe, and a small table on which he put his portable typewriter, but there was also something else very important – a telephone. "This then was for years the 'office' of the *Völkischer Beobachter* in England," he remarked.[5] It was just a few minutes' walk from the South Wimbledon train station, and not far from the Common where he sometimes rode horseback.

Every three to four months he made a trip to Germany in order to confer with his superiors at the newspaper's headquarters in Munich. This provided him with an excuse to confer with its Editor-in-Chief, Alfred Rosenberg, who was one of about a dozen men in Hitler's immediate entourage. From these visits evolved an exchange of correspondence between London and Munich. Rosenberg would ask Thost to do personal favors for him in Britain, or to undertake special assignments formulated by the inner circle of Party leaders known as the *Reichsleitung*. By doing this, Thost learned about the latest political maneuvers in Germany.

For nearly a year both the German Embassy and the British Foreign Office took no notice of Thost's articles and activities. However, in July 1931 his journalistic contributions and his role as a Nazi organizer began to attract the attention of some Jews and other anxious individuals in Britain. August Cohn, a barrister practising at 3 Hare Court, Temple, EC4, submitted a formal complaint to the Attorney General.[6]

> It has come to my knowledge that the correspondent of a Hitler newspaper (a German living here) is acting as agent for the Hitler movement and carrying on active propaganda "for the liberation of Germany" among young Germans in this country.

Cohn enclosed a copy of a letter that had come into his possession which was sent by a Nazi agency in Hamburg to Party members abroad, and turned out to be the first memorandum written by Dr. Hans Nieland, the recently appointed head of the *Auslandsabteilung* (Foreign Department) of the *NSDAP*.[7]

> To all Party Comrades abroad.
>
> To those who are engaged in the struggle against liberals and Marxists, against those who have brought low our once proud Reich: comrades who take pride in the way their Party was recognized by the elections of 14 September 1930; the wave of National Socialism continues to grow despite efforts to the contrary by her enemies. . . . Hitler has relegated to *Reichsorganisationleiter* Gregor Strasser the task of establishing a Foreign Department, and that is why I am getting in touch with those of you abroad. Party Members who are so devoted to the cause at home are sure that comrades abroad will not stand idly by but will join in the struggle to secure freedom within Germany.

Nieland went on to say that he was assigning specific geographical areas to key individuals:[8] Europe and the Near East to Lange; Africa to Willy Grothe; North America to Max Lahts; South America to Ruete; Australia and New Zealand to Ewald; India and East Asia to Siegfried Droessler. His intention was to facilitate the dissemination of propaganda among Party Members and better

3

coordinate their activities. Overseas colleagues had henceforth to defray their own expenses, since the party's central Treasury was fully committed. He concluded by issuing instructions for setting up *Ortsgruppen* in foreign cities which would report to him regularly.

When the Attorney General received Cohn's complaint about Thost and its accompanying enclosure, he forwarded both of them to the Foreign Office where several of the staff wrote comments, referred to as minutes, into an interoffice memorandum that circulated among the various departments. One person penned, "I do not see that Mr. Cohn has any ground for his rage. The Nazis are only organizing propaganda among German subjects resident in England (and other foreign countries). This is a perfectly legitimate proceeding, which concerns only German internal politics, and in no way affects this country." Someone else wrote, "The Italian Fascists have always been organized here." Still another observed, "I don't see what we can do about this, and I feel it would be unwise to make any protest."

For the time being, therefore, Thost continued behaving as he always had, and sent a Report dated 23 August 1931 to Rosenberg describing how he was conducting his business. In it he told of a three-hour conversation he had with Clare Sheridan, the niece of Winston Churchill.[9] Although she was an outcast in her family because she was a pacifist and had friends who were Bolsheviks, Thost thought that she might be persuaded to write favorably about the National Socialists if he could make her see things his way. He sensed that after meeting Mussolini in Rome, she had become interested in Fascism and wanted to visit Germany to gather material for articles on contemporary affairs. When Count Bernstorff invited her to stay with him at his chateau in Schleswig-Holstein, Thost offered to accompany her and provide any needed assistance. Already she had shown sympathy with the Party's positions on war and peace, France and Poland, and Germany's hopes for revitalization, so Thost was eager to encourage these inclinations.

> I know what sort of woman I am dealing with, but I also know how important it is to influence favourably her articles, which will be read by millions in England and America. I know her ideas and I am able to guide the conversation accordingly.

In the same report, Thost asked Rosenberg for details about Party Comrade Hans Berthold who ran a news and information service at 30 Neue Grünstrasse, Berlin SW19. He wanted to know about him because several of Berthold's letters to the editors of British newspapers had been published, and Thost realized how useful Berthold could be in countering the anti-Nazi attitudes of British journalists abroad. He also asked whether Berthold was writing on his own initiative, or on behalf of the Party. He insisted that Berthold use more idiomatic English in his releases because people in Britain knew little of German politics and even less about the *NSDAP*, and would therefore need accurate translations of the speeches by Party leaders. Thost therefore offered to supply Berthold with young British "nationalists and anti-Semites" to help him with translations, suggesting that they need not be paid very much – an annual salary of 300 Deutschmarks perhaps – yet they could generate a great deal of good propaganda.

Also mentioned in Thost's discursive communiqué to Rosenberg was the major economic crisis that had shaken Britain during that summer and resulted in a significant Cabinet realignment. Several Labour spokesmen joined with a group of anti-Semites and blamed the depression on the machinations of Jewish-controlled financial institutions, especially the Bank of England. A pamphlet by Arthur Kitson, an outspoken opponent of the banking establishment who had written several anti-semitic articles published in Germany, was enclosed.[10] Thost recommended that Kitson be introduced to Party theorists like Gottfried Feder so that they could exchange ideas.

Thost's final plea was that Rosenberg do something to convince *The Times'* correspondents in Germany to write more positively about the *NSDAP*.

When Thost wrote his lengthy account for Rosenberg he had already been in London for nearly a year, and had accomplished much in the way of legitimizing the Nazi Party in the eyes of the British authorities and press. However, he had not yet openly taken a leading role in the German community. With urging by Hans Nieland and the *Auslandsabteilung*, and no apparent popular or official British opposition, the time seemed right for him and other Nazis to create their own organization.

NOTES

1  Thost file, BDC.
2  H. W. Thost, *Als National Sozialist in England* (2d ed., Munich, 1940), p. 23.
3  *Ibid.*, p.21.
4  Bernstorff to *Auswärtiges Amt*, 14 October 1930, dispatch 2308, PAB, Bonn.
5  Thost, *National Sozialist*, pp. 25–27.
6  Cohn to Attorney General, 12 July 1931; PRO, FO 395/457, p. 2019, f. 171.
7  Nieland's Circular Letter No. 1 of 1 June 1931, *ibid.*, ff. 172–75.
8  It is customary to omit first names in German documents. Where we have been able to make positive identifications, we have done so.
9  Thost to Rosenberg, 23 August 1931, Rosenberg Papers, *Bundesarchiv*, Koblenz.
10  For background on Arthur Kitson, see: L. Wise, *Arthur Kitson* (London, 1946); also *The Times*, 4 October 1937, p. 19; *New York Times*, 2 October 1937, p. 21; and *Who's Who* (London, 1933), p. 1836.

# 2 FOUNDING THE LONDON *ORTSGRUPPE,* 1931–1932

When Hans Nieland of the *NSDAP's* Foreign Department sent his first circular letter to all Party members abroad at the beginning of June 1931, he urged them whenever possible to form local groups, or *Ortsgruppen.* A half dozen compatriots constituted a *Zelle* (cell), a dozen a *Stutzpünkt,* and twenty or more an *Ortsgruppe.* Eventually a nation-wide network of such organizations were recognized as a *Landesgruppe,* the equivalent of a *Gau* or province. Under the *Führerprinzip,* or chain of command, Nieland could grant official Party recognition to an *Ortsgruppe* as well as appoint the leader of each local group. However, in the early stages, being new to the job and not knowing the names and personalities of Germans already in London, Nieland allowed groups to select their own leaders, subject to his approval.

The *Ortsgruppenleiter* (local group leader) then appointed a Secretary, Treasurer, Propaganda Warden, Steward, and perhaps a few other minor officers. Once a month each Secretary was expected to send a report to Nieland detailing the activities of his group, and this had to be reviewed and duly signed by the *Leiter.* Monthly dues amounting to three Marks were collected from each member by the Treasurer who retained one Reichsmark for local expenses and forwarded what remained each quarter to the Hamburg headquarters. Ordinary Party members in Germany paid only two Marks per month as dues, but those working abroad were considered to have opportunities for better employment than those living at home in a depressed economy, therefore they were expected to bear the higher cost. Each group had a Propaganda Warden who received special indoctrination materials from Nieland which would be distributed to the members. Once an *Ortsgruppe* had been created, it was far easier to attract members from the German community. This was the situation confronting Hans Wilhelm Thost upon becoming the correspondent for the *Völkischer Beobachter* in September 1930. During his first year he was too preoccupied with his journalistic obligations to begin organizing an *Ortsgruppe,* but in early September

1931 a rambunctious twenty-one year old named Rolf Wunderer arrived from Germany. Like Thost, he had joined the Party in 1929, and after completing his *Gymnasium* came to London where he found a job and began to look for other young Germans who shared his political enthusiasm.[1] To do this, he frequented the restaurants in Soho such as Schmitt's and Pogg!ioli's on Charlotte Street as well as Lyon's Corner House and the specialized social clubs which catered to foreign visitors. Thost also introduced him to the British Fascists who met regularly each Wednesday evening at 16-A Craven Street.

In time Wunderer compiled a list of Germans sympathetic to the Nazi cause, and toward the end of October sent handwritten invitations to forty people to attend an organizational meeting of the *NSDAP*. He was unable to afford the necessary postage himself and asked Thost and another Party Member, Arthur Heinrich von Loesch, to defray the cost. On the appointed evening, many more than those invited crowded into a Viennese restaurant in Soho to drink German beer, sing German songs, hear patriotic poems, and listen to remarks by Dr. Thost. The fervor created was so great that Wunderer was able to report to Nieland the next day that an *Ortsgruppe* had been founded. Twenty-eight who were present expressed their intention to join the Party, and Thost was chosen as the *Ortsgruppenleiter*, with Wunderer as Secretary. Von Loesch lost no time acquainting a friend in Göttingen of these new and exciting developments.[2]

> The *Ortsgruppe* here has not yet developed very far. It is led by Dr. Thost, the correspondent for the *Völkischer Beobachter*. Once a week we attend meetings of the Imperial Fascist League, which runs along the same lines as Herr Graefe, General Ludendorff, etc. Afterwards we get together at an Italian cafe where Dr. Thost skillfully keeps the conversation flowing.

Von Loesch was typical of those in attendance. He had been in London only a little more than two months, and was slated to return home in March. Like many other twenty-three year olds, he was taking the opportunity to study abroad before settling into a career. He joined the *NSDAP* in Göttingen at the beginning of 1931 and spent the next six months actively participating in the *Ortsgruppe* there. Because he was very short-sighted and hesitant in his walk, he had not tried to join the *SA*, but instead contented himself with organizational and propaganda work. In a letter to his friend Adolf Kaempffer he wrote:[3]

> The Englishman is very eager to hear more about Hitler, and I can thank my Party affiliations for providing me with many invitations and interesting conversations. People here are very appreciative of such clarifications. They are astounded to learn just how reasonable Hitler is, when they imagined him as someone who dined on at least one Jew each day.

He then asked Kaempffer to send him a copy of *Mein Kampf* and several pamphlets by Feder and Rosenberg as well as other publications which would explain the aims of the Nazi Party and be suitable for Party members and others in Britain who might take an interest. He concluded with a plea for material concerning Nazism and Christianity, as he saw a need to convert "a few German pastors." In this same letter Loesch expressed a sense of isolation from his home-land, and said how much he longed to have news of Party activities and the latest number of storm trooper deaths at the hands of the Communists.

Back in Hamburg it was Nieland's job to minimize this sense of separation, which he tried to do in a variety of ways. Besides dispersing printed matter, he urged Party members to visit him at his office when they came back to Germany, combining his wish to be cordial with learning the latest news about each foreign group. He sent out a series of lecturers who were supposed to provide meetings with a sense of occasion as well as ideological purity. Within one week of the formation of the London *Ortsgruppe*, the new recruits were summoned at short notice to hear a talk by Herr Lange, the chief of European Party affairs in Hamburg.[4]

A week-long visit by Alfred Rosenberg in November 1931 should have aroused great excitement, but he was hardly noticed, and spent his time with a mere handful of Party faithful, applauding their initiative and encouraging their growth as an *Ortsgruppe*. Not until he had been in London for six days did the *Evening Standard* mention his presence: "An architect by training, he runs the Nazi press and is Hitler's expert on foreign affairs in the Reichstag. He is, in fact, the brains of the Nazi Party."[5]

Rosenberg was very disappointed with his reception in Britain, according to the *Daily Herald*: "I came here to inform myself about the state of mind of Britain, [but I have] not seen any British public men or women of note."[6] To a *Manchester Guardian* correspondent he observed, "My visit here . . . has no political signifi-cance at all . . . my business has been entirely connected with the affairs of newspapers which are controlled by the Hitler Party."[7] The *Daily Mail* suggested that Rosenberg's mission was to disseminate Hitler's ideas and to determine the probable political and financial reaction in England should the Nazis come to power, which Rosenberg predicted would occur in 1932.[8] However, when the *Daily Herald* asked him whether Hitler would seize control by force, he brushed the idea aside: "That suggestion is being put round by his political enemies. . . . It is not necessary to make a *coup d'état*."[9]

The British Foreign Office was unsure about Rosenberg's intentions during his trip to London, and so made enquiries of Horace Rumbold, their Ambassador in Berlin, who replied on 4 December:[10]

> As for the purpose of Rosenberg's visit, we agree that he probably intends both to make propaganda for his own party and to collect facts about English polit-ical life. It seems quite likely, however, that a third reason is to prepare the way for his Chief [Hitler] who may very likely wish to visit England and, if possible, to make the acquaintance of leading British statesmen before the time, which may

be soon, comes for his party to take an active part in controlling the destiny of Germany.

Rosenberg, who is responsible for the Nazi programme, of which we sent home a translation in our dispatch number 881 of October 31st, 1930, probably owes his leading position in the party chiefly to Hitler's support. He is said not to be on such good terms with some of the other leaders, notably Göring, who seems on one occasion to have asked him uncomfortable questions about his reputed stay in Paris during the War.

After the War he settled in Munich where he made friends with Hitler and imbibed the tenets of National Socialism then in its infancy. He edited a large number of political and general works, including one called *International High Finances* and another entitled *Traces of the Jews in World History*. As well as the *Völkischer Beobachter*, now the principal Nazi journal, which he has edited for ten years, he has also for a long time been responsible for two Nazi periodicals entitled Der *Weltkampf* and the *Monatshefte* respectively.

Following Rosenberg's visit, he and Thost tried to persuade the readers of the *Völkischer Beobachter* that all had gone well. They emphasized the cordial treatment accorded the distinguished Nazi visitor by the British press, with the exception of the allegedly Jewish-dominated Socialist paper, the *Daily Herald*. Contrary to the expectations of anti-Nazis, Rosenberg acknowledged that he had been allowed complete freedom to voice his opinions and set forth the principles of National Socialism. He also implied that Hitler would not be coming to Britain, and that he had come in his place.

By January 1932 the character and strength of the London *Ortsgruppe* changed dramatically. Recruits were beginning to receive new red membership books containing their individual party numbers, and as many as one hundred Germans attended special social events, most of whom were not Party members but people eager to learn more. Regular meetings no longer took place in public restaurants, but in private rooms rented from Mrs. E. M. French at 46 Cleveland Square, Paddington, W2. Several new officers were appointed. A 24-year-old Berliner by the name of Count Adelbert von Recke was named Treasurer. He was a law student who had joined the Party in November 1930 and come to London a few months later.[11] The job of keeping track of newspaper releases was given to another Berliner, the 22–year-old Johannes Wassermann.[12] His membership in the Party was more recent, dating from the beginning of November 1931. Edmund Himmelmann, a long-time resident of London, was asked to be Steward.[13] Born in Heidelberg in 1906, he moved to London when he was about 18, and by the early 1930s had a job as a translator in the London office of the Heidelberg Automatic Platen Co., an importer of German printing equipment. He became a Party member in January 1932.

To exert firmer control over the groups that had recently come into existence, Hans Nieland decided to visit Holland and England. He stayed in

London from 15–19 January, and soon after returning to Hamburg sent the following report to his superior, Gregor Strasser.[14]

> In London I spoke before about 200 people. Our group there was only formed a little while ago, but numbers already about 50 Party Members. The *Ortsgruppe* is directed by an employee of the Embassy who made an excellent impression on me. The group has already secured its own meeting place and therefore has achieved a considerable degree of togetherness. My trip to London was also of a private character, so as to avoid any foreign policy repercussions. In accordance with the Führer's instructions, I avoided any public interviews. There was only a short notice in the English press indicating my presence in London. Thus my informal efforts to organise the overseas German community contrasts with the more formal mission to London recently undertaken by Rosenberg.

At this time an important change occurred within the London *Ortsgruppe*. Hans Wilhelm Thost stepped down as leader because of journalistic demands on his time, and Ernst Neumann, Doctor of Jurisprudence, took his place. Nieland did not know either Thost or Neumann, and therefore was not able to appoint the *Ortsgruppenleiter*. He could only confirm an on-the-scene selection. Interviewed by Robert Bruce Lockhart, a reporter from the *Evening Standard*, Nieland appeared to be a strong and charismatic leader.[15]

> Hitler's emissary . . . is a blue eyed, strongly-built young man, with the dueling scars which are the outward mark of a German university education . . . [He] is not here to establish contacts with English politicians. His sole concern is with his own countrymen . . . he is the commander of all the Nazis abroad, and he is here in order to organize the Nazis in England into a local group . . . on the right side of forty . . . he is an ardent believer in Hitler's star, and is appalled by the gigantic task with which he himself has been entrusted . . . he hopes within a short time to emulate the success of Mussolini . . .

As Lockhart's 1932 diary reveals, he followed closely the activities of the London *Ortsgruppe*.[16]

> [Wednesday, 13 January]. This morning Thost came to tell me that he had heard from Rosenberg. I was to go to Munich at once to see Hitler. I made all arrangements to go on Thursday . . . Dashed back at 5:30 to Shoe Lane only to find that Gilliat was against my going tomorrow because he has no one to replace me. Rather absurd – a Hitler interview has some value today. Tomorrow it may be too late.
>
> [Friday, 15 January]. Gave luncheon to Thost, a Nazi correspondent here. He's a mild fellow, had been with a girl all night, and was dying for a beer. He was with Hitler and Goebbels in the Brown House – sitting on the stairs and joking together – at the time of Stennes row. When they went out they bought a paper (Jewish *Tageblatt*) with the headline: "Hitler Holds Goebbels a Prisoner in the Brown House"!

[Saturday, 16 January]. At nine thirty this morning went to see Herr Nieland, the Nazi M.P. who is visiting London in order to organize the local German Nazi group. . . . He tells me there are 20,000,000 Germans abroad, and he hopes to do as well as Mussolini. . . .

August Cohn was simultaneously reminding the Home Office and the Foreign Office of the inappropriate activities of the fledgling Nazi group. Although his information was somewhat misleading – he alleged that Thost was the local leader of the group and his residence in Wimbledon was the group's headquarters – he was the lone voice calling for action by British authorities.[17]

> In my submission it is not only an impudent but highly improper proceeding to carry on propaganda among the subjects of a foreign state resident here which has for its avowed object the overthrow of the Government, if not of the Constitution of that State. . . . I would submit with the utmost respect that national as well as international interests would seem to make it desirable that the organisation established here should be uprooted by canceling permits of residents of all its officers and members and that in this case "the celebrities" should be the first to go.

The Foreign Office was equally ill-informed.[18] One officer said, "Dr. Thost calls occasionally on the News Department and has been in London since February 1931, and is an ardent Hitlerite. Beyond that we have no information about him." Another observed: "I don't suppose there is anything to be done about the Nazis organising themselves over here, so long as they don't propose to subvert His Majesty's Government." A third agreed, but with the proviso that "they don't break the law." A fourth added: "Presumably we could and would take action against the Nazis here if it could be shown that they were preparing in this country illegal action against the constitutional regime in Germany." The original commentator responded to this suggestion with a question.

> But could we? I was under the impression that we had in the past given asylum to a large number of political refugees (of whom Mazzini is perhaps the most famous) who while in England have carried on subversive propaganda against the constitutional regime in their countries without being molested by us. In recent times de Valera carried on a violent agitation in the U.S.A. against the constitutional regime in Ireland and Moslem nationalists are carrying on a similar agitation at this moment. Surely the U.S. Government could not stop them except in special circumstances even if they wanted to.

With respect to Thost, the Foreign Office reminded the Home Office:

> He would, of course, be breaking the law of England if he were to publish defamatory libels against the German Government which might affect friendly relations between that Government and His Majesty's Government but there is no evidence of his doing this, and, as you know, prosecutions for this type of seditious libel

are very rare, and the authorities are always unwilling to launch them, as they may well do more harm than good.

What is striking about these commentaries, written in early 1932, is the designation of Nazis who lived in London as political refugees, whereas a few years later they were referred to as German exiles.

Under its new leader, Ernst Neumann, the London *Ortsgruppe* was left alone by the authorities. Neumann was born in Frankfurt-am-Main in 1885. He initially pursued a legal career which led him eventually into diplomatic service. He assumed the position of Consular Secretary at the German Embassy in London in October 1929, one year before Hans Wilhelm Thost came to England. Unlike Thost, Neumann was not a member of the *NSDAP*, presumably because it might have jeopardized his chances for promotion in the Foreign Ministry. Clearly, however, he was sympathetic to the movement by 1930, evidenced by a letter from Party headquarters in Munich, enclosing blank membership forms for him to distribute.[19] In the autumn of 1931 when a successor to Thost was needed, Neumann already had the great advantage of being respected and accorded prestige by the German community in London. Since his principal task was to convert Germans to the Nazi cause, the fact that he was not a member of the Party was overlooked. Partisans were expected to make this kind of pragmatic tactical judgment if it served the long-range goals of the movement.

By March 1932 the initial euphoria of fellowship enjoyed by those in the *Ortsgruppe* gave way to a certain amount of internal dissension, hinted at in a note from Rolf Wunderer to Gregor Strasser.[20]

> The *Ortsgruppe* London of the *NSDAP* is sending, in the name of the group leader, its Secretary, Party Member Rolf Wunderer, to Hamburg, Berlin, and Munich to talk there with the leaders of our movement about matters which are important for the prestige of our movement in England as well as for the continuation of the local group in England.

Wunderer's discussions with Nieland in Hamburg and with Strasser in Munich concerned allegations that Thost had exceeded his authority, had put on airs, and caused embarrassment to the Party. Wunderer alleged that Thost had boasted to a woman in London that it would not be long until the Swastika would fly over the German Embassy and that he would be the new Ambassador; that a lecture Thost gave at the Oxford University Union had been met with derision and alienated much of the audience, especially Jews; that a negative report from the German Embassy to the Foreign Office about Thost had caused Wunderer to be denied admission to aircraft installations; that Thost was passing confidential information to other Party colleagues; and that Thost was supercilious, and not sufficiently serious toward his newspaper job.[21]

It did not take long for this criticism to reach Thost's superior, Alfred Rosenberg, who straightaway confronted him. Thost naturally attempted to vindicate himself while discrediting Wunderer. He began by reminding Rosenberg that Wunderer was young and inexperienced, having only recently finished school and come to London. Both men joined the Party in 1929, but Thost, being ten years older, had served with distinction in the First World War, and had visited Britain since childhood, and so claimed a better command of English. In his current job he had lived in London for 18 months, gaining experience and meeting people, thus he hoped that if it came down to one man's word against another, he would prevail.

In a further effort to disparage Wunderer's claims, Thost enumerated instances of Wunderer's indiscretion to Rosenberg. In speaking to a Member of Parliament, Malcolm Bullock, he had ridiculed Hermann Göring; he had also accused Nieland of issuing stupid orders to Germans abroad. The ultimate insult occurred when Wunderer told William Patrick Hitler, a nephew of the Führer, that he had been sent to London to keep track of Thost.

Thost's vigorous defense came from feeling betrayed, since he had assumed that he and Wunderer were on good terms with each other. He would have been the first to agree that the local group lacked experienced senior Party members as leaders, but this was because those few Germans who were in London when Thost arrived in September 1930 were no longer in England, and some of the newer arrivals were jealous of Thost's prestige and popularity. Acting as spokesman for the dissidents, Wunderer had unwittingly become the dupe of an unrepresentative faction, according to Thost. Nonetheless, Thost was prepared to vigorously defend himself against these gross calumnies which he refuted one by one.[22]

As to Wunderer's story that Thost would be the first German Ambassador of a new Nazi regime, Thost protested, "Dr. Neumann tells me that this statement has been spread all over London by some German lady, but I am at a loss to say who she is. I am not especially intimate with any German woman, and if I were, I certainly would not talk such nonsense." Thost eventually discovered that the alleged conversation had taken place at the German Club in late 1930 or early 1931, and involved someone he could not recall. He maintained that this was undoubtedly an example of early efforts by the German Embassy to discredit National Socialists.

As for his lecture in Oxford before the Anglo-German Club, the heckling and disruption by Jews and Communists occurred only during the opening minutes of the speech. The President of the Club restored order by reminding the audience that their guest had been invited expressly to describe National Socialism and should be given a chance to do so. At this point the hecklers rose ostentatiously and left the hall, allowing Thost to continue addressing his audience. Wunderer stayed for only the first ten minutes in order to catch the last train back to London, so witnessed only the early commotion, not the subsequent rapt attention accorded Thost. Moreover, he pointed out that if his lecture had really been such a public-relations disaster, why had he subsequently been asked to the Anglo-German Club's annual banquet and to the Oxford branch of the League of Nations Union.

Independent evidence supports Thost's contention. The Oxford undergraduate newspaper, *Isis*, covered the speech at some length.[23]

On Saturday last Doktor Thost, the representative of the National-socialist press in London, delivered a most interesting speech to the club on the subject of National-socialism.

Dr. Thost pointed out that it was particularly interesting for members to hear something about this great movement, since the time was not far ahead when it would impress its stamp on Germany. He then indicated the economic, political, and psychological events which led up to the birth of National-socialism; chief among these events was the too hasty switch-over of Germany from an agrarian to an industrial state. The division of the people into international Marxists and property-owning bourgeois was a very dangerous one, and it is only due to the genius of Hitler that the national self-assertion has been united with the desire for social justice.

Turning to the questions of the day, Dr. Thost explained that it was the aim of the Party, after the cancellation of reparations, to stem the cut-throat economic competition which was ruining all of the nations of Europe. In this connection he emphasized the fact that the cancellation of reparations does not imply that of private obligations and that Germany's commercial debts will be strictly honoured.

As regards the Eastern question, he pointed out that the Versailles settlement must be revised for three reasons: first, it was impossible to maintain the corridor as it was, since it cut German territory in two; secondly, Poland only owed its existence to the fact that German troops had defeated the Russians during the war; and thirdly it was impossible ever to come to a reckoning with Bolshevist Russia, since every German government had to envisage the possibility of an attack by Polish nationalists.

Dr. Thost concluded by once again emphasizing the fact that the National-socialist party was not an aggressive movement, as its opponents always stated, but that its intentions were peaceful.

As a result of Wunderer's allegations, Rosenberg ordered Thost to refrain from giving any more public lectures. However, Thost urged his Chief to reconsider on the grounds that anti-Nazi German journalists were speaking out and attracting public attention, and therefore National Socialism should be defended against unjust accusations. He urged Rosenberg to reconsider the ban, and suggested that in future he should request permission to address the British public.

Thost initially denied Wunderer's third claim that he had been refused permission to inspect an airfield, but two weeks later he admitted that early in 1931 he had sought to visit Aldershot in order to gather background material for an article to appear in the *Völkischer Beobachter*. The War Office politely explained that no private viewing of airfields was possible, but that he was welcome to attend any functions open to the public. Eventually he wrote his story after visiting Croydon.

In seeking to exonerate himself, Thost acknowledged that occasionally he may have been indiscreet, but whatever confidences he shared were authorized by Dr. Neumann. Consequently, when he went to Germany in November 1931 and was told by Rosenberg that he was contemplating a trip to London, Thost thought it appropriate to tell the good news to a few other trustworthy Party members. Most upsetting to Rosenberg was Thost's mention of "Mr. M" to Wunderer. Thost protested that he had never indicated "Mr. M"'s true name or purpose in visiting Berlin, but had only procured his airfare through a Party member at the Mitropia travel agency in London. Since only a few people were present when "Mr. M." visited Rosenberg in Berlin, it must have been one of these who told the German Foreign Ministry.

Thost's extended vindication of his conduct included a reiteration of his own qualifications for his former position as *Ortsgruppenleiter* compared to the inexperience of his critics. For this reason Thost was stunned to learn that it was Neumann who was behind Wunderer's criticisms. In retrospect, it was ironic that he had given Neumann as a reliable source for Rosenberg to contact in connection with Wunderer's allegations. Not only had he confided in Neumann by talking about Wunderer's complaints, but he had shown Neumann a draft of the response he intended to send to Rosenberg. Neumann had said that he put little faith in Wunderer's judgment, but justified his perfidy on the grounds that Thost had not consulted with him on several occasions. He advised Thost not to make a fuss in case it would jeopardize his job with the Party newspaper, and suggested that he not mention anything about this matter to the *Ortsgruppe*. Thost agreed, but resented the betrayal and determined to defend his reputation where it counted, back in Germany.

Once Thost understood that Neumann was manipulating Wunderer, it was not difficult to elicit an admission from him that Otto Bene had been the one who furnished both Wunderer and Neumann with the testimony from the anonymous German lady. When confronted, Bene protested his innocence and said that he had not intended to land Thost in trouble with party superiors, but had only told Neumann what seemed appropriate under the rules of Party discipline.

Begun with such enthusiasm in October 1931, the London *Ortsgruppe* was badly divided by the time Neumann left in April 1932. The aura of mutual trust had given way to suspicion and backbiting. Yet, if anything characterized the Nazi movement as a whole, it was infighting at every level. Rosenberg was perpetually at odds with Goebbels, while Gregor Strasser, who was ultimately responsible for Party Members abroad, tried to split the Party and challenge Hitler's leadership by the end of that year. At the lowest level of party organization, therefore, the *Ortsgruppe* combined hearty fellowship with latent distrust.

This duality became obvious when Hans Erich Bening arrived in Britain at the same time Thost was fending off accusations against him from Wunderer and others. Bening claimed to be a Party Member, which was true, having joined in August 1931, but he also said that he came as Hitler's special emissary in charge of press and propaganda for Northern Britain. This was a far more dubious assertion by the untried twenty-two year old from Marburg, and was promptly squelched by the London *Ortsgruppe* which published a formal denial of Bening's role and stated that he spoke without party authorization.[24] At the same time, the members of the *Ortsgruppe* at Cleveland Square were assuring the British that they were not engaged in propaganda but merely getting together to chat, read German-language periodicals, and attend lectures.

Bening's behavior attracted the kind of publicity that the Nazis in London deplored, and they were relieved when he returned to Germany in the autumn. While wishing to recruit Germans to their cause, they were always in fear of alienating the British authorities by interfering in domestic politics. Although Thost and Bene and others within the *Ortsgruppe* were able to conceal their internecine struggles, they were unable to keep Party factionalism from surfacing as it did with Bening. Gradually the newspapers became aware of Nazi activity in England, from Rosenberg's visit in November 1931 and Nieland's trip in January to Bening's brief stay in April 1932. As yet, however, the Nazis were not thought to pose a threat to British domestic tranquility.

NOTES

1 Wunderer file, BDC. His account of the origins of the London *Ortsgruppe* appeared in the *Völkischer Beobachter*, 13 February 1934.

2 Loesch to Adolf Kaempffer, 10 October 1931, BDC.

3 *Ibid.*

4 *Völkischer Beobachter*, 13 February 1934.

5 *Evening Standard*, 3 December 1931, p. 6.

6 *Daily Herald*, 7 December 1931, p. 2.

7 *Manchester Guardian*, 7 December 1931, p. 12.

8 *Daily Mail*, 7 December 1931, p. 14.

9 *Daily Herald*, 7 December 1931, p. 2; See also *The Times*, 7 December, p. 11.

10 H. Rumbold to Foreign Office, 4 December 1931, PRO, FO 371/15216, C9099, ff. 219–23.

11 Von Recke file, BDC.

12 Wassermann file, BDC.

13 Himmelmann file, BDC.

14 Nieland to Strasser, 23 January 1932, NA microcopy T-580, roll 55.

15 *Evening Standard*, 16 January 1932, p. 6.

16 K. Young (ed.), *The Diaries of Sir Robert Bruce Lockhart, I* (London, 1973), 199–200.

17 A. Cohn to Home Office, 26 January 1932, PRO, FO 395/468, P683, ff. 136–41. See chapter 1 for Cohn's earlier approach to the Attorney General.

18 *Ibid.*, ff. 132–33.

19 Biographical information about Ernst Neumann can be found at the *Auswärtiges Amt*, Bonn. See also W. Schmidt to Neumann, 10 November 1930, BDC.

20 Wunderer to Strasser, 17 March 1932, NA microcopy T-580, roll 56, file 396.

21 Thost to Rosenberg, 5 April 1932 and 14 April 1932, pp. 13–14; and Rosenberg Papers, *Bundesarchiv*, Koblenz, NS8-117, pp. 9–12.

22 Thost to Rosenberg, 18 April 1932, *ibid.*, pp. 15–17.

23 *Isis*, 11 February 1932. The article was signed by the initials M. O. R. M., presumably those of Maury Micklejohn, the Secretary of the Anglo-German Club.

24 *Daily Herald*, 23 March 1932, p. 1. See also *ibid.*, 5 April 1932, p. 2 for the refutation by the London *Ortsgruppe* of Bening's authority as well as Bening file, BDC.

# 3 OTTO BENE
# *ORTSGRUPPENLEITER,*
# 1932–1935

Born on 30 September 1884 in Altenberg near Hamburg, Otto Wilhelm August Gottfried Bene eventually returned to his place of origin and died in Hamburg on 16 April 1973. Little is known of his childhood except that he completed seven of the nine years of formal education at his local gymnasium or secondary school. Between 1907 and 1909 he represented a Hamburg firm in Canton, China. Returning to Germany, he continued to work in Hamburg until the outbreak of war when he was among the first to volunteer. In the army he rose to the rank of an artillery lieutenant but was badly wounded in the line of duty and received the coveted Iron Cross, second and first class.[1] He was released from active military service in 1919, but continued to serve in the national militia, the *Stahlhelm*, until 1926.

In 1927 he came to London to work in the office of a Hamburg chemical firm, Promonta, located in Regent Street, and took lodgings in the City at 39 Great Tower Street, EC3. Promonta was taken over by the British firm, Savory & Moore, in the early 1930s, but it was not a problem for Bene because by this time he was one of a very few who received a salary from the National Socialist Party.[2] The steady growth of the London *Ortsgruppe* kept him fully occupied, as there were already 50 to 100 Party members in London in 1932–33 as well as a continual stream of visiting Germans. He was also fortunate to have the help of an adjutant, Baron Tassilo Krug von Nidda, a businessman who came to Great Britain the same year Bene did, and joined the Party in August 1932. They shared much in common, although Bene was older by ten years. Von Nidda at first lived at 45B Linden Gardens, W2, but after marrying a British subject, moved to Etchingham Park Road, N3. He combined his work as an importer–exporter with being an effective Party organizer.[3] The Secretary of the *Ortsgruppe* was Edmund Himmelmann, one of its original founders. Like Bene and von Nidda, he had been in business in London since the 1920s and shared a flat with Bene from time to time.[4] The group's Treasurer, Reinhold Boehm, joined the *NSDAP* in Germany in December 1931 and came to London in the spring of 1932.[5] A man in his early twenties, he was given responsibility for the Hitler-*Jugend*.

Neither the Home Office nor the Foreign office paid much attention to the *Ortsgruppe* until the autumn of 1933, ten months after Hitler came to power. Then, the Special Branch of Scotland Yard began to cover the local Nazi meetings regularly. Sergeant William East was assigned the task of infiltrating the group, and for the next few years was trusted as a sympathetic observer. His report of 9 November, describing a meeting at 102 Westbourne Terrace, W2, is the earliest surviving description by an outsider.[6]

> About 110 party members, all Germans, assembled in a large room. . . . The proceedings commenced by the entry into the room of a storm trooper in uniform carrying a large banner bearing the Swastika emblem. He was followed by Otto Bene, leader of the movement in this country, Baron von Nidda, adjutant to Herr Bene, Edmund Himmelmann, party secretary; Reinhold Boehm, party treasurer and member of the *Hitler-Jugend* movement, and another unknown member of the movement, all wearing Nazi uniforms. . . . Others present were Dr. H.W. Thost, Elsbeth Häussner, niece of Himmelmann, Himmelmann's sister, and the woman secretary of the Anglo-German Club. . . . The assembly rose at the entry of the flag and made the Nazi salute with the greeting "Heil Hitler". Herr Bene then addressed the meeting.

Bene reminded his listeners of the solemn occasion they were commemorating that evening. Ten years ago Hitler tried to liberate Munich from socialism and put an end to the Weimar Republic, but he failed, and his Nazi comrades died in the attempt. He repeated the claim that at the end of the Great War Germany had been betrayed from within by Socialists and Jews, yet from those defeats arose the National Socialist movement which was now triumphant. Following his remarks, four new Party Members were introduced, and each took an oath of allegiance to the Party, the German State, and the Führer. Bene then continued:[7]

> Herr Hitler had issued strict orders that Germans in this country were to refrain from the distribution of Nazi propaganda in any form unless expressly asked to do so by an acquaintance, not German, in this country. In that case they would be given literature to hand on to the enquirer. He emphasized that it is strictly forbidden for any Nazi to discuss or participate in English politics and particularly they were not to fraternise with members of Fascist organisations here such as the British Fascists.

Baron von Nidda spoke briefly, reiterating the need to avoid political topics with British acquaintances, especially controversial subjects like India and Ireland. An announcement was made that the local group had raised 14 Pounds for the unemployment relief fund in Germany. The meeting went on for three hours and concluded at about 11 p.m. with everyone joining together to sing the *Horst Wessel* marching song.

One year later Inspector Hubert Morse of Special Branch was able to provide a particularly detailed glimpse of the inner workings of the *Ortsgruppe* when he obtained a circular letter from Bene specifying the obligatory and optional meetings for members. [8]

1. My address is now No. 5 Cleveland Terrace, W2. All letters are to be addressed to me personally. Telephone – Paddington 9194.

2. The next duty meeting is on 18th October at 8 P.M. in the small hall at the Porchester Hall, W2, when the flags presented to us at Nuremberg will be handed over. All members must attend this meeting. Owing to lack of space, the meeting is for members only.

3. Contributions, as well as the special contribution for Nuremburg, are to be paid in, at the latest, at the next Duty meeting.

4. Following the proposal of the Instruction Leader, Party Member Dr. Roesel, I appoint that:

A. All Party Members will take part in the evening instruction classes. <u>This is compulsory</u>. The classes are divided into three groups and will be held in my house.

Men's Section 1
Men's Section 2
Women's Section 3.

B. Section 1 will meet on the following days:
31-10; 14-11; 28-11; 12-12.
Section 2 will meet on: 24-10; 7-11; 22-11; 5-12; 19-12.
Women's section: 1-11; 16-11; 29-11; 13-12.

These days must be noted. No further reminders will follow.

C. Party Member Dr. Roesel will take charge of Section 1. Party Member Dr. Schinnerer will take charge of the Women's Section.

D. Duty meetings for all members of the branch have been arranged for Thursday 18th October; Wednesday 21st November; and Thursday 20th December in the small hall at the Porchester Hall, at 8 P.M.

E. Debates, to which guests will be admitted, have been fixed for Thursday 8th November and Thursday 8th December, at the small hall of the Porchester Hall at 8 P.M.

The Instruction Classes and Duty Meetings are to be attended regularly so that every member gives one evening a week for the Movement.

5. On Thursday 15th November a dance will be held in the large hall at the Porchester Hall. Tickets at 2/each may be obtained at the Instruction Classes.

6. I draw your attention again to the order that you are not allowed to partici-

pate in British politics and particularly you are not to associate with Fascists. We are guests in the country and must behave accordingly.

Heil Hitler!
*Landesgruppenleiter*

Although most of these instructions seem clear enough, a few points deserve particular attention. In item #1 Bene is warning members not to address any mail to the Nazi *Ortsgruppe* or *NSDAP* headquarters, but rather to him privately, so that less attention would be paid to his incoming letters.

In item #3, the allusion to "contributions" is vague, but probably refers to the most important of the annual appeals throughout Germany, the Winter Aid Fund.

Item #4 underlines the fact that men and women were segregated for the purposes of instruction, one of many instances in the Third Reich when women were treated different from, and often subordinate to, men.

For the first time, Bene used his new title, *Landesgruppenleiter* (National Leader), at the end of the letter, indicating his promotion from *Ortsgruppenleiter* (Local Group Leader). This happened in June 1934 and meant that he was henceforth in charge of Nazi groups not only in London, but also throughout the United Kingdom of Great Britain, Northern Ireland, and Eire. The London group dominated the activities of the *NSDAP* in Britain, however, since the vast majority of Party members at any given time lived in or near the metropolis.

A large hall that seated upwards of 1,200 people was the usual venue for special events such as Hitler's birthday, or the anniversary of coming to power by the Nazi Party. On these occasions, as many as 50 invitations were issued to *Ortsgruppen* in Europe and the adjacent islands. From the spring of 1934 on, the favored meeting place was Porchester Hall on Porchester Road, but when this was not available, Victoria Hall in Bloomsbury Square, WCI was used. On May Day that year the Nazis appropriated the traditional Communist celebration and showed a film titled *Hans Westman*, a thinly disguised account of the Nazi martyr, Horst Wessel, who was allegedly murdered by Communists, and whose memory was rekindled in the Party's marching song. As with many other meetings, a special guest appeared: Herr Josef Wagner, a member of the Prussian State Council and *Gauleiter* of Westphalia. According to the *News Chronicle*, 1,200 invitations were sent, but 1,500 "managed to squeeze into the hall."[9]

On 30 January 1935, Franz Xaver Hasenoehrl of the Propaganda Ministry came to London to commemorate the second anniversary of Hitler's coming to power,[10] and a few months later State Secretary Fritz Reinhardt of the Finance Ministry in Berlin arrived to reiterate the familiar themes of Hitler's desire for peace, and how all Germans abroad should serve as emissaries of friendship. Inspector Morse attended this event and estimated that the crowd exceeded a thousand people.[11] On 12 November 1935 two of Rudolf Hess's adjutants, Alfred Leitgen and Karl Heinz Pintsch, spoke to a large audience at Porchester Hall before the showing of Leni Riefenstahl's film, *Triumph of the Will*.[12]

Gatherings of the *NSDAP* took place at other venues besides Bene's flat or Borough halls. In August 1934, for example, Party members enjoyed an outing aboard the German passenger ship *Monte Rosa* which was moored in the Thames near Greenwich. Inspector Morse counted 400 German visitors, 100 of whom were members of the London *Ortsgruppe*. There were also a further 300 passengers and 100 crew members who had their own shipboard *Ortsgruppe*. Each of the group leaders spoke words of welcome before the festivities began. Edmund Himmelmann's niece, Elsbeth Häussner, attracted a good deal of attention with her singing and dancing, and two young men were spotted wearing British Union of Fascists' lapel pins.[13]

Besides sponsoring Party politicians, the *Ortsgruppe* would occasionally invite a German artist or celebrity to give a presentation to attract a wider, non-Party audience. The poet, Hans Friedrich Blunck, was the guest lecturer at Victoria Hall on 17 October 1935. Blunck began by saying how important it was for Germans abroad to understand their country's cultural policy, especially in view of the many distortions perpetrated by the foreign press. It soon became apparent that he was referring to the recent Nuremburg laws regulating the relations between Aryans and Jews in Germany. He lamented that Jews had been allowed to rise in society and exert so much influence, but expressed relief that Jews would henceforth be controlled in so many ways that the next generation in Germany would grow up free of their influence. He assured his audience that Jews were not being persecuted, merely assigned their proper place.[14] In addition to paying an entry fee of one shilling at Party meetings, the members were reminded of the obligatory sessions each month. Bene announced that "admission cards may be obtained from me at Cleveland Terrace, London, W2. These will be unobtainable on the evening itself."[15] On the other hand, outsiders were discouraged from attending. Admission was usually by German passport, or some other official evidence of German nationality. This effectively excluded unwanted agitators such as ordinary British subjects, Fascists and British Communists, and avoided the *Ortsgruppe* being accused, as the Communists were, of staging incidents that provoked police brutality. It also minimized anti-Nazi press coverage.

Many of the celebrations and activities in the German community were jointly sponsored by the *Ortsgruppe* together with other organizations such as churches, the Anglo-German Academic Bureau, the *Deutsche Verein*, the war veterans organization, the YMCA, and the German Embassy. Only gradually did the Nazis take over many of these groups, and in the meantime they kept seeking ways to improve their image with Germans who were not yet Party members.

Spouses of Party members, whether or not they belonged to the *NSDAP*, took an active role at school functions, church fêtes, memorial services, weddings, hospital visits, and musical events. Nazis and non-Nazis often combined forces when they took sight-seeing tours and rambles in the countryside, and jointly sponsored sports competitions. Members were obliged to undertake obligations that could separate them from other Germans abroad, but in many respects they passed for ordinary citizens. German Jews and political refugees, however, felt excluded, and often formed their own sub-communities within neighborhoods or churches.

In the first year of the Third Reich anti-Nazis could still make common cause with Party members, as happened when several German journalists in London wrote to the *Manchester Guardian* protesting British news coverage of the Nazi experiment. Their letter appeared on 1 April 1933 and urged the British press to stop sensationalizing events in Germany. While they admitted that significant changes were taking place, they resented the use of the term "atrocities" which they said induced a war psychosis among the British. Of the 16 journalists who signed the letter, some were ardent Nazis like R. G. Roesel, Theodor Seibert, and Hans Wilhelm Thost; some were non-committal; and some proved later to be staunchly anti-Nazi, such as Albrecht Graf Montgelas, Paul Sheffer, and Jona von Ustinov. Soon after this it became difficult if not impossible for Germans holding differing views to act together on anything having to do with Germany.

In accordance with the *Fuhrerprinzip* of the Third Reich, the *Ortsgruppenleiter* was responsible for all communication between the *Ortsgruppe* and Party headquarters in Germany. Since Party members were not allowed to make direct contact with any organization in Germany, they had first to submit requests to the *Ortsgruppenleiter* who in turn forwarded them to the *Auslandsorganisation* which passed them to the appropriate official or Ministry. Replies often took weeks or months to arrive because the Nazi bureaucracy was prone to avoid making policy decisions.

Another of the responsibilities of the *Ortsgruppenleiter* was to send periodic Stimmungsbericht (mood reports) to the *Auslandsorganisation*, describing the atmosphere of the host country, its current political preoccupations, its controversies, and its attitudes toward Germany. Most of these accounts did not survive the war, but occasionally one did, often in the files of some other organization. This happened in the case of a summary sent by Otto Bene to Rudolf Hess, the Führer's deputy, asking whether he would like to receive reports from London on a regular basis.[16] Undoubtedly the only reason that this document survived was because it was enclosed in a letter from Bohle to Hess.

Another instance of a surviving letter was one from Bene to Gottfried Aschmann of the Foreign Ministry in June 1934. The usual injunction was invoked: regard the enclosure from my deputy, Karl Markau, as secret.[17]

Markau's concern was that German church policy was dominating the British press, with the result that people in England were beginning to think that Nazis were forcing the churches to adopt their official brand of Christianity. Walther Heide, of the Foreign Press Bureau in Berlin, speculated that newspapers like *The Times* must be obtaining inside information from dissidents because they were so well informed. "Those pastors who transmit such information, either knowingly or not, are plainly guilty of treason," he declared, urging that the church issue be resolved immediately in order to undercut British criticism of the situation.

Markau described two encounters he had with British acquaintances who partially sympathized with Germans who resented Eastern Jewish immigrants flooding into Germany, but did not understand why the Nazi regime was persecuting Jews who had lived there for many years. An Anglican churchgoer based his objection to intimidation directed toward the German churches on the principles of religious tolerance. Bene and Markau were very concerned about this controversy, and did everything they could to diminish the rancor it was causing. Little did they expect that in less than a fortnight they would be faced with an even more upsetting event: the Nazi bloodbath of 30 June 1934 which decimated the upper ranks of the SA and other "counter revolutionaries."

In contrast to Bene's fragmentary surviving reports to the *Auslandsorganisation* in Berlin is a series of letters he wrote to Rolf Hoffmann between November 1934 and May 1935. Hoffmann was in charge of a foreign press office outside Munich. On 3 November Bene wrote to him responding to his request for copies of several English publications to give to Rudolf Hess, who wanted samples of British political viewpoints. Bene obliged by suggesting the following as representative: the *Manchester Guardian*, the *Daily Express*, the *Daily Herald*, the *Irish Times*, the *News Chronicle*, the *Week* (Communist), and the *Black Shirt* (British Union of Fascists).[18]

Ten days later Hoffmann asked Bene for an article which had appeared in the *Daily Telegraph* of 6 November concerning Oswald Mosley's legal action against the *Star*, a request that originated from Ernst Hanfstaengl, head of the Foreign Press Office and one of Hitler's political cronies.[19] On 22 November Hoffmann sent Bene several brochures announcing a forthcoming book, *Germany's Hitler*, which was advertised by its London publisher, Hurst & Blackett, and asked him to promote its sale as much as possible and forward any book reviews to him. Hoffmann's next request was for a regular subscription to the *Jewish Chronicle* as well as a copy of an article by Lord Rothermere which had appeared in the *Daily Mail*.[20]

On 22 January he asked for three copies of the 18 January *Daily Mail* covering Ward Price's interview with Hitler. Since he had been in the audience, he was curious to see how much would be told to the British reading public.[21]

By mid-February Hoffmann's requests escalated. He asked Bene to discontinue sending the *Irish Times*, but start to forward the *Jewish Daily Post* and any items of interest from the *Contemporary Review* and the *Nineteenth Century and After*. He also wanted a copy of a recent article in the *Observer* by its editor, J. L. Garvin, as well as cuttings from *The Times* describing the recently-issued government White Paper.[22]

In April Bene responded to Hoffmann's query concerning an anti-Semitic speech given by Oswald Mosley that appeared in the *Daily Mail* of 29 October 1934, saying that unfortunately extra copies of that issue were no longer available. However, since Mosley had recently given a similar speech, Bene enclosed a cutting from the *Daily Mail* of 25 March 1935.[23]

Bene and his lieutenants complied with these requests from Munich, operating, in effect, as a clearing-house for a wide range of commissions.[24] Occasionally the *Ortsgruppe* was asked to perform a risky political task, as in early January 1935 when Hoffmann wanted Bene to offer assistance to Mr. Luttmann-Johnson of the London January Club, a gentleman who had been recommended to him by the German Automobile Club in Munich.[25]

> This Englishman is very pro-German, and would like to work for the enlightenment of his friends concerning the new Germany. Recently he visited Germany for several weeks, and was much impressed. In the near future he will get in touch with you and will request some propaganda material and seek some clarifications of certain issues. As far as we are concerned, we have no objections to his doing so.

Bene had to be cautious about any dealings he had with British subjects, given the policy of not proselytizing, but he provided information about Nazi Germany when asked. Thus, a few weeks after receiving Hoffmann's request, he made contact with Luttmann-Johnson at a gathering of the German community.[26]

In April 1935 Hoffmann made another potentially difficult request of Bene.[27] A friend of his, Gordon Woods, who was adjutant to the recently-deceased Miss R. L. Lintorn-Orman, the founder of British Fascists Ltd., the earliest Fascist organization in Britain, asked if at least some members of the *NSDAP* would attend her funeral at St. Giles in the Fields on Denmark Street, off Charing Cross Road. He mentioned that "Miss Lintorn-Orman was the first one to congratulate Hitler's government in 1933 at the rebirth of Germany." Bene declined this plea with unaccustomed brusqueness.[28]

> Because of the existing Party regulations, we cannot attend the memorial service. Besides, the organization of British Fascists is so unimportant that it is not worth our while, and would only mean a politely private gesture on our part.

In addition to his regular correspondence with officials in Germany, Bene had to cope with unexpected and sometimes embarrassing episodes that reflected poorly on the Nazi regime. In February 1934 two young S.S. men arrived at Croydon airport wearing uniforms, although they had come as private citizens and had no official sanction. The London newspapers quickly pounced on the story, the *Daily Telegraph* proclaiming: "Storm Troopers Stay in London."[29]

Otto Bene assured the press that the two men were only visitors on holiday and had inadvertently worn their uniforms while traveling; they were being housed by personal friends; and were given civilian clothes to wear while in England. He assured everyone that they would be returning to Germany very shortly.[30]

Plausible as this story seemed, the facts were not quite as Bene stated them. The German Embassy's Press Attaché, Sigismund FitzRandolph, in his dispatch to the Foreign Ministry in Berlin, admitted that a member of the British Fascist organization had invited the two German youths to visit him in order to promote Anglo-German solidarity, and they had accepted, not realizing that it was contrary to Party regulations to fraternize with any British political group on British soil. He made a clear distinction between entertaining British Fascists in Germany, and associating with them in England.

The British Foreign Office knew that this incident would trigger questions to the Home Secretary in Parliament, so they asked the German Embassy to clarify the situation immediately. They contacted Bene, who assured them that he had addressed the problem, minimized the damage, and would send the offending officers back to Germany on the first available flight. What was noteworthy about this rather trivial incident was that professional diplomats deferred to the *Ortsgruppenleiter* to dispense discipline and smooth things over, confirming that the power to control the situation rested with the National Socialists.[31]

Bene did his best to keep himself and the *Ortsgruppe* out of the press, but it was not always possible. From time to time newspaper articles gave rise to questions in Parliament as to whether Nazis were conducting themselves properly in Britain. The Home Secretary repeatedly assured Members that there was no cause for alarm, and that he saw no reason to investigate. However, they were encouraged to report any evidence of a compromising nature and assured that it would be forwarded to the appropriate authorities. On one occasion Bene was trapped into giving an interview with a reporter from the *Daily Express* because he used the ploy of showing Bene the proposed story, riddled with inaccuracies and misunderstandings.[32]

> I have great respect for your Scotland Yard . . . and we do nothing illegal. I have my house here in Westbourne Terrace, where members of the Party may meet. But we have no connection with Fascist organisations. We have nothing to do with Sir Oswald Mosley or with the Italian Fascists. Many members of the German Embassy come to us, for they are Nazis. But we make no propaganda among English people. That would be abuse of the hospitality of this country.

Not satisfied with this, the interviewer persisted, citing "the case of a young German domestic who received a letter demanding to know why she had neither taken part in Nazi activities in London; nor contributed to the Party's funds." Bene responded that he could not comment without knowing the name and address of the individual involved, but the reporter said that he could not provide this information without compromising the person. The resulting article thus read:

> Herr Bene was unwilling to say where the Nazis meet. He was unwilling to show me a copy of the circular letter sent Germans in London. He did not tell me that this letter was sent out not by the Nazi club, but by the German Embassy itself. Actually the Nazis have met at hotels in Bayswater, but they change the venue of their meetings frequently.

The most sustained effort to expose Bene and the London *Ortsgruppe* came from Paris and was instigated by Willi Münzenberg, a German Communist who fled his homeland when the Nazis came to power and eventually became the coordinator of Western European propaganda for the Comintern. To Bene's great discomfort, the *Pariser Tageblatt*, a left-wing newspaper run by several German refugees, released an article about the London *Ortsgruppe* on 22 May 1934 that became the basis of a book published by Münzenberg titled *The Brown Network* which contained a series of exposés of Nazi groups throughout the world.[33]

The book's Comintern origins were not immediately apparent, but the volume was the first major attempt to disclose the widespread activities of Nazis abroad, and included the names of individuals and organizations. However, in this case, the Comintern's reputation for successfully infiltrating organizations suffered a setback with regard to the accuracy of its findings. Münzenberg identified ten Party Members in England from among the several hundred in the London *Ortsgruppe* in 1934–35, but because this section of the book was more than a year out of date, it is riddled with errors: Thost's name was given as Troost, Tonn's as Tann, and Bene's office and personal residence were incorrectly sited as Bush House and South Kensington.

The source of many of the mistakes in *The Brown Network* was misinformation contained in the original article in the *Pariser Tageblatt*. For example, the political head of the *NSDAP* in Britain who dominated Ambassador Hoesch was identified as Fritz Randolf. Actually, this man's name was Sigismund FitzRandolph, and he was never connected with Alfred Rosenberg's *Aussenpolitisches Amt*. As a lower-level functionary, he was hardly "Hitler's direct political commissioner" who stood "above Ambassador von Hoesch in all party questions." Similarly, it was unlikely that "He also serves as liaison with the English Fascists whom he supplies with ample funds from German financial sources." Had this been true, FitzRandolph would have been expelled immediately from Britain, rather than having been allowed to stay until the outbreak of war in 1939. FitzRandolph may have supplied material about the Third Reich to Oswald Mosley for use in his newsletter, the *Black Shirt*, since his job entailed distributing news releases, but it is harder to judge whether he furnished Lady Houston with information for her *Saturday Review* articles.

By the time the *Brown Network* appeared, FitzRandolph was the liaison between Goebbels' Propaganda Ministry in Berlin and the German Embassy in London, and this gave him ample opportunity to embellish his reports, but it would not have enabled him to exert extraordinary power over von Hoesch or any other career diplomat in the German Embassy.

The article in the *Pariser Tageblatt* said comparatively little about Otto Bene, describing him only as the head of an organization to which all Germans in Britain belonged, whereas the London *Ortsgruppe* and the British *Landesgruppe* restricted membership to those enrolled in the Nazi Party. Two newspapers were identified as fronts for the *NSDAP*: the *Neue Londoner Zeitung* and the *European Herald*. It was alleged that the first went out of business because it was too blatant in its pro-Nazi propaganda, whereas it had tried to steer a middle course, and was, if anything, anti-Nazi prior to Hitler's coming to power. Neither Bevis, the editor of the *Neue Londoner Zeitung*, nor Van Hoek of the *European Herald*, were members of the *NSDAP*, and Van Hoek was Dutch, not German. His assistants, Ava Geisel and E. Popovitch, were not Party Members either. The *European Herald* started as a German language paper and gradually broadened its content to include articles in French and Spanish. Its eventual demise was due in part to the lack of support by the Nazis, so it should never have been seen as favorable to the *NSDAP*.[34] Another claim made was that all Germans in London were under strict control of the Party, and on May Day 1934 were required to attend a large rally at the Royal Albert Hall. In fact, that meeting took place at Porchester Hall, and although three employees of a shipping firm who missed this gathering were reported as having lost their jobs, no mention of this was made in the British press.

In *The Brown Network*, Lothar Streicher, the son of Julius Streicher – "the Nuremberg pornographer and extreme anti-Semite" – is portrayed as having often visited England as his father's emissary. "The British police threw him out of the country because, in his zeal to appease his father, he was too rabid for English sensibilities."[35] As a student, Julius Streicher's eldest son made only one visit to England lasting seven weeks, arriving on 8 August and departing on 26 September 1934. He was a young member of the *NSDAP*, and like many his age, traveled abroad during the summer holidays, but being the son of one of Hitler's inner circle, he was closely observed by Special Branch. On 25 August 1934 Hubert Morse recorded that Lothar was staying at 50 Pont Street, SW1, "the address of a Mrs. Clark, stated to be a BUF member." Since consorting with anyone who was a member of the British Union of Fascists was strictly forbidden by the London *Orstgruppenleiter*, he was reprimanded. There is no evidence to suggest that he engaged in propaganda or called attention to himself, nor was he asked to leave the country.[36]

*The Brown Network* was also incorrect about Frederick Willis, described as a naturalized German citizen working in the diplomatic service in London who specialized in propaganda and was eventually deported.[37] In fact, Willis never came to London. Münzenberg may have learned about him from an article that appeared in the *Jewish Chronicle* of September 1933 which said that Willis was being transferred from Rome to London to "be in charge of the Press Department with the title of Counsellor of Embassy."[38]

> At a banquet given in his honour in Rome . . . light was thrown upon a less official aspect of his work, when the German Ambassador wished him luck, and Herr Willis revealed his intention of intriguing with Sir Oswald Mosley for a Nazi revolution in England.

This story originated from conjectures made by the *Daily Herald*'s diplomatic correspondent who might have known that the Propaganda Ministry was in the process of hiring someone to become Press Attaché at the German Embassy in London. The post was in fact given to FitzRandolph, and Willis continued to work in Berlin for the next two years doing propaganda in connection with the Saar.[39]

Being continually exposed to inflammatory misstatements, the British press and public opinion were convinced that the London *Ortsgruppe* was a center of espionage and subversion. The reality was far more subtle: its priorities were to keep track of Party Members abroad; to attract German citizens who did not belong to the Party to become members of the *NSDAP*; to remind ethnic Germans who had become citizens of another country of their Teutonic roots; and to improve the image of the New Germany in the eyes of non-Germans. Most importantly, its function was to provide a base for Party activities where Nazis could support one another, socialize, be reminded of the Party's expectations. Unlike the Communists, who belonged to the same cell or work group and acted clandestinely, the Nazis were gregarious and felt more at ease when surrounded by fellow Brown Shirts who were drinking German beer and singing their favorite songs. Individually they might try to win converts to their movement, but collectively they banned together in the *Ortsgruppe* to witness to the strength of the Third Reich abroad, subject at all times, however, to the strict rules and discipline transmitted by the *Ortsgruppenleiter*.

NOTES

1 Bene file, BDC, as well as the Netherlands State Institution for War Documentation, Amsterdam.

2  Report from Vernon Kell to Robert Vansittart, 4 December 1933, PRO, FO 371/16751, C10679, ff. 72–80.
3  Von Nidda file, BDC. See also: PRO, FO 371/20739, C4198, f. 181.
4  Himmelmann file, BDC.
5  Boehm file, BDC.
6  PRO, FO 371/16751, C10434, ff. 67–71.
7  *Ibid.*
8  26 October 1934, PRO, FO 371/17731, C7342, ff. 185–88. Bene's Circular Letter dated 9 October was enclosed.
9  *News Chronicle*, May 1934, undated press cutting at the Wiener Library, London. See also Report of H. Morse, 2 May 1934, PRO, FO 371-17730, C2983, ff. 90–94.
10 Report of H. Morse, 28 January 1935, PRO, FO 371/18868, C1070, f. 155.
11 *Ibid.* 3 May 1935, PRO, FO 371/18868, C3764, ff. 229–34.
12 Special Branch Reports, 9 and 13 November 1935, PRO, FO 371/18869, C7704, and C7756, ff. 311–19.
13 Report of H. Morse, 30 August 1934, PRO, FO 371/17730, C6000, ff. 158-62.
14 Report of W. East, 18 October 1935, PRO, FO 371/18868, C7384, ff. 192–97.
15 *Ibid.*
16 Bohle to Hess, 14 March 1934, PAB: *Chef der AO*, Vol. 49, No. 116.
17 Heide to Aschmann, 4 June 1934, NA microcopy T-120, roll 3217, file 7607-H.
18 Bene to Hoffmann, 3 November 1934, NA microcopy T-81, roll 35, folder 20.
19 Hoffmann to Bene, 12 November 1934, *ibid.*
20 Hoffmann to Bene, 22 November 1934; Bene to Hoffmann, 26 November 1934; and Hoffmann to Bene, 30 December 1934, *ibid.*
21 Hoffmann to Bene, 22 January 1935, *ibid.*
22 Hoffmann to Bene, 15 February 1935, *ibid.*
23 Hoffmann to Bene, 14 March, and Bene to Hoffmann, 25 April 1935, *Ibid.*
24 Hoffmann to Bene, 4 May 1935, *ibid.*
25 Hoffmann to Bene, 3 January 1935, *ibid.* Hoffmann spells the name Luton-Jonson, but he probably intended F.M. Luttmann-Johnson.
26 Bene to Hoffmann, 19 January 1935, *ibid.*
27 Hoffmann to Bene, 3 April 1935, *ibid.*
28 Bene to Hoffmann, 5 April 1935, *ibid.*
29 *Daily Telegraph*, 21 February 1934, p. 14.
30 *Ibid.* See also: *The Times*, 21 February 1934, p. 16.
31 FitzRandolph to *Auswärtiges Amt*, 21 February 1934, NA microcopy T-120, 2706/HO31341-342.
32 *Daily Express*, 29 August 1934, p. 9.
33 *The Brown Network; The Activities of the Nazis in Foreign Countries* (New York, 1936). See especially pp. 132–33 and 267. The title page cites no author or editor.
34 Little is known about Bevis other than a brief allusion to him in Kell's report to Vansittart of 4 December 1933, PRO, FO 371/16751, C10679, ff. 72–80. MI5 conjectured that Bevis conspired with the Nazis to discontinue his paper, but the surviving copies do not indicate this.
35 *The Brown Network*, p. 132.
36 Lothar Streicher file, BDC. See also: reports of Hubert Morse of 25 August and 3 September 1934, PRO, FO 371/17730, C5828 and C6226, ff. 157–73.

37  *The Brown Network*, p. 267.
38  *Jewish Chronicle*, p. 25. Willis file, BDC.
39  AA to Willis, 13 June 1934, NA microcopy T-580, roll 86, file 418.

# 4 ESTABLISHING A NAZI BROWN HOUSE

Between December 1931 and April 1933 the National Socialists in London used two rooms at 46 Cleveland Square, W2, as the nearest thing they had to a Party headquarters. By the spring of 1933, however, the number of Party members in the *Ortsgruppe* had risen to nearly one hundred, and a public building like Porchester Hall was inadequate for closed meetings of the members. Therefore they began in earnest to seek premises that the London *Ortsgruppe* could call their own. On 26 April 1933 Otto Bene was able to inform his superior in Hamburg, Ernst Bohle, that he had been able to rent space in Bayswater near Lancaster Gate for a new *NSDAP* headquarters at the Park Gate Hotel, 12 Stanhope Terrace, W2. For Bene, this was a dream come true.[1]

I would request that the enclosed letter be given to the proper authorities. Its publication means a good deal to me because we must try to make our stay at the hotel a paying proposition. It has not been easy to find something suitable for our home. For much of the time the problem has been expense, and then, we were the headquarters, and perhaps there might be problems with the Jews, etc. Also we have been too many, with 80 people twice a week. I think that the present solution is a good one. The owners are pleased to have their rooms rented, and they like to make additional money on the serving of food and drink. Five of our Party Members are also moving in full time. Others will follow. In time we shall hope to rent all twenty rooms in the hotel. Then we shall be completely to ourselves. Please send us everyone who is going to England, even if they are not Party Members.

The rate for rooms and all meals except lunches is reasonable: between £2–10-0 and £3 per week including Sundays. Rooms rented by the day can either include meals or not. We shall make sure that everyone is treated fairly. The location is very central, ten minutes to Piccadilly Circus and fifteen to the City.

Hopefully this venture will succeed. For the first few weeks we shall have to put money into the scheme but there is no use complaining, for without a home the *Ortsgruppe* will disband here.

It did not take the British press long to hear about the premises. On 29 April *The Times* printed a brief notice, "Nazi Club in London," without referring to the Park Gate Hotel, and glossed over any political purpose it might serve. Otto Bene was appointed President of the Club, and was quoted as saying that Party members would not meddle in British politics, nor could British subjects join the organization.[2]

A few days after this article appeared, Colonel Josiah C. Wedgwood raised the subject during Question Time in the House of Commons. He asked the Home Secretary whether the Nazis were establishing a "Brown House" in London like the Party headquarters in Munich called the *Braunes Haus*. Sir John Gilmour replied, "I have no information indicating that there is any intention of starting such an institution in this country."[3] A week later Wedgwood repeated his question, focusing attention on the private hotel newly leased by the Nazis. "May I ask whether he [the Home Secretary] thinks that we need to treat this Nazi house differently from the Bolshevist house which was raided?"[4] It seemed to members like Jimmy Maxton that the Government was favoring the Right at the expense of the Left, as in the case of the imminent visit to London of Alfred Rosenberg. "May I ask the Rt. Hon. gentleman why he refused a request from me a fortnight ago to permit Mr. Leon Trotsky to come to this country, a much more distinguished figure in world politics, and now allows this man [Rosenberg] to come in."[5] The Home Secretary explained that the Government felt obliged to discourage overt propagandists like Trotsky, while it hesitated to interfere with internal matters such as private meetings of the National Socialists.

Meanwhile, Ernst Bohle, the head of the *Auslandsorganisation*, wrote to his superior in Munich, Rudolf Schmeer, urging him to assist the London *Ortsgruppe* in any way he could concerning the new facility. "In Party Member Bene we have one of our most sensible local group leaders abroad, whose ability can well be corroborated by both Party Comrade Schumann of the *Aussenpolitisches Amt* in Berlin and Party Comrade Rosenberg."[6]

During that summer the Park Gate Hotel was featured in an article in the *Daily Herald*, "Nazis Send Cash and Speakers to Convert Britain."[7]

Fascist propaganda is being broadcast under the guise of speeches to the League of Nations Union, local Rotary clubs, University societies, and similar bodies. An English "Brown House" has been established in a hotel in the West End of London as the headquarters from which this campaign is conducted. The chief of the Nazi propaganda organisation is Dr. Thost, whose nominal position is that of London correspondent of the official Nazi newspaper, the *Volkische Beobachter*. His activities have recently been reinforced by a certain Herr Otto Bene. Herr Bene accompanied Alfred Rosenberg . . . on his recent visit to London for the purpose of "explaining" Nazi aims and to lay the foundation for the Hitlerite propaganda machine in Britain.

Such publicity distressed the Nazis who were doing their best to deflect attention from themselves. However, in mid-September the *Daily Herald* scooped all the other papers with a shocking story: "Murder Incitement in London Nazi Club."[8] Their reporter discovered that the names of 33 Germans who had recently been deprived of their citizenship appeared on a poster inside the hotel.[9] Above their names someone had written, "If you meet one of them, kill him. And if he is a Jew, then break every bone in his body." It was pointed out that many on the list were distinguished national figures, such as three former leaders of the German Social Democratic Party: Rudolf Breitscheid, Otto Wels, and Philip Scheidemann, the first Chancellor of the Weimar Republic. Authors like Leon Feuchtwanger and Heinrich Mann were listed, as were journalists and editors like Prof. Georg Bernhardt of the *Vossische Zeitung*, Friedrich Stampfer of *Vorwärts*, and Willi Münzenberg, a leading Communist propagandist. Most of the people actually lived in Paris or Prague, but Breitscheid, Bernhardt, and Albert Grzesinski, a former Prussian Minister of the Interior and Police President of Berlin, were in London, having recently arrived in order to attend an unofficial inquiry into the Reichstag fire. Their presence made the hand-written threat immediate and ominous.

The next day's *Daily Herald* announced on its front page, "Nazis Hold Panic West End Rally."[10] The *Ortsgruppe* had become alarmed when it learned of the paper's disclosure of the offensive poster, and promptly removed it while announcing a rally to be held on the evening of 14 September. More than 200 Germans gathered to hear speeches and sing songs, but their underlying concern was the damaging article which they feared would prompt police action.

For about a month the *Daily Herald* kept silent on the subject of Nazis, but on 17 October it ran an article on page 3 with the headline, "London Nazis Move in Hurry."[11] This dealt with the fact that during the previous week the Party vacated the Park Gate Hotel and moved to the top floor of a block of flats in Westbourne Terrace. Six members were said to be living at this location, while others remained in Bayswater. The move was confirmed by Otto Bene in a note to E. W. Bohle on 14 October.[12] "The address change announced to you several days ago is no longer valid, since we were not allowed to move into the house we had rented. Please address all mail for us to Otto Bene, 102 Westbourne Terrace, London, W2 – Paddington 9194." Jewish landlords were blamed for denying occupancy to the Nazis.

Some years later, in an article titled "In London – Nest of Nazis," which appeared in the *Empire News*, Detective Sergeant William East of Special Branch, Scotland Yard, identified the author of the threats on the poster.[13] A left-wing German student, Gustav Werner Knop, tipped off the *Daily Herald* and then told East how he had become involved in the episode. To begin with, he lived in the same household as a Labour Member of Parliament.[14]

He was interviewed and confirmed to me that he had taken the poster away with him. On the advice of the M.P. he had sold the story to a London daily. . . . After further questioning Knop told me, trembling with fear, who he thought had put up the poster. I asked him of what he was afraid, and he replied that he was in great fear of reprisals from the Nazis here in England. Having told me that he thought the perpetrator of the poster was a Nazi named Erich Dinse, he saw to it he did not go back to the Nazi headquarters in Bayswater.

Erich Dinse came to England in March 1933, two years after joining the Party.[15] He was a Berliner by birth in 1907, and worked as a salesman. Being a dedicated *Alter Kämpfer* may have triggered his decision to put up the poster and adorn it with threatening remarks, but East wanted to verify Dinse's responsibility for the deed, so went to one of the social evenings held aboard the *Monte Pascoal* which was moored along the embankment of the Thames. Pretending that he understood very little German, he joined the heavy drinkers and positioned himself near several of the leaders of the *Ortsgruppe*. He heard Himmelmann say to Dinse in German, "You sheep's-head; you nearly spoiled our evenings like these." Dinse indicated that he did not understand what was meant, so Himmelmann added, "by sticking that notice up."

With this information, the British authorities felt justified in refusing to extend Dinse's visa, since he had entered the country as a student, but had not yet begun his studies. "The Nazis knew full well why he had been sent back, and Dinse, though an ardent Nazi, spent four weeks in a concentration camp for being indiscreet and undisciplined while in London."[16]

From the German records it is clear that Dinse was already in trouble with the Nazi Party.[17] Bene had written to Party Headquarters in Munich complaining of Dinse's rash act, and he eventually came before a *Kreisgericht* (district Party court) charged with determining whether he should be disciplined or expelled from the Party. Dinse plead extenuating circumstances: as an *Alter Kämpfer* who was among those who helped bring the Nazis to power in January 1933, he and his comrades were accustomed to using hyperbole like "breaking the bones of all Jews." He acknowledged that newer Party members might take offense at this rough language, but he pointed out that they were not old enough to remember the "time of struggle" in Germany. He produced several other *Älten Kämpfer* as character witnesses during his trial, all of whom testified that Dinse had not damaged the reputation of the Party. The court exonerated him, but year later he was expelled from the *NSDAP*.[18]

Meanwhile, Colonel Vernon Kell, head of MI5, was closely following the revelations by the *Daily Herald*, as he reported to Sir Robert Vansittart, Permanent Under-Secretary of the Foreign Office.[19]

In October 1933 accusations were made in the *Daily Herald* about the Club [*Ortsgruppe*] being used as a centre for propaganda. Inquiries showed that the meet-

**35**

ings were entirely confined to Germans and that beyond instructions binding upon all members of the party to speak in favour of Hitler and his regime, no outward propaganda was going on.

Negative publicity induced the proprietors of the Park Gate Hotel to terminate the lease with the *Ortsgruppe*, necessitating a move to Westbourne Terrace. The new premises were similar to those the group had occupied in 1931–32 at 46 Cleveland Square, but gone was Bene's dream of a permanent headquarters. Sergeant East quoted him as saying:[20]

> Party Comrades, this is no "Brown House" but the personal residence of myself and Party Comrade Himmelmann. You are free to come here when you like, but we have particular evenings when we wish to gather together as many as possible of our people who are in this country. The second Thursday evening in each month is a strictly Party evening when only those with a membership card will be admitted. On other Thursday evenings you may bring your friends for discussion and entertainment.

The eviction from the Park Gate Hotel served to spark the interest of the Metropolitan Police Special Branch which decided to begin infiltrating National Socialist meetings. As one member of the Foreign Office admitted, "It was a clever feat of Sergeant East to be present at this meeting."[21] Henceforth, Party members had to be much more circumspect coming and going from Westbourne Terrace. Bene directed them "to disburse in groups of three or four persons so as to avoid any comment from neighbours or passers-by."[22]

On 29 January 1934 Bene and Himmelmann had to move out of their flat at 102 Westbourne Terrace to another at number 27, typifying the dilemma that German organizations in London faced: an acute shortage of space in which to live as well as congregate. To address this problem, the *Ortsgruppe* met on 12 December 1933 to explore possible solutions.[23] Attending from the German Embassy were First Secretary Ernst H. Rüter, Second Secretary Theodor Auer and Press Attaché Dr. Sigismund FitzRandolph. Otto Bene and Baron Tassilo Krup von Nidda were there in behalf of the National Socialist Party, and Theodor Seibert represented the German Press Association. The German community's chief social organization, the *Deutsche Verein*, sent its Secretary, the London solicitor Eduard Cruesemann, while the Catholic Church Rektor Schnitzler and the Lutheran pastor, Fritz Wehrhan, came as well. There were also delegates from the Anglo-German Academic Bureau and the German Engineering Group. It did not take long for them to agree on the need for a *Deutsches Haus*.

Otto Bene applauded this idea, pointing out the needs of the growing *Ortsgruppe* which already numbered upwards of 300, and would undoubtedly increase to 500–600 in the coming year. Their requirements included space for secretarial help, small conference rooms, a large hall, lodging accommodations, and a small restaurant. The Anglo-German Academic Bureau already had adequate office space, but badly needed a lecture hall as well as classroom space for language lessons. The *Deutsche Verein* favored the establishment of a *Deutsches Haus*, provided that it could be reserved for their own social evenings. Pastor Wehrhan was enthusiastic because currently German youth had nowhere to meet, nor did the various churches have a place to congregate.

It became apparent as they talked that their expectations warranted a fairly elaborate building, not merely four or five floors of a typical West End house. Soon they were back to considering a small hotel like the one the *Ortsgruppe* had leased earlier that year. The Montague Hotel in Bloomsbury was mentioned as the kind and size of building that might be rented, and Eduard Cruesemann was delegated to explore this possibility and assess the legal implications of operating a private hotel.

There were some doubters, like retired naval Captain Otto Karlowa. He asked where the money would come from for such an extensive undertaking, and could a strictly German center be established in London without incurring criticism from the press and the public. Others looked to German business firms in Britain as well as from the Reich Treasury and the *NSDAP* headquarters in Germany to provide start-up costs. Everyone agreed that once such a house was established, it should be self-sustaining.

At the conclusion of this exploratory session, Otto Bene urged that the German Embassy take responsibility for coordinating the search for accommodation; deciding when to call the next meeting of the planning committee; and using its staff to prepare a solicitation letter which would be sent to potential contributors. The Embassy agreed, and began doing the preliminary work for a meeting of the planning committee to take place 7 February.[24] Convening at the Embassy was significant, as Bene well knew. It helped convert the planning for a *Deutsches Haus* into a national undertaking rather than a purely Nazi Party project, and this would increase its appeal among Germans as well as defuse British criticism.

By April 1934 the components were assembled, and a letter proposing a goal of £7,000 was drafted and distributed. It was restrained in its tone, contrasting markedly with the handbills posted in German organizations and clubs:[25]

> ATTENTION – A German House Should Arise in London – London is the business metropolis of the world. For a long time London has been on the way for German pioneers carrying German work to new markets. London is also the gathering place for Germans who build for the Fatherland a bridge of understanding to the British people.

The principal German organizations in London as well as eight Protestant and Catholic churches endorsed this appeal, and in spite of their intentions to be non-partisan and non-political, no one could miss the name of Hitler's chief representative in London – Otto Bene – at the head of the list.

Meanwhile, Special Branch of Scotland Yard knew about the project and monitored its progress. On 25 April Inspector Hubert Morse reported on the planning session in late March when the aims of a *Deutsches Haus* were discussed, although he mistakenly stated that Ambassador Hoesch and Hans Wilhelm Thost were involved. He also revealed that the German Government had declined to subsidize the undertaking, but said that the Nazi Party leaders had promised £2,500 if the rest of the money could be raised.

Morse guessed that there was a reason the Nazis wanted to provide accommodations for visitors:[26]

> The motive behind this, of course, is the necessity from a Party point of view, to get hold of German visitors here and look after them socially in order to keep them as far as possible from contamination by anti-Nazi propaganda whilst in London.

He also made an astute observation that was not apparent in the Minutes and reports kept by the Germans.

> There is also a hitch occasioned by the reluctance of the old-established German Social Club here, the *Deutsche Verein*, and also the Anglo-German Academic Bureau, to relinquish their individuality and go entirely into the Nazi Party camp.

Morse concluded by saying that the real barrier to the scheme was financial, especially in view of German business stagnating abroad. Three weeks later Ernst Rüter confirmed this when he informed the planning committee that so far only one thousand Pounds had been subscribed, a most disappointing return from the 1,500 letters sent to firms and individuals.[27] Rüter wondered if the time had come to give up the idea of acquiring the Montague Hotel, and think about something more modest. Compounding their problems, late in August, for the fifth time in two years, the *Ortsgruppe*'s lease was broken.[28]

> The premises at 27 Westbourne Terrace, W2, which have been in the occupation of the London *Ortsgruppe* of the *NSDAP* since the 29th January, 1934, have been suddenly sold over the heads of the occupants to a firm named Sidney Van den Bergh and Co., 11 Albion Mews East, W2, provision merchants, whose intention it is to convert into flats and sublet.

The owners of this company were Jewish, increasing the sense of outrage felt by the *Ortsgruppe*.[29]

> This proceeding is interpreted by the *NSDAP* representatives as a manifestation of Jewish intrigue against the Party; the more so as several other houses in the same street are for sale and are alleged to be more advantageously purchasable

and more suited for subletting than No. 27. This has revived the question of the founding of a combined German centre in London to be known as the *Deutsches Haus*.

As of late February 1935 only £1,500 had been subscribed, leading Bene to seek help from Berlin.[30] He proposed approaching Franz Xaver Hasenöhrl, head of the Foreign Department of the Propaganda Ministry, and perhaps even Goebbels. Ambassador Hoesch recommended seeking the advice of Hans Dieckhoff of the Foreign Ministry. Raising funds from any Ministry promised to be difficult, especially for a project outside Germany, since the Mark was so devalued. Dieckhoff confirmed that he had no available funds, but directed Bene to approach the Propaganda Ministry.[31]

The last known meeting of the planning committee took place at the German Embassy on 5 June 1935.[32] Only eight committee members were present, while eleven were absent, symptomatic of the discouragement that was setting in.

The German community had by this time become used to renting Porchester Hall, having met there since the autumn of 1934 when the *Ortsgruppe* moved from Westbourne Terrace to Cleveland Terrace. Surviving records of the Paddington Borough Council include accounts of most of their meetings in both the large and small halls.[33] Meeting rooms were generally booked in the name of the German Club or the German Colony, with no mention of the Nazi Party. However, only Party members could attend. The following schedule indicates how frequently they used the Small Hall.

1934: 29 June; 13 July; 18 October; 8 and 21 November; 6 and 20 December.

1935: 10, 25 and 30 January; 7 and 21 February; 14 and 28 March; 11, 18, and 30 April; 9 May; 13 June; 15 August; 7 November.

1936: 5 March (meeting postponed until 19 March during the period of mourning for George VI); 2 April; 14 May; 11 June; 9 July; 13 August; 29 October; 3 and 12 November.

1937: 21 January; 5 and 11 February; 18 March; 7, 15 and 20 April; 20 and 26 May: 24 June; 15 July; 5 August; 15 October and 9 December.

1938: 13 January; 10 February; 10 March; 7 and 21 April; 12 May; 10 June; 14 July; 4 August; 24 November and 8 December (both cancelled).

The gaps in scheduling may reflect the great flurry of activity in early 1937 when Otto Karlowa took over as *Landesgruppenleiter* and reorganized the leadership roles within the group. Eventually the original London *Ortsgruppe* subdivided into two, and later three, sections. Predictably, the summer months were slow since many went on holiday, especially from late August through the end of September.

Meetings that took place in the Large Hall had various purposes. Since there was enough space to accommodate 600 to 1,200 people, it was ideal for dances, films, parties, and lectures. These appeared on the following schedule:

1934: 1 May (reception); 29 June (dance).

1935: 29 January (cinematographic exhibition); 14 February (concert); 21 March (dance); 1 May (reception); 25 May (dance); 25 June (social evening); 16 July (dance); 4 October(reception); 12 November (film showing); and 28 November (dance).

1936: 17 January (dance); 31 January (lecture); 14 February (dance cancelled); 18 March (dance); 19 June (dance); 15 July (meeting); 2 October (meeting); 20 October (dance); 8 December (concert).

1937: 12 January (dance); 25 and 28 January (meetings); 25 February (dance); 4 March (meeting); 30 April (meeting); 11 June (dance); 21 October (meeting); 19 November (dance).

1938: 2 May (meeting); 27 May (dance); 22 July (dance); 30 September (Harvest Festival meeting, cancelled); 21 October (dance, cancelled); 18 November (dance, cancelled).

Certain occasions were always celebrated in the Large Hall, a pattern established over the years. In honor of May Day 1938 and Hitler's recent birthday, Karlowa reminded the crowd that they had gathered in this place for the past five years, providing stability and continuity for those separated from their homeland.[34]

When the Large Hall was unavailable, the community was not without adequate alternatives. On 9 November 1937 it hired Paddington Hall for a joint memorial service recalling the armistice of 1918 and the Nazi martyrs of Munich in 1923. A month later the same hall was used for a German children's Christmas party. Paddington Council also administered small and large swimming baths which were used by the German community increasingly from the spring of 1936 until the late summer of 1938. Several organizations also had their meetings at Seymour Hall which was under the jurisdiction of the Marylebone Borough Council.

Germans maintained a low profile when they came together in these halls, and only rarely did they incur criticism. However, the visit by Ernst Wilhelm Bohle unleashed an avalanche of complaints. As head of all German citizens abroad, he was scheduled to speak in the Large Hall on 1 October 1937. Respected and feared by all *Auslandsdeutsche*, his appearance promised to fill the hall to overflowing. Therefore, five days beforehand, the Paddington Town Clerk appealed to William Strang, the head of the Central Department of the Foreign Office, because "on the present occasion . . . the Mayor had received a violent letter of protest from Mr. Brendon Bracken, M.P. for North Paddington."

Edmund Himmelmann, Secretary of the German colony, assured the Paddington Council that the meeting would proceed peacefully, especially since Ambassador von Ribbentrop would be present. Admission was restricted to German citizens and those of German descent, and in order to secure tickets, people had to show their passports or other forms of identification. As with all such meetings, the police would be evident as well as representatives from the Borough Council.

Strang's response to the Clerk was that the Foreign Office had no official role in this sort of activity. Although Strang knew that Bohle was coming to London, he was unaware of plans to have him speak at Porchester Hall. In any case, he maintained that "it was entirely a matter for the Paddington Council to decide."[35] In answer as to whether it was too late too call off the meeting without creating an "incident," he acknowledged that a certain amount of blame would be levied, whatever happened.

To everyone's relief, the Paddington meeting took place without incident, but the Marylebone Borough Council was less fortunate in their letting of Seymour Hall several months later. Again, Brendon Bracken submitted the complaint, this time against hiring the hall for an Anglo-German *Komeradschaft* dance on 18 March by Major T. S. Chalmers. Several Labour members tried to rescind the booking, suggesting "that the Council do disagree . . . as relates to the letting of the Seymour Hall to Major T. S. Chambers," but the motion was defeated.

During February and March, letters and petitions poured in to all departments of the Marylebone Council from groups such as the Marylebone League of Youth, the St. Marylebone Labour Party, the St. Marylebone Trades Council, the St. Marylebone's Peace Council, the Amalgamated Union of Upholsterers, Morley House of Regent Street, and the Marylebone Communist Party.[36] Complaints appeared in the local press.[37] G .E. M. de Ste. Croix, Secretary of the St. Marylebone Labour Party, characterized the dance as a celebration of the *Anschluss* with Austria. The *Daily Worker* questioned why Seymour Hall was closed to Communist meetings but open to Nazi ones.

The dance would have taken place as scheduled had not the organizers themselves cancelled it "as the result of exceptional circumstances which arose," by which they undoubtedly meant the annexation of Austria by Germany.[38] This aroused deep indignation throughout the British Isles, and was followed in September 1938 by the Czech crisis which brought about a profound change in Anglo-German relations. The *Oktoberfest* was suddenly cancelled by the Paddington Council because Porchester Hall was designated as an air raid evacuation center.[39]

The Munich Agreement, signed in late September, did not allay people's fears or convince them of Germany's good faith. Both the Labour and the Municipal Reform members of the Paddington Council voiced their doubts about leasing their facilities to Germans. A special meeting was called for 20 October.[40] Mayor Lt. Col. J. B. P. Karslake presided, and Councilor L. F. Thurlow moved that "the Baths Committee be instructed that in no circumstances shall any premises under their control be let to foreign nationals." Since all of Porchester Hall, including the swimming baths, came under the jurisdiction of this sub-committee, the phrase "foreign nationals" needed clarification, and Thurlow amended the motion to read, "no hall under the authority of the Baths Committee shall be let to any branch of the German Nazi organisation."[41] He contended that ratepayers should not be forced to subsidize facilities used by groups repugnant to them. It had cost the Council £4,944 to maintain Porchester Hall during the past year, and another £1,000 would be needed for the current year. He went on to say that about one-third of the residents of his ward, Maida Vale, were Jewish, and they could hardly be expected to view the situation with indifference.

His remarks made their way into the local *Bayswater Chronicle*:[42]

> The Council would also be told that these meetings were conducted by "well-behaved, nice Aryan people." These were not ordinary social functions but secret gatherings. He hoped that as a result of that meeting the public in Paddington would know who was pro-Nazi and who was not.

Popular as this sentiment was, some members of the Paddington Council opposed Thurlow's motion. Councilor G. de Swiet (Labour) recalled having attended one of the German meetings the previous May and found it perfectly innocuous, causing him to question the need to change the current policy, provided that Councilors were allowed to continue attending such meetings. As to the implications of barring the press from their gatherings, Swiet posited that the Germans feared accurate reporting more than misrepresentation of their activities in newspaper columns. In either case, he declared that there were not sufficient reasons to keep Germans from using Porchester Hall.

Municipal Reform Party Councilor and Vice-Chairman of the Baths Committee, R. J. P. Campbell, also dissented, pointing out that there had been "obvious misrepresentation" in Thurlow's remarks. "The Council do not let any halls under their control to the German Nazis, but to the German Colony, and the German Swimming Club. The Honourary Secretary of the organisation lives in Paddington and is a ratepayer." This reference provoked laughter among his listeners, which led Campbell to continue more passionately.[43]

> His personal attitude was that they must be prepared to do everything possible to *defend personal liberty*. While the Germans were given the liberty to live in this country, it was only right that they should also have the liberty to hire halls when they wished. He knew the difficulties of getting respectable lettings. The Germans had behaved themselves like ladies and gentlemen. (disturbances) "For God's sake," he urged, "let us hold on to our personal liberties here. It is the only way to preserve world peace." (uproar)

On the 9th of November 1938, the Jews in Germany were subjected to a horrific attack that included systematic plunder and assault known as

*Kristallnacht*. The following Monday the Baths Committee met in emergency session to reconsider their policy. It was not a meeting open to the press, but the local newspaper learned what had transpired. "Recent events in Germany are probably responsible for the decision which it is understood was reached by the Baths and Washhouses Committee."[44] At the next meeting of the Borough council on 24 November the following regulations were adopted.[45]

(1) That admission to the meetings be granted to any members of the Paddington Borough Council by prior arrangement with the hirer.
(2) That facilities will be given for the admission of accredited representatives of recognised Press agencies.
(3) That no uniforms shall be worn.
(4) No singing of any songs containing objectionable references to the Jews or to the Nationals of any country with which this country is on friendly terms.

While these stipulations apparently allowed the *Ortsgruppe* to request the use of Porchester Hall, the following clause effectively denied them access.

We have intimated to the hirer that in view of the antagonistic feelings now being manifested in regard to anti-Jewish measures in Germany, it would be desirable that no further applications for the hire of the Hall should, at present, be made.

Thwarted once again, the *NSDAP* decided to solve their congregational needs by exploiting a recent Nazi acquisition in London. As a result of the annexation of Austria by Germany, the Austrian Legation in Belgrave Square had become their property, so Karlowa and the *Landesgruppe* moved there, where they were able to have instruction classes, visiting lecturers, receptions, and dances. The Nazis regarded this as giving the Austrians the opportunity to have their London diplomatic base be the Party's much longed-for *Deutsches Haus*.

The residents of Paddington and Marylebone were relieved that their public halls were not going to be contaminated by either Communist or Nazi meetings in the future, but they still suffered from protesters, as reported to the British Foreign Office in March 1939.[46]

Dr. Velhagen of the German Embassy rang me up this afternoon to say that there had been a demonstration outside No. 28 Cleveland Terrace – the headquarters of the German community in London – with shouts of "down with the Nazis", "Out with the Nazi spies".

The Foreign Office assured the German Embassy that adequate police protection would always be provided, but they warned that one of the inconveniences of a democracy was the freedom to protest. The rented house at 28 Cleveland Terrace would still be vulnerable to public clamor, but the National Socialists could retreat behind the guarded gates of the former Austrian Legation.

## NOTES

1 Otto Bene to Ernst Bohle, 26 April 1933, *Bundesarchiv*, Koblenz, Schumacher Collection, 296. See Also: NA microcopy T-580, roll 56.
2 *The Times*, 29 April 1933, p. 13.
3 *Parliamentary Debates*, 5th series, Vol. 277 (3 May 1933), col. 838.
4 *Ibid.*, Vol. 277 (11 May 1933), col. 1682.
5 *Ibid.*
6 Bohle to Schmeer, 2 May 1933, Schumacher Collection. See note 1 above.
7 *Daily Herald*, 15 July 1933, p. 3.
8 *Ibid.*, 14 September 1933, p. 1.
9 For a discussion of deprivation of citizenship, see: J. P. Fox, "Nazi Germany and Emigration to Great Britain," in G. Hirschfeld (ed.), *Exile in Great Britain* (Leamington Spa, 1984), pp. 42–43.
10 *Daily Herald*, 15 September 1933, pp. 1–2.
11 *Daily Herald*, 17 October 1933, p. 3.
12 Bene to Bohle, 14 October 1933, Schumacher Collection. See note 1 above.
13 William East, "In London – Nest of Nazis," *Empire News*, 6 October 1940, p. 9.
14 *Ibid.*
15 Dinse file, BDC.
16 East, *Empire News*, 6 October 1940, p. 9.
17 Dinse file, BDC.
18 In 1939 Dinse was reinstated to the Party.
19 Kell to Vansittart. 4 December 1933, PRO, FO 371/16751, C10679, ff. 77–78.
20 Report of William East, 9 November 1933, PRO, FO 371/16751, C10434, ff. 67–71.
21 *Ibid.*, f. 66.
22 *Ibid.*
23 At the *Auswärtiges Amt* in Bonn there is a series of reports dealing with the *Deutsches Haus*, filed under "German Embassy Archives, London, bundle 179." Hereafter this collection will be referred to as *Deutsches Haus*.
24 *Ibid.* Minutes of 7 February 1934 meeting are misdated 9 February 1934.
25 *Ibid.* Copies of the April 1934 form letter and handbill are also in the Report of 24 March 1934.
26 Report of Inspector Hubert Morse, 25 April 1934, PRO, FO 371/17730, C2943, ff. 84–89.
27 *Deutsches Haus*. Circular letter of 14 May 1934.
28 Report of Hubert Morse, 25 August 1934, PRO, FO 371/17730, C5828, ff. 156–57.
29 *Ibid.*
30 *Deutsches Haus*. Hoesch to Dieckhoff, 27 February 1935.
31 *Ibid.*, Dieckhoff to Hoesch, 7 March 1935.
32 *Ibid.*, Report of 7 June 1935.
33 Metropolitan Borough of Paddington, Minutes of Council, Vol. IXX, can be found at the Marylebone Library. The lettings of both the Small and Large Halls of Porchester Hall is filed under "Committee on Baths and Washhouses."
34 *Deutsche Zeitung in Gross Britannien*, 7 May 1938, p. 3.
35 PRO, FO 371/20740, C6770, ff. 112–14.
36 *Ibid.*, 17 February, 21 March and 28 April 1938, pp. 282, 415–17.

37 *Record and West London News,* 19 March 1938, p. 2; 26 March, p. 7; 2 April, pp. 2 and 5; *Daily Worker,* 12 March 1938, p. 5.
38 Metropolitan Borough of St. Marylebone, *Minutes of the Proceedings of the Council and Reports of Committees,* 17 February and 10 March 1938, pp. 292, 416–17.
39 *Bayswater, Paddington, Kensington and West London Chronicle,* 30 September 1938, p. 8.
40 *Ibid.,* 14 October 1938, p. 4, and 21 October 1938, p. 1.
41 Paddington, Minutes, p. 536.
42 *Bayswater Chronicle,* 21 October 1938, p. 1.
43 *Ibid.*
44 *Ibid.,* 18 November 1938, p. 1.
45 *Ibid.,* 25 November 1938, p. 1.
46 PRO, FO 371/22988, C3830, ff. 285–86. Memo dated 22 March 1939.

# 5 THE EXPULSION OF HANS WILHELM THOST

On 29 October 1935, a Scotland Yard officer personally delivered a sealed envelope from the Home Office to Hans Thost, the London correspondent of the *Völkischer Beobachter*, at his lodgings, 316 Combe Lane, Wimbledon.[1]

> I am directed by the Secretary of State to say that he has had under consideration the question of your continued residence in the United Kingdom and has decided that he is unable to permit you to prolong your stay further. You should therefore make arrangements to leave the country not later than the 18th November 1935.

This came as a terrible shock to Thost, since it not only brought discredit on the Nazi regime, but also jeopardized his career as a newspaper reporter. He hastened to seek the advice of Ambassador Leopold von Hoesch, hoping to salvage the situation. Von Hoesch immediately sent a low-level member of the Embassy staff, Second Secretary Dr. Albert Hilger Van Scherpenberg, to make inquiries at the Foreign Office.[2] Van Scherpenberg was able to secure an appointment with Rex Leeper, the Australian who headed the Foreign Office Press Department, and asked why the British Government was taking this action. Leeper would not give a direct answer, and said only that it was Foreign Office policy not to provide reasons for such a decision.

Van Sherpenberg reminded Leeper that the Germans had provided a full explanation to the British as to why they found it necessary to oust Pembroke Stephens, the *Daily Express* reporter from Germany, in the spring of 1934. Nonetheless, Leeper remained adamant, and pointed out that no explanations had been forthcoming in the autumn of 1933 when Noel Panter was asked to leave Germany. Van Scherpenberg countered that Panter had not been the official correspondent for the *Daily Telegraph*, and warned that if Thost were forced to leave, there would be additional reprisals against British journalists in Germany.

46

After their acrimonious exchange, Leeper informed his colleagues, "I have never met Herr Van Sherpenberg before, but his manner throughout was nervous and uncomfortable. The Embassy are no doubt frightened of Dr. Thost."[3] Since Thost was influential in Nazi Party circles, but not in diplomatic ones, Leeper may have thought that the German Embassy would be blamed for Thost's removal, especially since Ambassador von Hoesch and a number of his diplomatic colleagues were not yet members of the *NSDAP*.

Upon returning to the German Embassy, Van Sherpenberg told Hoesch that he detected the vaguest hint that more information might be forthcoming if the expulsion order were broached at a higher level. Accordingly, the next day von Hoesch made an appointment to see the highest ranking Foreign Office person available, Deputy Under-Secretary Orme Sargent. Neither the Foreign Secretary, Samuel Hoare, nor the Under Secretary, Robert Vansittart, was in London at the time. Sargent revealed that the Home Office decision was based not on Thost's journalistic work, but on his non-professional activities, and beyond this he could not comment because he did not know the details.[4]

Van Hoesch was relieved that military espionage was not involved. To the German Foreign Ministry he wrote:[5]

> The English Government had carefully chosen the mildest form of expulsion in order to avoid as far as possible any disruption between their two governments over the Thost case. If His Majesty's Government had acted without due regard for Anglo-German relations, then an arrest with a subsequent trial would have been considered, something which was to be avoided if at all possible. In the light of my conversations and those of others in the Embassy with Thost, concerning his non-journalistic activities during the past month, it becomes clear that he committed certain indiscretions, of course with the best intentions and with a desire to serve the German cause.

While not going into details, Ralph Wigram, head of the Central Department of the Foreign Office, confirmed the charge against Thost in a letter to Sir Eric Phipps, British Ambassador to Germany.[6]

> The reason is that his continued presence here is considered undesirable, as there is proof that amongst his activities has been espionage. The case on the facts is definite and we have for some time wondered if it would not be the right thing to get rid of him.

Clearly, there was a significant difference between the way that the Germans and the Foreign Office perceived Thost's offense. Von Hoesch and Thost were convinced that it was something he had done during the past month which incurred British wrath, while Wigram makes it clear that the problem was of longer duration. No doubt he had in mind, among other things, the Special Branch report of early 1935 in which Thost is characterized as having a "tendency to intrigue on his own which does not meet with Party approval here."[7]

In explaining the situation to Sir Eric Phipps, Wigram indicated that the Foreign Office intended to use the recent expulsion of a British Consul at Hanover in order to justify the removal of Thost. "Now, although we have no intention of connecting his departure ostensibly with the Aue case, the latter did bring things to a head and has produced this decision at this particular moment." Capt. W. R. Aue had been accused by the German Government of transmitting information about certain defense facilities in the region near Hanover to the British Embassy in Berlin. On the surface, Aue appeared quite innocent: a retired officer from the British army in India, who ran a bookbinding business. The British viewed his reports as ordinary consular communiqués, while the Germans saw them as espionage, since the information concerned military installations.[8] Wigram also told Phipps that Vansittart did not mind if the Germans were deceived into thinking that Thost was the *quid pro quo* for Aue's expulsion.

Thost and von Hoesch continued to be puzzled about the reasons behind the deportation order. However, a review of Thost's career in London provides numerous clues. Besides his journalistic endeavors, Thost had many other interests and undertakings, people with whom he came in contact, and semi-political commissions from officials in Germany. His position in Britain was markedly enhanced once Hitler became Chancellor in January 1933. No longer was he simply the London correspondent for a lunatic-fringe newspaper. He now represented the official and increasingly powerful *NSDAP* press. His Party Comrades continued to hold him in high regard and recognized him as one who, like themselves, had struggled for years to attain power. From now on, the British would accord him greater respect, as someone who had contacts in the New Germany and who could get things done.

Between 1930 and 1935, Thost served Alfred Rosenberg in a dual capacity: as London correspondent to the Editor-in-Chief of the *Völkischer Beobachter*, and as an *Alter Kämpfer* in the inner circle of the *NSDAP*. As an experienced Party comrade, he kept Rosenberg informed about Party matters, ran errands for him, complained about the unpatriotic spirit of other Germans, and occasionally asked favors of him.

A month after Hitler came to power, Thost asked Rosenberg to investigate Wilhelm von Richthofen, who had been loudly proclaiming his political contacts in Berlin, and who therefore wanted the German Embassy in London to provide him with a job. Thost knew of several ambiguous episodes in von Richthofen's past, and wanted background information and assurances of his character. One example of von Richthofen stretching the truth was his alleged friendship with Count Bernstorff, Councilor of the Embassy, who, he said, had been at Oxford with him. In fact, while at university, von Richthofen had actually merely joined the Oxford movement, a religious group.

Thost suspected that Wilhelm Richthofen was an unhappy man who had tried various careers without success, having come to a meeting of the London *Ortsgruppe* brandishing an expired *NSDAP* membership card, and then writing friends in Berlin lamenting the absence of an *Ortsgruppe* in London. Thost's unease with von Richthofen's past prompted him to caution Rosenberg not to confuse this man with Gunter von Richthofen who, along with Eduard Ritter von Schleich, made the daring flight to England in 1932.[9]

From other sources it appears that Wilhelm von Richthofen was indeed hard pressed for money and tried every means of securing employment.[10] Having joined the *NSDAP* in the spring of 1932 with card number 738662, he proceeded to ignore the monthly dues. By October of that year he was dropped from the Party, but a few months later when Hitler came to power he persuaded the *Auslandsorganisation* to restore him to full membership. However, the pattern of not paying dues persisted, and by the spring of 1934 he was again dropped from the Party. This time it took a *Kreisgericht* hearing to reinstate him because he was also accused by Prince Wittgenstein of "uncomradely behavior." The Prince had invited von Richthofen to attend his wedding in Warsaw, and had even lent him money for the train fare. Von Richthofen then boldfacedly borrowed more money from the bride's family on the pretext that he did not have enough to make the return trip to Germany. Afterwards he refused to repay the loans, which led Thost to believe that he would be an embarrassment to the Party. Uncertain of this assessment, Thost requested instructions from Rosenberg.

Among Thost's most important assignments was the arrangement of Alfred Rosenberg's visit to London in the spring of 1933. As much as Rosenberg wished to bypass the German Foreign Ministry, as he had in November 1931 when travelling to Britain as an informal emissary of the *NSDAP*, this time the Party was in power, and he had to go through designated channels. After seeking the advice of "Lord H.", Thost suggested that Rosenberg delay announcing his intention to make an official visit until Sir Robert Vansittart was back in London on 5 May. Unlike the Foreign Secretary and other politicians who held office only when their party was in power, Vansittart was the Permanent Under-Secretary of State, and the most influential person in the Foreign Office.

Although it was necessary to arrange Rosenberg's visit through the German Embassy in London, Thost thought it well not to alert them too far in advance.[11]

People like Bernstorff and Van Scherpenberg will do everything they can to put a spoke in your wheel. I think it best if I first find out when the people you wish to see will be in London, and then you inform the Embassy of your intention. It will then no longer be possible for those gentlemen to intrigue against you.

The spring of 1933 provided Thost with two opportunities to address public gatherings, one in a committee room of the House of Commons and the other at the Oxford University German Club. The former was arranged by Edward Doran, Member of Parliament for North Tottenham, and Thost took as his topic, "The True Meaning of Germany's Attitude toward the Jews."[12] Thost later looked back upon this evening meeting of 26 April as a high point in his London journalistic career. About 50 people attended, one-third of whom were M.P.s. Not surprisingly, the *Jewish Chronicle* was unimpressed.[13]

> Indeed the meeting was treated with such marked indifference by the Members generally that Dr. Thost . . . can be under no apprehension as to the true feeling in the House, and the non-representative character of the auspices under which his lecture was given. . . . He admitted that in the case of many Jews the loss of jobs is a terrible tragedy, and that the Nazis were perfectly aware of it, but he asked whether it was not also a tragedy for Germans to lose their jobs. . . . Dr. Thost was asked a number of direct questions to which he gave evasive replies. When it was pointed out to him that a comparison of census figures for 1910 and 1925 showed a decline of over 50,000 in the Jewish population of Germany, he replied that the 1925 figure did not include those Jews who had renounced their faith or who had become Communist. He was also asked whether the German Government had deprived Jews of their full civil rights as citizens, because in his address he had referred to them as aliens. His reply was that as the Jews claimed to be a nation they were regarded as foreigners in Germany. Dr. Thost's evasiveness evoked complaints from several Members.

At one point in the proceedings Major Henry Adam Proctor moved a resolution "deploring the attitude of the German Government toward the Jews, as tending to destroy the spirit of good will which should exist between the English and the German people." This was duly seconded by J. T. Morris. Doran, who had called the meeting, tried in vain to avoid any expression of sentiment on the part of those present, but the motion passed unanimously by voice vote.

Thost's appearance in Oxford on 18 May drew far more local attention. As the *Manchester Guardian* recorded:[14]

> [He was] the centre of a rowdy demonstration of undergraduates and other members of the October Club, the Communist organisation. Before the meeting began students in red shirts distributed anti-Fascist pamphlets among the audience. When Dr. Thost arrived, the *Red Flag* was sung and there was hissing and shouting of "down with the butcher." Having made their protest, the interrupters marched out and Dr. Thost then gave his address.

Thost acknowledged that there had been excesses in the Nazi revolution, but said that these must be put into perspective and compared with the far more devastating upheavals of the French Revolution, the Russian Revolution, or even Cromwell's coming to power. As for the Jews losing jobs, they would now be allowed employment proportional to their percentage in the overall population, or about one and a one-half percent. Those Jews who had fought in the

Great War or who had lost fathers and sons could retain their posts within the German economy.

Thost scarcely had time to savor this second public appearance when a severe remonstrance came from Rosenberg after his official trip to London.[15]

> The haste of our conversation in London made it impossible for me to discuss with you a half-personal, half-official matter, which has been brought to my attention from many quarters. More than once Englishmen whom I met claimed that your temperament did not seem suited to London. In spite of your fitting in well, you apparently misjudge the English psyche and accordingly have difficulty making personal acquaintances. It was also felt that you either ignored or misunderstood suggestions made to you, so that I was confronted on four or five occasions with complaints that were polite but went so far as to ask that you be recalled.
>
> The situation in London is such that the correspondent for the *Völkischer Beobachter* is virtually assumed to be a political representative of the Party; and since this unfortunate situation exists, I think it appropriate that in the near future you exchange your London post for another. Rest assured that I appreciate your work very much and I know how much you tried to help the *Völkischer Beobachter* continually and extensively. In addition you have written many valuable articles. Of course it is understood that you will continue working for us in future. I even think that you may be able to work directly for the *Völkischer Beobachter*'s editorial offices in Germany.

Working in Berlin was the dream of many overseas Nazis who longed to be in Germany in the spring of 1933 during the struggle to consolidate the new regime, but this ambition was highly disconcerting to Thost, who had recently remarried and was planning to bring his wife and household furniture to London. Naturally, he did not like being reprimanded and leaving Britain under a cloud, so defended his conduct as best he could, returning to Germany briefly to confront Rosenberg. As a result, Thost was allowed to remain in London and move into his new married quarters at 316 Coombe Lane, West Wimbledon, SW 20.

During 1933 Thost kept Rosenberg informed about the activities and attitudes of an assortment of foreigners living in Britain, whether they were pro- or anti-German. Always interested in undermining the Soviet Union, Thost described a conversation he had with Vladimir von Korostovetz, a Russian diplomat under the Czarist regime who now headed the Ukranian independence movement in London and was responsible to Hetman Skoropadsky in Berlin.[16] Korostovetz claimed that the Jewish writer for *The Times* and other newspapers, Poliakoff, was a paid agent for the Poles and was trying to make contact with the Italian Fascists.[17] Thost puzzled over why he had been introduced to Korostovetz by Van Scherpenberg, who was no friend of National Socialism.[18]

Thost was not always consulted by Rosenberg, as he thought he should be, especially regarding internal Party matters or *Völkischer Beobachter* politics. In early 1934 Rolf Wunderer, who had helped to found the London *Ortsgruppe* in 1931, applied for a job with the *Völkischer Beobachter* after being recalled to Berlin. Because of slanderous remarks Wunderer had made about him, Thost strongly opposed employing the young troublemaker, suggesting that Rosenberg talk to some of the old-timers in the London *Ortsgruppe*, like Bene, in order to gain a more accurate assessment of Wunderer. According to Thost, Wunderer and the first leader of the London *Ortsgruppe*, Dr. Neumann, had done much to split the membership and create an atmosphere of suspicion. Furthermore, Wunderer took far too much credit for establishing the local group, and had no business publishing a recent article in the *Völkischer Beobachter* which disclosed the names of Party members and provided the *Jewish Chronicle* with additional anti-Nazi ammunition.[19]

During the early 1930s, Thost's relations with other journalists were ambivalent. At times he felt he was on good terms with some of the British press, while at other times he felt that editors like Robert Bruce Lockhart had misled him badly. In the spring of 1933 Thost warned Rosenberg that Lockhart was no longer to be believed. "I don't trust Lockhart an inch any more."[20] Thost had been told that in the autumn of 1931 when Rosenberg visited London Lockhart had been asked by the British authorities to keep an eye on the Nazi leader. His subsequent report was highly critical of Rosenberg's boastful manner, and by 1933 Thost felt that Lockhart's paper, the *Evening Standard*, was more hostile to National Socialism than the left-wing *Daily Herald*. When anti-German articles were brought to his attention, "Lockhart always innocently washes his hands," according to Thost. Lockhart's attendance at a banquet honoring the Zionist leader, Chaim Weizmann, convinced Thost that he was hopelessly under Jewish influence, as Lockhart sardonically noted in his diary.[21]

> Dined at home. Disturbed by Thost, the Nazi correspondent. After asking him to write an article in reply to the Brown Book on the "Hitler terror" we have now turned it down. . . . All very awkward for me, as Thost, who came to my home to see me, accused me of having a Jewish secretary, and England of having Jewish watch-dogs in all important posts.

Thost believed that because the *Daily Telegraph* had half Jewish ownership, this accounted for the hostile views of its correspondent in Berlin.[22] However, his real *bête noire* was Norman Ebbutt, the Berlin correspondent at *The Times*, about whom he said, "At the moment Ebbutt's reports are scandalous. He bluntly claims that right, justice, and liberty are turned upside down in Germany, and that every criminal would be pardoned if he shouted 'hurray for my German Fatherland.'"[23] Ebbutt's fondness for drink gave Thost the opportunity to propose an idea to Rosenberg. He suggested that the Nazis arrest Ebbutt, not on political grounds, but for drunken behavior. This would not only embarrass him personally, but also *The Times*, since Lady Astor abhorred alcoholic beverages, and her husband was one of the proprietors of the newspaper. Rosenberg vetoed this suggestion.

A year after Hitler became Chancellor, Thost decided that enough time had elapsed since his arrival in London that he could seek clarification of his financial position with Rosenberg. He reminded him of their recent conversation in Germany, and pointed out that his salary no longer covered his augmented business expenses. Besides doing a certain amount of official entertaining to reciprocate invitations, he had to prepare several special reports, and pay for information about conditions in the East End of London. In addition, he was subject to both British income tax and deductions from his salary by the German government. Worst of all were unexpected dental expenses for him and his wife, plus his wife's gynecological treatments in Britain and Germany which involved her returning to Lübeck with their child. He also hoped to purchase a car, paid for by the *Völkischer Beobachter*, since many of the other German reporters in England had automobiles.

He explained to Rosenberg that he had already secured a 300 Mark advance on his January salary, which he planned to supplement with a further 700 Marks, and then repay the full RM 1,000 during the course of 1934. At his mother's death the previous June, he and his sister were left equal shares in the estate of 250,000 Marks, but delays had ensued because a third party contested the will. However, he planned to honor the debt once he realized his inheritance. Meanwhile, he asked whether the newspaper would pay for his British tax obligation of £11-3-9, and provide £20 per month as an expense allowance from which he would cover the cost of operating a car.[24]

Rosenberg agreed to all these requests, yet was concerned that Thost's journalistic conduct was causing criticism by both the British and the Germans. For instance, having his name appear in the British press was definitely undesirable, as had happened when the *Observer* called attention to his protest against showing the anti-German film *Whither Germany*, because it was "enemy propaganda" that badly distorted what was happening in the New Germany.[25] Rosenberg was also critical of an article that Thost inserted in the *Völkischer Beobachter* implying that there was a conflict of interest in the British Cabinet, since the Secretary of War was also a Director of a large chemical firm. This inference of economic self-interest and corruption could not be tolerated, according to Rosenberg.

Toward the end of 1933 revised guidelines for foreign correspondents were adopted, but Thost told Rosenberg that it was difficult to interview government officials and members of the Cabinet because almost everything they said was off the record; reporters could never cite their sources. It was easier to quote opposition politicians who were willing to voice their opinions, as was true of Lloyd George, who he hoped to interview, and who, as a Welshman, was much less reticent to talk to the press corps.[26]

Complaints about Thost continued to escalate. In a memo sent by the Munich office of the *Völkischer Beobachter* to Berlin, it was noted that Thost had scarcely covered the royal wedding of the Duke of Kent and the Princess Marina, nor had he given enough importance to the disarmament debate in the House of Commons. The editors in Munich were beginning to question whether it was worth the expense of maintaining a reporter in London if what he provided could be gleaned from the wire services.[27]

By early 1935 even the Home Office and the Foreign Office knew of the Nazi *Orstgruppe*'s dissatisfaction with Thost. As Special Branch reported, Thost was in "bad odour with the London Group at present."[28] Consequently, when the British authorities decided to ask Thost to leave, there were many reasons why the Germans might have welcomed their decision. They acknowledged that his career in London had been controversial, and Rosenberg admitted receiving complaints about him over the years. However, there was no evidence that Rosenberg seriously contemplated removing him in 1935. He valued Thost's forceful reporting of the news, and the many small favors he did for him, and he was never bothered by his ideological shortcomings. In fact, his National Socialist credentials were impeccable, and he worked tirelessly for the Party and the Nazi regime. Therefore, whatever the reasons were behind expelling Thost, they were not based on internal German fault-finding.

Thost was correct in assuming that his expulsion stemmed from his non-journalistic activities, but he and Ambassador von Hoesch could only speculate which ones had determined his fate. He admitted to the Ambassador that on one occasion he had made some indiscreet remarks about Winston Churchill while on the telephone to his newspaper in Germany, and perhaps the line had been tapped when he'd asked his editor whether Churchill could be linked somehow to a recent American scandal involving the sale of arms.[29] In his political memoirs, Thost reiterates that his expulsion was connected somehow to criticism of Winston Churchill. "Private circles in touch with Downing Street indicated that Churchill had complained to the Foreign Office about my attacks on him and had demanded my expulsion."[30]

There are two problems with this explanation. First, the evidence that Thost was not ousted because of his journalistic endeavors is overwhelming. Second, there is nothing in the Foreign Office files suggesting that Churchill, or someone on his behalf, lodged complaints about Thost. Ambassador Hoesch may have been closer to the truth when he told the German Foreign Ministry that Thost "became a bit too friendly with Markgraf Csaky-Pallavicini, who lives here and has a rather unsavoury reputation. He introduced Thost to two other agents, Elliott and McKeigue. Thost discussed various projects with them for influencing English public opinion and even the possibility of winning Churchill over."[31] Hoesch went on to say that Thost had previously been warned not to consort with Pallavicini, the same person suspected of being a paid agent for the enemies of Germany by Fritz Hesse of the *Deutsches Nachrichtenbüro*.

Writing to Hitler's personal adjutant, Major Fritz Wiedemann, Thost later confirmed that the treacherous Graf Pallavicini "was the real author behind my expulsion."[32] It is certainly possible that there were foreigners acting as informants for the British. The Marquis Alphonz de Csaky-Pallavicini was head of the Consular section of the Hungarian Legation in London during the early 1930s, and although he was reassigned elsewhere at about the time Thost left Britain, there is no reason to suppose that there was a connection between their departure dates. Pallavicini may well have been anti-Hitler, for after the Nazis occupied Hungary in 1944, he joined the resistance movement.[33] He and Thost may have hatched schemes to propagandize the British public in the early 1930s, but this would not have been grounds for expulsion, especially as a great number of propagandists were allowed to remain in Britain.

One of the most intriguing explanations of Thost's expulsion in 1935 surfaced as recently as 1978. In his book *Most Secret War*, Reginald V. Jones recounts meeting Thost unexpectedly in Oxford shortly before he was asked to leave Britain. At the time, Jones was one of Frederick A. Lindemann's (the future Lord Cherwell) protegés at the Clarendon Laboratory, doing potentially sensitive experiments for the Air Force.[34]

> Arising from my friendship with Carl Bosch, an opportunity for quick thinking soon arose. He was as much interested in military matters as I was myself, and he told me that the Maginot Line was not as impregnable as it was supposed to be because corrupt contractors had put in considerably less concrete than they had been paid for. On Friday 1st November 1935 he told me that he was off to London for the weekend. I was staying in Oxford until Monday, when I would have to go to Farnborough for the vital infra-red trials about the exhaust gases, but of course I did not tell him about this. My Saturday was normal up to tea time, which I spent with others from the Clarendon, as usual, in Elliston and Cavell's. On our return we found a tall stranger, a German, in the laboratory and he explained that he was looking for Carl Bosch; he himself was Dr. Hans W. Thost, the correspondent of the *Völkischer Beobachter* (the "People's Observer"). I said that I was pretty sure that Bosch had gone to London, but that I would telephone his digs. Returning from the telephone, I found that one of my colleagues had taken Thost into my room, where my infra-red detecting equipment was assembled ready for packing. Now a newspaper correspondent might easily be a cover-occupation for a spy, and here he was in the room along with equipment which was about to be used in a secret trial. If he spotted it, and started to ask questions, it could be awkward. I therefore thought that it would be a good idea to give him something to think about, and generally distract his attention. So on the spur of the moment I invented a preposterous story which seemed harmless enough at the time, but could have had unforeseen and unhappy consequences if we had lost the coming war.

I told Thost that I had a certain amount of sympathy with Hitler, and could see why he had pushed out the Jews. Thost almost clicked his heels together with an "Ach, so!" and said that if it were not for the Nazis he would not have his present job. But I went on to wonder whether Hitler had done such a good thing for Germany after all. "What do you mean?" asked Thost. "Well", I replied, "they are very clever and if they started to plot against Germany there could be trouble. For example", I added, "I know that there is a great anti-Nazi organiza- tion run by the Jewish refugees in Britain." With a highly sibilant "Sso!" Thost pulled out a pencil, stretched his arm to expose a stiff white cuff and started to write notes upon it. "Oh yes", I went on, "I thought everyone knew about it. Why, the headquarters are here at Oxford!" "So, here in Oxford!" repeated Thost at the same time inscribing it on his cuff. "Not only that," I added, "but here in this Laboratory. The headquarters is in that room over there, and Franz Simon is the head of it." "Franz Simon," wrote down Thost. I then said that any friend of Bosch's was a friend of mine, and since Bosch was away I would be delighted to offer him dinner. "No, no", said Thost, "I must get back to London at once!" And off he went.

Three weeks later I read on the placards as I went to dinner "R.A.F. SPY SCARE". Being interested in both spies and the R.A.F., I bought a paper but the story conveyed nothing to me – it concerned a Dr. Goertz who had been arrested for making a sketch of the aerodrome at Manston in Kent. Two days later I had a letter from my mother, who had the same interest in spies, saying how glad she was that they had got Dr. Goertz, and how sorry she was that Dr. Thost had got away. I was puzzled because there was no mention of Thost in my paper, and I could not remember having told her that he had visited me in Oxford. So I wrote home asking her how she knew about Thost.

She replied that if only I would read a decent paper like the *Daily Sketch* instead of *The Times*, I should be better informed. She sent me the article from "The Sketch" and there, undoubtedly, was Thost's photograph alongside that of Goertz. It turned out that Thost was one of Goertz's acquaintances, at the least, and that he had been made *persona non grata* by the Home Office because the secu- rity authorities were convinced that he was a spy, without having enough evidence to convict him. So this was round No. 2 of the escapade – I really had had a German spy in the room, and had distracted him from the infra-red apparatus with this cock-and-bull story about the anti-Nazi organization.

We thought no more of it for the next two years; but in August 1937 there was a bout of expulsions of newspaper correspondents between Britain and Germany. We had expelled three correspondents, the Germans retaliated, and this had raised the question of whether newspaper correspondents were really spies or not. As I later heard the story, Simon and Nicholas Kurti were over in Paris doing some low temperature experiments with the big electro-magnet at Bellevue, when they were astonished by an article in a paper published by the Jewish émigrés (probably the *Pariser Tageszeitung*), which said that the British had been thoroughly justified in their action. One of their own reporters had somehow obtained a copy of Thost's report back to his masters on how he had come to be so unsuccessful as to be expelled from Britain. In it he said that while he was in London he had obtained evidence of a great anti-Nazi organization run by the Jewish refugees in Britain, with its headquarters in Oxford and headed by the Jew Simon. Thost had gone up to Oxford to investigate the matter and had succeeded in penetrating the headquarters where he had spoken to two Englishmen. One had immediately gone to the telephone to warn the Jew Simon of Thost's presence, and Simon had clearly used his influence with the English police to get Thost thrown out of the country.

Simon and Kurti came back to Oxford with this astonishing story, having no idea of the true explanation. At least, this is how I heard the story at the time, although it must be mentioned that Nicholas Kurti has no recollection of reading the newspaper in Paris. But Thost certainly published in 1939 a book *A National Socialist in England 1930–1935* in which he stated that he had reported on the activities of Jewish emigrés in England. Fortunately, all ended very well; but when, at the end of the war I was shown a list of all the men to be rounded up by the Nazis if their invasion was successful, there was Simon's name. . . .

On the surface, this account seems to settle the question of why Thost was asked to leave England. It is difficult to imagine a more astute observer than Jones, who later was privy to many of Britain's technical wartime secrets, yet what can be learned about Thost from other sources does not support Jones's story. There is no other independent evidence either in official British or German sources linking Thost to a German espionage organization like the Gestapo or the *Abwehr*. Not all the British archives are yet available, but it is likely that a hint of this would have surfaced in the files currently open to scholars.

Why Thost wanted to see Carl Bosch is puzzling, since Bosch did not know him nor did he ever have any contact with him thereafter.[35] It is perfectly possible that Thost wanted merely to interview him as a German scientist working in Britain.

Jones concluded that Thost was a spy because of the way in which the *Daily Sketch* article linked him with the recently-arrested Hermann Goertz.[36] However, when one compares the *Daily Sketch* account of Goertz's indictment with the coverage in other newspapers, the link is more tenuous. For example, at the Goertz hearing, Major William D. Hinchley-Cooke of MI5 noted that "the name Thost occurred in some notebooks belonging to Dr. Goertz." In them was found the entry, "Thost was until recently the London representative of a German paper."[37] This reference was the only allusion to Thost throughout the extensive pre-trial hearing and subsequent trial and conviction of Goertz. For Goertz, who clearly was working for German Air Intelligence, to have Thost's name and telephone number in his notebook tells us very little about their possible connection, and certainly does not provide evidence of Thost's affiliation with a spy operation. More likely, Thost like other prominent Nazis abroad, was a logical person for Goertz to contact in order to obtain general information or introductions. For years, Thost had been covering the British scene for the *Völkischer Beobachter* and was therefore the likely person to contact if someone were in Britain for a few months.

On the other hand, there was some evidence to support the suspicions surrounding Thost's espionage activity. For example, in a letter he wrote to another of Hitler's adjutants, Wilhelm Brückner, he said:[38]

> In November 1935 my expulsion from England unfortunately caused quite a scandal. I can only say this much here. I worked to the best of my conscience and ability, while at the same time seeking to avoid anything directly against England. The reason for my expulsion was because I wished to be informed about the activities of certain German emigrants. . . .

In his memoirs, Thost acknowledged that he felt it was his duty while residing in London, "to report to the German authorities anything which could harm the Fatherland. . . . I can now openly admit that I sometimes informed Berlin of certain Jewish and emigré currency transactions which were brought to my attention."[39]

During the 1930s Germans going abroad, whether temporarily or permanently, were severely limited in the amount of currency they could take with them. Refugees tried to smuggle out as much money as they could, and sought ways of recovering their former property and assets through third parties. From the Nazi point of view these activities were illegal, and in fact treacherous. Anyone remaining in Germany who connived in such unlawful export of currency or transfer of assets was harshly punished. Thus, it was not unusual for Thost to have been contacted by one or more German agencies to report any suspicious accumulation of wealth by emigré Germans in London. Perhaps it went back to the autumn of 1933 when an unidentified agent called "M" was in London on a special mission for the Propaganda Ministry to look into the expenditures and financial resources of certain Germans resident in Britain.[40] "M" may have asked Thost to keep an eye on some of these individuals and inform him of their activities. Thost probably did not welcome this request, since he later apologized, but justified it as being his patriotic duty to the Party and the nation.

Typical of Thost's reports on Germans abroad, whether refugees or not, was a letter he sent to Rosenberg in which he included information supplied to him by a German student at Trinity College, Cambridge, Herbert Kuhlmann.[41] Kuhlmann joined the Nazi Party in January 1932 and was anxious to demonstrate his fervor by exposing the behavior of a visiting German political scientist, Dr. Hermann Heller, who he alleged was not only a Communist, but also a half-Jew. Thost transmitted this information to Rosenberg with the suggestion that if Kuhlmann's allegations were true, perhaps a way could be found to recall Heller to Germany.

These two instances demonstrate why, in Thost's mind, the most likely reason that he was asked to leave Britain was not that he spied on British military installations or personnel, but that he maintained close surveillance on German refugees abroad.

Thanks to the release of Thost's file by MI5 in 2002,[42] it is finally possible to reconstruct the British decision to force Thost's departure. The newly-available material is surprising in one respect. MI5 was suspicious of Thost within nine months of his arrival in London, and in July 1931 it requested a tap be put on his telephone, and all his incoming mail be opened and selectively photographed by the Post Office. Ironically, Thost complained to his local postman the next month that his letters seemed to take a very long time reaching him from Germany, but he never seems to have guessed at the real cause of their delay. This monitoring of his communications continued until his departure in November 1935, and raises the question of why he came to the attention of the British security service so early in his sojourn in London.

The answer lies in the fact that he was seen consorting with three known German intelligence agents: Eric von Salzmann of the German publishing group, *Scherlverlag*; Friedrich Glimpf of the *Telgrafen-Union*; and Karl Heinz Abshagen, journalist for various German papers such as the *Rheinisch Westfalische Zeitung* and the *Hambuger Nachrichten*. All three were working for organizations run by Alfred Hugenberg, who MI5 regarded as a control within German intelligence by virtue of being in charge of the *Deutscher Uberseedienst*.[43] Although MI5 knew very little about Thost early in the summer of 1931, they discounted his natural propensity to cultivate the acquaintance of other German journalists in London, but became concerned about his occasional meetings with Germans already under surveillance. Salzmann and Abshagen were apparently not considered sinister, since they were allowed to remain in London as journalists well after Thost was asked to leave.

The other dimension to Thost's ultimate ouster emerged in the summer of 1933. It had to do with a former RAF officer, Major Christopher Draper, who visited Munich in October 1932 as the guest of an old friend and German flying ace.[44] Draper was given a tour of the Nazi *Braunes Haus*, and afterwards had a half- hour conversation with Hitler at a nearby airfield. Returning to London, Draper met Thost, who inferred from their conversation that the Major was sympathetic to National Socialism. Thirty years later, Draper recalled how Thost "approached me with the suggestion that I might do a lecture tour in and around London on behalf of the Nazi Party, for which I would be paid three Guineas lecture plus travelling expenses."[45] Draper went on to say: "I felt that by putting forward the German attitude, I would at least be doing my tiny bit towards a better understanding. I do not think I gave more than half-a-dozen lectures in all."

Once Hitler came to power, non-German Nazi sympathizers like Draper were especially valuable to the Third Reich. Therefore, Thost kept in touch with Draper, and in late June or early July 1933 invited him to lunch. After much food and wine, Draper realized that he was being recruited to undertake low-level intelligence work for the Nazis. Thost wanted him to contact an official in Hamburg who would instruct him as to what kind of information was wanted. The offer was tempting, because Draper was out of work and short of cash. However, he was also concerned about crossing the line into espionage. Through an acquaintance, he was able to secure a meeting with Percy Sillitoe, later head of MI5, who encouraged him to play along with the Nazis, while keeping MI5 informed.

Thost, from his meager resources, paid for Draper's one-way airfare to Hamburg on 24 July 1933. There, he met with Herr Degenhardt, who outlined the sort of non-secret publications the Germans were interested in. As Draper wrote later: "What they wanted were performance figures for British aeroplanes and engines, particulars of armament, output of aircraft factories and the composition and size of R.A.F. squadrons."[46] He was told that he would be provided with mail drop addresses in both Germany and Holland, and he was instructed not to post his reports from Britain, but from Calais or Ostend. Similarly, German letters to him would be sent from somewhere in England so as not to arouse postal suspicions. Degenhardt gave Draper RM 230 to cover his expenses while in Germany as well as his return boat fare.

Once he returned to Britain, Draper secured a job with an aircraft company and felt less need to work for German intelligence. To cover himself, he told MI5 about his contact with Degenhardt by way of Thost, and was urged to continue furnishing information choreographed by the British. This lasted one year, and sealed Thost's fate. MI5, the Foreign Office, and the Home Office were all eager to rid themselves of Thost, who they had come to regard as a troublesome Nazi journalist. Thus, when the British Consul Aue was required to leave Germany, it seemed expedient to complete the exchange by demanding Thost's departure from London.

NOTES

1  R. R. Scott, in behalf of the Secretary of State for Home Affairs, Samuel Hoare, to H. W. Thost, 29 October 1935, PAB.
2  Von Hoesch to AA, 1 November 1935, AA archives, A3927.
3  Leeper's memo of 31 October 1935, PRO, FO 371/18868, C7381, ff. 290–91.
4  Sargent's memo of 1 November 1935, PRO, FO 371/18869, C7431, ff. 302–3.
5  Von Hoesch to AA, 1 November 1935, AA archives A3927.
6  Wigram to Phipps, 31 October 1935, PRO, FO 371/18869, C7406, ff. 298–301.
7  Report of H. Morse, 19 January 1935, PRO, FO 371/18868, C766, ff. 146–50.
8  PRO, FO 371/18869, C7567, ff. 304–10.
9  Thost to Rosenberg, 28 February 1933, Rosenberg Papers, *Bundesarchiv*, Koblenz, NS8-117, p. 23.

10  Wilhelm von Richthofen file, BDC.

11  Thost to Rosenberg, 1 April 1933, Rosenberg Papers, *Bundesarchiv*, Koblenz, pp. 27–28. See also: R. Cecil, *The Myth of the Master Race* (New York, 1972), pp. 169–75.

12  *The Times*, 27 April 1933, p. 8.

13  *Jewish Chronicle*, 28 April 1933, p. 28.

14  Press cutting dated 19 May 1933 from the *Manchester Guardian*, in the possession of the Wiener Library. The microfilm of the *Manchester Guardian* of this date which is in the Colindale Library does not contain this item, and it is possible that the Wiener Library cutting is incorrectly dated.

15  Rosenberg to Thost, 17 May 1933, Rosenberg papers, *Bundesarchiv*, Koblenz, pp. 29–30.

16  General Skoropadsky had been Hetman, or ruler of a puppet Ukranian state, during 1918 when the Germans still controlled the region under the terms of the Brest–Litovsk Treaty. See occasional references to him in W. H. Chamberlin, *The Russian Revolution*, 2 vols (New York, 1935).

17  The allusion may be to V. Poliakoff, who wrote an article on "Jews in Germany" for *The Times*, 3 April 1933.

18  Thost to Rosenberg, 9 March 1933, Rosenberg Papers, *Centre de Documentation Juive Contemporaine*, Paris, No. CLXIII-315.

19  Thost to Rosenberg, 28 February 1934, Rosenberg Papers, *Bundesarchiv*, Koblenz, pp. 36–37. See chapter 2 for further information about Rolf Wunderer.

20  Thost to Rosenberg, 9 March 1933, Rosenberg Papers, *Centre de Documentation*.

21  K. Young (ed.), *The Diaries of Sir Robert Bruce Lockhart* (London, 1973), I, 271; entry for 1 September 1933.

22  Thost to Rosenberg, 28 February 1933, Rosenberg Papers, *Bundesarchiv*, Koblenz, p. 23.

23  *Ibid.*

24  Thost to Rosenberg, 7 January 1934, *Ibid.*, pp. 33–34.

25  *Observer*, 11 February 1934, p. 18.

26  Rosenberg to Thost, 13 September and 3 November 1933; and Thost to Rosenberg, 2 December 1933; in Rosenberg Papers, *Bundesarchiv*, Koblenz, pp. 31–32.

27  Memos to Amann and Weiss, 30 November 1934, *ibid.*, p. 49.

28  Report of H. Morse, 19 January 1935, PRO, FO 371/18868, C766, ff.146–50.

29  Hoesch to AA, 1 November 1935, AA archives, A3927.

30  Thost, *Als Nationalsozialist in England, 1930–1935* (Munich, 1939), p. 364. This is also quoted in the *Jewish Chronicle*, 14 July 1939, p. 24.

31  Hoesch to AA, 1 November 1935, AA archives, A3927. Identifying Elliott and McKeigue has been impossible.

32  Thost to Wiedemann, 12 November 1938, BDC.

33  C.A. Macartney, *A History of Modern Hungary, 1929–1945*, No. 6, Edinburgh University Publications (Edinburgh, 1961), II, 384, 522.

34  R.V. Jones, *Most Secret War* (London, 1978) and the American edition titled *The Wizard War* (New York, 1978), pp. 26–28. Lindemann became the scientific adviser for Air Intelligence and liaison with MI6 in 1939.

35  See letters from Jones to Barnes, 15 August 1985, and Bosch to Barnes, 26 September 1985.

36  *Daily Sketch*, 19 November 1935, p. 1.

37  *Daily Herald*, 27 November 1935, p. 6.

38  Thost to Brückner, 20 January 1938, BDC.

39   Thost, *Als Nationalsozialist*, p. 364–65.

40   Thost to Rosenberg, 11 September 1933, Rosenberg Papers, *Bundesarchiv*, Koblenz, p. 31.

41   Thost to Rosenberg, 13 March 1933, and 11 September 1933, Rosenberg Papers, *Bundesarchiv*. See also Kuhlmann file, BDC. Kuhlmann was rewarded for his support of the *NSDAP* with appointment to both the *SS* and the Ribbentropbüro.

42   MI5 file on Thost, PRO,KV2/952–53.

43   MI5 file on Salzmann, PRO,KV2/910-14. Also MI5 file on Abshagen, PRO,KV2/388.

44   MI5 file on Draper, PRO, KV2/952; also KV2/365.

45   Christopher Draper, *The Mad Major* (Letchworth, 1962), p. 137.

46   *Ibid.*, p. 142.

# 6
# APPOINTMENT OF A NAZI CONSUL-GENERAL

On 4 February 1936, a Jewish Yugoslav student, David Frankfurter, shot to death Wilhelm Gustloff, the *NSDAP*'s *Landesgruppenleiter* in Switzerland. If this had taken place two and a half years later it would have touched off a savagely orchestrated persecution of Jews throughout Germany, but in 1936 it had the effect of further discrediting Nazi activity abroad. The Swiss authorities were outraged that a foreign student had so little regard for their hospitality that he could commit such an act, but they also blamed intensifying Nazi provocation. For the past few years there had been increasing concern throughout Switzerland that the Nazis were taking over German social clubs, youth organizations and cultural activities, and many Swiss were angered by the way a German emigré journalist, Berthold Jacob, had been lured to Switzerland in the spring of 1935, and then forcibly smuggled back into Germany and imprisoned. At the end of that year, the Swiss Federal Assembly dismissed its chief stenographer, Hans Kettelmann, because of his Nazi activities.

Thus, two weeks after Gustloff's death, the Swiss authorities outlawed the *Landesgruppe* at the same time that they apologized to the Third Reich for the untoward incident. Elsewhere in Europe similar events occurred. The Netherlands sought to separate the National Socialist members from the rest of the German community, and Sweden expelled the resident *Landesgruppenleiter*.

In Germany, Gustloff was elevated to the pantheon of Nazi martyrs. Elaborate measures were taken to return the fallen hero's body, and at his funeral Hitler delivered the eulogy which was broadcast widely by radio. In it he claimed that innocent Germans were being harassed, especially by Jews, and this was part of a large international Bolshevik conspiracy.

The assassination of Gustloff had peculiar and unexpected consequences for Otto Bene and the *Ortsgruppe* in London. In a letter of 19 March, the head of the Reich Chancellery, Hans Lammers, explained to Foreign Minister Neurath, Hitler's great concern for the safety of his many *Landesgruppenleiter* abroad, and his wish to increase their security by officially attaching them to the diplomatic service.[1] They could then enjoy the privileges and immunities accorded Consuls and Ambassadors, and foreign governments would think twice before prosecuting members of the *NSDAP*, or seeking their expulsion. Hitler thought it important for the *Landesgruppenleiter* to affiliate with their respective German embassies, as was done with military and naval attachés. A *Landesgruppenleiter* would become a "Party Attaché," reporting directly to the *Auslandsorganisation* in Berlin, and would be paid from the Party's treasury. Upon taking his post in a foreign country for the first time, a "Party Attaché" would register with his host government as a staff member of the German Embassy or Consulate.

In less than a week, the *Evening Standard* leaked the news that the German Government was already seeking British approval to grant Otto Bene an Exequatur as "Germany's New Consul-General. . . . In one sense the appointment may be regarded as a sop to the Radical element in the Nazi Party."[2] Until now, Bene's task as *Landesgruppenleiter* had been to "organise the German Nazis abroad and to keep an eye on anti-Nazis and German refugees in this country. He will now be able to carry out officially those duties which hitherto have lacked both the stamp and the efficiency of official control."

The *Evening Standard* article produced excitement and alarm at the British Foreign Office. Beginning on 28 March and lasting for nearly a month, the topic generated a flurry of departmental queries and comments. It was pointed out first of all that no request for an Exequatur had yet been received by the Treaty Department, so that whatever the Press might say was mere speculation. However, there were differing views as to whether to approach the German Embassy about the rumors, or wait, in case the story proved false.[3]

On 8 April 1936, C. J. Norton of the Central Department noted that in German circles the *Landesgruppenleiter* (Bene) was already being treated like a Consul-General, but this did not satisfy him; he wanted the prestige and immunity which came with the official designation. Bene was rumored to have gone to Berlin to try to clarify his position, leaving the Second Secretary, Wolfgang Egon zu Putlitz, as acting Consul-General. Norton expressed the view that for the time being it would be best to refrain from querying the German Embassy until Bene was actually named to the post, at which point the British Government could reject him.[4] Orme Sargent disagreed.[5]

> As Bene's appointment has been mentioned in the *Evening Standard*, I do not see why one of us should not call attention to this report in private conversation with some member of the German Embassy and indicate that we hope it is not true, since such an appointment would be very embarrassing to us. I think some such private and unofficial intimation might strengthen the hand of Herr [Ambassador] von Hoesch.

What worried Sargent in particular was the possibility of the German

Government conferring the title of Consul-General on Bene even though the British Government refused to officially recognize the designation. This would pressure Germans in Britain to defer to Bene as though he held diplomatic rank, and would greatly enhance his power within the German community.

C. W. Baxter advocated delivering a private warning to the *NSDAP*, enumerating the potential consequences, since this would give satisfaction "both to the Embassy and to a large part of the German community here. The hint can be given plainly but unofficially, and will give infinitely less offense than a later official refusal."[6]

Sir Robert Vansittart was confident that there were ample arguments the Foreign Office could employ should it become necessary to justify their rejection of Bene's appointment.[7]

> We have nothing against Herr Bene personally. The objection to his being given consular rank and consular privileges is based solely on the fact that he has for some years been the head of the *Landesgruppe* in Britain and Ireland. . . . The *Landesgruppe* is known to be in touch with 1,500 Germans and naturalised British subjects of German descent. It is obvious that, whatever may be thought of the propagandist and other activities of this organisation, it is a potential centre of espionage in future and also for sabotage in an emergency. . . .
>
> The real object of the Nazi Party in arranging for Herr Bene to be appointed Consul-General in London is to enable him to exercise more effective control over German residents in this country. In other words the acquisition of consular rank will make it easier for Herr Bene to carry on political activities in this country, and even to extend those activities. It would make it more difficult for us to deport or expel him if we took exception to his activities. It is clear that these reasons, as given in the preceding paragraph, are not entirely suitable for use in the House of Commons or in reply to an enquiry from the German Government. I should think, however, that it would be possible for us simply to take the line that we think it undesirable that a man who has for some years been the representative in London of the *Landesgruppe* of the Foreign Organisation of the Nazi Party should become the official German Consul-General in London. I do not see why we should give more detailed grounds for our objection.

Two days later, on 17 April, Bene's appointment as Consul-General was formally announced in Berlin, but news of it did not reach the British Foreign Office for several days.[8] On 21 April the head of the Foreign Office Central Department, Ralph Wigram, stated that it was vital "to act at once," and sought authorization for an informal conversation the next day with Adolf Marschall von Bieberstein, First Secretary at the German Embassy.[9] He intended to make clear that the British Government would find it difficult to accept Bene as Consul-General.[10]

> If Baron Marschall asked the reason, I would say that he did not think that certain recent activities of Herr Bene would – so far as we are concerned – facilitate the

discharge of his duties as Consul-General. I would refuse to give any further information: and add that I was only speaking to avoid any further unpleasantness.

That same day Vansittart reported that the Foreign Secretary, Anthony Eden, was agreeable to Wigram's proposed action, as was the Treaty Department.[11] However, everyone was warned not to expect too much from a veto of Bene's appointment, since even if he failed to become Consul-General and Putlitz continued in this role, they would have to fully cooperate with Bene.

On 22 April Wigram spoke to Baron Marschall von Bieberstein and simply told him directly that it would be difficult for His Majesty's Government to grant Bene an Exequatur, and to his relief, he was not asked for an explanation.

Internally, the British Foreign Office was supported in its resolve to block Bene's appointment as the result of a private talk between Captain Franz von Rintelen and C. J. Norton that had taken place on 27 March. Although a former Nazi Party member, von Rintelen was actually at odds with the Nazi regime at this time and was applying for British citizenship, but, prompted by the report in the *Evening Standard*, he volunteered the following information of interest to Norton:[12]

> He asked me to treat what he said as confidential and to believe that he had no interested motives as he had himself applied for British naturalisation. . . . He said that many German residents in England viewed this appointment with anxiety and even alarm. Some of them had some time ago signed a protest to Berlin against this man's activities, on the ground that they themselves had, during many years residence in England, improved the atmosphere of relations between the two countries which was being endangered by the conduct of hotheads such as Bene. This protest had, with incredible stupidity, been referred by Herr Hess to Bene himself, who therefore had a list of his enemies in this country.

Rintelen conceded that Bene had recruited relatively few new members into the Nazi Party, and those that he had were of many stripes, yet he sensed that no German in Britain would feel safe knowing that he or she would have to deal with a National Socialist Consul-General, since the power to revoke visas and force a return to Germany terrified non-Nazis. Norton concluded by saying, "Capt. von Rintelen still visits Germany, and any betrayal of his confidences would be very unfortunate."[13]

Bene's situation was undoubtedly influenced by the sudden death of Ambassador Leopold von Hoesch on 10 April. This, combined with Wigram's hint to Baron Marshall von Beiberstein, convinced the German Government to postpone consideration of the Consul-General issue. Besides, they recognized the need to mend fences following the Nazi military occupation of the Rhineland in early March. Bene therefore maintained a low profile throughout the summer and early autumn.

In October no formal request had yet come to grant Bene an Exequatur, and "he himself apparently felt alarmed by our attitude and left England," according to Wigram.[14] "Toward the end of May Dr. FitzRandolph, the Press Attaché at the German Embassy, who is known to be an active member of the Nazi Party, complained privately at the Foreign Office about our attitude towards Herr Bene." From various secret sources, it was discovered that Bene hoped to have his appointment confirmed by the British Government once a new ambassador replaced von Hoesch. These rumors were confirmed by Chargé d'Affaires Prince Otto von Bismarck who asked Wigram, off the record, what the British had against Bene, and indicated that it was very likely when Ambassador von Ribbentrop assumed his duties, he would probably press Bene's claim.

Wigram again urged decisive action by the Foreign Office.[15]

> I have consulted MI5 whose view is that it would be most unwise to consent to this appointment. To do so, they think, would certainly be greatly to strengthen the position of the Nazi organisation over here; and I have no doubt that it would make it more difficult for us to take action against the organisation later.

Anthony Eden offered another point of view which jolted some of his colleagues: "If, as I take it, the Nazi organisation of Germans in this country is not illegal, won't it be rather difficult to maintain that Herr Bene's connection with it renders him unfit to be Consul-General?"[16]

Vansittart lost no time expressing his disagreement with the Foreign Secretary.[17]

> An organisation for eventual sabotage and espionage more powerful than any yet known is growing up under our noses, and we are doing nothing about it. We are now likely to be asked again to take on its head as Consul-General, and MI5 warn us that it would be most unwise for us to consent to it. In the face of this I don't think we can possibly do so, however much Herr von Ribbentrop presses in order to strengthen his own position in Germany.

Eden agreed to ask MI5 whether they had enough evidence to implicate Bene in espionage, and if so, would it be sufficient to preclude his being confirmed as Consul-General, or even prohibit his return to London. "Failing such direct evidence against Bene, does MI5 consider that the National Socialist Party Organisation in London, of which Bene is or was *Landesgruppenleiter*, is involved in espionage or other activities detrimental to British interests . . .?"[18]

Vernon Kell and MI5 had very definite views concerning Otto Bene. To the Attorney General, Russell Scott, Kell observed that Bene was not his prime target. "What I feel is that it is the organisation rather than the individual at the head of it, which is definitely dangerous." Nevertheless, Kell had a number of reservations concerning the *Landesgruppenleiter*.[19]

On the surface it might appear that Bene's activities in England are concerned solely with members of the Nazi party here, with the organisation and discipline of the Party and with their social gathering; that so long as they commit no breach of the law, they and their activities are of no concern to us.

On the other hand, he was well aware that those in charge of the *Ortsgruppe* inevitably shaped its collective personality.[20]

The case against Otto Bene on our records may be summarised as follows.
(1) There is evidence that, as head of the *Landesgruppe*, he works in close touch with the *Hafendienstamt* [Harbor Service] which is in liaison with the Gestapo for the purpose of supervising the activities of German nationals in this country and for maintaining Party discipline.
(2) There is evidence that, as head of the *Landesgruppe*, he in some sense controls the *Schlichter* [Nazi Party disciplinary official] whose activities involve an infringement of British sovereignty. . . .
(3) There is evidence that, in one case only, he has performed counterespionage duties by reporting to the *Hafendienstamt* on a British subject visiting Germany in circumstances which appeared suspicious to the *Landesgruppe*.
(4) There is evidence that the *Landesgruppe* is used as an instrument of German foreign policy to the extent that Otto Bene has played a prominent part in working for the creation of a pro-German feeling in Great Britain. That is of course unexceptionable in itself but it is difficult to resist the inference on general grounds that this is done as part of a policy whose ultimate object is to neutralise Great Britain and separate her from France. . . .
(5) There is evidence that, as head of the *Landesgruppe*, he is responsible for the maintenance of *Deutschtum* among Germans in this country and naturalised British subjects of German descent. We have known for some time that the Nazi Party were attempting to win over the people whom they described as "old German", i.e. Germans who have been long resident in the United Kingdom, including those who have been naturalised as British subjects or have been born in British territory and therefore, *ipso facto*, have British nationality. . . . In the event of war between Great Britain and Germany, after all German subjects had been deported, the "old Germans" – British subjects – would remain in this country as ready-made machinery for the organisation of sabotage and espionage there.

It should be noted that all German merchant seamen temporarily stopping at British ports came under the jurisdiction of the *Hafendienstamt*, and were therefore subject to the *Landesgruppe* in England. Bene would almost certainly have had little contact with them, but would have left this to his subordinate, Capt. Eduard Jäger. As for item #2 concerning the *Schlichter*, this was the way the *Landesgruppe* disciplined its own members. The *Schlichter* would hear disputes, investigate Party irregularities, and in extreme cases, deprive someone of his or her membership pending an inquiry by a higher Nazi Party court in Germany. Kell's third allegation defies proof because there is no way of knowing who the

British subject was, and what his alleged purpose was for going to Germany. As Kell readily admitted, there was nothing about Bene which could justify his expulsion, but should the *Landesgruppe* be mobilized sometime in the future for purposes of sabotage and espionage, it could indeed become a threatening presence.

MI5's response to Eden's queries were recorded on 23 October.[21]

1. MI5 have no positive evidence and have never suggested that they had positive evidence that Bene was engaged in espionage in this country.
2. MI5 have no positive evidence that the National Socialist Party Organization in London is at the moment involved in espionage or other activities detrimental to British interests; but what they do maintain is that the headquarters of the Nazi Organisation in London are in touch with some 1,500 people, some being British subjects of German extraction. Since the Nazi Party in Germany has unprecedented power over the individual, it can direct the energies of every member of the party in any desired direction.

MI5 further contended that Bene was an undesirable candidate for Consul-General even if he resigned as leader of the Party in Britain.

Given this information, Eden still found insufficient grounds to refuse Bene an Exequatur as long as he would not continue as *Landesgruppenleiter*.[22]

For some months the Germans kept Bene in limbo, declining to clarify his status, but leaving open the possibility that he would eventually become Consul-General. Consequently, the Foreign Office began to relax a bit toward the end of November.[23]

It is worth remembering that we were told at one time that Herr von Ribbentrop was at once going to raise the question of the appointment of Herr Bene as Consul-General, and was going to make it a test case. But as far as I know he has never said a word on the subject, and his silence seems to show that he thinks wiser not to embark upon a frontal attack, in which he might be seriously defeated, but rather to work by underground channels. . . .

As late as March 1937 the situation was still not clear. The Foreign Office thought it unlikely that he would return to London, but no successor as *Landesgruppenleiter* had been announced. A *News Chronicle* item in February suggested that Wolfgang von Langen might be reassigned from Rome to London, but this was thought unlikely.[24] Finally, on 30 April 1937 it was announced in Berlin that Bene had been designated the new Consul-General to Milan as well as German Commissioner on questions of resettlement in the disputed area of the Tyrol.[25] At long last he had achieved his goal of enhanced respectability and prestige. No longer would he dominate the lives of 300 Party comrades in London and threaten non-Party Germans. Best of all, he had gained what many faithful Party members dearly coveted, an entree into the diplomatic service. It may have taken ten years to rise from humble representative of a German chemical firm to becoming Consul-General, but it had been accomplished without enduring the rigorous admission requirements of the German Foreign Ministry. His sense of having arrived is especially evident in a letter which he wrote to his former boss, Ernst Bohle, urging him and his wife to come to Milan, and inviting members of the *Auslandsorganisation* to call at his office if they were in Italy.[26] Meanwhile, the post of *Landesgruppenleiter* was filled by Otto Karlowa, who had been *Ortsgruppenleiter* in London for the past two years.

Only after Bene was reassigned to Milan did Kell inform the Home Office of Bene's communications with the *Hafendienst* (sometimes referred to as the *Inspektionsamt*) of the *Auslandorganisation*.[27] Bene had described the activities and whereabouts of a former German Communist, Paul Halster, who had acquired British citizenship and was currently a Director of the Enfield Cable Works of London. He was concerned lest Halster contact other Communists when traveling back to Germany. Similarly, in 1936 the *Hafendienst* asked Bene to locate Dr. Dietrich Sandberger of Tübingen, who was thought to be living temporarily in Britain. Another assignment involved delving into "the character and reliability" of an engineer, Dagobert Rudorff, who had lived for a time in the United States before coming in 1933 to London where he had joined the Nazi Party. It is not apparent what aroused the suspicion of the *Inspektionsamt*, but Rudorff was summarily dropped from the Party in May 1939.

As *Landesgruppenleiter*, Bene was provided with the information that the sister of a Jewish woman in Stuttgart worked at the German Embassy in London. However, because the Embassy could not find an employee by the name of Ries, Bene was asked to make inquiries and try to locate her. On another occasion he was questioned about a Jew named Eissenberger who was trying to dispose of some property in Germany by selling it to British subjects.

The British Government's sense of triumph and relief in having foiled Bene's appointment as Consul-General in London was short-lived. On 3 February 1938 the Germans promulgated a decree requiring all citizens who had been abroad for more than three months to register with the nearest German Consulate, purportedly "to unite the German nationals abroad in an effective and comprehensive whole for maintaining their relations with the home country."[28] Once registered, each person had to update any changes to his or her status or address. Heads of households were responsible for registering all members residing with them, and failure to do so within a reasonable length of time resulted in a fine of RM 5-100. Anyone who knowingly or persistently refused to register was "declared to have lost his German nationality."

Commenting on this new regulation, *The Times* suggested that the Nazis were motivated in part by a wish to impose tighter control on Germans abroad because they suspected that many lacked sympathy with the Third Reich, and it was therefore necessary to bring them more firmly under *NSDAP* discipline.[29]

The British Foreign Office reacted promptly and negatively to several impli-cations of this decree.[30]

> It is wholly contrary to the practice which nations have hitherto followed in such matters. It is commonly accepted that naturalised subjects may be denaturalised; what the state has given it can take away. . . . But that refusal to report to a consulate should in itself be an excuse for depriving a natural born subject of his nationality is something new.

In addition to being concerned about registration as a means to deny Germans their citizenship, there was a subtler issue.[31]

> This law opens up a very serious prospect. It is to be anticipated that most of the refugees from Germany will refuse to report and will be only too glad to be deprived of their German nationality. The practical effect, so far as we are concerned, will be that the refugees who are here will become stateless, and we shall be unable to send them back to Germany even if they are convicted of serious criminal offences.

While admitting that clear statistics on immigration were difficult to compile, and in many cases there were "no means of saying who is a refugee and who is not," the Foreign Office acknowledged that "there can be no doubt that the number of refugees who find their way into this country and succeed in remaining here is already large and is steadily increasing."

It is possible to calculate the approximate rate of growth in the number of Germans who remained in Britain.[32] During the five years 1933–1938, Germans registering with the police increased by about 10,000, which would not in itself be conclusive, because many of these undoubtedly returned to Germany. However, "the Traffic Index figures" showed that "the excess of arrivals over departures is just over 11,000." Thus, by both measures, approximately 2,000 additional Germans stayed in Britain each year, and this number accelerated to 400 each month for a potential annual increase of about 5,000. The recent annexation of Austria promised to swell these totals even more.

In the same Foreign Office memo, the shift from a concern with the plight of Germans having to register with their Consulates to the predicament in which His Majesty's Government found itself, was significant.[33]

> It is therefore clear that the tide is much stronger now than it was even two or three years ago. . . . It is perhaps worth considering, on grounds of national policy, whether the time has not come to stop, or at least check, this flow of refugees. Ten thousand is, of course, not in itself a large figure – certain smaller countries have taken twice that number. Almost all of the 10,000 have however settled in London, and from ordinary observation there is already a real danger of the spread of anti-Jewish feeling.

Refugees from Germany contributed substantially to British life, especially "in the realms of research, science, medicine, etc." Therefore, if they continued to emigrate, Britain would be subjected to an increasing drain on its financial resources, since refugees were allowed to take only 8–9 percent of their personal assets with them when emigrating. With the augmented harassment of Jews, it was assumed that more and more would be driven into exile, and the only effective way to limit this influx would be to require all those leaving Germany and Austria to secure visas from British Consuls, undoubtedly risking retaliation by the Germans.

In April 1938 the *Daily Sketch* drew even wider implications from the Nazi requirement that all German citizens abroad had to register.[34] Its article, "Chain of Nazi Girl Agents in Britain – Gestapo Agents Here to Organise Them," claimed that there were an estimated 25,000 German and Austrian girls currently working in Britain who reported to Gestapo agents posing as journalists, businessmen, and even refugees. Many of these young women were employed as domestic servants by politicians, civil servants and military personnel, and were therefore in a position to overhear sensitive conversations or observe local industrial and training facilities. Therefore, registration with the German Consul-General in London was an effective way to monitor them. Otherwise, as one Nazi Party Member admitted, "of every 100 German propagandists we send to England, 90 return here with half their National-Socialist training undone, and full of all kinds of democratic ideas."

The *Daily Telegraph* informed its readers of the kinds of information that German registrants were required to provide, revealing a chilling picture of the way Nazis could use the data.[35] In addition to their names and addresses, they had to indicate the date and place of their birth, marital status, and religion. There was a pointed question about race, and another probed how they had obtained their citizenship papers. Details concerning their passport, current employment, and prior military service were asked, as well as their last address in Germany before going abroad. The *Telegraph* tried to confirm complaints by registrants that there had been additional questions, but a German consular official refused to comment, giving the excuse that there were too many people being processed.

The pressure being exerted on ordinary Germans living and working in London soon surfaced in the media. On 1 June 1938 a story appeared in the *Daily Herald* about an Austrian girl who had been denied an extension of her visa by the German Consul-General in London even though the British authorities had already extended her work permit for another year.[36] The German justification for this action was based on the fact that she worked for a Jewish family. Some months later the British Foreign Office learned more details from the Home Office.[37] "At the instance of the Home Office the Special Branch of the Metropolitan Police made enquiries of the *Daily Herald* who referred them to

Mr. Lucien Fior, a solicitor," who confirmed that he knew of several cases where Austrian girls had been warned not to work for Jewish employers. Identified as Karoline Maresch, the woman alluded to in the *Herald* article entered Britain on 27 November 1936 with a British work permit valid for one year. Through the Anglo-German Agency she secured a position with Mrs. Sattin on 21 December and remained with her for one year. When she tried to extend her German visa, she was told to leave her present employer, which she did in April 1938, and returned home.

Between June 1938 and the outbreak of war in September 1939, there were countless other examples of German consular interference in the private lives of their nationals abroad. In fact, it was rather taken for granted by the British that this would occur, given the inexorable pressure by the Nazi Party to impose its ideology upon the German bureaucracy and diplomatic service. Thus, what seemed unthinkable in the spring of 1936 when Ambassador von Hoesch was still alive and Otto Bene stood ready to be named Consul-General, became acceptable two years later. A Nazi stalwart, von Ribbentrop, had been named German Ambassador, and Putlitz, the quiet and covert anti-Nazi, found it necessary to join the *NSDAP*.

Ironically, the focus of the British Foreign Office centered on Bene becoming Consul General, whereas Hitler's goal was to upgrade Nazi leaders abroad in order to provide them with greater prestige and protection in the wake of the Gustloff assassination in Switzerland. The British seemed to have entirely overlooked this objective, concentrating solely on the danger implicit in combining Party leadership with Consular authority. Consequently, the Nazis exploited this oversight and increased their pressure on recalcitrant Germans living and working abroad.

NOTES

1 Lammers to Neurath, 19 March 1936, NA microcopy T-120, roll 913, frames 384134-136.
2 *Evening Standard*, 24 March 1936, p. 6.
3 PRO, FO 371/19942, C3143, f. 108.
4 *Ibid.*, f. 108v.
5 *Ibid.*, f. 109.
6 *Ibid.*, f. 110.
7 *Ibid.*, ff. 110v-11.
8 For Bene's appointment, see: *Mitteilungsblatt der Auslandsorganisation*, No. 27 (April 1936), p. 2.
9 PRO, FO 371/19942, C3143, f. 111.
10 *Ibid.*
11 *Ibid.*, f. 112.
12 *Ibid.*, ff. 114–15.
13 *Ibid.*

14  PRO, FO 371/19942, C7296, ff. 245–47; memo of 8 October 1936.

15  *Ibid.*, ff. 237–37v.

16  *Ibid.*, f. 238; minute of 17 October 1936.

17  *Ibid.*

18  *Ibid.*, f. 239.

19  Kell to Scott, 24 April 1936, PRO, HO 45/25385, pp. 5–14.

20  *Ibid.*

21  *Ibid.*, PRO, FO 371/19942, C3143, ff. 240–41.

22  *Ibid.*, ff. 243–44.

23  Memo of Orme Sargent, 26 November 1936. PRO, FO 371/19915, C8427, ff. 186–88.

24  PRO, FO 371/20739, C1879, ff. 42–43; minute of 9 March 1937. See also: News Chronicle, 4 February 1937, p. 13.

25  *Mitteilungsblatt der Auslandsorganisation*, No. 49 (May 1937), p. 2.

26  Bene to Bohle, 29 July 1937, AA Archives, Bonn, Chef AO, Band 42.

27  HO 45/25480, document no. 690642/87. John Lloyd of the Home office Record Management Service permitted examination of this previously unavailable material.

28  "Law regarding the Duty of German Nationals Abroad to Report to the Authorities," 3 February 1938, PRO, FO 371/21649, C1047, ff. 191–95.

29  *The Times*, 11 February 1938, p. 14.

30  PRO, FO 371/21650, C1564, ff. 227–44.

31  *Ibid.*

32  *Ibid.*

33  *Ibid.*

34  *Daily Sketch*, 8 April 1938, p. 3.

35  *Daily Telegraph*, 12 April 1938, p. 7.

36  *Daily Herald*, 1 June 1938, p. 3.

37  PRO, FO 371/21652, C12607, f. 127.

# 7 THE NAZI TAKEOVER OF GERMAN NEWS AGENCIES

By the early 1930s there were three major German news agencies supplying material to foreign correspondents and newspapers in Germany and abroad. One was a subsidiary of the Ullstein newspaper chain, with a bias towards democracy and socialism. The second was middle-of-the-road in its orientation, and generally went by the sole name of Wolff. The third and most recent was the creation of the right-wing press baron, Alfred Hugenberg, and in its name embodied its rapid mode of communication: the *Telegrafen-Union* or *T-U*. All of these relied primarily on land lines and underwater cables for the transmission of their news, while a fourth agency, *Transozean*, sent its reports by wireless.[1]

As long as Heinrich Brüning was Chancellor and the Social Democrats controlled the shaky coalition in the Reichstag, the Ullstein service was favored by the German Government. If early news leaks occurred, Ullstein carried them, and reporters looked to them for the definitive text of official speeches and releases. When Brüning was replaced by Franz von Papen in the summer of 1932, Ullstein underwent a gradual eclipse which eventuated in its demise at the hands of the Nazis the following year. Von Papen and his successor as Chancellor, Kurt von Schleicher, used either Wolff or the *Telegrafen-Union*, although Wolff was viewed as increasingly suspect because of its reliance on staffers who were democratic in their sympathies, some of whom were Jewish. Hitler's assumption of power changed the mixture in favor of the *Telegrafen-Union*, since Hugenberg was a member of the new Cabinet. T. J. Breen, the British press attaché in Berlin, described what happened.[2]

> The Nazis undermined the [Wolff] service by holding up official reports for hours or even days. A favorite trick was to withhold the text of Hitler's speeches on the ground that they needed revision. In the meantime the *Telegrafen-Union* agency was able to publish the text. Hugenberg being a Cabinet Minister naturally helped his agency in every possible way until he was expelled from the

Government. By that time Wolff's back had been financially broken and it was only a matter of time until the Nazis or the *Telegrafen-Union* swallowed it up.

By the autumn of 1933 the Nazis decided that none of the big three agencies would be allowed to survive in their present form. However, Goebbels realized that his *NSDAP* cronies were not trained well-enough to run a news agency, so Hugenberg was called upon to reorganize them, retaining only as many skilled non-Socialist personnel as necessary from the older news services. The result was the *Deutsches Nachrichtenbüro* or *DNB*, which was officially inaugurated at the end of November 1933.[3] Although nominally private, 70 percent of its shares were controlled by the Government, and it soon assumed the role of official Nazi news and information agency. Only one of Wolff's former directors, Dr. Gustav Albrecht, was included on the board of the *DNB*, while Otto Mejer, Baron von Besseren Thalfengen, and Dr. Reetz came from the *Telegrafen-Union*. The Editor-in-Chief of the *Völkischer Beobachter*, Wilhelm Weiss, was the official Nazi representative on the new board.

Breen found the *DNB*'s General Director, Otto Mejer "an energetic man, an ex-Naval officer, and though a Nazi outwardly, an orthodox nationalist inwardly,"[4] but Rex Leeper was less impressed. "I met Herr Mejer at dinner at the German Embassy last week. I was not attracted by Herr Mejer who is very much the ex-naval officer of the Prussian type."[5]

Repercussions resulting from the formation of the *Deutsches Nachrichtenbüro* were felt by representatives of the other foreign news organizations in Germany, like the Associated Press, Reuters, and Havas. In particular, Reuters and Havas had a longstanding exclusive arrangement with Wolff under which they exchanged news items and shared correspondents, but the newly-formed *DNB* was unwilling to continue this special relationship.[6]

> They stated that the existing contracts with Reuters and Havas were "Versailles" contacts, i.e. Reuters and Havas had everything and Wolff got nothing. There was a certain amount of justification, because German governments in the past, anxious to have Reuters and Havas friendly, never insisted on their rights. Thus Havas have the sole right of distribution in South America, Spain, and elsewhere, while Reuters reserves North America, China, etc., and other important domains. The new company are insisting on absolute reciprocity. Hitherto again *The Times* and other newspapers here were not allowed to take the Wolff service by Reuters. They had to be content with the *Telegrafen-Union*, a very inferior service. The *Deutsches Nachrichtenbüro* want to change all this. You may have noticed that Reuters has been trimming its sails to the Nazi breeze of late. It is hoping in that way to get better terms. Reuters agent here wants this information treated most confidentially.

London was similarly worried about the ability of Reuters to remain neutral, despite assurances from its correspondent in Berlin. Breen and Leeper agreed that Wilson Harris, Editor of the *Spectator*, was "probably right" in suspecting that Reuters accepted everything sent to them by the *DNB* and printed it as their own.[7]

In the course of the *DNB*'s takeover of the pre-existing agencies in London in late 1933 and early 1934, many of the *Telegrafen-Union* staff were dismissed, while most of the Wolff correspondents were retained. The *T-U*'s representative, Friedrich H. Glimpf, survived the cuts but was soon transferred to Calcutta, while Wolff's agent, Iona Ustinov, was allowed to stay in England. Neither was a Party Member at the time, although Glimpf joined in 1937.

When the Wolff agency opened an office in London after the First World War, it encountered a good deal of anti-German sentiment. Consequently, one member of staff whose German name was Jona Ustinow changed it to Iona Ustinov in order to seem to be Russian. His wife, Nadia Benois, was in fact Russian. They were sent to London in the early 1920s, where a son, Peter, the future actor and author, was born in 1921. Until 1924 they lived in a furnished flat in Ridgemount Gardens, Bloomsbury, and then moved to an unfurnished one in Carlisle Mansions near Victoria. In addition to his work for the *Wolffbüro*, Iona Ustinov became a Press Attaché to the German Embassy which used an office in the Reuters building, 9 Carmelite Street, EC4.[8]

Being much interested in music and art, the Ustinovs courted a wide circle of British friends who were not only valuable sources of news, but also provided them with opportunities to review performances by German companies such as the Berlin Philharmonic Orchestra under Furtwängler. "Klop", as Iona was familiarly known, was a special favorite within the German community, and a frequent toastmaster at official functions. As his wife later recalled:[9]

> So life went on, rich and varied, until 1933 when the hideous shadow of Hitler looked for the first time on our horizon. I was full of apprehension, but Klop, being an optimist, believed that all would be well. He regarded Hitler as a complete nonentity and could not agree with me that his appearance portended disaster. However, slowly but surely our relations with the German Embassy started to deteriorate.

About 1927 Ustinov had been authorized to hire an assistant, and he chose his old friend and *Wolffbüro* colleague, Felix Banse. Banse was born in 1889, which made him three years older than Ustinov. The two men complemented each other nicely, Banse being a shy and retiring bachelor who preferred to work at night, while Ustinov was sociable and charming and tried to avoid business duties in the evening. Both shared a hearty distaste for the Nazis. Banse took a flat at 27 Hogarth Road, SW5, less central than the Ustinovs'.

During 1933 German journalists and news agencies came under the jurisdiction of the Propaganda Ministry, and as such were subject to the decrees of 7 April, requiring proof of Aryan ancestry. Accordingly, the Propaganda

Ministry asked the *Auslandsorganisation* whether Ustinov and Banse were qualified under the new rules to represent the *Deutsches Nachrichtenbüro* in London.[10] Otto Bene admitted that he knew very little about Banse because of his nocturnal habits and solitary ways, only that his political persuasion was similar to Ustinov's, "left wing and anti-Nazi. . . . From the National Socialist point of view, I put as little worth on his [Banse] continuing here as I do with von Ustinow, who is currently trying to pull all strings to make himself loved by the leading National Socialists."[11] Sir Vernon Kell, head of MI5, remarked about Ustinov that his work for the *Wolffbüro* brought him about £70 a year, and he was thought "to be doing a certain amount of propaganda work on behalf of the present regime," although he was "not fully in favour with the Nazis because of his Jewish wife."[12]

Against these impressions conveyed by Bene and Kell is the statement by Ustinov's wife. "The Nazis had been regarding Klop with ever-growing suspicion and animosity, while he had been almost boiling over with contempt for them."[13] Reconciling these divergent opinions rests on believing with Ustinov that the right-wing lunatic manifestations of Nazism would be short-lived, and that he could meanwhile persevere and perform his duties. Equally important to him was keeping his job in the prevailing economic depression, since he was anxious neither to return to Germany nor seek employment somewhere else.

For a time Ustinov and Banse were considered candidates for employment in the Propaganda Ministry's press section, but a negative report from Bene, in addition to a required civil service questionnaire, combined to stymie this possibility. Banse had no hesitation answering the questionnaire, since he was confident that his family had no skeletons in the cupboard; his father had been a long-time director of the Wolff agency, and his lineage was correctly Aryan.[14] However, Ustinov "flatly refused" to fill it out, according to Nadia. Fritz Hesse, Ustinov's successor at the German News Agency in London, said it was more than that. "The Propaganda Ministry had asked Herr Ustinov to submit proof of his Aryan ancestry, and taking offense at this, he wrote back that 'Herr Dr. Goebbels should first prove his own Aryan origins and then he would do likewise.'"[15]

On 4 October 1933 a decree was issued which further narrowed Ustinov's chances of surviving close scrutiny by the Propaganda Ministry and the *NSDAP*. Titled *Schriftleitergesetz* (Law for Editors), it restricted employment to Aryan German citizens whose spouses were Aryan as well.

Shortly after this, Banse had a heart attack and returned to Germany, to be replaced by Johannes Jacobi, a twenty-five year old journalist who had undoubtedly been chosen by the Propaganda Ministry, and who further complicated Ustinov's tenure in London. First, the Ministry ordered Ustinov back to Berlin "for 'consultations', which he very wisely refused to do." Next, he was threatened with dismissal, but friends in high places were able temporarily "to save the situation" until Nadia returned from Berlin where she had gone for medical treatment. Then he was fired. Nadia later wrote, "The battle for Klop lasted a few weeks, but it was evident to him that he could not possibly remain at his post. Besides he did not wish to. He had suffered enough having to work for that contemptible crowd."[16]

Left unresolved was Ustinov's future. He naturally hesitated to forfeit his German citizenship until he had acquired British papers, and he knew that this process could be lengthy. As his son Peter later revealed, his father applied secretly for British citizenship "with the help of Sir Robert Vansittart." [17] He cleverly published his intention to become a British subject in a Welsh-language newspaper, "which defied the expertise of German intelligence."[18] Ironically, this move accorded him political, but not economic, security, as he never again succeeded in his subsequent careers: bookkeeper, free-lance journalist, art critic, and art dealer; the Nazis had effectively deprived him of his chosen profession as a journalist, the job he did best and was most suited for.

In March 1935 Fritz Hesse arrived in London to take charge of the *Deutsches Nachrichtenbüro*, still located at 9 Carmelite Street. He was experienced at living abroad, being the son of a German diplomat who relocated every few years. As a flag-bearer in the German Army during the First World War, he was badly wounded in the stomach at Ypres where a Canadian surgeon rescued him. Soon after arriving in London he mentioned this to Sir Robert Vansittart. "I added that I had been wounded in 1917 and owed my life to the care I received at English hands and that I should like to do something to show my gratitude."[19] This episode also convinced him that he was peculiarly well-suited to interpret the British to the Germans, "work for a better understanding" between the two nations, and "do what I could to help in preventing a war."[20] From 1917 to 1919 he was a prisoner of war in England, and when he was released he turned to the study of law and geography at the universities of Munich and Berlin. Due to rampant inflation in 1923, he was forced to abandon his studies, so for the next few years he became a freelance journalist associated with the *Telegrafen-Union* news agency. By 1931 he was one of their three chief editors along with Otto von Rittgen and Friedrich Gericke, under the direction of Otto Mejer.[21]

When the *Telegrafen-Union* was absorbed into the official *Deutsches Nachrichtenbüro*, Hesse retained his job for six months, but the purge of Röhm and the *SA* on 30 June 1934 seriously undermined his position. He was not in any way directly involved, but had close connections with particular elements within the military, especially the disgraced and executed General Kurt von Schleicher. As a result, Goebbels declared that he was politically unreliable, and demoted him to the *DNB*'s foreign desk. Both Bernhard Wilhelm von Bülow and Gottfried Aschmann of the Foreign Ministry came to his aid and urged reconsideration, whereupon he was appointed head of the London office of the *DNB* in London, and simultaneously joined the Nazi Party.[22]

American officers interrogated him ten years later and described him as unimpressive looking, very correct in his manner, but quite animated when engaged in conversation. A short, balding, middle-age patrician, he spoke "flawless English – spiced or clarified when necessary by an occasional French, Latin or German expression."[23]

When Hesse succeeded Ustinov, he found Ambassador von Hoesch cool and suspicious. Not only had the Ambassador valued Ustinov's independence of mind, but he clearly assumed that Hesse had been sent by Goebbels to spy on the Embassy. After a few months, however, von Hoesch relented and gave Hesse his confidence and ultimately his friendship. For Hesse's part, he thought that von Hoesch was particularly well qualified to be the German Ambassador to Great Britain, having known many of the political leaders since his youth, and been on good terms with the Royal family. He commented that "Hoesch had only one 'fault': he was not a Nazi, and came from the Stresemann era."[24]

Each day Hesse briefed von Hoesch on the latest items of news and told him the content of *DNB* dispatches before they were sent to the agency's headquarters in Berlin. Occasionally the two differed concerning how best to influence Hitler. Von Hoesch was inclined to tone down criticism of Germany for fear that it would spur Hitler into becoming more aggressive, but Hesse argued that the Führer would probably learn about any outspoken remarks by Churchill and others, so they should be included in his reports. Hesse believed that Hitler relied more on the accuracy of *DNB* telegrams than the official and longer dispatches from German diplomats.[25]

Von Hoesch's unexpected death in the spring of 1936 precipitated the appointment of Joachim von Ribbentrop, an ardent Nazi, as the next Ambassador to London. Hesse was pleased with this choice, since he was already well acquainted with von Ribbentrop by whom he had almost been hired until Goebbels indicated his hostility towards him. As told to his American interrogators after the war, he held von Ribbentrop in high regard.[26]

> A well qualified, sober statesman fit for the post of Foreign Minister. While discounting the widespread picture of Ribbentrop as an inept, clumsy fool who persuaded Hitler that Chamberlain would never go to war over Poland, he [Hesse] does admit that his [Ribbentrop's] major shortcomings were impatience, and an overbearing attitude toward subordinates. Had he been even the greatest diplomatist of our times, he could not have acted in any essentially different manner inasmuch as he had no actual final authority in shaping foreign policy. "I know that Ribbentrop very often suggested ideas that were turned down. I know for a fact because many times he complained that he had been asked for advice, had submitted his report and that precisely the opposite course had been taken."

In February 1938 von Ribbentrop was recalled to Berlin to become Foreign

Minister, and was eventually replaced by Herbert von Dirksen, leaving Hesse in his dual role as *DNB* representative and press adviser to the Embassy.

On a visit to Paris in 1938 Hesse was asked by Otto Mejer, his superior in Berlin, to observe the *DNB* office there. His report comparing the agency's operations in the two capitals not only provided useful information about the operation of the *DNB* in France, but also indicated Hesse's priorities as *Büro* chief.[27] Whereas the Paris office divided its own work from that it provided for the Embassy between two men, London combined these two aspects, presenting Hesse himself with the chance to have daily contact with the Embassy. Paris used a paid agent to provide news from governmental sources, whereas Hesse always had someone from the London *Büro* at official press conferences and briefings by the Foreign Office. Paris had access to the more general and less detailed services of the Havas agency, while London relied on Reuters and the Associated Press plus a specialized news service dedicated to covering affairs in Parliament. Although the Paris office clipped from 50–60 French newspapers and covered sports and business more than any other kind of news, Hesse used only a dozen or so sources which covered stories in more depth and detail.

Because Hesse cleared his *DNB* reports with the German Ambassador before sending them to Berlin, von Dirksen often shared them with colleagues in the Foreign Ministry. Sometimes these were accurate, but in many cases, they contained idle gossip.

The Munich Crisis in September 1938 prompted Ambassador Dirksen to announce that all employees of the *DNB* were under his jurisdiction and were therefore entitled to diplomatic immunity in case hostilities should commence. On the list presented to the British Foreign Office, besides Fritz Hesse, were Baron Dr. von Hahn, Heinz Cramer, Otto Stadler, Willy Konnertz, Herman Furth, Edgar Schmidt, and Harald Boeckmann. All but von Hahn were Party members, yet the Press Department had scarcely heard of any of them.[28]

> Neither [Hahn nor Cramer] has made any particular impression upon me, and each is cut to the same pattern. Their activities are of course, closely coordinated by Dr. Hesse who is also, in these days, a somewhat infrequent visitor. They probably do as much propaganda as news gathering.

It was agreed that there was little likelihood that the *DNB* representatives would be granted diplomatic status. One British official suggested that His Majesty's Government request immunity for British journalists in Berlin.[29]

> I take it that these gentlemen are journalists pure and simple, and as we have always strenuously opposed attempts to claim diplomatic status for persons whose duties are not wholly or predominantly of a diplomatic character, I think we should firmly decline to accept them for inclusion in the Embassy staff – at least insofar as entering their names on the list of privileged persons is concerned.

I imagine that the underlying object was to endeavour getting these people out of the country without hindrance as members of the Ambassador's suite if certain eventualities had come to pass as the result of the recent crisis.

Early in January 1939 Hesse traveled to Germany to consult with Foreign Minister von Ribbentrop, and subsequently conveyed the substance of their conversation to Sir Horace Wilson. In July he was again entrusted with a message for von Ribbentrop which said that Britain was willing to contemplate a mutual defense pact with Germany for the next 25 years. He also attempted to convince von Ribbentrop and his advisers that the British would stand by Poland and regard seizure of Danzig as a *casus belli*, but notwithstanding this warning, Hitler was convinced that the British were bluffing and would again back down as they had at Munich in September 1938.[30]

When Hesse returned to London in mid-August, he was unaware that the Nazis were negotiating a non-aggression pact with the Russians, effectively eliminating all need for an understanding with Great Britain. Nonetheless he continued his efforts to persuade von Ribbentrop, Hess, and Göring that the British were prepared to fight if Germany marched into Poland. The Nazis condescended only slightly, offering a last-minute proposal to withdraw on condition that Germany be allowed to occupy Danzig and retain a road across the Polish Corridor.

Hesse knew that these terms would be unacceptable to the British, who were already beginning to round up potential enemy aliens. On the evening of 2 September, he took refuge in the German Embassy and communicated with Berlin by telephone and telegraph over lines which he knew were being tapped.[31] Years later another German press attaché, Sigismund FitzRandolph, described how he and some other members of the Embassy staff delayed their evacuation, waiting aboard a steamer in the channel to learn the results of Hesse's fruitless negotiations.[32]

After the war the British suspected Hesse of having had covert links with German intelligence. He had difficulty convincing them that his occasional scoops or inside information came from legitimate and official sources, especially George Stewart, Prime Minister Baldwin's Press Secretary. Hesse truly believed that Stewart and other British officials trusted him more than did his Nazi friends, and understood his desire to promote better Anglo-German relations. FitzRandolph confirmed that he had often witnessed Hesse chatting with Stewart at their club in St. James, particularly on one occasion when he overheard some inside information about the 1936 abdication.[33]

Since Hesse wrote about his activities and thoughts while in London in his memoirs, he naturally justifies his own actions, and shifts blame onto others. However, there is no doubt that Hitler seriously undermined his journalistic career, causing him to look back on it with a mixture of disappointment and resentment. He probably deserved to be recognized as far more influential than he was given credit for. He lamented how his talent had been wasted and over-looked, but recognized that the Nazis had achieved what they had wanted: an official German News Agency in London headed by a Party Member subservient to the Third Reich who was too candid and pessimistic.

There was one other semi-official German news agency transmitting news by wireless during the 1930s. The *Transozean* service supplemented its transmissions throughout the world from Auen with conventional telegraphic links *via* the Europa Press. Both *Transozean* and *Europa* had offices in major European capitals. In London, both of these were combined at 7 Museum Mansion, Great Russell Street, WCI. Günther Tonn, a journalist in his forties who had joined the *NSDAP* in November 1933, was in charge. His assistant was Norbert Tonnies who became a Party member in 1937 and left for Stockholm at the outbreak of war.[34] Both Tonn and Tonnies maintained a low profile while in Britain, although Tonn was among a handful of Nazi agents listed in the *Brown Network*. Unlike Ustinov and Hesse, however, Tonn never had close ties with either the German Embassy or the British Foreign Office, and was therefore a distinctly subordinate figure.

NOTES

1   PRO, FO 395/485, P196, ff. 172–74; P1968, ff. 175–83; P2325, ff. 184–95; FO 371/16762, C11012, ff. 460–71.
2   PRO, FO 395/515, P199, ff. 367–73. Hugenberg resigned on 29 June 1933.
3   *The Times*, 29 November 1933, p. 13. See also PRO, FO 395/485, P2774, ff. 205–8.
4   Breen to Willert, 18 January 1934, PRO, FO 395/515, P199, ff. 367–73.
5   Leeper minute of 24 January 1934, *ibid.*
6   Breen to Willert, *ibid.*
7   Leeper minute of 24 January 1934.
8   Nadia Benois Ustinov, *Klop and the Ustinov Family* (London, 1973); Peter Ustinov, *Dear Me* (Boston, 1977); letters of Peter Ustinov to J. J. Barnes, 22 November 1979 and 31 January 1980.
9   N.B. Ustinov, *ibid.*, p. 186.
10  *Wolffbüro* Berlin, to Propaganda Ministry, 2 November 1933.
11  Bene to *Auslandsorganisation* Hamburg, 15 December 1933; *Auslandsorganisation* Hamburg to Propaganda Ministry, 19 December 1933, BDC.
12  Kell to Foreign Office, 4 December 1933, PRO, FO 371/16751, C10679, ff. 72–80.
13  Ustinov, *Klop*, p. 187.
14  Propaganda Ministry memos, 11 September and 10 November 1933, NA microcopy, T-70, roll 89, frames 3607457-58, 3607463. Banse's completed questionnaire was sent to the Wolffbúro in Berlin on 31 October 1933 and can be found in the BDC.
15  F. Hesse, *Das Spiel um Deutschland* (Munich, 1953), p. 37.
16  Ustinov, *Klop*, pp. 188–89.
17  P. Ustinov, *Dear Me*, p. 80.
18  *Ibid.*

19  F. Hesse, *Hitler and the English* (London, 1954), p. 11; translation of the title cited in note 15.
20  *Ibid.*
21  Hesse papers, *Bundesarchiv* Koblenz: Kl. Erw. 276-2.
22  *Ibid.* Hesse's membership card can be found in his file at the BDC.
23  12 July 1945, NA RG165; G-2 Division Interrogation, PWB/SAIT/23/25.
24  Hesse, *Das Speil*, p. 37.
25  *Ibid.*, pp. 16–27 and 40.
26  Interrogation of Hesse, 12 July 1945.
27  Hesse to Mejer, 28 June 1938, Hesse Papers, *Bundesarchiv* Koblenz, Kl. Erw. 276-1, pp. 16–19.
28  PRO, FO 372/3247, T12488, ff. 301–7.
29  *Ibid.* See also PRO, FO 372/3247, T14553, ff. 342–45.
30  Hesse, *Hitler and the English*, pp. 62, 68–72.
31  *Ibid.*, p. 80.
32  S.S. FitzRandolph, "To Whom It May Concern", 22 January 1954, Hesse papers, *Bundesarchiv* Koblenz, Kl. Erw. 276-4, p. 31.
33  *Ibid.*, and Hesse, *Das Spiel*, pp. 36–37.
34  BDC, and PRO, FO 371/20741, C7066, ff. 221–32; and FO 371/ 19942, C5497, ff. 167–73.

# 8 PARTY AND *SS* MEMBERS IN THE GERMAN EMBASSY

In 1933 the German Embassy in London was staffed by nine career diplomats. In addition to the Ambassador, Leopold von Hoesch, there were: the Counselor, Count Albrecht Bernstorff; First Secretaries Ernst Rüter and Prince Otto von Bismarck; Second Secretaries Günther Henle, Theodor Auer, and Albert van Scherpenberg; Third Secretary Werner von Fries; and Head-of- Chancery Friedrich Wilhelm Achilles.[1] With two exceptions, von Bismarck and Auer, they were distinctly unenthusiastic or hostile to the Nazi seizure of power, as the following letter to Herman Göring indicated:[2]

> The present Reich government may well wonder where the unfavorable reports about the New Germany originate. I cannot help but think that such adverse publicity comes from many of the German Embassies abroad, and from foreign Jewish journalists. For the moment I suggest you pay special attention to the German Embassy in London. As a National Socialist I feel it is my duty to protect the New Germany from such calumnies. I urge you to remove from the diplomatic service, as soon as possible, Ambassador von Hoesch, a gentleman of the Stresemann, pin-stripe tradition and someone who is heartily disliked by the English people and even by the Queen. With him should go Count Bernstorff, a left-wing democrat.

In London, Nazi Party faithful like Hans Wilhelm Thost added their voices to those who condemned the offending Embassy officials. In a letter of 26 March 1933, written jointly to Rudolf Hess and Alfred Rosenberg, Thost alleged that Count Bernstorff had been a great embarrassment to the cause of National Socialism because he had formally received delegations of British Socialists and trade unionists who protested Nazi policy toward the Jews, and he had granted an audience to Thomas Mann at a time when he was under sentence of treason in Germany for being a Communist.[3]

Allegations like these resulted in Bernstorff's recall from London in June 1933, and after a few months of obvious make-work at the Foreign Ministry in

Berlin, he submitted his resignation. The Nazis' worst suspicions about him were confirmed when he accepted a directorship of the Jewish-owned Wassermann bank. To resign from his chosen profession must have been very difficult for him because he had come from a family of diplomats, including an uncle who had represented Germany in Washington during World War I and had tried to keep the Americans neutral. Born in 1890, he was one of five German Rhodes Scholars to enter Oxford in 1909. He studied at Trinity College for the next two years, and in 1914, on the eve of war, entered the *Auswärtiges Amt*. His experience in pre-war Britain and his excellent command of English recommended his appointment to London after the war in 1922. For the next decade he devoted himself to improving Anglo-German relations, winning the respect of many in Britain. There was no mistaking the warmth of esteem and affection in which he was held. As Edith Bagnold recalled: "He was nearly a giant, perhaps six foot six, certainly at one time weighing twenty stones, somehow younger than in young-middle-age, blonde as a baby; bald, but with the remains of curling tendrils above his ears . . . "[4]

After resigning from the *Auswärtiges Amt*, he spent much of his time traveling. When war broke out in September 1939, he was in Switzerland and delayed returning to Germany. For his failure to come home immediately, he was imprisoned at Dachau, but once released he avoided Nazi clutches until the attempt on Hitler's life in July 1944 when he, along with many others, was rounded up, put in prison, and finally executed on the eve of Germany's surrender. Among his contemporaries abroad, Bernstorff was seen as the epitome of German traditional values: a man of integrity, gentility, and conviviality. The journalist Robert Bruce Lockhart eulogized: "He spent his last four years in England in fighting Nazism both in Germany and in his own Embassy in London, and in warning his British friends in high places that Hitler was a dangerous lunatic."[5]

Another diplomat that Thost excoriated was Albert van Scherpenberg. As the son-in-law of Hitler's future finance minister, Dr. Hjalmar Schacht, he enjoyed a degree of immunity and never succumbed to pressures to join the Nazi Party during his professional career.

Ernst Rüter, at the age of 48, was one of the more senior German representatives in London. In 1933 he was not a member of the Nazi party, and his assignment in London ended in mid-1934 when he returned to Berlin to take a post in the *Auswärtiges Amt*. He applied to join the *NSDAP* in October 1937, but unbeknownst to him there was a file in the central membership office edged in red and stamped with the word "Warning", indicating that he was distrusted by the Party and should not be admitted, except after thorough scrutiny. It took a special request from the *Auslandsorganisation* to remove this designation which showed clearly that Rüter had been among the hostile diplomats serving in London.[6]

Another Second Secretary whose card carried a warning label was Günther

Henle. Prior to assuming his post in London in late 1931, he had been on assignment in Latin America as well as in Berlin. Born in 1899, he grew up in the pre-Nazi era, and found that as a staff member at the German Embassy in London during the Weimar years, he remembered with nostalgia the cultural events that had been sponsored in 1932: "Furtwängler symphonies, concerts, the engagement of German opera ensembles at the Covent Garden opera house, the commemoration in 1932 of the centennial of Goethe's death . . . all these were magnificent high points. . . ."[7] Henle never tried to join the Nazi Party, and it is unclear why he was blacklisted.

Chancellor Friedrich Achilles also avoided becoming a member of the *NSDAP*. Born in 1880, he entered the German diplomatic service at the turn of the century, came to the German Consulate-General in London in 1904, was assigned elsewhere for some years, and returned to London in 1920. Until the outbreak of war in 1939 he was in charge of the Embassy's Chancery, but lacked enthusiasm for National Socialism.

The same cannot be said for Second Secretary Theodor Auer. A few months after Hitler became Reich Chancellor, the thirty-four year old indicated his support by applying for Party membership, and was admitted in January 1934. Soon afterwards he was transferred from London.

Of the nine senior staff in 1933, the most prominent pro-Nazi was Otto von Bismarck, grandson of the nineteenth-century statesman. Born in 1897, he briefly entered the *Auswärtiges Amt* in 1915–16, after which he served on the Russian front until the end of the war. Trying his hand at politics, he was elected to the Reichstag in 1924, but became disillusioned and re-entered the diplomatic service. While posted in Stockholm he married Ann-Marie Tengbom, and in 1928 they came to London where they lived for the next eight years, becoming consummate hosts at 9 Stanhope Street, W2.

In 1933 Otto von Bismarck joined the Party and took over Bernstorff's duties as Embassy Counselor. Next to Ambassador von Hoesch, he was the most important German representative in London. As early as 1931 he recognized that Hitler was someone who would soon achieve political power.[8] His older brother Gottfried was already a Party member, and later joined the *SS*. There was irony in following his brother into the Party because Gottfried became increasingly disillusioned, and in July 1944 was one of those accused of treason in the failed bomb plot against Hitler. Until early 1937, von Bismarck was the *Verbindungsmann* (liaison) between the Embassy and the *Ortsgruppe*, ensuring that Party directives were made known to the entire diplomatic staff.

Since only von Bismarck and Auer were Party members during the early thirties, they were unable to impose a National Socialist agenda on the Embassy. However, this soon changed, as happened in the wider German community.

Ambassador Leopold Gustav Alexander von Hoesch reacted to National Socialism with mild interest tinged with a skepticism borne of years of experience in the *Auswärtiges Amt*. He first became a diplomat in 1907 at the age of 26 and was posted to Peking. His credentials were impressive, having studied law at Geneva, Heidelberg, Munich, and Leipzig. The next few years found him assigned to Paris, Madrid, and London; the last as Third Secretary from 1912 to 1914. During the first phase of the Great War he served in the Army and received the Iron Cross, Second Class, and later transferred into the *Auswärtiges Amt* and was sent to Sofia (1915–16), followed by a tour of duty in Constantinople (1916–17). In 1918 he took part in the negotiations at Brest-Litovsk which culminated in Russia withdrawing from the war. His postwar career took him to Oslo (1918–19), Madrid (1919–20) and finally, Paris (1921–32). Appointment to the French capital signaled the high regard in which he was held by the Weimar Republic, and this was confirmed in 1924 when he was appointed Ambassador. In 1932 he became Ambassador to the Court of St. James where his colleagues, without exception, held him in high esteem. According to Günther Henle:[9]

> Both in intellect and as a politician, Hoesch far surpassed his predecessor. Overall he was one of the most brilliant personalities produced by the German Foreign Service between the two world wars. An elegant and adroit diplomat of world-wide experience, he was also possessed of a keen political intelligence. He was, however, by no means free of snobbishness or of a sizable dose of vanity. Of the social success that he revered and preferred to seek in aristocratic circles, he was assured by his tall, slender figure, his perfect manners and pleasing personality. . . . Although a bachelor, he knew how to make the German Embassy a centre of social and political life, and under him it was generally regarded as the "smartest" embassy in London.

As a career diplomat, von Hoesch had been accustomed to representing his country regardless of its political leanings. Accordingly, whether it was the Second German Reich or the Weimar Republic, von Hoesch assumed that he could ignore the stridently political aspects of Hitler's policies, and proceed more or less as usual. He therefore ignored as far as possible the Nazi Party members and the *Ortsgruppe*, but learned that this was counter to Berlin's expectations. In April 1933 he received instructions to show public recognition of the Nazis and to include them henceforth in diplomatic functions. Otto Bene reported to his superiors in Hamburg that a slightly embarrassed von Hoesch summoned him to consult about how to implement this new directive.[10]

> Bearing in mind that we are living in England and must take all things into consideration, we have decided to hold a reception at the Embassy on the 30th of April in the evening to which all Germans, in so far as they can be located, are invited. The Ambassador will speak to the guests briefly in his role as chief of the colony here. Now I am intrigued to discover whether some of the Jews, who usually put on quite an act around here, will show up. The Embassy is, after all, absolutely

inundated by them. Unfortunately they still have German passports and legally are recognized as German citizens.

During 1933–34 an additional career diplomat joined the Embassy, Leopold von Plessen. Since he was a cousin of Otto von Bismarck, it might have looked as though strings were being pulled in order to bring another Nazi sympathizer to 9 Carleton House Terrace. Paradoxically, von Plessen was definitely not a member of the *NSDAP*, which may account for his brief stay in London. By the end of 1934 he had returned to Berlin. His replacement as First Secretary was Adolf Marschall von Bieberstein, a man whose position with respect to the Nazi movement was clear. As related to the Foreign Office by Horace Rumbold, the British Ambassador in Germany,[11]

> Many young men of good family with a certain amount of money gave it all away to the movement in the first flush of enthusiasm and now have no more to give. For instance, young Marschall von Bieberstein, the son of the ex-Ambassador in London, has I hear on unimpeachable authority, sold his estates and given the money to the Nazi movement –and is now completely ruined.

When the Nazis came to power, von Bieberstein had apparently lost little time applying for membership in the Party, and was admitted on 1 May 1933.

In 1934 another First Secretary arrived in London. Harald Bielfeld was appointed as the new head of the Embassy's Commercial Department, and although he was not a Party Member at the time, he joined in 1936, becoming one of three top diplomats, other than the Ambassador, whose allegiance could be claimed by the Party: von Bismarck, Marschall von Bieberstein, and Bielfeld. Among the lower ranks at the Embassy was a young attaché by the name of Hans Otto Meissner, the son of Hitler's head of Chancery, Otto Meissner. He joined the *NSDAP* in December 1936. Two years later, while posted in Japan, he also became a member of the *SS*.

There were several notable exceptions to the trend toward nazifying the Embassy. From 1934 to 1936 two distinctly anti-Nazi diplomats were assigned to London: Second Secretary Wolfgang Egon Gans Edler Herr zu Putlitz, and Dr. Eduard Brücklmeier, both of whom felt compelled to join the Party when war broke out in 1939. Putlitz sought refuge in Holland, while Brücklmeier met his death as one of the bomb plotters in July 1944.

The year 1936 brought significant changes to the German Embassy. In April, Ambassador von Hoesch suddenly died, under possibly mysterious circumstances. Rumors were rife that he had been poisoned, but it is much more likely that his heart attack was genuine. Von Hoesch's death created a vacuum which Hitler filled with his favorite expert on Britain, Joachim von Ribbentrop, who soon made it clear that von Hoesch's old-fashioned ways would be relegated to the past. He indicated that five out of eight posts held by non-Party members were too many, and henceforth the Embassy would represent the Nazi movement in all respects.

Von Ribbentrop shared the attitude of many Nazis that the German diplomatic service was not to be trusted. Officials concerned with Party membership abroad agreed on this point. "As long as the diplomatic representation of Germany is not National Socialist, the *Gau Ausland* [*Auslandsorganisation*] performs many other tasks of which little is known up till now."[12] These included giving advice to Germans living abroad about emigration, consular affairs, returning to Germany, financial liquidations abroad, retention of German citizenship, and property ownership in the former German colonies. "It is significant that many abroad are now turning to us for such matters rather than to the official state representative here and abroad."[13] The *Gau Ausland* was advised to follow the example of domestic *Gaue* and begin keeping files on diplomats and other personnel so that they would know, for future reference, which ones were reliable and sympathetic.

The investigation of diplomats often led to their replacement by members of the *NSDAP*. According to von Ribbentrop, "only convinced National Socialists . . . could represent Germany effectively abroad."[14] This policy achieved its object, because by 1935 the British Consul-General in Hamburg commented on the extent to which the *Auslandsorganisation* was able to control career diplomats abroad:[15]

> While it is difficult to form an accurate estimate of the organisation's political influence in foreign countries, its importance seems to be steadily on the increase. A member of my staff was recently informed that German Ambassadors and Ministers generally consider it advisable to pay a visit to this organisation when home on leave of absence. The Ministry for Foreign Affairs and German diplomatic representatives abroad also have contact with it and, I gather, find it a considerable nuisance. Diplomatic commissions have been instructed to work in the closest touch with the Party representatives, and it is expected that the latter be invited by German missions to any functions with Germans living in their country.

There were other areas the *Auslandsorganisation* sought to dominate or manipulate. Relying on the decree that *NSDAP* members were expected to conduct themselves at all times so as to bring honor to the Third Reich, it required any serious breaches of behavior be reported directly to headquarters. Accordingly, the *Auswärtiges Amt* instructed its diplomats and consuls to cooperate and relay incidents of misconduct by Party members overseas.[16]

Foreign missions were also expected to display the latest publications of the German Propaganda Ministry, but the routine practice of giving pamphlets to visitors aroused heated controversy. A case in point involved the English translation of a speech that Goebbels delivered at Nuremberg on 13 September 1935 attacking the Soviet Union. On 10 December during Question time in Parliament, Neill Maclean asked the Foreign Secretary if it was a breach of diplomatic privilege for the German Embassy to distribute written material containing attacks on a nation with whom Britain enjoyed normal and friendly relations.[17] The official response was a willingness to look into the matter, but behind the scenes the Foreign Office expressed decidedly contradictory views. Some thought it perfectly normal for embassies to leave a variety of publications on tables and counters for visitors to peruse or take away with them, especially since foreign missions enjoyed extra-territorial status. This being the case, the British could not interfere, provided that the distribution of propaganda took place within embassy property. By contrast, others heartily disagreed.[18]

> Even if it is usual for diplomatic missions to have available versions of important declarations by national statesmen, nevertheless, when it comes to distributing copies of them to callers at the Embassy, the propriety of the action must surely depend upon the nature of the declaration distributed. There are certain limitations on the propaganda which it is permissible for foreign missions to carry on in the country to which they are accredited and unless I am mistaken, warnings or intimations have in recent times been given both to the Abyssinian Legation and the Italian Embassy in cases where we thought they had gone too far.

FitzRandolph, the German Embassy's Press Attaché, minimized the importance of the pamphlets, saying that because they were expensive to translate and print, they were not very numerous. Moreover, major Nazi speeches and press releases were usually covered in the British press. He naturally defended displaying material at the Embassy since he was employed by the Ministry that printed Goebbels' speech, and was probably responsible for supplying the propaganda in the first place. He admitted making the mistake of sending copies of the speech to several Members of Parliament, and vowed to limit the distribution of similar material only to those requesting it.[19]

Von Ribbentrop had his reasons for mistrusting the official German diplomatic establishment. He held a grudge against von Hoesch dating back to the pre-Nazi era when he was working in Paris for a French champagne company, and was never invited to official Embassy functions. Negotiating the 1935 Naval Agreement with Britain from behind von Hoesch's back was his way of taking revenge.

Once von Ribbentrop succeeded von Hoesch in 1936, he was able to transform Germany's diplomatic representation in Great Britain. Like other Nazis, he was aware that even the *Auswärtiges Amt* in Berlin had resisted nazification. Of the 92 senior officials who held posts in late 1936, only 31 were members of the *NSDAP*, and a mere handful had been inducted into the *SS*.[20] Von Ribbentrop set himself the task of filling all the positions at the German Embassy in London with Party Members. He recognized that this would take time, but meanwhile he intended to alert the British that they would soon see changes such as plain and outspoken discourse replacing the former diplomatic niceties of protocol.

Arriving in London on 26 October, von Ribbentrop hastened to present his credentials to King Edward VIII, an event which drew little attention from the press. By contrast, the formal presentation of Exequaturs to George VI, after Edward's abdication, was quite another story. It took place at Buckingham Palace, and was described in detail by the *Daily Herald*.[21]

> Herr von Ribbentrop wore full levée dress. When his name was called he advanced toward the King, halted, clicked his heels and raised his right arm in a full Nazi salute. Then he made three steps forward, clicked his heels and saluted again. Once more he advanced three paces, stopped and clicked his heels for the third time and gave the King a third Nazi salute. The King bowed in formal acknowledgment and the reception went on.

The German Embassy vehemently denied the report in some papers that von Ribbentrop had greeted the monarch with the words, "Heil Hitler!", but readily admitted that he had raised his arm as Germans were used to doing, in "a salute of honour to rulers all over the world."[22] The *Evening Standard* cartoonist, David Low, portrayed the incident using the caption, "Yes, you may go out, Ribbentrop," possibly mocking a schoolboy's request to be excused. The article about the event carried the headline, "Untimely Nazi salute misinterpreted at high function."[23] At this point in his tenure as Ambassador, it was fashionable to portray von Ribbentrop as an uncouth buffoon, not yet recognizing his potential to undermine Anglo-German relations.

The arrival of Herr and Frau von Ribbentrop gave the Germans in London an opportunity to put on a big show. The interior of the Embassy at 9 Carleton House Terrace was completely refurbished in spectacular Nazi fashion, including lowering and covering over the original finely-plastered ceilings, but the façade of the house, designed by John Nash in the early nineteenth century, could not be altered. Second Secretary and head of the Consular Department, zu Putlitz, described the chaotic scene.[24]

> Since the coronation of the new King, George VI, was to take place in June 1937, work went on at high pressure in the German Embassy so that the new interior might be ready in time for the receptions and dinner parties which Ribbentrop planned for the occasion. As the walls were not drying quickly enough, great coke ovens were placed immediately beneath my offices and burned night and day for a week, so that the temperature became unbearable. However, all the energy expended was not wasted, and at the opening of the Coronation festivities the last German workman had departed for home.
>
> The dignified and time-honoured interior of the old Embassy was no longer recognizable. In our offices every single stick of furniture had been replaced. We

were now supplied with mahogany writing tables, cream coloured telephones and armchairs upholstered in green and red leather.

Upstairs, the drawing-room, enlarged by demolishing intervening walls, was now one hundred feet long, with vast mirrors at either end which added to its sense of spaciousness. It is only fair to say that the planning and decoration, designed by Speer, Hitler's personal architect, left nothing in taste and would have done credit to the Hotel Waldorf-Astoria in New York. Various German museums had been ordered to supply paintings to adorn its walls, but as was only to be expected, their curators had refused to part with their best pictures and sent only second-rate stuff. So most of the pictures were trash, although the head of a horse by Lenbach was worth looking at, and also a long-haired Lucrezia by Lucas Cranach, who was about to thrust a dagger into her bare bosom. Ribbentrop often stood before the latter masterpiece blowing his cigar smoke into the lovely suicide's face.

One of von Ribbentrop's secretaries, Erich Kordt, estimated that the work cost not three, but five million Marks – more than the German Foreign Ministry spent on all their buildings throughout the world in a given year. Here again, von Ribbentrop's ability to bypass the Ministry's constraints and secure funds directly from Hitler greatly facilitated his schemes of grandeur.[25] Second Secretary Günther Henle echoed the sentiments of many with longtime connections to the Ministry.[26]

> While the style and furnishings of the Embassy formerly had been in keeping with the aristocratic tastes cultivated in London, the ostentation of the Third Reich and the showy luxury of Berlin's Kurfurstendamm now became the order of the day, doing much to destroy the respect for Germany that had been so laboriously built up after the First World War.

Not surprisingly, the extensive remodeling of the German Embassy came to the notice of the House of Commons. The Government was asked how many foreign laborers were carrying out the work, with the implication that British workers were being deprived of jobs. Concern was also registered that many unscreened foreigners were suddenly descending upon London. The Government gave assurances that to date – January 1937 – about 145 German craftsmen had been admitted into the United Kingdom, and only a few more would join the approximately 130 British workers who had been employed by the Germans to assist with the project.[27]

His more elaborate quarters allowed Ribbentrop to import additional diplomatic and consular personnel, although not all of them were utilized effectively.[28]

> The new Ambassador had also brought with him a dozen so-called orderlies some of whom were the usual type of young *SS* men who imagined that they would be living in grand style in London. Instead they were put to polishing floors and

door knobs, washing crockery and doing other domestic chores for Frau von Ribbentrop, which made them highly indignant. They too were under the strict discipline of an *SS* sergeant. . . .

Contemporary and later accounts confirm the increase in von Ribbentrop's diplomatic and personal staff. The German Military Attaché described how "a swarm of young men had turned up on Ribbentrop's staff who were remarkable not only for their complete ignorance of foreign affairs but for their willingness to believe any and every story they were told."[29] Erich Kordt remembered that many were hired in anticipation of von Ribbentrop's arrival in London, while others were drawn from his own *Dienststelle*. A former businessman and Ribbentropbüro colleague, Martin Luther, came to London especially to help with the refurbishing project, while others with no Foreign Service experience were made Honorary Attachés or adjutants.[30]

In order to determine the effect of appointing Nazis to the German Embassy staff, one needs to know the approximate number of personnel employed before von Ribbentrop became Ambassador. These figures were requested by a Member of Parliament in 1935, but the British Government could only say that between 1929 and 1935 there had been an increase from 25 to 33 regular staff members, not including Chancery servants or household domestics.[31] The gradual growth stemmed in part from the addition of military and naval and commercial attachés plus shorthand typists. By the spring of 1936, a similar question in Parliament drew the response that there were a total of 36 diplomats and their clerical staff.[32]

How do these figures compare with the tabulation kept by the German Foreign Ministry? A list dated February 1936 gives the names of 42 diplomats and clerks, while one dated in July indicates only 33. Perhaps seasonal turnover in staff, changes following the death of von Hoesch, and ambiguity as to the exact nature of the work being done, accounts for these discrepancies.[33] Given these figures, it would not be amiss to number the Embassy staff on the eve of von Ribbentrop's arrival in London as 36, nine to twelve of whom were career diplomats, while the others were support staff (messengers, doormen, and chauffeurs) who worked either at the Embassy itself, or at the Ambassador's Residence. One year later, in July 1937, the German Foreign Ministry listed 15 career diplomats, 29 clerks, and 15 domestics as Embassy personnel, a marked increase of 23. Then in April 1938 the British Foreign Office asked that the list be revised, and this time it tallied 16 career officials, 30 clerical workers, and 22 domestic servants, for a total of 68.

Throughout these years only ordinary employees of the German Foreign Ministry were listed. There was no way to know how many orderlies and assistants von Ribbentrop imported from Berlin or other German agencies. This may explain why, in answer to a Parliamentary Question in May 1939, the Foreign

Secretary estimated that the German Embassy Staff, including domestic servants, numbered about 88.[34]

Although it is impossible to know who made up von Ribbentrop's unofficial entourage in 1936–38, the question of his influence over the 36–46 diplomats and clerks remains. During the latter half of 1937, there were 15 senior officials administering the German Embassy in London. Von Ribbentrop presided, with Ernst Woermann as his Counselor and second in Command. There were three First Secretaries: Harald Bielfeld, Erich Kordt and Eduard von Selzam; and four Second Secretaries: Eduard Brücklmeier, Alexander von Dornberg, Wolfgang zu Putlitz and Oskar Schlitter. Holding the rank of Attaché were Herbert Behlau and Heinz Thorner, while Prince Ludwig von Hessen und bei Rhein was an Honorary Attaché. From the pre-von Ribbentrop days, there remained the Assistant Commercial Attaché, Walter Maria Weber; the Press Attaché, Sigismund FitzRandolph; and the Chancellor, Friedrich Wilhelm Achilles.

There is clear evidence that von Ribbentrop put pressure on his senior colleagues in the Embassy to join the Nazi Party. Five were already members: Bielfeld, Dörnberg, FitzRandolph, Schlitter, and Thorner. In his memoirs, Putlitz describes the recruitment. Woehrmann was asked by von Ribbentrop why he was not a Member, and when he replied that he had never been asked to join, he received a personal invitation from the *Ortsgruppenleiter* the very next day. *NSDAP* membership files show that he applied to be a member on 27 April 1937, and was formally admitted in December. Similarly, Putlitz and Brücklmeier were given one week to apply. With von Ribbentrop's backing, Brücklmeier was granted membership in December 1937, having been refused in 1934.

Although Erich Kordt had been a close aide to von Ribbentrop before coming to London, he had never joined the Party, but with urging, he applied in July 1937 and was admitted in November. Commercial attaché Walter Weber had already applied in January 1937 and was accepted in August. Prince von Hessen joined shortly before coming to England, while Herbert Behlau decided to act before Ribbentrop left London in February 1938, and received his Party card in July. Similarly, once it became apparent that von Ribbentrop would be chosen Foreign Minister, Theo Kordt, Erich's brother, proceeded to join, but was not admitted until August 1939 on the eve of World War II. First Secretary Selzam might have gone ahead had not his marriage to an American made him suspect, and probably would have disqualified him.

These new *NSDAP* members did not automatically mean that Nazis were taking over the Embassy staff, because several of them were either indifferent or antithetical to their new status. Nevertheless, it was becoming increasingly clear that being a Party member was required of anyone hoping for promotion or transfer to a desirable post. As Putlitz later wrote, "a refusal would have certainly meant the end of our careers."[35]

It is interesting to note the lengths to which Eduard Brücklmeier went to advance his prospects. He not only accepted von Ribbentrop's offer to accompany him to Berlin in February 1938 as his personal assistant, but he also followed von Ribbentrop's recommendation that he join the *SS*, a privilege conferred only on his closest staff members. Brücklmeier had trouble disguising his true feelings concerning these supposed honors, and eventually was ousted from the Party for unreliability. He was among those executed for being involved in the bomb plot against Hitler in July 1944.

As Foreign Minister from February 1938 on, von Ribbentrop had to approve all senior appointments to key missions like London, and he made sure that most of them were Party Members. During 1938–39 six Second Secretaries were sent to London: Georg Federer, Josias von Rantzau, Adolf Velhagen, Georg Vogel, Karl Waluschek von Wallfeld, and Wolfgang Welck. Furthermore, two new attachés were added: Egbert J. Geyer and Wolfgang Jasper. Of these, all were *NSDAP* members except Federer and Rantzau. By 1939 it was the exceptional diplomat who declined to join or was refused admission to the Nazi Party, attesting to von Ribbentrop's success.

When von Ribbentrop became Foreign Minister, the staff numbered about 2,300; by the time the war ended it had increased to about 10,000. Within the Ministry, the Department of Protocol rose from three to 50, while the Press Department went from seven to 200.[36] Whatever else may be said about him, von Ribbentrop was certainly an effective "empire builder," determined to curb, as much as possible, the traditional independence of the *Auswärtiges Amt*, and make the German Embassy in London a model of nazification.

Did the military attachés in London also succumb to Nazi political pressure? Following World War I, the Weimar Republic wanted to underline its peaceful intentions by not attaching army and navy officers to foreign missions. However, Hitler's immediate predecessor as Chancellor, General Kurt von Schleicher, revived the practice by sending Brigadier General Leo Geyr von Schweppenburg to London in late 1932. Von Schweppenburg spoke English well, and was able to allay Ambassador von Hoesch's fears that the German military was trying to re-enter the political arena.[37]

For a while von Schweppenburg also functioned as Air Attaché until he was joined in 1935 by Luftwaffe Colonel (later Lieutenant General) Ralph Franz Albert Wenninger in 1935. Air power was fast becoming a dominant consideration, especially once the Nazis repudiated the restrictions imposed by the Treaty of Versailles and openly began to rebuild the Luftwaffe. Von Schweppenburg departed in late 1937, and was followed by Colonel Anton von Bechtolsheim.

A Naval Attaché, Captain Erwin Wassner, also came to London in 1933. He served until the summer of 1937 when he was transferred, and replaced by Captain Leopold Siemens.

**96**

As European nations rearmed during the 1930s, the number of military personnel attached to missions abroad increased. During the Rhineland crisis of March and April 1936, Major Reinhold Kitschmann was sent to London to work with von Schweppenburg, and when he unexpectedly died two years later, Captain Albrecht Soltmann assumed the post of Assistant Military Attaché. The summer of 1938 brought Commander Burkardt von Mullenhem-Rechberg to London as an Assistant to the Naval Attaché, and when the Czech crisis worsened, Captain Eberhard Spiller and Chief Engineer Dietrich Schwencke arrived to assist Air Attaché Wenninger. Surprisingly, of these eight military attachés and their assistants, only one – Reinhold Kitschmann – was a member of the Nazi Party.

The same cannot be said of the clerical staff. Prior to von Ribbentrop's arrival, only eight of the 30 clerks, typists, and telephonists who worked in the Embassy were members of the *NSDAP*, whereas by the autumn of 1937 seventeen were Nazis. Typical of someone who joined the Party after assuming her duties as a secretary in the German Embassy in 1937 was Helga Hellwig, a former student at the London School of Economics. Another woman, Edith Krüger, worked for the Foreign Ministry until March 1936 when she switched to the *Ribbentropbüro*, and was brought to London as Ribbentrop's private secretary. Within a year she applied for membership in the *NSDAP*.

Those who came to London as replacements during von Ribbentrop's tenure were more than likely Party Members. From early 1936 until the outbreak of war, of the 62 clerical staff, 33 belonged to the Party, and since many of these were women, far fewer of whom joined the *NSDAP*, it is significant that half of them were Nazis. Because there was no distinction made between those in the *Landesgruppe* and those who worked for the Embassy, everyone was expected to attend *NSDAP* meetings, instruction groups, and social events.

Domestic servants were less likely to join the Party than clerical personnel. From 1937 to the outbreak of war, 83 individuals worked either for the Embassy, or privately for diplomatic families, as cleaning women, cooks, doormen, messengers, firemen, chauffeurs, and mechanics. The Ambassador had his own household staff, about half of whom were women, and only one was a Party member; of the men, 13 were enrolled. In all, about one-third of the 33 domestic staff were Party members.

Before 1939 there were occasional attempts to give quasi or actual diplomatic immunity to Party members abroad. Professional diplomats, German as well as others, disapproved, but Nazi leaders, especially E. W. Bohle of the *Auslandsorganisation*, repeatedly challenged official protocol. We have already seen how Otto Bene, the *Ortsgruppenleiter* in London, was suggested as Consul-General, but the British refused to allow a key political figure to assume a position in which he could bully German citizens.[38] For this same reason great alarm spread in January 1937 when Bohle's *Auslandsorganisation* merged with the *Auswärtiges Amt*, threatening to force the issue of granting diplomatic immunity to Nazi officials. If this had occurred, it would have been far more difficult to demand their recall.

This question arose again when Britain expelled three journalists plus a former *Ortsgruppenleiter*, Wolfgang von Langen, recently arrived from Italy.[39] As reported in the *New York Times*, Bohle was determined to protect Party members from unwarranted pressure and reprisal while they were abroad. Under the headline, "Diplomatic status sought for Nazis," he was quoted as saying that he intended to force "foreign governments to recognize and protect National Socialist Party officials and groups in their territories."[40]

> Through the absorption of the National Socialist Party's foreign section into the Foreign Office, the unity of Party and State is made clear to the world abroad and is established beyond contradiction. German Party organisations in other countries, therefore have a character resembling that of diplomatic legations . . .
>
> However, the Party's foreign section is concentrating on convincing foreign nations that these groups abroad are in no sense forms of political agitation but representatives of the German Reich, resembling the German Reich's diplomatic representatives.

Once Britain was at war, journalists and other Germans in London had to fend for themselves. They could not claim diplomatic privilege, nor could they leave Britain unless transport was available and permission granted. In fact, only those in the German Embassy who held diplomatic or clerical rank could be included in the Ambassador's entourage and obtain safe conduct out of Britain. Domestic servants and minor consular officials were not eligible for exit permits, and many were forced to remain in Britain throughout the war. There was an exception was made for about 27 Embassy servants who were married.[41]

Von Ribbentrop's elevation to Foreign Minister in February 1938 necessitated the appointment of a successor. In late March the name of Herbert von Dirksen, a career diplomat since 1918, was proposed. At age 56 he had considerable experience, having been Ambassador in Moscow (1928–33) and Tokyo (1933–38). From Berlin, the British Ambassador, Neville Henderson, commented: "Dirksen is by no means a Party enthusiast. He has, I understand, always been Baron von Neurath's nominee for London."[42] The former Foreign Minister was not a Party enthusiast, but it is worth noting that von Dirksen had already taken the precaution of becoming a Party member.

In London, those in the Foreign Office had mixed reactions to von Dirksen's nomination. Orme Sargent suspected that von Ribbentrop had an ulterior motive in supporting him. "Herr von Ribbentrop is not going to allow himself to be overshadowed by his successor."[43] F. K. Roberts was ambivalent. "Herr von Dirksen sounds personally sympathetic, but he is an invalid [he was a severe asthmatic] and is obviously not the sort of man to cut much ice in Nazi circles. In fact the choice suggests that the German Government are not for the present very interested in London."[44] Others were more positive. William Strang, head of the Central Department, observed:[45]

> I knew Herr von Dirksen well in Moscow. He is quiet, sensible, easy to deal with. Both he and his wife will do their duty well, but will not try to cut a figure. Frau von Dirksen can sometimes be disconcertingly frank. Herr von Dirksen will probably not have any great influence with the German Government. What German ambassador has? It does not really matter much who is German Ambassador in London. German diplomacy nowadays is conducted through Herr Hitler's speeches and Herr Hitler's acts. But Herr von Dirksen is probably as pleasant a man as they could have chosen.

Permanent Under-Secretary, Alexander Cadogan, agreed with Strang.[46] "I traveled across the Pacific and Canada with the von Dirksens. They were both very agreeable. He, I should think, is able and sensible. She is rather formidable, and I suggest she is a better Nazi than he is."

Von Dirksen had his share of detractors as well. Putlitz characterized him as a "heavily built, unimaginative and reactionary bureaucrat," and some regarded the family as *nouveau riche*.[47] Von Dirksen's grandfather had been a peasant in Schöneberg when that part of Berlin was a separate village, and as the city expanded, land values rose enormously, making the von Dirksens millionaires. After the First World War, von Dirksen's step-mother, who lived in a fine mansion on the *Margaretenstrasse*, "was the first Berlin hostess to throw open her doors to Hitler and the Nazis."[48]

Putlitz is our best source concerning Gestapo agents in the German Embassy in London, since he was involved in plots against the Nazis while he was posted there.[49] It is important, therefore, to make a distinction between Gestapo and Abwehr agents. The latter functioned abroad in classic espionage roles, which is why it was assumed that the German Embassy became a haven for them. However, as we shall discover later, there were very few Abwehr agents in London during 1930s.[50] Gestapo personnel, on the other hand, did not ordinarily function abroad, since their job was to focus on internal security and counter-espionage. However, under certain circumstances, Gestapo agents were assigned to combat anti-German activities outside the Third Reich, which included surveillance of German nationals, either refugees or Nazi Party Members.

Putlitz named two Gestapo agents assigned to the Embassy in London during von Ribbentrop's tenure, Herr Schulz and Herr Mittelhaus, but gives no further details about these two men. There was also an *SS* Sergeant, Scharschewski, whose responsibility it was to maintain discipline among the younger *SS* orderlies and adjutants.[51] It has been impossible to identify Schulz, as this name is too common, but there is a file on Werner Mittelhaus at the Berlin Document Center. Born in Berlin in 1898, he served in the German army during World

War I, and then joined the *Schutzpolizei* from 1920 to 1927, eventually becoming a *Kriminalpolizei*. He was sent by the Gestapo to London in October 1936 and remained there until June 1937. "I was put in charge of the expansion of the German Embassy in London," he later wrote, an allusion to his promotion to *Kriminalsekretar*.[52]

Putlitz gradually realized that he was under suspicion by von Ribbentrop or one of his subordinates at the Embassy. From an electrician involved in remodeling the Embassy, he learned that hidden microphones had been installed in some parts of the building. He also discovered that one of his colleagues, Herbert Behlau, had combed through his office files once when he went briefly to Germany.[53]

Von Ribbentrop's suspicions were, in fact, correct. Putlitz was functioning as a double agent, recruited by an émigré German newspaper correspondent whom he dubbed "Paul X" who had been in Britain since about 1929 with his wife, Gabrielle, and son, Hugo, and had applied for British naturalization. Whoever he was, he was able to contact Vansittart directly. One family fit this portrait almost exactly: the Ustinovs.[54]

As head of the Consular Department, Putlitz lacked access to diplomatic correspondence, since his brief included only emigration, passports, and the status of refugees. However, he was free to monitor the activities of Nazis, which was of utmost interest to the British. Officially, his Embassy job involved harassing German Jews and other refugees from Germany who wanted to remain in Britain, and facilitating Nazis in their work, without attracting the attention of the British. Periodically Putlitz made a show of meeting with E. N. Cooper of the Home Office in order to review difficult cases, although he later revealed that "We had come to an agreement that I should give him the full details of the various cases privately, and then he could decide what action to take."[55] Likewise, "Otto Bene, the Local Group Leader, was also often in my office dictating harsh instructions or listening to my protests to Cooper which I made sound convincingly Nazi. But since Bene was not particularly bright, he never realised that I was acting, or that Cooper never took any of my protests seriously."[56]

Putlitz boasted about having warned the British about several distinctly undesirable Nazis who had sought entry into England, enabling the Foreign Office to exclude them.[57] He also relished the discovery that von Ribbentrop had retained the services of a Russian-born, German-speaking journalist known as Petkov, who provided him with useful high society gossip at the rate of £100 per month.[58] Petkov's real name was George Popoff, and his reports were usually handed to the Head of Chancery, Friedrich Wilhlm Achilles, who locked them in his safe. However, on one occasion Putlitz chanced to read one of these, describing information which had been gleaned from a relative of Neville Chamberlain during a weekend house party. When this report was passed to

"Paul X" and Vansittart, Putlitz took malicious delight in having provided the pretext to eject Popoff from the United Kingdom.[59]

That the German Embassy could have been a center of Nazi activity in London, at first seemed highly unlikely. But, like every institution in the Third Reich, nazification proceeded relentlessly, and far from escaping its impact, the diplomatic and consular service succumbed inexorably, especially when the ardent and ambitious Joachim von Ribbentrop became German Ambassador to the Court of St. James.

NOTES

1 British *Foreign Office List* and *Statesman's Yearbook.*

2 H. G. Sasse, *100 Jahre Botschaft in London* (Bonn, 1963), pp. 63–64.

3 Thost to Hess and Rosenberg, 26 March 1933, *Bundesarchiv* Koblenz, Rosenberg papers, NS8/117, p. 26.

4 R. Reventlow (ed.), *Albrecht Bernstorff zum Gedächtnis* (Berlin, 1952), p. 40.

5 R. B. Lockhart, *Friends, Foes and Foreigners* (London, 1957), pp. 141–42.

6 Rüter file, BDC.

7 G. Henle, *Three Spheres* (Chicago, 1971), p. 36.

8 Lockhart, *Friends,* p. 31.

9 Henle, *Three Spheres,* p. 31.

10 Bene to the *Auslandsorganisation,* 26 April 1933, *Bundesarchiv* Koblenz: Schumacher collection, p. 296.

11 H. Rumbold to the British Foreign Office, 13 March 1931, PRO, FO 371/15213, C1692, f. 212.

12 Reichskommissar Nord to Oberste Leitung der PO der *NSDAP,* 7 March 1933; NA microcopy T-580, roll 56, file 293.

13 *Ibid.*

14 E. Kordt, *Nicht aus den Akten* (Stuttgart, 1950), p. 69.

15 Phipps to Simon, 30 March 1935, PRO, FO 371/19968, C2835, f. 188.

16 Memo from *Auswärtiges Amt,* 16 July 1934, NA microcopy M-942, roll 1, frame 0536.

17 *Parliamentary Debates,* Commons, CCCVIII (10 Dec. 1935), cols. 755–56.

18 PRO, FO 371/18869, C8181, ff. 320–29.

19 FitzRandolph to German Foreign Ministry, 12 December 1935, NA microcopy T-120, roll 3217, file 41/13.

20 Estimates of Party membership within the upper levels of the German Foreign Ministry were made by Paul Seabury in *The Wilhelmstrasse: A Study of German Diplomats under the Nazi Regime* (Berkeley, 1954), p. 63.

21 *Daily Herald,* 5 February 1937, p. 1.

22 *Evening Standard,* 5 February 1937, p. 2.

23 *Ibid.,* 13 February 1937, p. 7.

24 Wolfgang Gans Edler Herr zu Putlitz, *The Putlitz Dossier* (London, 1957), pp. 127–28.

25 Kordt, *Nicht aus den Akten,* p. 154.

26 Henle, *Three Spheres,* p. 33.

27 *Parliamentary Debates,* Commons, CCCXIX (28 January 1937), cols. 1057–59.

28 Putlitz, *The Putlitz Dossier,* p. 118.

29 Leo Dietrich Franz Geyr von Schweppenburg, *The Critical Years* (London, 1952), p. 148.

30  Interrogation report of Fritz Hesse, 12 July 1945, p. 6; NA, Military Archives Division.
31  *Parliamentary Debates*, Commons, CCC (16 April 1935), col. 1676.
32  *Ibid.*, CCCVIII (20 Feb. 1936), col. 1953.
33  Here we are indebted to Dr. Maria Keipert at the PAB for providing these lists and other relevant documents.
34  *Parliamentary Debates*, Commons, CCCXLVII (8 May 1939), col. 43.
35  Putlitz, *The Putlitz Dossier*, p. 114.
36  E. Davidson, *The Trial of the Germans* (New York, 1966), p. 151.
37  Von Schweppenburg, *The Critical Years*.
38  See chapter 6.
39  See chapter 15 for a discussion of the expulsion of German journalists in 1937.
40  *New York Times*, 23 August 1937, p. 3.
41  For lists of Embassy staff permitted to leave Britain, see: PRO, FO 372/3329, T11789, ff. 61–82; and T11791, ff. 91–99.
42  N. Henderson to the British Foreign Office, 29 March 1938, PRO, FO 371/21706, C2190, f. 321.
43  *Ibid.*, 30 March 1938, ff. 322–23.
44  *Ibid.*, 29 March 1938, f. 321.
45  *Ibid.*, 30 March 1938, C2514, f. 322.
46  *Ibid.*, 31 March 1938, f. 323.
47  Putlitz, *The Putlitz Dossier*, p. 143.
48  *Ibid.*
49  *Ibid.*
50  See chapter 17.
51  Putlitz, *The Putlitz Dossier*, p. 143.
52  Mittelhaus file, BDC.
53  Putlitz, *Laske, London und Haiti* (Berlin, 1965), p. 128.
54  See chapter 7 for a discussion of Ustinov's work in London.
55  Putlitz, *The Putlitz Dossier*, p. 97.
56  *Ibid.*
57  See chapter 15 for details of the Ludwig case.
58  For the British decision to expel Popoff, see chapter 15.
59  Putlitz, *The Putlitz Dossier*, p. 134. 59.

# 9 BONHOEFFER AND THE STRUGGLE FOR CHURCH AUTONOMY

On 30 July 1933 Dietrich Bonhoeffer preached at two different German-speaking congregations in London: the *Reformierte St. Paulskirche* of 3 Goulston Street, E1, and the *Deutsche Evangelische Gemeinde zu Sydenham*, Dacres Road, SE23. The Goulston Street church had about 50 parishioners, mostly working class and trades people whose families had lived in Whitechapel long enough to have forgotten some of their native German language and acquired a proficiency in English, whereas the church in Syndenham catered mostly to business and professional people, numbering about 30. Both parishes were served by Pastor Friedrich Singer, but he was soon to retire, and on this particular Sunday Dietrich Bonhoeffer was auditioning as his replacement. He impressed both congregations, and was offered the job, which he accepted after several weeks of soul-searching.

In some ways it looked as though he was running away from a promising career in Germany, since he held a position at the Friedrich Wilhelm University in Berlin, and would have no difficulty securing an advantageous pastorate if he wanted a change from the academic life. However, during the course of July 1933 the status of the Lutheran Church altered radically within Germany, and Bonhoeffer seriously doubted whether he could subscribe to the new entity. He had, until recently, been a pastor within the Prussian Evangelical Federation, but as of 15 July, this Federation, together with other parts of the Lutheran church, merged to become a new state-controlled *Deutsche Evangelische Kirche* (German Evangelical Church), referred to by the Nazis as the *Reichskirche*.

Equally disturbing to him was the rewriting of the Church's Confession of Faith in response to Nazi importuning. One paragraph in particular troubled him, for it excluded non-Aryans from serving as Lutheran clergy. One potential victim of this edict was his good friend and fellow pastor, Franz Hildebrand, whose Jewish ancestors had long since converted to Christianity, but because of this change he would eventually be deprived of his vocation. The so-called

"Aryan paragraph" was totally at variance with traditional Lutheran doctrine, and consequently Bonhoeffer did not see how he could continue to function as a pastor within the newly-defined church.

During the several months delay before assuming his new posts in London, he inadvertently became a pawn in the hands of the pro-Nazi wing of the *Deutsche Evangelische Kirche* which ousted its presiding Bishop, Friedrich Bodeldschwingh, because he was not a member of the *NSDAP*, and replaced him with the former military chaplain, Ludwig Müller, favored by the *Deutsche Christen* (German Christians) who were determined to impose Nazi values on the Church. Müller was highly suspicious of Bonhoeffer because knew that Bonhoeffer objected to the direction that the church was taking, and therefore informed him in October 1933 that he was unfit to represent the *Reichskirche* abroad. As a faithful Party member, Müller had no intention of allowing him to spread anti-Nazi propaganda among émigré Londoners who were already predisposed to being critical of what was going on in Germany.

Bonhoeffer's response to Müller's allegation was to agree that he could not be expected to promote the National Socialist agenda of the *Reichskirche*, but he asserted that he could effectively minister to the needs of the German community in London. Moreover, he assured Müller that he would refrain from attacking the *Deutsche Christen*, and seek only to interpret what was happening in church circles in Germany. He pointed out that as a well-known ecumenist, he could scarcely remain totally silent regarding issues of church and state. Furthermore, it would reflect poorly on Germany and the church if he were forbidden to assume the posts in the churches that were expecting him.[1]

Although characterized by the British Embassy in Berlin as "a stupid man," Müller realized that on this occasion he was outflanked.[2] Grudgingly he gave his permission, and by mid-October Bonhoeffer was fully installed in the vicarage at 23 Manor Mount in Forest Hill, a large Victorian house on a hillside south of Horniman Park where he had two private rooms and no central heating. A caretaker lived in the basement, and there was a girls school under the direction of Fräulein Witte in a separate wing of the house. Bonhoeffer quickly settled into a routine of delivering sermons, organizing youth groups, teaching children, and counseling refugees.

His two churches kept him very busy, but he nevertheless continued to monitor what was going on in Germany. He found the religious rally held at the *Sportspalast* in Berlin on 13 November 1933 especially troubling, as speaker after speaker mocked the traditional Lutheran emphasis on the Bible and the Confession of Faith, and extremists proposed dispensing with the Old Testament because it recapitulated the crimes and perversions of the Jewish people.

The German pastors, as well as other clerics in Britain, were not slow to react. About two weeks after the *Sportspalast* meeting, six of them met in Bradford and jointly sent a protest to the governing body of the *Reichskirche*. They deplored the excesses that were being perpetrated by those calling themselves *Deutsche Christen*, and urged Bishop Müller to adhere to his promise to maintain purity in church teaching that was being threatened by Nazi ideology.[3] Because of complaints like these, Müller's formal consecration as Reich Bishop, scheduled for December 1933, was indefinitely postponed.

On the other hand, the crisis within the *Reichskirche* went far deeper than whether or not it was able to control the rumblings of a lunatic fringe. Its clergy were forbidden to speak publicly on controversial matters affecting Church-State relations, and if they did, their jobs would be in jeopardy. On 7 January 1934 four German pastors in London made it abundantly clear whom they blamed. "For the sake of our consciences and the Gospel, we support the statements of the Pastors Emergency League and withdraw our confidence in Reich Bishop Müller."[4] These pastors also addressed a similar letter to President Paul von Hindenburg, expressing their dismay at the ways in which the *Deutsche Christen* were undermining the *Deutsche Evangelische Kirche*. They pointed out that such internal church strife reflected poorly on Germany in the eyes of foreigners, and they maintained that Germans abroad would find it harder to retain close ties with people at home if their church was in disarray. It was their firm conviction that further fragmentation was inevitable as long as Müller was Bishop.[5]

Müller responded to this criticism by suspending Martin Niemöller and 50 other pastors throughout Germany. Bishop Theodor Heckel, the head of the *Reichskirche* Foreign Affairs Office, tried to moderate between the antagonists and soothe tempers, especially among the clergy in England.[6]

> I would like to emphasize that pastors abroad are obliged to exercise the utmost political restraint. Just as the frontline soldier is unable to appreciate the whole of the strategy but only the most immediate task he is to carry out, so overseas pastors must make a distinction between their special assignments and the overall direction of the German Evangelical Church at home.

By early February 1934 Bishop Heckel realized that his epistolary admonitions were insufficient, and that he and his colleagues at the church's Foreign Affairs Office would have to enforce discipline personally. Accordingly, along with two associates, he traveled to London and conferred with the German pastors on 8 February, with negotiations continuing the following day.

Who were these pastors that stolidly opposed Müller and the *Reichskirche*? Were they all staunch anti-Nazis like Bonhoeffer? Of the four who ministered to six churches in London, three were Nazi Party members, or would soon be. The eldest was Fritz Wehrhan, who was born in 1872.[7] He was given permission in 1920 by the British authorities to revive German church worship in London, and his initial responsibility was the *Deutsche Evangelische Christuskirche* on Montpelier Place, off the Brompton Road, SW7. In the late spring of 1933 he also succeeded to the pastorate of the *Deutsche Evangelische St. Marienkirche*, 46 Cleveland Street, W1. He served these two parishes for the remainder of the 1930s, residing at 19 Beverley Road, SW13. In 1933 he applied for membership in the *NSDAP*, and was admitted on 1 May 1934.

Next in seniority was Gustav Schönberger, who was 26 years younger than Wehrhan, and was in charge of only one church, the *Hamburger Lutherische Kirche* in Dalston, near the German Hospital on Ritson Road, E8.[8] Schönberger was the most dedicated of the three, having been a Party member since October 1933, just before Bonhoeffer arrived in London. Like Wehrhan, he was married, and lived at 19 Graham Road, E8.

Julius Rieger began as pastor at the *Deutsche Lutherische St. Georgskirche*, 33 Little Alie Street, E1, in 1930.[9] Like Wehrhan and Schönberger, Rieger remained at his church throughout the 1930s, and also served as pastor at the Seamen's Mission. He joined the *NSDAP* at the beginning of January 1934 in the midst of the mounting controversy over Müller and the *Deutsche Christen*.

Outside London there were four German Evangelical pastors in early 1934: Ewald Steiniger in Newcastle, Wilhelm Hansen in Bradford, Karl-Heinz Schreiner in Liverpool, and Martin Böckheler in Hull. All but Steiniger became members of the *NSDAP*: Böckheler on 1 May 1934, Hansen on 1 October 1934, and Schreiner in April 1936.[10] What impelled these pastors to join the Nazi Party is puzzling, because all of them were outside Germany when the Nazis came to power and did not witness first-hand the escalating Nazi fervor overwhelming German politics. Perhaps being exiles fanned the flames of their patriotism. At the end of 1933, Schönberger explained his decision.[11]

> I spent two years at the front, where I fought and bled for my country. With my own eyes I saw many of my best friends pay with their lives for their service to their fatherland. . . . In my youthful enthusiasm I regarded their death as a sacred legacy . . . we had to fight on so that their death for Germany should not have been in vain or even be forgotten. But what had become of Germany? A land of injustice and corruption, subject to the whims of black and red rulers alike. As a pastor it was not my business to take part in politics, let alone party politics . . .
>
> Then the National Socialist Party came into power, a party that didn't want to be a party, with a programme having a moral and religious basis. That's why I became a member of the movement. Another reason . . . was the realization that the lower ranks of the Party hierarchy were not permeated with the same deep morality and religion as the Führer and his ideas, that many of them believed they could simply change the colour of their hearts from red to brown, and that not a few agitators – for as such I regard the movement of the 'German Christians' – would seek to use the movement to climb to positions of influence. The proclamation of the Gospel might well be prevented in consequence, so destroying the very fundament upon which the fatherland could be constructed . . . For this reason it seems to me absolutely necessary to collaborate for the sake of the Church of Christ and for the sake of the national community in which God has

placed us. That this is best done as a Party member is self-evident . . .

And I believe that already there may be opportunity to collaborate in the way I have just mentioned. After the National Bishop's sorry performance, the Party is trying to coordinate our youth work. This might perhaps be possible in Germany but not for us here . . . Today I shall make representation to the *Obergruppenleiter* who, I am convinced will listen to me because I am a member. In no circumstances shall I allow any deviation from the clear line we must follow in our work.

The confrontation of 8–9 February 1934 between Bishop Heckel and the German pastors in Britain went as anticipated. Heckel alternated threats with sweet reasonableness. As in the past, he called for moderation, asking that the *Reichskirche* be given time to weed out the hotheads, and he cautioned against further dividing the Church. However, he made it abundantly clear that the "Aryan paragraph" was not open to negotiation. It must stand as written. None too subtly, he hinted that opposition to what was transpiring in Germany by German churchmen living abroad would result in grave consequences, since it bordered on disloyalty to the state, and he alluded to rumors suggesting that the *Auslandsorganisation* might revoke the passports of troublesome clergy outside Germany. In the name of national unity and support of the Nazi regime it was imperative, he concluded, that the pastors in question cease their complaints and sign a declaration of support. At this point in his speech, Bonhoeffer, Rieger, and Steiniger ostentatiously walked out of the conference. Seemingly undaunted, Heckel urged those remaining to approve a statement of solidarity purporting to be the "unanimous" opinion of the German pastors, but he failed.[12]

While still in London, Bishop Heckel and two associates from Berlin also had an audience with George Bell, Bishop of Chichester and a staunch supporter of Bonhoeffer. Bell warned the delegation from Germany that British opinion was highly disturbed by what was happening in the *Reichskirche*, but Heckel took little notice of Bell's complaint, knowing that it was only a matter of time until sufficient pressure would be brought to bear upon the recalcitrant pastors that they would have to conform.

During his brief visit, Bishop Heckel detected the existence of a few parishioners who thought Bonhoeffer involved his congregation too much in politics, and this gave him hope of instigating dissension and eventual victory. Pursuing this goal, he wrote to Baron Bruno von Schröder, the head of the Association of German Churches in Great Britain and Ireland, asking if the Declaration "unanimously agreed to" on 9 February had yet been circulated. Schröder, who was by then a firm supporter of Bonhoeffer, replied that nothing had been done, since the Declaration had never been approved, and therefore would not be distributed among the German congregations.[13]

Bonhoeffer's campaign against Müller and the *Reichskirche* began to show signs of success, underscored toward the end of March 1934 when he received an invitation to Lambeth Palace from Cosimo Lang, the Archbishop of Canterbury, who had pointedly refused to see the Nazi church officials. Then, on 10 May, George Bell used the international forum provided by a meeting of the Universal Council for Life and Work to issue a pastoral letter expressing his growing alarm at what was happening in the *Reichskirche*. Bonhoeffer had suggested this idea, and provided Bell with the evidence to support his concerns.

Additional help for Müller's opponents came from Germany in the town of Barmen. The churches there steadfastly clung to the old Confession of Faith, and defied the takeover by the *Reichskirche*. They called themselves the *Bekennenden Kirche* (Confessing Church) and condemned as "false doctrine" the teachings of the pro-Nazi *Deutsche Christen*, but at the same time tried to stay within the legal parameters of the Third Reich.

Toward the end of August 1934 Bonhoeffer was given another boost in morale from the delegates of the Ecumenical Federation assembled on the island of Fano off the coast of Denmark. Like the Bishop of Chichester, they expressed their grave concern about events within the *Reichskirche*. By this time, however, Bonhoeffer had no illusions about his notoriety and that of his fellow pastors in Britain. Already Müller was muttering about treasonable activities, and Heckel continued to berate them from his office in Berlin. In fact, according to one of the delegates at the Fano conference, the pressure from Heckel was no longer subtle, but explicit: Bonhoeffer must leave London.

"When I asked what his [Bonhoeffer's] reply had been to the Bishop's order, he said with a grim smile: 'negative'," and then added: "I told him he would have to come to London and get me if he wanted me out of that church."[14]

As long as Müller was merely the Reich Bishop *pro tem*, many hoped that there would be a change in the church administration, but this became moot on 23 September 1934 when the Reich Synod at Wittenberg formally consecrated him, and thereby sanctioned his future repressive measures, including the arrest and imprisonment of several South German bishops. The *Bekennenden Kirche* responded to this injustice by calling a Synod in Dahlem, a suburb of Berlin, to establish an Emergency Church Government which would provide an alternative administrative structure, separate from the *Reichskirche*. This resulted in the release of the dissident bishops, and a formal distancing between the spheres of church and state. As Bonhoeffer's biographer explained, "Hitler publicly disassociated himself from the Reich Church; indeed, he declared that professions of loyalty to the Third Reich and its Führer could not be identified with commitment to any one of the groups in the Church."[15]

To complicate matters, Bonhoeffer was confronted with a personal dilemma. The leaders of the *Bekennenden Kirche* approached him about founding a seminary in Germany which would train students as opposition ministers. He knew that if he accepted this offer and returned to Germany, he would be far more vulnerable to state control than he was in London. Fortuitously, he still had the support of all the German pastors in London, even Schönberger, who had become *Ortsgruppenleiter* of a new Nazi group in Dalston. As Bonhoeffer wryly observed, Schönberger's Hamburg Lutheran Church had become more or less synonymous with his *NSDAP* cell.[16]

It is interesting to speculate why Party members like Schönberger, Wehrhan, Rieger, and Böckheler continued to tolerate Bonhoeffer's dissent from the *Reichskirche*. No one doubted that this young and outspoken pastor was persuasive, yet there must have been other reasons why they stood by him. As residents in a foreign but democratic nation like Britain, perhaps it seemed easier not to obstruct Müller and Heckel and the others. As Nazi Party members, they may have thought they were redeeming the tarnished reputation of their movement by condemning the excesses of the *Deutsche Christen*. It was less than six months since Hitler and the *SS* had ruthlessly put down Röhm and his *SA* followers, so it was still popular to praise the Nazi seizure of power and approve purging radical elements that corrupted the idealism of the new regime. As foreigners in Britain, they may have rationalized that Müller and his partisans were giving Germany and the Church a bad name, and it was their duty to resist.

Pending Bonhoeffer's decision about whether to return to Germany and establish a seminary, he had unfinished work in London. Once he found out that the *Bekennenden Kirche* had authorized an independent governing body, he urged the German churches in Britain to sever their connection with the *Reichskirche*, and affiliate with this new entity. To this end he organized a meeting of the German pastors and elders on 5 November 1934 at Christ Church, Montpelier Place.

On 10 November Baron Bruno von Schröder and Pastor Fritz Wehrhan, on behalf of the *Reichskirche* in Britain, formally notified Bishop Heckel of their intention to seek affiliation with the *Bekennenden Kirche*. Heckel reacted immediately to this news, and telephoned the German Embassy to ask postponement announcing this decision pending clarification of events in Germany. The Embassy responded that they could not interfere unless instructed to do so from Berlin.[17] The Bishop then addressed the German pastors directly, lamenting the way they were dividing the Church, and reminding them that the *Bekennenden Kirche* had no legal status in Germany, and was only an unofficial movement. This message roused the pastors in Britain to send a circular letter to all German churches abroad, explaining why they had acted as they did, and inviting others to join them. They reminded their colleagues that they had all united in 1928 under the umbrella of the Prussian Evangelical Church Federation, and now it was time to unify within the *Bekennenden Kirche*.[18]

As was probably inevitable, there was at least one defector among the German pastors in Britain. Karl Heinz Schreiner was persuaded by his fellow-Bavarian and good friend Heckel to return to Berlin and dispel any notion of unanimity. He let it be known that he disapproved of Reich Bishop Müller, but admitted that this would not make him switch allegiance to the *Bekennenden Kirche*. From Berlin he tried to win over Baron von Schröder and Pastor Rieger, arguing that he had not found the situation in Germany as desperate as Bonhoeffer pictured it. "We don't have to play at being confessing heroes," he said.[19] Schröder and Rieger were not persuaded, however, and Schreiner never again acted in conjunction with the other pastors.

In letters dated 28 November and 10 December 1934, Bishop Heckel went over the heads of the dissident pastors and addressed the parish congregations directly, implying that their pastors had acted unconstitutionally, without the knowledge and consent of their parishioners. He criticized the circular letter they had sent to churches abroad, and accused them of superseding his authority as head of the Foreign Affairs office of the *Reichskirche*.

Not until January 1935 was there a response to Heckel's allegations. Challenging his assumptions, several parishes enlisted a member of the Sydenham congregation, Eduard Cruesemann, a solicitor and Secretary of the *Deutsche Verein*. Together they decided to schedule open meetings of parish councils at which the pastors would explain their repudiation of the leaders of the *Reichskirche* and their decision to affiliate with the *Bekennenden Kirche*. They also censured the Bishop for trying to alienate them from their parishioners.[20]

Obviously, this was an inherently unequal contest, since the *Reichskirche* could threaten the churches with termination of their subsidies, and withhold their pastors' pensions. In London they were also capable of depriving Rieger of the income he derived from his ministry to the German sailors. Some parishes would be able to survive if they had a generous congregation, but most churches could not.

As the months went by, there was trouble from another quarter. The churches in Germany which made up the *Bekennenden Kirche* were themselves growing more timid and divided. They were finding it difficult to negotiate with the *Reichskirche* which until now had barely tolerated them. In the face of this mounting pressure from both the *Reichskirche* and the *NSDAP*, Bonhoeffer realized that his options and those of his fellow-pastors were gradually narrowing. He was also feeling overwhelmed by his responsibilities to his two parishes as well as his obligations to the ecumenical movement. Frustrated, he explored the possibility of finding a temporary replacement.[21] However, he refused to seek help from the *Auslandsorganisation* because he wanted nothing to do with Heckel. Pastor Schönberger offered to find someone, but Bonhoeffer knew that he would insist that the person was a Party member.

By the end of November 1934 it became known among the clergy of London that Bonhoeffer intended to return to Germany sometime in the New Year. Otto

Bene, in his capacity as *Landesgruppenleiter* of the *NSDAP* in Britain, was informed of this, and he in turn wrote to his superiors in Germany.[22]

> I am informed by the most trustworthy of people that Pastor Bonhoeffer, who is leaving Forest Hill to take up a chair in Germany at the beginning of next year, is to be replaced by a Pastor Hildebrand from Germany. This Pastor Hildebrand is supposedly of Jewish blood. I fervently request that next time, you send a Party Member to be pastor at Forest Hill.

Although we do not know the identity of this "most trustworthy" source, it was presumably Pastor Schönberger, who held the position of *Kulturwart* (director of cultural affairs) in the *Landesgruppe Gross Britannien*.

Once Bonhoeffer realized that he had perhaps done all that he could in London, he reluctantly decided to return to Germany and accept his next challenge: establishing a *Bekennenden Kirche* seminary. Accordingly, on 10 March 1935 he said formal farewells to his congregations, and although he returned four more times that year, he was no longer able to stand in the way of nazification as applied to the German churches. His biographer, Eberhard Bethge, confirmed this judgment: "It seems doubtful whether, without Bonhoeffer's strong backing, the congregation in Britain would have been able to overcome their misgivings in the face of Berlin's threats of financial and legal sanctions."[23]

Bonhoeffer's successor at Sydenham and at *St. Paulskirche* was, predictably, a Party member: Martin Böckheler from Hull. Both parish councils nominally had the ultimate authority to call a pastor, but they hesitated to call Franz Hildebrand, since he was an unknown quantity. Furthermore, they were uncertain whether Bonhoeffer would stay permanently in Germany or return to London, and therefore it was expedient to hire a known personality, especially since Bonhoeffer had recommended him. At first, Böckheler had a temporary appointment, but when it became apparent that Bonhoeffer would remain in Germany, he was fully installed and moved into 23 Manor Mount, SE23 at just 31 years of age.[24]

When Böckheler began his ministry, he was in a stronger position than most of the other German pastors in London because he was able to live solely on what he earned from his two parishes, whereas it was typical to receive only part of one's salary from parishioners, and the rest from the *Reichskirche* in Germany. Moreover, as a Party member, he recognized that he was able to take certain risks. "I became godfather to a child of a Jewish refugee couple, and my sister who lived with me and I looked after Dietrich Bonhoeffer's twin sister, Sabine Leibholz and family when they took refuge in London."[25] He also came to appreciate why most German churchgoers enjoyed such a remarkable degree of autonomy.[26]

> Most of them were naturalised [British subjects] because of their negative experiences during the First World War. For this reason the German congregations

in London were quite independent. Therefore the *NSDAP* could, in my opinion, not exert any pressure on the German congregations, at least not any direct pressure. The church committees were formed mostly from these old naturalised members; since any newcomer normally did not or could not stay for good in England.

On the other hand, he knew all too well that the *Landesgruppenleiter* kept any eye on all the German pastors, in particular Julius Rieger, who ministered to so many refugees.

In his letters Böckheler praised the support and comfort that he and the German pastors derived from their contacts with British clergy, youth groups, and other ecumenists. He told how a combined British and German choir had performed Bach's *St. Matthew Passion* in German at *St. Paulskirche* and *St. Marienkirche* in 1939 before the outbreak of war, and how proud he was to have sung the part of Christ.

Schönberger reached the height of his influence in London's Nazi community just at the time when the German pastors were struggling to find a way to negotiate with the *Bekennenden Kirche*. Ironically, his tenure as *Ortsgruppenleiter* in Dalston was short-lived, according to a Special Branch report of early 1935.[27]

> In pursuance of Herr Hitler's policy of excluding clergy as far as possible from the secular leadership of the Party, Pastor Schönberger has been replaced in the leadership of the Dalston *Ortsgruppe* by Herr Schmidt of Schmidt Brill and Co., bullion dealers, 63 Hatton Garden, EC1. Schönberger will act as Deputy and take charge of the cultural side of the *Ortsgruppe*.

Schönberger's influence was felt far beyond the Dalston *Ortsgruppe* and the several groups which made up the *Landesgruppe* because he was the Editor of the *Gemeinde-Bote*, a weekly journal distributed to all German churches throughout the United Kingdom. A comparison of the magazine published in 1932 and 1934, reveals that in 1932 the articles were overwhelmingly religious in tone and content, with only occasional mention of political news. By 1934, religious items are eclipsed by information about the activities of the *Auslandsorganisation*; celebrations in Germany of Hitler's birthday, and the crowd which greeted him on May Day; appearances by Göring and other Nazi leaders; a forthcoming Party rally at Nuremberg; holidays sponsored by the Nazi-controlled *Arbeitsfront* (including one to the Isle of Wight); and major diplomatic conferences involving the Führer or his chief lieutenants. Each issue had a section titled *Deutsche Chronik* that described current events in Germany. It was initially written by Pastor Rieger after he took several trips to Germany and was favorably impressed. Then suddenly, in July 1935, his name no longer appeared, perhaps as a result of his repeated and friendly exposure to Bonhoeffer. Several others continued the column for awhile, including "Stover" who focused on anti-

Semitic speeches by Goebbels and Streicher.[28] These must have been too strident for the editor, since the byline soon changed to "Pastor B", presumably Böckheler, and became more moderate.

As often as possible, the *Gemeinde-Bote* implied that the church and the state were partners with the *NSDAP*. On the occasion of President Hindenburg's death in August 1934, services were held at *St. Marienkirche*, Cleveland Street, with Pastor Wehrhan officiating; among the mourners were Ambassador Leopold von Hoesch and *Landesgruppenleiter* Otto Bene.[29] Schönberger made the point more explicitly in a *Festschrift* honoring the 70th birthday of Baron Bruno von Schröder, an outspoken anti-Nazi, whose family were benefactors of the German Hospital,[30] a connection he mentioned in an article published in *Wir in die Welt*, a semi-Nazi publication in 1935.[31] In both pieces he credited the churches, more than any other institution, with welding together the German people living in London by perpetuating a common religion, heritage, culture, and song. The Nazi Party, he said, had contributed significantly toward the unity of émigré Germans by allowing Party members and non-Party people to worship together. Everyone was encouraged to gather for church-sponsored memorial days, festivals and holy days, despite their differences of opinion and politics. This was an appealing portrait until it became known that parishes were struggling mightily to retain their autonomy against Nazi influence and domination.

Once Bonhoeffer left London, the parish most successful in withstanding Nazi pressure was the *Deutsche Lutherische St. Georgskirche* at 33 Little Alie Street, led by Julius Rieger. While Bonhoeffer was still active, both the *Deutsche Evangelische Gemeinde* in Sydenham and the *Reformierte St. Paulskirche*, Goulston Street, were preeminent in welcoming and helping to support newly-arrived refugees from Germany, but once he was gone, *St. Georgskirche* attracted the majority of them. In 1936 Bonhoeffer sent one of his seminary students to London to assist Rieger as Curate, and after Martin Niemöller's sudden arrest in 1937, Franz Hildebrand left Dahlem and became Rieger's assistant.

The year 1937 further demonstrated Rieger's determination to resist nazification. In October *St. Georgskirche* was due to celebrate its 175th anniversary, and various Lutheran dignitaries, including the head of the *Bekennenden Kirche*, Karl Koch, received invitations to join the festivities during which Rieger studiously ignored Bishop Heckel. This snub resulted in the withdrawal of funds promised to *St. Georgskirche* for the restoration of its organ, and not until June 1938 were the 2,000 Marks released.[32]

A typical response to the anniversary invitation came from a pastor abroad. He explained that he would very much like to attend, but Bishop Heckel would have to approve his coming, and the less he had to do with him the better. Without obtaining permission from the Church's Foreign Affairs Office, he dared not risk appearing.[33]

I must remain humble and be content that I can somehow help my weak parish survive, which is unfortunately not possible without the financial assistance of the Church Foreign Office. Please understand that my hands are not only tied but chained.

Throughout the 1930s the German churches in London were able to find various ways to resist Nazi ideology. They often declined to confer with representatives from the *Reichskirche*, and openly opposed the idea of establishing a *Deutsches Haus* in London. In 1937, when Ambassador von Ribbentrop tried to reorganize the German Hospital, Baron von Schröder, in his dual capacity as Chairman of the German Church Association and the Hospital's Board of Directors, refused to fire Jewish doctors, and arranged for Jewish patients to continue receiving kosher meals from the hospital's kitchen.[34] A year later, when Bishop Heckel relayed the latest Reich legislation forbidding mixed marriages, they ignored the injunctions.

Perhaps typical of the relations between the German churches in London and the Nazi authorities was an exchange which took place at the annual meeting of the *Reichskirche* in 1936. As usual, Baron von Schröder presided, and in the course of the discussion one of the pastors lamented the number of traitorous clergy within the *Bekennenden Kirche*. Someone in the audience replied, "I hope you will not take it amiss if we have for years, willingly or otherwise, moved to the side of the *Bekennenden Kirche* through the influence of Bonhoeffer, and more recently Kramm."[35] A third person commented that it had become ideologically too difficult to work with the *Bekennenden Kirche*. Without a doubt, the German pastors and their churches had a difficult time resisting nazification after Bonhoeffer left England. They clearly lacked his fervor and determination, yet they tried to stem the rising tide. Some, like Rieger, were able to preserve their independence, while at least one, Gustav Schönberger, succumbed to National Socialism. The others, along with their parishioners, held fast to the middle ground.

When war came, Schönberger returned to Germany, whereas Böckheler and Wehran remained in London. Both were interned in 1940 under Regulation 18-B, and were eventually shipped, with other internees, to Canada. Once Böckheler was interned, Rieger took charge of Bonhoeffer's former parishes, and was summarily dropped from the *NSDAP* membership files in 1941 because he failed to maintain contact with the Party.

Unlike other organizations, the German churches in London were not entirely overrun by the Nazis. On the contrary, to a greater or lesser extent, they served as places of refuge for the victims of Nazi tyranny – before, during, and after the war.

NOTES

1   Eberhard Bethge (ed.), *Dietrich Bonhoeffer: Gesammelte Schriften*, II (2d ed., Munich, 1965), 125–34; also Bethge, *Dietrich Bonhoeffer: Man of Vision Man of Courage* (New York, 1970), p. 250.

2   "Personalities in Germany," PRO, FO 371/18866, C244, f. 2.

3   29 November 1933, Bethge, *Gesammelte Schriften*, II, 147–48.

4   *Ibid.*, II, 158.

5   *Ibid.*, II, 159–60.

6   Gerhard Niemöller, *"Die Deutschen Evengelischen Gemeinden in London und der Kirchenkampf,"* *Evangelische Theologie*, III (1959), 135, Heckel's letter was dated 31 January 1934.

7   Wehrhan file, BDC.

8   Schönberger file, BDC.

9   Rieger file, BDC.

10  See their respective files, BDC.

11  Bethge, *Bonhoeffer: Man of Vision*, pp. 260–61.

12  Niemöller, *Evangelische Theologie*, pp. 135–36.

13  Heckel to Schröder, 8 May 1934; and Schröder to Heckel, 25 May 1934, *ibid.*, p. 139.

14  Henry Smith Leiper, "The Acts of the Apostle – Dietrich Bonhoeffer," in W. D. Zimmermann and R. G. Smith (eds.), *I knew Dietrich Bonhoeffer* (London, 1966), pp. 91–92.

15  Bethge, *Bonhoeffer: Man of Vision*, p. 318.

16  D. Bonhoeffer to J. Winterhager, May 1934, Bethge, *Gesammelte Schriften*, I, 179–80.

17  Bethge, *Bonhoeffer: Man of Vision*, p. 321.

18  Bethge, *Gesammelte Schriften*, I, 188–89.

19  Bethge, *Bonhoeffer: Man of Vision*, p. 322.

20  German Pastors to Reichskirche Foreign Affairs Office, 21 January 1935, in Bethge, *Gessammelte Schriften*, I, 194.

21  Bonhoeffer to Winterhagen, mid-May 1934, Bethge, *Gesammelte Schriften*, I, 179–80.

22  Bene to AA, 30 November 1934, NA microcopy T-580, roll 381, file 49.

23  Bethge, *Bonhoeffer: Man of Vision*, p. 328.

24  Böckheler file, BDC.

25  Martin Böckheler to J. J. Barnes, 9 September 1986 and 7 January 1987.

26  *Ibid.*

27  Report by Hubert Morse, 4 March 1935, PRO, FO 371/19968, C1957, f. 178.

28  Gemeinde-Bote, 18 August 1935, p. 5; and 15 August 1935, pp. 3–4. The Dietrich Bonhoeffer Church of Sydenham has a nearly complete run of this weekly publication from 1932–38, except for the year 1933.

29  *Ibid.*, 19 August 1934, pp. 4–5.

30  G. Schönberger (ed.), *Siebzigsten Geburtstag in Dankbarkeit* (London, 1937), pp. 30–35.

31  G. Schönberger, *"Die Deutsche Kolonie in London,"* *Wir in die Welt*; published by the *Verband Deutscher Vereine im Ausland* (Berlin, 1935), p. 93.

32  Niemöller, *Evangelische Theologie*, p. 141.

33  *Ibid.*, pp. 141–42.

34  P. Schwarz, *This Man Ribbentrop* (New York, 1943), p. 217.

35  Niemöller, *Evangelische Theologie*, p. 141. Dr. H. W. Kramm lived in Oxford during the latter 1930s and early 1940s. In 1943 he became pastor to the bombed-out congregation of the *Deutsche Evangelische St. Marienkirche*, 46 Cleveland Street, W1.

# 10 NAZI INFILTRATION OF BUSINESS AND LABOR

During the 1930s the Nazis had no difficulty controlling the two organizations in London concerned with business and employees: the German Chamber of Commerce (*Deutsche Handelskammer*) and the German Labour Front (*Deutsche Arbeitsfront*). Officially, the Chamber was not under direct Nazi administration, since it was made up of both German and British firms; rather, National Socialist influence came through those who presided over the Chamber, most of whom were members of the *NSDAP*. As for the *Deutsche Arbeitsfront*, known more commonly as the *DAF*, it was the creature of the Nazi regime, both in its inception and function.

Until the end of 1934, London had no German Chamber of Commerce. Previous to this time, individual Germans lived independently in the city as representatives of some aspect of Germany's overseas trade, such as the Leipzig Fair, but on 12 December, a group of German businessmen met at the Victoria Hotel, Northumberland Avenue, to found a *Deutsche Handelskammer*.[1] They formed a steering committee and selected Karl Markau as its head. Representatives from German industry in Berlin, Hamburg, and Aachen attended the meeting to lend their encouragement and support, and there were consultations with the German Embassy staff in London as well as with the *Auslandsorganisation* in Hamburg where the brother of Rudolf Hess, Alfred, was the advisor to Nazi groups abroad concerning foreign trade. At this meeting it was stated that "membership will be open to Jews," a motion seconded by no less a stalwart Nazi than Otto Karlowa, the Local Group Leader (*Ortsgruppenleiter*) for Central London.[2] This concession to Jewish businesses in Britain was undoubtedly intended to forestall local protests or boycotts by British firms.

In March 1935 the Articles of Incorporation for the German Chamber of Commerce were submitted to the Board of Trade for its scrutiny and approval by the Solicitor and President of the *Deutsche Verein* in London, Eduard

Cruesemann. The Board of Trade then consulted the Foreign Office, which had no objections, so the project was allowed to proceed.[3] Premises were secured at Shell Mex House, Strand, WC2, and the membership grew steadily, reaching about 700 in 1938, 400 of whom were German companies, and the rest, British.[4]

The Chamber hosted annual dinners at the Savoy Hotel. The guest lists included prominent diplomats and businessmen as well as leading Nazis such as von Ribbentrop's personal press attaché, Theodor Böttiger, and the head of the German Commercial School in Ealing, Kurt Frauendorf.[5] Scheduled around the holidays were speeches by British and German leaders in commerce and government. In January 1939, *Ministerialdirektor* Emil Wiehl, chief of commercial policy for the German Foreign Ministry, and R. S. Hudson, Parliamentary Secretary for the Department of Overseas Trade, both spoke about ways to increase world-wide trade.[6]

The initiative for holding meetings did not always come from the Germans. On 20 February 1936 a representative group of London and Birmingham merchants hosted a lunch in honor of the Chamber and its President, Karl Markau, who spoke about the positive role being played by trade fairs in promoting international commerce.[7] Here and elsewhere Markau emphasized the business aspects of the German Chamber. At a meeting in the spring of 1938, he went out of his way to make this clear. "I think it fitting to observe that this Chamber, like all others established in Britain, is a completely free and voluntary union of those who are involved in trade between our two countries."[8] This tactic was so effective that even MI5 excluded the Chamber of Commerce from its list of proscribed Nazi organizations, and Karl Markau was not among those expelled by the British as war approached in 1939.

Not unexpectedly, Markau did his best to promote Germany's image in his speeches and occasional letters to the press. In response to allegations that the German motor industry was dumping cars on the British market at prices below cost, he sent a letter to *The Times* denying this, and then proceeded to dispute another accusation, that German factories were clandestinely being converted to war production.[9]

> May I respectfully point out that in my opinion preaching such doctrines is nothing but preaching trade war, and if this spreads to all countries I do not see how we can ever come to a peaceful settlement in Europe. For instance, German importers of wool cloth from Bradford, could, with the same right, say that as the Bradford mills manufacture cloth for the British Army and Navy, Germany cannot buy any longer from Bradford, as in doing so she would assist the British War Department.

In November 1936 the first issue of a projected monthly periodical appeared: the *Journal of the German Chamber of Commerce for the United Kingdom*. The writing in its columns was not overtly National Socialist, and in fact, in its April 1937 issue there was a proposal that language training be encouraged in each other's country. However, it ceased publication with Volume IV, no. 8, in August 1939.

Assuming the Presidency of the Chamber when he was 60 years old, Karl Markau was highly respected in the London *NSDAP*. A Berliner by birth and education, he did advanced work in physics at the University of Berlin before the First World War. During that war he served on the staff of Field Marshall Paul von Hindenburg, and in the 1930s came to England as the technical director of Supra-Electro Motors Ltd. of London.[10]

While living in East Croydon he joined the Nazi Party, receiving his membership on 1 May 1933. Early in 1935, at the time he was assembling plans for the new Chamber of Commerce, he was appointed Deputy *Landesgruppenleiter*, which meant that he was second in command to its leader, Otto Bene. Within the *Landesgruppe Gross Britannien* he was the appointed adviser on economic questions, thus clearly tying the fledgling Chamber of Commerce to the *Landesgruppe*. Nevertheless, it can be said that Markau was more circumspect than most in combining his Nazi activities with his Chamber duties.

Between 1935 and 1939 three men served as Secretary of the Chamber: Reinhold Lassen, Thomas Knatz, and Enno Becker. Born in 1911 in Hamburg, Lassen completed his secondary education and then worked for firms in Hamburg and Berlin. He came to London in January 1934, intending to apprentice with a shipping firm for one year and become more proficient in English. He ended by staying five years, assisting Markau both at the Chamber of Commerce and in the *Landesgruppe*. His membership in the Nazi Party was approved shortly after he reached London, thus making it feasible for Markau to select him as the first Secretary of the Chamber.[11]

Little is known of the next Secretary, Thomas Knatz, except that he was born in 1906 in Berlin, applied for membership in the *NSDAP* in June 1936, was admitted to the Party that October, and practiced law.[12]

More is available, however, concerning the third Secretary, Dr. Enno Johann Becker. He was born in 1897, a native of Duesseldorf, and a World War I veteran. His wife was English, which probably accounts for why he settled in Birmingham in 1931. There he started his own ball bearing factory, which he managed personally for seven years. In 1934 he joined the Nazi Party, and soon thereafter organized an *Ortsgruppe* in the Birmingham area. By 1937 he was put in charge of economic affairs for the *Landesgruppe* in London until August 1938 when he and his wife left England for Germany to begin a new life in the Third Reich.[13]

If the German Chamber of Commerce was the acceptable face of Nazism to the British, the German Labour Front (*Deutsche Arbeitsfront*) was at the other end of the respectability spectrum. Referred to as the *DAF*, it was Hitler's answer to the trade union movement in Germany which he abolished upon taking power in 1933. Under its leader, Robert Ley, it sponsored a number of auxiliary operations, including welfare, package holiday tours, youth training schemes, and job information. Foreign observers looked suspiciously at the organization, as the following official Canadian report indicates.[14]

> The *Deutsche Arbeitsfront* (German Labour Front) aims at registering all Germans abroad according to their various trades and occupations. It is subordinate to the Party Organisation, and under a recent ruling which came into force in March, 1937, officials of the Deutsche Arbeitsfront must be members of the Party. . . . The organisation is part of the whole scheme for consolidating Germans abroad, and its records provide a very useful source of information for the Party authorities.

This same report listed the regulations governing membership in the *DAF*.

TASKS:

I. The German Labour Front is the organization of working Germans of the brain and the fist.

The aim of the German Labour Front is the formation of a real people's service-community of all Germans. It will take care that everyone may take his place in the economic life of the nation, spiritually and physically, that will qualify him for the greatest achievements and thereby enable him to render the greatest usefulness to the *Volksgemeinschaft*.

The Foreign Organization of the German Labour Front has received through the Reichsleader of the German Labour Front, Pg. Dr. Ley, the commission to carry out the task of the German Labour Front according to its meaning, for the citizens of the German State (Reich) who live in foreign countries.

These tasks encompass the following fields of activities:

(a) Taking care socially of all members;
(b) Creation and administration of benevolent institutions for the members, for the purpose of maintaining the livelihood of the German Labour Front members within a frame of the means available, or to give capable fellow countrymen possibilities for advancement.
(c) Moulding of spare time habits and fostering of community spirit in the meaning of National Socialist Society "Strength through Joy," whose sponsor is the German Labour Front.
(d) Vocational and Post-school Education.
(e) Instructing all foreign-country members about the social, political, economical, and cultural developments within the German State.

CONDITIONS FOR ADMISSION:

(1) Membership can be obtained by all working citizens of Germany who are not in a state of permanent disability at the time of making application, provided

they fulfill the conditions regarding the obtaining of Reich citizenship as provided for in the law of 15.9.1935 and its ordinances for execution.

(2) Membership and adherence to the German Labour Front includes automatically membership in the N.S. "Strength through Joy." Membership in the German Labour Front is obtained through tendering a prescribed declaration of intention to join, and through payment of admission fee in the amount of dues "class A I," and payment of the first monthly dues. Admission is only valid following ratification by the District Administration of the Foreign Organization of the German Labour Front.

(3) With the declaration of intention to join the applicant for admission acknowledges for himself the binding character of these directions.

(4) Every member admitted to the GLF receives a membership card or membership book which remains the property of the GLF. and, on request, is to be returned to the competent Sub/District Administration against receipt.

(5) Membership and adherence to the GLF is not transferable.

Just how much pressure there was on Germans working abroad to join the *Deutsche Arbeitsfront* was a matter of dispute. The Germans claimed there was never any coercion involved, but others, like Member of Parliament Geoffrey Mander, were convinced otherwise. In December 1938 he asked in the House of Commons: "Is the Home Secretary aware that many of these German nationals feel afraid not to belong to this organisation because of what might happen to their relatives in Germany?"[15] In reply, Sir Samuel Hoare asserted, "In any case brought to my attention, in which intimidation has been proved, appropriate action will at once be taken." The year before, John Parker, Labour member from Romsford, read aloud a Labour Front schedule of meetings for the month of October 1937.[16] Parker took particular exception to the requirements spelled out at the end of the document where members were told to be present at all meetings "in their own interests", and the veiled threat implied by the phrase, "Apologies for absence will only be accepted if sent in advance in writing." He summarized his objections succinctly.

> It seems to me that if there is a foreign political party organising itself in this country in that way, the Government of this country ought to be aware of the fact and ought to do something to prevent it. It does not seem at all desirable to have foreign political parties organising themselves with this degree of detail and compulsion in this country.

The extent to which Germans were forced to join the *Deutsche Arbeitsfront* is not an easy question to answer. Motives for enrolling were as complex and varied as they were for joining the Nazi Party itself. Large numbers clearly applied to one or the other out of a sense of conviction, while others did so purely from expediency. Since membership in the *NSDAP* was restricted from time to time, some felt that joining the *DAF* might eventually facilitate entry into the Party itself. As the 1930s went on, certain categories of jobs required membership in the *DAF* as well as the Party, while in other cases it was more a question of job opportunity and promotion. Thus, it is clear that affiliation with the *DAF* did not presuppose Nazi Party membership, nor did all Party members necessarily join the *DAF*.

Consequently, the British authorities were uncertain as to the overall strength of the *Deutsche Arbeitsfront* in Britain. Estimates ranged from about 350–600, but the latter figure may have been a combined *DAF* and *NSDAP* count.[17] It was acknowledged that there was a significant overlap, so that it is impossible to be precise, especially since *DAF* records for Britain have not survived the way that Nazi Party files have.[18]

As mentioned above, those who belonged to the *Deutsche Arbeitsfront* were expected to attend monthly meetings. These were quite distinct from the regular gatherings of the *Ortsgruppe*, which were limited strictly to Nazi Party members. The *DAF*'s monthly sessions were scheduled according to occupation or type of employment, and a glance at the calendar for October 1937 shows their range and diversity.[19]

> 3 OCTOBER: Women employees to meet at 4:00 P.M. in the German Commercial School, 46 Eaton Rise, London, W5.
>
> 8 OCTOBER: Sales people to meet at 8:00 P.M. in the Tatler Tea Room, Brighton. This was the so-called Sussex branch or "cell".
>
> 9 OCTOBER: Technicians to meet at 8:00 P.M. in the German Commercial School.
>
> 17 OCTOBER: Women employees to meet at 4:00 P.M. in the German Commercial School.
>
> 18 OCTOBER: Surrey branch to meet at 4:00 P.M. in the Benhill Street Adult School, Sutton.
>
> 26 OCTOBER: Catering workers to meet at 8:30 P.M. in the Landesgruppe headquarters, 5 Cleveland Terrace, London, W2.
>
> 27 OCTOBER: Tradesmen to meet at 8:00 P.M. in the Westgate House, London, WCI.

Members of the *Deutsche Arbeitsfront* were given a respite from monthly meetings during August and September. The *DAF* office also closed from mid-August to mid-September during the summer holidays.

In London, the head of the *DAF* was Heinz Juettner, who doubled as Secretary of the German Commercial School (*Deutsche Handelsschule*), 46 Eaton Rise, W5. As long as Juettner was in London, this location served as the main office for the *DAF*, but after his departure, the office moved to 28 Cleveland Terrace, W2. Founded in 1929, the *Handelsschule* also served as a meeting place for the *Ortsgruppe* in Ealing (West London). During the day, however, the school provided courses in trade and industrial arts, language training, and other business-related subjects.[20]

Juettner was only 24 years old when he arrived in London in February 1936 to take charge of the *DAF* office. He joined the Nazi Party in May 1930, at about as young an age as he could, and was assigned his first job in Paris. During the two years he was in London before returning to Paris, he not only combined his Commercial School and *DAF* jobs, but also acted as Secretary to the *Ortsgruppe* in Ealing.[21]

The leader of the Ealing *Ortsgruppe* was Kurt Frauendorf, who worked closely with Juettner in behalf of the *Deutsche Arbeitsfront*. Older by ten years, Frauendorf had been in London since 1932, representing the German Commercial Information Service. In the mid-1930s his office was at 34 and 39 Maddox Street, W1, and he combined being *Ortsgruppenleiter* for Ealing with serving on the staff of the *Landesgruppenleiter*, Otto Bene, as the *DAF* representative for all of the United Kingdom. Under Bene's successor, Otto Karlowa, he continued performing these two Party functions.[22]

There were other Germans affiliated with the *DAF* during the 1930s. Most were Party Members, and further details about them can be found in the Appendix. These were:[23] Bruno Anton, Kurt Blessing, Max Ebel, Herbert Engert, Kurt von Heising, Eduard Jäger, Werner Kuhlmann, Bruno Sauk, Ludwig Steinmetz, and Johanna Wolf. Anton, for example, headed the catering sub-group within the *DAF*, while Blessing was responsible for those involved in technical occupations. Ebel was the *DAF* representative within the Dalston *Ortsgruppe*, succeeding Sauk in that post. Within the Ealing *Ortsgruppe*, Engert was responsible for National Socialist welfare and the Winter Relief Fund, two programs sponsored by the *Deutsche Arbeitsfront*. Captain Jäger served both the *DAF* and the *Landesgruppe* as "harbor leader", superintending the German seamen in British ports. Steinmetz was in charge of sales for the *DAF*, while Wolf was head of the women's section of the Ealing *Ortsgruppe*, and was involved with organizing the domestic servants who joined the *DAF*.

Domestic servants formed a large and mostly untapped reservoir of potential *DAF* membership, as shown by the 13,576 work permits granted to foreign women and girls between 1 April 1937 and 31 March 1938: 7,007 were issued to Austrians, 2,210 to Swiss, and 1,267 to Germans.[24] Following the *Anschluss* of 1938, Austrians automatically came under German law and were eligible for membership in the *Deutsche Arbeitsfront*, but the problem of recruiting them lay in their short tours abroad, about one year on average.

Typical of British opinion concerning foreign domestics was the question posed in the House of Commons by Sir G. Fox addressed to the Home Secretary, Sir Samuel Hoare. "Does the Right Honourable Gentleman think that it is in the national interest that German servants employed in this country should be compelled to go to this organisation and to give information of what they have heard in the houses where they are employed?" To which Hoare replied: "I should certainly disapprove of any action of that kind."[25]

Snooping and reporting undoubtedly took place, but probably on a limited scale, since most servants were not members of the *DAF*, let alone the Nazi Party. To be sure, it was possible to instill in Germans, and later in Austrians, the notion that it was their patriotic duty to assist their government in whatever ways were appropriate. Perhaps the best summary of this responsibility appeared in a Foreign Office report for early 1939: "Evidence has been produced that members of the German Labour Front are expected to keep their eyes open with a view to furnishing the German authorities with any information of an economic or military character which they may chance to obtain."[26]

Among those in Britain who paid attention to the fate of foreign domestics, questions arose about the largest of the hiring organizations, the Anglo-German (Employment) Agency, 53–54 Haymarket, SWI, which was run by Mrs. E. A. L. R. Thomson, a British subject of German descent. This agency had nothing to do with the *Deutsche Arbeitsfront*, but rather dealt directly with prospective employers in Britain and qualified servants from Germany and Austria. On average, an employer would have to pay £5 to cover the servant's travel expenses to Britain, plus an additional amount to the agency, and a finding fee. In 1938 so many complaints reached the London County Council that it authorized an inquiry through its Public Control Department. In its report to the Home Office, the Control Department noted that Mrs. Thomson had been licensed by the County Council "continuously since 8 January 1931, and during that time a steady flow of complaints as to the manner in which it has been conducted has been received by the Council."[27] A common objection was that the Agency promised to provide servants who possessed certain skills, but who were, in fact, found wanting. In her defense, Mrs. Thomson said she had to trust the references required of foreign applicants, even though they were impossible to verify.

Complaints of a more serious kind surfaced in 1938. The Agency was portrayed as anti-Semitic in the columns of the *Jewish Chronicle*, where it was labeled a centre of German espionage.[28]

As a result, MI5 investigated, and did not like what it found. Mrs. Thomson turned out to be the wife of Alexander Raven Thomson, one of Sir Oswald Mosley's chief lieutenants in the British Union of Fascists.[29]

> A complaint was received at the Home Office in April, 1938, from Mr. Leonard Goldhill, a British Jew, that the Anglo-German Agency, 53 Haymarket, had refused to supply his wife with a domestic servant, "because acting under orders from the German Government, German-Austrian girls under the age of 45 are not allowed to work for non-Aryan persons."

Responding to this complaint, Mrs. Thomson blamed a staff member of the Agency who inadvertently misinformed the Goldhills, because there was no prohibition against placing servants with Jewish families. When pressed, she admitted that she felt it her duty to mention to German and Austrian girls that

**123**

if they worked for Jews, they might incur the displeasure of their government for ignoring the Nuremberg Laws.

The MI5 report also pointed out that the Thomsons were known to have had contact with the German *Landesgruppenleiter*, Otto Karlowa. Here again, there is no reason to think that the Anglo-German Agency was in any sense taking orders from the Nazis or the *Deutsche Arbeitsfront*, but it was their predisposition as pro-Fascists to further the policies of the Third Reich.

When in 1939 the British authorities began to expel a growing number of Nazis, those connected with the *Deutsche Arbeitsfront* figured high on their list. Johanna Wolf, Eduard Jäger, Kurt Frauendorf and Gunther Schallies were among the first to be asked to leave.

Anna Johanna Ottilie Wolf came to the attention of the British authorities during the summer of 1938 in a case involving the intimidation of one German woman by others. Wolf was then 42 years old, and had been a member of the Nazi Party since December 1937. Her stay in London predated this by some time, however; she first entered Britain as a domestic servant in April 1934. At the time of the inquiry into her *DAF* and Ealing *Ortsgruppe* activities, she was living at and working for the household of Mrs. Challis, 1 Linden Gardens, W2.[30]

As the story was reconstructed by Special Branch, Johanna Wolf sent one of her *DAF* subordinates, a cook named Hildegarde Wiesner, to have words with another German domestic servant, Sigrid Sander, who had worked a long time for Mrs. Rosina Fry. Since she had proved very satisfactory, Sigrid had been urged by her employer to consider applying for British naturalization. Wiesner came uninvited for a visit one evening late in May 1938 to warn Sigrid not to do this, and hinted broadly of the consequences which might befall her family in Germany if she went ahead. Furthermore, Wiesner informed her that it had been reported to the *Ortsgruppe* that she had voiced anti-Nazi remarks. The 27-year-old Sander was no doubt intimidated by the nearly 40–year-old Wiesner, but there was something more. In 1935, her brother, an outspoken Socialist, had been sentenced to ten years imprisonment at Siegburg and was still serving time, making him far more vulnerable to Nazi retribution than her parents.[31]

When Special Branch interviewed Sander, she was so frightened that she would not commit anything in writing by way of a statement against Wiesner or Wolf, but was only willing to tell her story verbally. As for Wiesner, Special Branch noted: "She has not come under notice of MI5 or this department as having engaged in political activity on behalf on the Nazi Party. Enquiries have been made of previous employers, and it has been confirmed that she is an ardent Nazi sympathizer."[32] As for Wiesner's superior, Wolf, who was in charge of all domestic servants for the *DAF* in Britain, nothing was done at the time, but in the spring of 1939, when the British authorities decided to expel three leaders of the London Nazi community, Wolf was one of them.[33]

Although Capt. Adolf Eduard Julius Jäger had been in London since 1929, he didn't join the Party until 1938. By contrast, Schallies was an *Alter Kämpfer*, having joined in 1931, well before the Nazis came to power.[34] It is not entirely clear, but Schallies was probably Heinz Juettner's successor, and therefore high on the Home Office list for deportation.[35]

In all four instances of expulsion – Wolf, Frauendorf, Jäger and Schallies – it is worth bearing in mind that their undesirability stemmed not from overt espionage in a military or professional sense, but from the inappropriate pressure they exerted on fellow Germans in the United Kingdom. Here, as elsewhere, the perpetrators of harassment were told to leave the country without any further explanation.

NOTES

1 *Mitteilungsblatt der Auslandsorganisation*, No. 18 (mid-January 1935), p. 3.

2 *The Times*, 13 December 1935, p. 18.

3 See Cruesemann to Board of Trade, 6 March 1935, PRO, FO 371/18879, C2713, ff. 113–32.

4 *Deutsche Zeitung in Gross Britannien*, 23 April 1938, p. 6.

5 *Journal of the German Chamber of Commerce for the United Kingdom*, II (January 1937), I.

6 The dinner of 23 January 1939 was covered in *The Times*, 24 January 1939, p. 7. For background, see Markau to Wiehl, 17 November 1938, *Documents and Materials Relating to the Eve of the Second World War*, Vol. II, Dirksen papers, 1938–39 (New York, 1948; reissued in Salisbury, N.C., 1978), pp. 54–56.

7 *The Times*, 21 February 1936, p. 11.

8 *Deutsche Zeitung*, 23 April 1938, p. 6.

9 *The Times*, 18 June 1938, p. 8.

10 See H. G. Kleinmann and S. Taylor (eds.), *Who's Who in Germany* (Munich, 1956), p. 759. There is also some material on Markau in the Berlin Document Center.

11 Lassen file, BDC, and *Deutsche Zeitung*, 24 December 1938, p. 3.

12 Knatz file, BDC.

13 *Deutsche Zeitung*, 6 August 1938, p. 6; and BDC.

14 "Report on Nazis in Canada," August 1938, FO 371/21652, C79035, ff. 48–51.

15 *Parliamentary Debates*, Commons, CCCXLII (22 December 1938), 3080–81.

16 *Ibid.*, CCCXXX (21 December 1937), 1862–64.

17 MI5 report of 8 October 1937, FO 371/20741, C7183, f. 272.

18 The BDC has more than ten million *NSDAP* membership files where we were able to find most of the Nazis who resided in Britain.

19 *Parliamentary Debates*, Commons, CCCXXX (21 December 1937), 1862–64. For schedules covering May and June 1938, see *Deutsche Zeitung*, 21 May, p. 4, and 25 June, p. 8.

20 A brief history of the *Deutsche Handelsschule* can be found in *Deutsche Zeitung*, I April 1939, p. 3.

21 Juettner file, BDC, and FO 371/21649, C332, ff. 114–22.

22 Frauendorf file, BDC. For his *Ortsgruppe* and *Landesgruppe* duties, see FO 371/19942, C5497, ff. 166–73; and FO 371/21652, C7841, f. 28.

23 *Ibid.*, C5497, f. 172; FO 371/20741, C7183, f.272.

24  These figures, compiled by the Home Office, were given to Parliament and cited in the *Deutsche Zeitung*, 21 May 1938, p. 7.

25  *Parliamentary Debates*, Commons, CCCXLII (22 Dec. 1938), 381.

26  LCC to HO, February 1939 in FO 371/23035, C2695, f. 291v.

27  Public Control Department Report, 30 March 1938, FO 370/549, L2752, ff. 207–8.

28  *Jewish Chronicle*, 6 May 1938, p. 44.

29  MI5 Report, October 1938 in FO 371/21652, C12607, f. 125.

30  Wolf file, BDC; and FO 371/21652, C12607, f. 159.

31  Sander case, *ibid.*, ff. 153–57.

32  *Ibid.*

33  E. L. Woodward and R. Butler (eds.), *Documents on British Foreign Policy, 1919–1939*, 3d series, Vol. V (London, 1952), p. 245; and Halifax to G. Ogilvie-Forbes, 3 April 1939, FO 371/23035, C4820, ff. 395–98.

34  Halifax to E. Kordt, 26 April 1939, FO 371/23036, C6054, ff. 93–95.

35  Jager file and Schallies file, BDC.

# II  MOSLEY'S BRITISH UNION OF FASCISTS

Among the many Fascist and proto-Fascist organizations which sprung up in Britain during the 1920s and 1930s, none was as prominent or important as the British Union of Fascists, organized by Sir Oswald Mosley. During his lifetime, the question on everyone's mind was whether he was collaborating with the Nazis. All too often, the affinity between the BUF and the Nazi regime seemed more than coincidental, as MI5 described in a memorandum to the Home Office in the summer of 1934.[1]

> Superficially, at any rate, the British Union of Fascists follow Nazi methods very closely. There is the same massing of banners, the same spot-light on the "Leader", the same defence force, the same facile promises of relief from economic stress, the same kind of excessive simplicity of thought wholly at variance with the complexities of life and the infinite variety of scientific facts. There can be no doubt, logically, they lead up to the same conclusion: to the capture of power at a general election, followed by the suppression of all opinion opposed to the policy of the Fascist government.

Begun in October 1932, the British Union of Fascists consciously modeled itself on the Italian fascists by wearing black shirts, adopting the fasces emblem (bundle of rods and axe), and using the raised arm to salute. Gradually, however, the symbolism became more Nazi in character: the BUF Headquarters on the Kings Road in Chelsea took the name Black House, an obvious allusion to the Brown House in Munich; the uniform was modified to more nearly resemble the one worn by the *SS*, and the fasces gave way to the flash in a circle. During the summer of 1936 the official name expanded to the British Union of Fascists and National Socialists. Even its marching song borrowed the same tune as the *Horst Wessel Lied*. In an interview granted by Mosley to Werner Crome, the London correspondent for the *Berliner Lokal-Anzeiger*, which appeared in the issue of 22 November 1936, the similarities were made even more explicit: the BUF was organized into divisions. The first was analogous to the Nazi *SS*; the second resembled the *SA*, while the third included the public at large.[2]

It is little wonder that when war hysteria gripped England in May 1940 after the Nazi invasion of France and the Low Countries, Mosley and other British Fascists were arrested and imprisoned under Section 18-B of the wartime regulations. One of the fears harbored by the British authorities was that Mosley, like Quisling in Norway, would collaborate with the enemy should the Nazis invade England. Hence his detention was pre-emptive. What concerns us here, however, is his past record, covering the years prior to the outbreak of war. Mosley's authorized biographer, Robert Skidelsky, had this to say about the widespread perception that there was a connection between the BUF and the Nazis.[3]

> The [British] Government never produced the slightest shred of evidence of any such foreign control in the case of the British Union; and all the ransacking of enemy archives since the war has failed to come up with any such evidence. Fascist parties all over the world operated as independent organizations. There was no central organization controlled by Berlin or anywhere else. . . . Mosley was undoubtedly sympathetic to the aims of German, Italian, and even Japanese foreign policy, but only insofar as they did not conflict with the maintenance of the integrity of Britain and its Empire. Rightly or wrongly, Mosley decided that there was nothing in Hitler's published aims that conflicted with Britain's interests.

Perhaps the more significant concern should focus on the ways he cooperated with the Nazis, trying to identify his aims with theirs, and seeking their assistance to further his own agenda. For many reasons, the year 1934 was crucial for the BUF. Its membership peaked that year, with an estimated 10,000 active members and 20,000–30,000 passive ones.[4] In January, Lord Rothermere dedicated his considerable personal financial resources as well as the editorial endorsement of his newspapers, the *Daily Mail*, the *Evening News*, and the *Sunday Dispatch* to Mosley and the BUF.

Not until the middle of 1934 did MI5 begin to report bi-monthly to the Home Office on Fascist organizations, focusing particularly on the BUF. Occasions such as a monster rally in Olympia Hall on 7 June for which 15,000 tickets were sold piqued their concern. Before this, no political gathering had been so large, and Mosley's stewards literally knocked heads together and forcibly ejected hecklers in typical Stormtrooper fashion. Even some of Mosley's conservative supporters were dismayed by the brutality shown that night, and Lord Rothermere quickly distanced himself from the organization.

Also during 1934 the British Union of Fascists defined and clarified its foreign policy, as noted in a memorandum by Special Branch that stated that the purpose of the BUF's Foreign Relations and Overseas Department was to maintain contact with Fascist organizations abroad.[5] The Department head was

128

George A. Pfister, M.A., Ph.D., D.Litt., who was reputed to be an Australian with Swiss parents. He lived at 118 Sutherland Avenue, W9, and maintained a business, the Reliance Translations Bureau, at 177–78 Fleet Street, EC4. Reputedly, one of his advanced degrees was from Heidelberg University, and he frequently traveled to the Continent.[6]

> Instructions have recently been issued to the effect that if any member of the BUF wishes to communicate with the German National Socialist Party he must do so through that Department. At the same time members were informed that they were not to apply for membership of any foreign political movement; and that it was the wish of the German National Socialist Party that no members should be admitted to the Union even as associate members.

Pfister maintained contact with Fascist organizations on the Continent in various ways.[7]

> One Richard von Stradiot has acted as liaison between the Nazi bureau for Austrian affairs at Munich and the British Union of Fascists. In the course of discussion he has advised Dr. Pfister and his colleagues of their mistake in having made contact with Prince Starhemberg and the Dollfuss brand of Austrian Fascists.

In July 1934 Pfister tried to act as an intermediary between Mosley and Hitler.[8]

> During the past ten days [Pfister] visited the German Nazi Party offices in London on several occasions to negotiate for a meeting through Herr Bene of Sir Oswald Mosely and Herr Hitler in Germany. Bene has definitely refused to arrange the matter and moreover has informed Dr. E. W. Bohle, leader of the foreign department of the Nazi Party in Hamburg, of his decision; and further, that Mosley is a person of little importance. He also expressed the view that no good would acrue to the Party and its aims as the result of such a meeting. Pfister intimated that he would attempt to bring about the meeting through other channels, but it is unlikely, in view of Bene's attitude, that he will succeed.

The "other channels" depended on Pfister's acquaintance with the editor of *Der Stürmer*, Julius Streicher, whose son Lothar was to come to London in the summer, and upon his return was supposed to convince his father to pave the way for a Mosley–Hitler meeting.

> The British Union of Fascists is making somewhat crude attempts to establish sympathetic relations with Fascist movements all over the world. It thus becomes part of a movement having a certain international significance. The Fascist in every country desires to see Fascism established everywhere. In furtherance of this conception, Dr. Pfister has supplied material for anti-Jewish propaganda regarding events in England to the Nazis, who have made it clear

that they consider it desirable that the British Union of Fascists should be anti-Semitic.

By the end of August the London *Ortsgruppe* and its leader, Otto Bene, were distancing themselves more than ever from the British Union of Fascists. Bene not only declined a BUF request that his members be permitted to attend a gathering of Nazis at Westbourne Terrace, but also forbid them to attend a forthcoming Fascist rally in Hyde Park. As Inspector Hubert Morse put it, "Herr Bene is definitely against any cooperation with Sir Oswald Mosley, whom he steadfastly regards as a political adventurer worthy of no serious consideration. His reports to the Foreign Department in Hamburg on this point have been consistently in this sense."[9] Not for the first time, the British authorities were opening and reading letters to and from the *Ortsgruppe*.

Bene's attitude and actions convinced Mosley that he had better set his Black House in order, and curb Pfister's activities. The BUF's Foreign Relations Department "closed down in consequence of alleged intrigues with Austrian Nazis," and Pfister was transferred to the Research Department.[10] In addition, "The personality of W. Joyce has proved to be a storm centre at National Headquarters. He is responsible for the recent eclipse of G. A. Pfister. . . ."[11] With Pfister sidelined, the BUF made fewer overtures to Nazi organization, both domestic and foreign.[12]

> The maintenance of relations with foreign Fascist movements is conducted with much greater secrecy than hitherto at National Headquarters. Some of Mosley's intimates are somewhat apprehensive regarding the delicacy involved in having relations simultaneously with the French Fascists and the German Nazis.

For their part, the Nazis increased the distance between themselves and the British Union of Fascists. When two leaders of the BUF, Major General J. F. C. Fuller and W. E. D. Allen, visited Germany in early 1935, they were met with a distinctly cold reception. Shortly thereafter, Pfister learned that a confidential circular forbidding communication with BUF representatives had been distributed to government offices. A succession of blunders by the BUF also annoyed Berlin.[13]

> The secret circular is said to state that Mosley had not sent congratulations concerning the return of the Saar to Germany; that a Nazi official who had visited Mosley reported unfavourably on his reception and the BUF generally; and that the visit of Fuller and Allen was unwelcome to the German Cabinet. It is also stated that the Nazi officials are antagonistic toward the BUF because Lady Mosley had virtually criticised Hitler when interviewed by a French journalist.

When Mosley learned that Pfister had complained to a German about shabby treatment of the BUF, he suspended him for six weeks without pay, "as he disobeyed . . . specific instructions that he was to cease communicating with Nazi officials."[14]

Somewhat surprising is the following comment made by MI5 about Pfister:[15]

> We know that a certain George Arnold Pfister was an agent for the Nazi Party on the staff at the National Headquarters of the British Union of Fascists until he was removed by Sir Oswald Mosley in March 1935, in consequence of something in the nature of his relations with the Nazi Party being discovered.

Unfortunately, there is nothing in the German records dealing with Pfister's dual role, but this was a distinct possibility.

At the height of BUF–Nazi disharmony, Diana Mitford Guinness met Hitler in Munich and became a convenient and adept liaison between the Fuhrer and her future husband, Oswald. The very next month Mosley had a private hour-long audience with Hitler, and in October 1936 Oswald and Diana were married secretly in Goebbels' house in Berlin.

Nazi–BUF relations were also influenced by the several British branches in Germany. Since January 1934 a group of English residents in Berlin had been meeting weekly, and as early as July 1933 a similar branch was started by two BUF members in Cologne, where, within six months, they claimed to have a membership of one hundred.[16] In November 1934 the Cologne branch came to the attention of the British Consulate because of an article in the *Kölnische Zeitung* describing the local ceremonies commemorating the Nazi Putsch eleven years before. At this gathering, Captain Levi, a former field artillery officer and President of the local branch of the BUF, said:[17]

> As leader of the British Fascists in Cologne it is my privilege to greet you. This is the first time that our movement has officially met the authorities of the Third Reich. On this sacred day we have marched up to honour Germany's warriors who bravely fought and died for their country. We also wish to remember the members of the *NSDAP* who lost their lives for the movement. It is our hope that these sacrifices and our ideals may lead to the triumph of Fascism in the whole world. My comrades, I ask you to give a hearty cheer for the Führer of the German Reich, Adolf Hitler, and for Sir Oswald Mosley.

On Armistice Day two days later, the British Consul went to the British Cemetery in Cologne to lay a wreath at the War Memorial, and to his considerable embarrassment, he encountered Captain Levi and about 20 British Fascists.[18]

> Captain Levi was perfectly respectful and did not attempt to make a speech. I must add, however, that I regard with some misgiving the activities of this branch of the British Fascists. Being men of little education, I fear that sooner or later they may do or say something to cause friction with the local authorities.

The British Ambassador in Berlin, Eric Phipps, believed that the best tactic in dealing with these demonstrators was to ignore them, while the Consul in Cologne remarked on the irony "that Capt. Levi is believed to be a Jew."[19]

The extraterritorial branches of the BUF may not have been informed that the policy regarding anti-Semitism had stiffened as a result of Mosley being accused of being soft on Judaism by Arnold Leese, the head of the Fascist League in London.[20] Beginning in September and October 1934, the BUF launched increasingly harsh attacks on the Jews, a change welcomed by William Joyce, Chief of Propaganda.[21] Illustrative of this more aggressive anti-Semitic stance was a telegram sent by Mosley to Julius Streicher and later published in *Der Stürmer*.[22]

> Please accept my very best thanks for your kind telegram. . . . I value your advice greatly in the midst of our hard struggle. The power of Jewish corruption must be destroyed in all countries before peace and justice can be successfully achieved in Europe. Our struggle in this direction is hard, but our victory is certain.

While trying to define its relations with Germany, the BUF was plagued, in the words of one of its officials, by having "drawn to itself almost every unstable person and adventurer of either sex."[23] In January 1935, Special Branch catalogued the curious mélange of characters who furtively assembled at Bourne Farm near Hawkhurst in Kent. The host was E. Brown, who was let out of prison on bail pending his appeal against a three-month sentence for breaking into the offices of the *Daily Worker* on the night of 22–23 November 1934 along with William O. V. Slater and two other BUF members, J. Bennett and W. Walters.[24] Among the other guests were two German nationals, Günther Tonn (misidentified as Thon) of the Europa Press, and another journalist named Ahn.[25] William Joyce and another BUF leader completed the group.

Joyce called the meeting to confront Brown, Slater, Bennett, and Walters with the rumor that they were about to become bodyguards and stewards for Captain Cecil Barry Blacker, a *persona non grata* with Mosley on account of a visit to Germany during which he posed as third in command of the BUF. He actually held no official rank at all, but was merely a Fascist who had persuaded several Germans in the cinema industry to let him distribute Nazi films in the United Kingdom. It was always a problem to restrain eccentric followers like Blacker whose past history gave no hint of his predilections. He was born in London on 22 August 1893, and during the First World War was a lieutenant in the Fifth Dragoon Guards. After the war he came to the attention of the police and the magistrates for incurring more than 40 fines for traffic violations, which may have contributed to his reputation as someone who was always short of money. In 1934 he resided at 2 Great Chapel Street, W1.

In spite of directives from both sides not to work together, the BUF and the

London *Ortsgruppe* occasionally cooperated regarding suspicious sympathizers, as in the case of Gordon Perry.[26]

> An Englishman named Gordon Perry called on Herr Bene at 5 Cleveland Terrace, W., and offered his services as agent for the Gestapo in this country. He stated he had been employed by the Saar Commission as a police officer at Saarbrucken, and asserted that he is an ardent believer in the aims and future of the Party. On being told that the matter was not one to be dealt with by Party leaders here, Perry asked Bene to forward some information for him to the Gestapo head-quarters in Berlin, "by his [Bene's] secret channel." Perry was then told that the Party wished to have nothing to do with him, and at the same time informed him that no secret channel for sending information to Berlin existed and that the Party uses the local letter-box for its communications.

Bene believed that Perry was an *agent provocateur*, acting in behalf of an anti-German newspaper or Jewish group. Therefore he was undoubtedly surprised to learn from William Joyce that Perry had come to the Chelsea headquarters of the BUF to offer his services as a liaison between the two groups, hinting that he was connected in some way with the Gestapo. Joyce found the man and his story suspect, and turned him down. Special Branch discovered that Perry was a British subject who had been educated in Germany and was attached to the Saar's international police force as an interpreter. Strongly pro-Hitler, his primary reason for approaching Bene and Joyce was that he needed a job. MI5 found it highly unusual that the BUF and the *Ortsgruppe* had alerted each other about Perry.

Later that year the British Union of Fascists sent a long memorandum to Bene which he then forwarded to the *Auslandsorganisation* in Berlin. MI5 somehow secured a copy of this, presumably by intercepting it through the post, and called it to the attention of the Home Office. Attributed to William Joyce, it enumer-ated the great strides that the BUF had made, and described the reorganization that Mosley instigated in 1935, setting a new goal, "to use the machine so created to capture Parliamentary power by means of the Ballot box."[27] MI5 conjectured that mention of this political strategy was meant to impress the Nazis, since they had captured power in this way. The noncommittal reply from the *Auslandsorganisation* was, "how interesting." Guarded cooperation continued between the two organizations, as indicated in the following report.[28]

> Colin Paul Julius Ross, a journalist and author of German nationality (Scotch descent), who came to this country from Germany on 4th April 1936 for a month's visit, has had a conversation with Sir Oswald Mosley, who was able to impress upon him the conviction that the BUF was an active and virile movement which was steadily gaining ground in Great Britain. In consequence of this inter-view, Ross, who is said to be a personal friend of Herr Hitler's, is touring the agricultural areas with a view to ascertaining the strength of the movement, and is later to visit the industrial districts with the same object.

Ross went to some length to keep his conversation with Mosley secret, but let it be known that he had connections within the Nazi hierarchy.

One of the great dilemmas facing the British Union of Fascists was persuading the Germans and the Italians that their numbers were growing, when the truth was that they had peaked in 1934. A steady decline in membership took place between 1935 and 1937 when the number of dues-payers ranged from five to ten thousand.[29] If this had been known by the Nazis and Fascists, they would have regarded the BUF far less seriously.

Growth and influence required money, and financial support for the BUF was lacking from the outset. Initially, Mosley attracted followers and funding because he was active in the Labour Party, and some of his colleagues were intrigued by the new political entity, but attracting capital was not easy. Perhaps this is why he decided to go to Italy in April 1933 to meet Mussolini. He made no effort to keep this visit quiet; on the contrary, he openly identified himself with El Duce. Was it, then, pure coincidence that a few months later a secret bank account was opened at the Charing Cross branch of the Westminster Bank into which foreign currency was deposited?

Before and after World War II, Mosley stoutly denied being given a subsidy by the Italian Government, but subsequently his son, Nicholas, described how funds had been put into the private checking account of Mosley's friend and lieutenant, W. E. D. Allen, *via* a Swiss account, beginning in mid-1933.[30] The arrangement ended in March 1935 when the spacious BUF headquarters in the Kings Road were relinquished in favor of more modest ones in Great Smith Street. Special Branch and MI5 suspected that foreign subsidies were involved, but were unsure how much weight to place on rumors of an Italian bankroll. In June 1934 the Home Office was told about these suspicions, and were also informed that the BUF had exceeded its income based on subscriptions.[31] Not until the autumn of 1935 did they conclude that Mosley was receiving funds from Italy, probably in recognition of his support of the Abyssinian war.[32]

After Sir Oswald was interned in May 1940 and the BUF records and accounts were examined, it became possible to confirm this hypothesis. The bank account which Nicholas Mosley alluded to was opened in July 1933, with W. E. D. Allen and I. H. Dundas as authorized signatories. In May 1935 a third BUF leader, G. J. H. Tabor, was also given access to the account. Deposits were generally in the form of drafts from foreign banks or bundles of foreign currency. The latter mostly consisted of Swiss francs, French francs, German marks, and American dollars. The following are the approximate amounts credited to the Allen–Dundas–Tabor account from its inception until its closure in May 1937: 1933: £9,500; 1934: £77,800; 1935: £86,000; 1936: £43,300; 1937: £7,630.[33] Given the circuitous nature of the deposits, many of them in cash, it has never been possible to prove what portion of the annual sums came from Italy. When questioned during the war, Tabor insisted that he knew nothing of the subsidies, and explained the amounts as deposits from British supporters who possessed foreign bank accounts and did not want it known that they were financing the BUF. MI5 viewed this explanation, together with the claim that significant amounts of money had come from BUF branches abroad, as highly specious.

This mystery surrounding the Italian connection is further complicated by a discrepancy in the amounts suggested by Nicholas Mosley, and those shown in the Charing Cross records. Nicholas thought the aid from Mussolini ceased in March 1935,[34] but the bank received large deposits throughout 1936, tapering off in the early months of 1937. As to the sum provided by the Italians, Nicholas estimated £5,000 per month, which is consistent with the totals for 1934–35, but not for 1933.

If Nicholas' recollection is compared with the contemporary estimates made by MI5, a possible scenario emerges. Presumably the Italians began modestly, more likely £1000 from July through December 1933, rather than the full £5,000 per month, with the rest of the year's total coming from other sources. For the year 1934, a monthly average of £5,000 would have totaled £60,000, leaving the additional £17,800 gleaned from elsewhere. Reports by Special Branch agree that there was a sudden halt to Italian payments in March 1935, for unknown reasons. Payments seem to have resumed in April 1935 (although Nicholas Mosley did not realize this), which would suggest the likelihood of BUF support for Mussolini's attack on Abyssinia. Yet, the BUF suffered a loss of income that spring which necessitated budget cuts, including relinquishing their Chelsea premises. How can these opposites be explained?

An MI5 report of October 1935 estimated Mosley's Italian subsidy at £36,000 a year, averaging £3,000 monthly. If Mussolini resumed payments at this reduced rate in April 1935, and the BUF received £10,000–£15,000 in early 1935 at the former rate, the total would be somewhere around £40,000, leaving £46,000, presumably held in a secret account.[35] There was another reduction of £2000 from February to July 1936.[36] If we suppose that the BUF received £3,000 for the first six months of the year, and a further £6,000 for the balance of the year, the total would come to £24,000, leaving an additional £23,000 in income from non-Italian sources.

In January 1937 Special Branch observed that it was common gossip that Mosley had been receiving secret payments from Italy, but they were at risk of being terminated if the organization continued to decline.[37] Accordingly, when the funds actually came to an end in March, Mosley was taken by surprise.[38]

More than one have stated that the financial dilemma in which the movement finds itself is caused by the stoppage of financial support which has hitherto been received from secret sources. It is clear also that the withdrawal of these subventions was threatened in 1936, especially after the failure of the much boosted Fascist march through East London. These threats forced Mosley to make extravagant claims regarding the enormous progress made by the movement in East London and eventually into entering the lists in the London County Council elections for that district in an endeavour to supply proof that his statements were true. The failure of the organisation to secure the return of a single candidate on 4 March was the final blow which resulted in the dilemma in which Mosley now finds himself.

It has always been puzzling why Mosley suddenly ordered drastic cuts in expenditure in March 1937, including an estimated 70 percent reduction in the salaries of his staff from the highest echelon of leaders like William Joyce and John Beckett through the secretarial and clerical workers, down to the chauffeurs and porters.

The source of the excess income for 1934–36 remains an enigma, especially for the last two years. It is tempting to speculate that it came directly from Germany, especially after the rapprochement with the Nazis in 1935. However, as MI5 concluded: "Suggestions that Mosley was obtaining funds from Hitler have been much more vague than those in the case of Mussolini."[39]

Throughout the 1930s, and to the present time, there has never been any firm evidence that the Nazis financed British Fascism. Whoever supplemented the Italian funds in 1934–36, they were also sufficiently disillusioned by early 1937 that they discontinued their largesse. When MI5 finally had firm confirmation that Mosley was being subsidized by foreign sources, it declared:[40]

> These facts inevitably have the consequence of putting the Fascist Movement in Great Britain in an entirely new light. Where it seemed to have roots in this country, these roots now appear to be very much frailer and to have been kept alive only by artificial means. Thus both the Communist movement and its re-agent, Fascism, are for all practical purposes dependent on foreign funds. Without such funds, Fascism, at any rate, would probably cease to exist. Mosley is in fact reported to have sent a message to Mussolini to that effect.

The fortunes of the BUF continued to slide during 1937 in spite of further fund-raising efforts. Ian Hope Dundas returned to London briefly from Rome at the end of October to report that the Italians continued to refrain from any more payments.[41] Efforts were also made to give the organization a more purely domestic tone by dropping Fascist from their name, and henceforth calling themselves merely the British Union. In early 1938 the weekly publication, Blackshirt, went onto a monthly printing schedule because orders were down to 12,000 from the 17,000 of a few years earlier. Further cuts in staff were also made, bringing the paid number down to 57, of whom 52 were at National Headquarters.[42]

Only as war seemed likely did membership rise again, and this trend continued after hostilities broke out. During 1938–39 it rose from 16,000 to about 23,000.[43] However, many of these people were not pro-Nazi, but rather anti-war.

Members of Parliament and others complained to the Foreign Office that British Fascists were distributing Nazi propaganda, and concluded that Mosley's group was but one of a number of channels through which Germans were disseminating their ideas. Defending himself in 1940 before the Advisory Committee established to determine if he should be interned under Defence Regulation 18-B, Mosley argued that although the BUF received a wide variety of Nazi publications, it was not a semi-official conduit for Nazi propaganda. He admitted that Abbey Supplies Limited, the BUF's distributing outlet for its own publications, occasionally responded to special requests of members by ordering a particular pamphlet or book direct from Germany, but otherwise there was no arrangement with the vast propaganda machinery of the Third Reich.

There turned out to be one curious connection which was not known at the time, but became apparent only during Mosley's 1940 interrogation. In 1938 a man named Bruening, who had worked for the BUF but lost his job due to the 1937 cutbacks, secured employment with the notoriously anti-Semitic semi-private agency called *Welt-Dienst* (World Service) in Erfurt where his work involved preparing publications for English-speaking markets. Abbey Supplies had a Standing Order of about a dozen copies of *World Service* each month. At the outbreak of war, neither Bruening's British citizenship nor his affiliation with the BUF counted in his favor, and he was interned in Stalag XIII-A as an enemy alien.[44]

Once it was known that Mosley had secretly married Diana Mitford Guinness, her sister Unity became a great liability to the BUF. She had once been an active member, but from the mid-1930s she had spent an increasing amount of time in Germany. On occasional trips back to Britain she embarrassed the family, pro-German as it was, with outlandish demonstrations of support for the Nazis, including wearing a Swastika armband. Mosley later admitted that he should never have allowed her to renew her membership, and urged her to stay in Germany and not publicize her presence in Britain.[45]

> Hitler's attitude to her is that of a man to a child. He is always laughing and making jokes, and she had a great sort of insouciance and charm and would say anything to him, which the Germans will not. . . . On the other hand, he would talk to my wife seriously, as a more or less grownup person and as a English woman. . . .

Crucial to the decline of the BUF was the Public Order Act of 1936 which gave the police both in and out of London the power to call off political demonstrations and marches. It also forbade the wearing of uniforms, robbing the BUF much of its power to either inspire or to intimidate. Moreover, it frightened prospective contributors, because the government was authorized to audit the finances of any organization deemed to be violating the law. Besides threatening contributions from individuals, this statute effectively put a stop to the secret subsidies Mosley had become accustomed to receiving. Faced with the organization's imminent bankruptcy, Mosley realized that he could no longer take a nonchalant attitude toward BUF finances. In 1940 he told the Advisory Committee:[46]

> The origins of my attempt to make money were these. I had had no part, I never played any part in commerce or industry, until the age of 40, for the simple reason that I started life, by an accident, with more money than I wanted and I was not interested in commerce at all. I have always given a certain amount of my fortune, a good deal of my fortune, to my particular political beliefs. I used to give in various ways to British Union during its early years a considerable amount of my fortune, but nothing which hurt me at all.

In the spring of 1937 he had dipped heavily into his personal capital in order to give an estimated £100,000 from his own estate, but none of his infusions constituted a long-term solution, so he was forced to consider alternative ways to make significant amounts of money quickly.[47] To accomplish this, he was guided by two acquaintances, Peter P. Eckersley and William E. D. Allen. During the 1920s, Eckersley compiled a distinguished record as Chief Engineer of the British Broadcasting Corporation.[48]

In 1929 he left the BBC and became a freelance consultant on all aspects of broadcasting. He was not only able to provide Mosley with technical advice, but he was also, "sympathetic to British Union," so Sir Oswald could count on him to support several clandestine money-making schemes with the utmost discretion.[49] Eckersley familiarized Mosley with the growth of private commercial radio stations like Radio Normandie and Radio Luxembourg, which were outside the jurisdiction of the BBC's monopoly but directed toward a British listening audience. These stations had many British listeners, especially during the hours when the BBC was not transmitting. Furthermore, advertisers who were spending about £400,000 on commercials would quickly recognize a new market.

In William Allen, Mosley had another staunch believer in British Fascism as well as an expert concerning all forms of advertising. Allen was, in fact, an old friend, a fellow Member of Parliament representing Belfast from 1929–31, and an early adherent of Mosley's new Party. Allen was never a member of the British Union of Fascists, but he wrote a very favorable article about it which was published in the *Quarterly Review* for October 1933, reprinted by the BUF, and distributed to its followers. As Director of the advertising firm of David Allen & Sons Limited, William was able to steer Mosley into profitable ventures based on commercial radio, especially because his firm retained Peter Eckersley as one of its consultants.

Mosley also had help from Captain Leonard Frank Plugge, a Conservative M.P. who founded the International Broadcasting Company Limited in 1930, and secured the license for the highly successful English-language commercial station, Radio Normandie. Mosley recognized that the French were unlikely to authorize another British-oriented station, but he hoped that other countries might sponsor broadcasts directed towards Britain.

The idea of exploiting commercial radio was also suggested to Mosley by one of the members of the British Union, Dudley Evans. Since the BUF was frustrated with not being able to secure any air time either on the BBC or on pirate stations such as Radio Normandie or Radio Luxembourg, Evans volunteered to approach his friend, Colin Beaumont, heir to the Channel Island of Sark (which he believed was outside the jurisdiction of the BBC), and try to persuade him to allow a radio station to be erected there. Beaumont was not a member of the BUF, but was known to be sympathetic to its goals. Moreover, he had at one time been involved with Captain Plugge, so he knew something about commercial radio.

According to Mosley, "Young Beaumont and I got on very well," and together they agreed on a 30-year contract whereby Mosley would create a holding company to finance the construction costs, and Beaumont would receive 25 percent of the profits.[50] A holding company had to be created in order to disguise Mosley's involvement from Beaumont's mother, the Dame of Sark, about whom Mosley confided, "The lady does not know that I was behind that at all, she has no idea of it, poor woman; she would be shocked."[51]

Mosley believed that commercial radio was one of modern history's great innovations, along with yellow journalism, the automobile, and the aeroplane. He admired Captain Plugge's creation of Radio Normandie, but noted that it could not be heard by British listeners west of Birmingham; and the same was true of Radio Luxembourg, which was controlled by the Havas news agency. Similarly, commercial stations broadcasting from the Irish Republic carried poorly beyond Lancashire.

Mosley's aim was to broadcast to the entire United Kingdom from locations beyond the jurisdiction of the British Government, such as Eire in the west, Sark to the south, and either Belgium or Denmark in the east. Accordingly, he concluded an agreement with Sark in the spring of 1937, and soon thereafter Sir Oliver Hoare, brother of the Home Secretary, agreed to handle negotiations regarding the acquisition of a station in Belgium. Predictably, the Sark location raised legal problems, and virtually guaranteed that the BBC would seek an injunction to block transmission from the Channel Islands. However, Mosley hoped to convince the courts that the Seigneurie of Sark was not bound by British law because of the autonomy granted to it by Elizabeth I.

The holding company created to negotiate these agreements was the Museum Investment Trust Limited. Mosley's solicitor, Gerald Keith, 18 Southampton Place, WC1, was named its Director, and Mosley provided one to two thousand Pounds capital. Museum Investment Trust served to mask Mosley's involvement in the operation, and took no part in operating the stations, only drafting and concluding contracts.

When the Advisory Committee of 1940 impugned Mosley's motives for establishing these radio stations, suggesting their connection with British Fascism, Mosley rejoined that political propaganda had been specifically prohibited in his contracts, and added, "It would be the act of a lunatic to use a commercial station for propaganda purposes because three-quarters of your advertisers would leave you at once and you would lose thousands a year."[52] In this connection, he maintained that the reason Lord Rothermere ceased supporting him publicly in 1934 was because he feared mass defections by those who advertised in his newspapers if it became known that there was any connection between himself and Mosley.

Time and again, Mosley protested that his motives for entering the radio advertising business were private and commercial, and had no ideological overtones. However, he admitted that there was an indirect relationship between his business affairs and the BUF.[53]

> The only link whatsoever with British Union was if I had not been concerned with British Union I should never have wanted to make money because I had plenty, although I had, and my friends all knew it and I did not disguise it, I had the intention that any money which I made in my business at all, in whatever sphere, should go in, in one way or another, to my beliefs.

In addition to trying to establish radio stations as income-producers for the treasury of the BUF, Mosley also explored the financial potential of the health-and-fitness fields. He concluded an agreement with Basil Stafford, the chief researcher for Chemical Research Productions Limited, to develop new and reliable patent medicines, confident that the public could be persuaded to buy effective, rather than quack, remedies which could then be advertised on his network of commercial stations.

The largest and most thoroughly developed of Sir Oswald's business ventures involved a contract for the construction and operation of a radio station in Germany. Not surprisingly, the Advisory Committee focused its attention primarily on this enterprise because of its possible implication for collaboration with the Nazis on the eve of World War II.[54]

As early as June or July 1937, Diana Mosley, Sir Oswald's wife, traveled to Germany and met with Hitler to broach the idea of joining with her husband in establishing an English-speaking radio transmitter on German soil which would broadcast to England. She stressed the mutual benefits of this scheme, especially the ability to send signals twenty-four hours a day. Hitler listened to her proposal, but was noncommittal. It was not the sort of proposition that Nazis usually supported, and both the Propaganda Ministry and the Wehrmacht raised objections. The former feared that the station might be used to embarrass or even attack the Third Reich, and the latter saw it as a potential risk for divulging military secrets. Thus, in October 1937 the Mosleys were informed that the proposal had been rejected.

In early 1938 Diana tried again. This time she returned to Germany accompanied by Frederick Lawton, a barrister who often traveled with her. She reopened the subject with Hitler, who finally relented, and agreed to meet with Mosley's representative, W. E. D. Allen, to discuss the matter. Allen's willingness to act as Sir Oswald's agent allowed Mosley to remain quietly in the background, avoiding direct contact with the Germans.

The Advisory Committee was naturally interested in how Mosley had managed to penetrate the bureaucracy of the Third Reich and secure such an unusual contract. What were his, and by implication the BUF's, connections with the Nazi regime? Mosley stated that he had met Hitler only twice: first, at Hitler's flat in Munich in the spring of 1935, and second, at Goebbels' house in Berlin which was the setting for Mosley's clandestine marriage to Diana Mitford Guinness. Mosley was anxious to protect Diana from the inevitable harassment she would suffer if it became known that she had married the leader of the British Union of Fascists, since his first wife had been hounded constantly by the press. "But there was one other reason which I did not publish," he added. "There is a legend in the Movement that if you marry, you cease to do any work. I therefore meant to keep it quiet for some time so that if they did find out, I could say, 'Well, you can see I have not changed at all, the Movement has been just the same. . . .'"[55] Aware that questions were always being raised about links between the BUF and the Nazis, Mosley stressed that Diana represented him personally, not the organization. Explaining why she was on such friendly terms with Hitler, he said:[56]

> Hitler of course is very fond of music and goes to Bayreuth every year. My wife talks German; . . . and she has this particular appearance which makes all Germans take to her. She was, before our marriage, a great friend of Frau Goebbels and of Frau Wagner, who was Hitler's great friend, and she knew Hitler and Goebbels very well, Göring not so well.

The Advisory Committee was not entirely convinced that there were not concealed ties between Mosley and Hitler. Asked if Diana had obtained the radio concession directly from Hitler, Mosley replied, "He does not deal personally with those sorts of things, but she had the advantage that she could get any door opened for her." In her memoirs, Diana confirmed how easy it was to gain access to Hitler's entourage.[57]

When from time to time I happened to be in Berlin I would telephone the *Reichskanzlei* to say I was at the Kaiserhof Hotel. Occasionally, in the evening, Brückner would ring up. *"Gnädige Frau, wollen Sie uns herüberkommen?"* I crossed the Wilhelmplatz and was shown in. Hitler was generally sitting by an open fire; quite a rarity in centrally heated Berlin. Sometimes we saw a film, sometimes we just talked. During these evenings at the *Reichskanslei* I got to know him fairly well.

Still unsatisfied, the Committee continued to search for reasons behind such an unusual concession. Mosley finally confessed that Hitler was indeed granting a favor to Diana, but he credited himself with having "had a certain knowledge of me by reputation which would lead them to the view that I should not swindle them in a business which was very liable to swindling."[58]

There was also an economic reason behind Hitler's agreement to subsidize the construction and operation of a radio station on German territory: "They were quite keen to do that because they had to build the station in their internal currency and they were repaid for building the station in external currency."[59] The projected cost to construct the station at Nordyk on Heligoland was about two million Marks, which would be amortized over a period of ten years and paid in sterling from Mosley's company. The initial contract was drawn up and dated 18 July 1938. Acting for Mosley was Bill Allen, while the German representative was Dr. Johannes Ebehard Franz Bernhardt, a Director of the Anglo-German company. Representing the Nazi regime was the well-known investment banker, Kurt von Schroeder, clearly the representative of the Nazi regime.[60] Schroeder was not only a Director of the Cologne banking firm of J. H. Stein, but he was also President of the Cologne Chamber of Commerce, and a member of the International Chamber of Commerce. These combined duties provided him with the pretext for traveling regularly to Britain, France, and the United States. Additionally, he was personally acquainted with Hitler and with Robert Ley, the Nazi Minister of Labour. Before the Nazis came to power he assisted the *SS* financially, and in 1936 joined its ranks, becoming attached to Himmler's personal staff in November 1938. As a Director of Mosley's radio station, he could therefore maneuver at all levels of the Nazi bureaucracy while protecting Germany's interests.

Mosley actually set up two companies in order to obscure his involvement. The holding company which negotiated the contract was called *Air Time Limited*, whereas *Radio Variety* was responsible for selling advertising and developing programs. Peter Eckersley was a Director in both companies, and because he had been the chief engineer of the BBC, Mosley calculated that this would impress people in the field of communications. When the Advisory Committee learned that there was a second company, it assumed that *Radio Variety* would be used to air political propaganda, which Mosley stoutly denied.[61]

142

If, for instance, I had been so foolish as to want to broadcast in peacetime from Germany I should simply have got my organisation to advertise it by leaflet distribution. "Mosley will speak at such and such a time from Hamburg" or on the Munich wavelengths, and you would get a perfect response at nighttime from any of those stations.

He reminded them that even a purely commercial station had to abide by certain restrictions stipulated by the Third Reich, and all news bulletins had to conform to Nazi guidelines. What mattered most, he emphasized, was the station's ability to make lots of money, since this venture had been a part of his financial planning since the spring of 1937. "I wanted to stress the chronology to show that I had been in this business for a very long time in terms of this enterprise, prior to getting any German business," adding, somewhat defensively, "This was my real business; [it was] not some political racket. . . . I had just as much right to go into Germany, if I could get in there, as Captain Plugge, the Conservative, had to go into France."[62]

Mosley was finally able to persuade the Advisory Committee that his radio stations, including the one in Germany, were primarily commercial in character, but he could not dispel the pro-Nazi image of the BUF. Moreover, he refused to condemn Hitler, and would not agree to fight against Germany unless Britain was threatened directly.

Retrospectively, there was an unexpected and curious twist to Mosley's entrepreneurial schemes. William Allen, his negotiator and front man, turned out to be more than a go-between for his business affairs. The Allen firm not only advanced money to the BUF Trust Limited and the New Era Securities Limited, but it was slated to share in the profits from any agreement made with Beaumont for a station on Sark. Their relationship entailed one other startling dimension.[63]

Allen himself, my father divulged later, worked for MI5 in the 1930s — and my father even knew of this at the time. In a statement he recorded in later life he said of Bill Allen – "Very much involved with MI5, made no bones about it, that is why he wasn't imprisoned in the war, of course, because he had done so much for them." Also, when asked whether he thought MI5 had used Allen to find out what was going on in the movement my father replied – "To some extent: probably reporting conversations with me which were probably largely fictitious: he is a tremendously boastful man . . . one of those men who simply lived in a dream world – a Walter Mitty world, as we would call it now." In addition, my father quarreled with Allen in 1938 on the subject of loans that the latter had made to *Air Time Limited*, and Allen had told him he was in danger of losing his "one surviving friend".

Ironically, Mosley's self-imposed detachment from events on the Continent caused him to be caught by surprise at the outbreak of war in September 1939, apparently not calculating that Britain would resist German aggression. From this point onwards, he and the British Union of Fascists survived in name only, since its candidates could never hope to win elections, and the projected radio stations had no chance of materializing.

A highly perceptive assessment of the British Union and Mosley was made by C. Wegg-Prosser, a disgruntled member of the organization who was once an active propagandist for the BUF, and a candidate for a seat on the London County Council as a Blackshirt in 1937. In mid-1938 he abruptly resigned, and sent the following letter of explanation to Mosley.[64]

> It destroys your claim to be a "British Movement" with a British outlook and methods, as distinguished from foreign movements. You retreated, it is true, from the Fascist name and the Fascist symbol which, once you used them, imitated the uniform of the German *SS*. Anti-Jewish propaganda, as you and Hitler use it, is a gigantic sidetracking stunt, a smokescreen to cloud thought and divert action with regard to our real problems. Hitler I cannot judge, but you I know are intelligent enough to agree that in places where no Jews exist (as in my home county), there may still exist injustice, poverty, exploitation, bad housing, low wages, dirt and degradation. Hitler attacks the Jews to whip up the luke-warm and critical; you do it to get a mass support in East London and other places. I tried to interest these people in real problems, unemployment, wages, housing, and so on. I watched with dismay the mentality which said "get rid of the Jews and you will automatically get rid of unemployment, slums, sweating." Further, I have always loathed the spirit which says "he is a Yid," therefore bad. I know and you know that vile and unprovoked assaults have been made on a single Jew by a group of Fascists; even looting has occurred. All that I have seen and read in recent months leads me to the same conclusion, your movement is the negation of everything that is British. Our people are fair, tolerant and humane. You introduce a movement imitating foreign dictators, you run it as a soulless despotism.

NOTES

1 MI5 to HO, 1 August 1934, PRO, HO 144/20142, pp. 10–22.
2 *Berliner Lokal-Anzeiger*, 22 November 1936.
3 R. Skidelsky, *Oswald Mosley* (London, 1975), p. 453.
4 *Ibid.*, p. 331; Nicholas Mosley, *Beyond the Pale: Sir Oswald Mosley and Family, 1933–1980* (London, 1983), p. 42.
5 Memorando, Special Branch, 1 May 1934, PRO, HO 144/20140, p. 114.
6 *Ibid.*
7 MI5 to Home Office, 1 August 1934, PRO, HO 144/20142, pp. 110–11.
8 Home Office Report, 17 July 1934, PRO, HO 144/20130, document 66136/34.
9 Report of Hubert Morse, 3 September 1934, PRO, FO 371/17730, C6226, ff. 162–73. See also: Special Branch Report, 25 August 1934, *ibid.*, C5828, ff. 154–57.
10 Special Branch report, 5 September 1934, PRO, HO 144/20142, p. 138.
11 MI5 to Home Office, 8 October 1934, *ibid.*, p. 221.
12 MI5 to Home Office, 13 December 1934, PRO, HO 144/20144, p. 269.

**144**

13  MI5 to Home Office, 20 March 1935, PRO, HO 144/20144, p. 109. See also N. Mosley, *Beyond the Pale*, p. 71.

14  MI5 to Home Office, 20 March 1935, *ibid.*

15  MI5 to Home Office, 22 October 1935, PRO, HO 45/2538, pp. 38–39.

16  Labor Research Department no. 269 (25 June 1934), p. 16, in PRO, HO 144/20141, p. 136.

17  *Kölnischer Zeitung*, 9 November 1934. Levi's speech was also enclosed in a dispatch from the British Consul in Köln to the British Embassy, Berlin, 10 November 1934, HO 144/20144, p. 315.

18  British Consulate, Köln, to British Embassy, Berlin; 19 November 1934, *ibid.*, p. 308–10.

19  MI5 report, 20 March 1935, PRO, Ho 144/20144, p. 109.

20  *Ibid.*

21  Mosley's switch to anti-Semitism is discussed in R. C. Thurlow, *Fascism in Britain* (Oxford, 1987), p. 104.

22  Quoted in the *Jewish Chronicle*, 17 May 1935, p. 18. A slightly different translation of this telegram appeared in the *Daily Herald*, 11 May 1935, p. 2.

23  Mosley, *Beyond the Pale*, p. 42.

24  Special Branch report, 10 January 1935, PRO, HO 144/20144, p. 209. See also: *Daily Worker*, 24 November 1934, p. 1; 26 November 1934, p. 1; 29 November 1934, p. 3; and 1 December 1934, p. 1.

25  Tonn appears in the Appendix; we have been unable to identify Ahn.

26  Report of H. Morse, 24 April 1935, PRO, FO 371/18868, C3710, f. 223.

27  MI5 to Home Office, 13 August 1935, PRO, HO 45/25385, pp. 16, 17–23.

28  Special Branch report, 24 April 1936, PRO, HO 144/20147, p. 236. There is an extensive file on Ross at PRO, KV2/532, p. 124a.

29  Thurlow, *Fascism in Britain*, pp. 122–23.

30  N. Mosley, *Beyond the Pale*, p. 30.

31  MI5 to Home Office, 18 June and 1 August 1934, PRO, HO 144/20141, p. 301; and 144/20142, pp. 108–22.

32  MI5 to Home Office, 22 October 1935, PRO, HO 45/25385, p. 38.

33  PRO, HO 45/25393, p. 34.

34  N. Mosley, *Beyond the Pale*, pp. 31–32.

35  PRO, HO 45/25385, pp. 38–39.

36  MI5 report of 10 July 1936, PRO, HO 144/21060, pp. 52–56.

37  Special Branch report, 28 January 1937, PRO, HO 144/21063, p. 408.

38  Special Branch reports,15 and 17 March 1937, PRO, HO 144/21063, pp. 253 and 238.

39  PRO, HO 45/25385, p. 39.

40  *Ibid.*, p. 38.

41  Special Branch report, 10 November 1937, PRO, HO 144/21064, p. 45.

42  Special Branch report, 10 February 1938, PRO, HO 144/21281, p. 24.

43  Thurlow, *Fascism in Britain*, p. 122.

44  For Mosley's interrogation by the Advisory Committee in July 1940, see HO 283/14, p. 31. It is highly probable that the Bruening whom Mosley mentioned, without indicating his first name, was the same as Clement Bruening who was interned in Stalag XIII-A by Feb. 1940. See PRO, FO 369/2564, K3552, ff. 160–64.

45  PRO, HO 283/14, p. 40.

46  PRO, HO 283/13, pp. 105–6.

47  J. J. Barnes and P. P. Barnes, "Oswald Mosley as Entrepreneur," *History Today*, XL (March 1990), 11–16.

48  For background on commercial radio see: P. P. Eckersley, *The Power Behind the Microphone* (London, 1941); R. H. Coase, *British Broadcasting: A Study in Monopoly* (London, 1950); A. Briggs, *The History of Broadcasting in the United Kingdom*, II (London, 1965).

49  Mosley, *Beyond the Pale*, P. 135.

50  PRO, HO 283/13, pp. 107–8.

51  *Ibid.*

52  *Ibid.*, p. 113.

53  *Ibid.*, p. 125.

54  Nicholas Mosley's biography of his father provides a few heretofore unknown pieces of this puzzle, but Home Office documents supply many more.

55  *Ibid.*, pp. 116–17.

56  *Ibid.*

57  Diana Mosley, *A Life of Contrasts* (London, 1984), p. 149.

58  PRO, HO 283/14, p. 31.

59  PRO, HO 283/13, p. 124.

60  Kurt von Schroeder file, BDC.

61  PRO, HO 283/13, p. 125.

62  PRO, HO 283/13, p. 114.

63  Mosley, *Beyond the Pale*, pp. 174–75.

64  PRO, MEPO 2/3043, p. 83.

# 12 NAZI INFLUENCE OVER THE BRITISH LEGION

After World War I, British and German war veterans pondered the problem of reconciliation between their two nations. They recognized the symbolic significance of frontline soldiers getting together in the pursuit of future peace, and reasoned that no one could speak more eloquently than they upon the horrors of war and the need to avoid a repetition of such a tragedy. Eventually this led the veterans in the United Kingdom and Northern Ireland who belonged to the British Legion to propose inviting Germans to join the existing international organization, the *FIDAC* (*Fédération Interalliée des Anciens Combattants*), which had previously excluded Germans. However, the French and the Belgians were vehemently opposed to this, arguing that the inter-allied association of ex-servicemen should comprise only those who had fought against the Central Powers; to admit Germans, Austrians, Bulgarians, and Czechs would entirely alter the character of the group and its sense of comradeship.

When the Nazis came to power, the British were even more desirous of promoting links with other veteran's organizations abroad, since doing so would allay fears of future German aggression. They argued that if veterans could come to trust their German counterparts, then they would be able to assure fellow countrymen that the Nazi revolution was strictly internal, and not a threat to the tranquility of Europe.

The year 1933 somewhat undermined this hope, especially after Hitler ordered Germany's withdrawal from the Geneva Disarmament Conference and the League of Nations. In spite of these actions, the Nazis tried to convince others of their good intentions, and in the spring of 1934 made private overtures to the British Legion, laying the groundwork for official recognition. Baron Hans von Redwitz, whose father was a Lieutenant General in the German Army, personally invited the Chairman of the British Legion, Sir John Brown, to visit Munich and meet with an informal group of former soldiers. In his mid-thirties, von Redwitz was well placed to arrange such an excursion, since his wife was Scottish, and they had lived in London for some time prior to Hitler assuming power.[1]

Before making up his mind whether to accept this invitation, Brown consulted Orme Sargent of the British Foreign Office who explained to him why such a visit was desirable.[2]

> The British Legion was in favor of establishing contact with analogous associations of ex-Servicemen in the ex-enemy countries; and if this had hitherto been impossible in Germany, it was because the ex-Servicemen were split up into so many different associations with divergent political views. The *Gleichschaltung* brought about by the Nazi regime has put an end to this, and the *Stahlhelm* insofar as it still exists as a separate body, may now be considered to represent all ex-Servicemen in Germany.

Sargent affirmed that the Foreign Office had no objection to Sir John accepting a purely personal invitation as long as he went as an individual, and not a representative of the Legion. However, he cautioned him to avoid being used by his hosts for Nazi propaganda.

Brown decided to take another official of the Legion with him, H. M. Bateman, but was annoyed to discover that Lieutenant Colonel Graham Seton Hutchison had also received an invitation from von Redwitz.[3] What disturbed both Brown and Bateman was that Hutchison, in spite of being one of the founders of the British Legion in 1919, now zealously advocated ultra right-wing causes after losing his bid for a Labour seat in Parliament in 1923. He was also the founder of the National Workers Movement which had distinct overtones of National Socialist and anti-Semitic ideology.

Representing the "Old Contemptibles" of the British Legion,[4] Hutchison extended von Redwitz's invitation to two friends, Colonel J. J. McCarthy and Robert F. Boss-Walker. McCarthy had served in the army in Rhodesia with him, and then did police work vital to military operations in East Africa during the war. Eventually he formed an organization of veterans known as the South African Police Association, with branches throughout the Empire. Hutchison knew that he could rely on McCarthy to keep an open mind about the Nazis because he shared Hutchison's enthusiasm for the New Germany.

Boss-Walker was introduced to Hutchison by his wife, an Australian who knew that Boss-Walker, a fellow Aussie, was spending the spring of 1934 attached to Number 57 Squadron of the RAF at Heyford, near Banbury. Since he was studying German, he welcomed an invitation to spend a few weeks in the Third Reich in order to improve his comprehension of the language.

This distinctly unofficial five-man British delegation arrived in Munich on Wednesday, 28 March 1934. The von Redwitzes and others, including press representatives, were on hand to greet them, and during the ensuing days the local press made much of their visit. However, Brown and Bateman soon became uncomfortable about the exaggerated claims that Hutchison was making to the German press. Not only did he tell journalists that the members of the delegation had come to improve Anglo-German relations, but he emphasized that they were there to independently assess the situation in Germany, unlike the British press which he characterized as anti-Nazi. Brown and Bateman were even more disturbed when Hutchison and McCarthy laid a wreath at a German war memorial commemorating the unsuccessful Munich Putsch of November 1923.

During their next few days in Munich the British delegation met many Nazi luminaries such as Rudolf Hess, General Franz von Epp, Major Ludwig Streil, Count Max von Armansberg, and T. E. Scharf, all of whom listened to Hutchison's boasts.[5] He regaled them with praise of his National Workers Movement, and told how it was supported by illustrious personalities like Lloyd George, Rudyard Kipling, Reverend Dick Sheppard, and Generals Pinney, Dunsterville and Fuller. He dismissed the British Union of Fascists and Sir Oswald Mosley as mere bourgeois Fascists who, if given a chance, would pave the way for Bolshevism.

Bateman conveyed his negative impression of Hutchison in a memorandum to the British Foreign Office. "I have never heard such violent attacks on the Jews, or praise for the Germans, as he gave. He was anxious to impress the Germans on every occasion, and they swallowed everything he said."[6] He was equally distressed with the way the others in their group, Colonel McCarthy in particular, "outdid the Germans in their condemnation of the Jews."[7] Even McCarthy eventually dissociated himself from Hutchison, and criticized him for never finding fault with Germany while losing no opportunity to criticize Britain. To the British Consul-General in Munich, D. St. Clair Gainer, he alleged that Hutchison was "completely insane",[8] and to Sir John Brown he admitted chagrin at having once been such a staunch friend.[9]

> The kindest thing one can say about him is that he is mad. He has got the bug and imagines that he is a second Hitler. I put the German Foreign Office wise and they will know how to receive him in Berlin. We were to see Hitler but Hutchison spoiled that as Hitler could not receive a revolutionary body from England, and that is what our friend represented us as being.

Sir Eric Phipps, the British Ambassador in Berlin, conveyed a similar message to the German Foreign Minister.[10]

> In the course of a conversation with the Minister for Foreign Affairs on 9 April, I took the opportunity of drawing attention to the fanciful claims which Col. Hutchison appeared to be making in Munich, and I suggested that, should the Chancellor receive him, it would be advisable to take his statements with a good deal of salt. Baron von Neurath replied laughingly that he was well acquainted

with Col. Hutchison, and he would see that the Chancellor, if he received the latter, should be fully warned of his unbalanced character.

Meanwhile, the Foreign Office and the Air Ministry were not happy to discover that, besides Boss-Walker, there was another potentially unreliable Australian attached to the RAF in Munich. "A sinister detail is that another member of the squadron is Flying Officer Frank Beaumont, whose wife is said to be a Czechoslovak, but in reality is a German, has a property near Munich, and is very thick with the Nazis. The Air Ministry has their eye on Flying Officer Beaumont."[11]

Hutchison realized that his traveling companions disapproved of his behavior, and decided to take the offensive and accuse the British Consul-General in Munich of turning McCarthy and the others against him. Not surprisingly, Gainer heaved a sigh of relief when the visitors departed, and wrote plaintively to Phipps, "Is there no way of keeping these people quietly at home, and preventing them from racing around Germany playing politics?"[12]

Although the delegation invited by von Redwitz failed to promote contact between veterans of the two countries, Hutchison succeeded in ingratiating himself with two of the Nazi organizations which catered to foreigners: Alfred Rosenberg's *Aussenpolitisches Amt*, and Margarete Gärtner's *Wirtschaftpolitische Gesellschaft*.[13] In fact, there is some evidence suggesting that the Nazis may have compensated Hutchison for his cooperation.[14] If Hutchison received any payment, it may have been done by covering his expenses in Germany, since Nazis were always loath to reimburse foreigners in currency other than Marks.

During the spring of 1934, Hutchison seems to have stayed in Germany, attached to Rosenberg's *Aussenpolitisches Amt*, but by January 1935 questions arose about how he was being financed, and once these surfaced, the Germans wanted nothing more to do with him.[15]

Hutchison appeared to many as a crank, but he was actually a complex and talented individual. In addition to his distinguished military record, he had served on the allied Commission to supervise a plebiscite in Upper Silesia in 1920–21. He then embarked on a career in journalism, and wrote highly successful adventure and spy stories under the pen name of Graham Seton. He was also considered a reasonably good artist. Nevertheless, the Nazis did not welcome his proposal to lead yet another British delegation to Munich. By this time they had heard that in Britain his previous trip was considered a fiasco by Sir Ian Hamilton, who advised the German Military Attaché in London that Hutchison was perceived as a person of no consequence.[16]

January 1935 was a particularly propitious time for Germany to seek better relations with the major European powers, since the plebiscite in the Saar was working to its advantage, thereby removing one key source of antagonism. Rudolf Hess approached Otto Bene about seeking a *rapprochement* between the

French, German, and British veterans. Laval had already been sounded out, and Hess asked Bene's opinion of Lieutenant Colonel Hutchison. According to Special Branch,[17] "This, in Herr Bene's opinion, indicates that Seton Hutchison has been putting himself forward in Germany; through channels outside Herr Bene's knowledge." Bene apparently told Hess, "If any dealings were had with Seton Hutchison, the plan would be doomed from the outset so far as this country was concerned. He urged that any approach should be made to the British Legion, as the leading ex-Service men's organisation here."

Although the details are not entirely clear, it seems that a formal invitation was sent to the British Legion in February 1935 by Joachim von Ribbentrop.[18] It was communicated to Colonel George R. Crosfield, the Legion's informal Secretary of State for Foreign Affairs, who asked a Member of Parliament, D. E. Wallace, to ascertain the reaction of the Foreign Office. On 1 March 1935 Crosfield met with Anthony Eden, then serving as Lord Privy Seal, who said that the Foreign Office had no objection to the Legion sending some of its officials to Germany for the purpose of holding conversations with their opposite numbers, but he "warned him that the object of this organisation no doubt included propaganda."[19] On 12 May its President, Frederick Maurice, raised the question with Sir Robert Vansittart who repeated Eden's warning to be wary of being used by the Nazis.[20] Meanwhile, the officers of the Legion, especially the Chairman, Major Francis Fetherston-Godley, canvassed local branches in order to learn whether they agreed with him that another trip to Germany should be undertaken. A proposal to this effect was presented at the Legion's annual conference in June when the Prince of Wales addressed his fellow veterans:[21]

> There is one point which your President, when I was speaking with him the other day, brought up, and which also commended itself to me, and that was that a deputation or a visit might be paid by representative members of the Legion to Germany at some future time. I feel that there could be no more suitable body or organisation of men to stretch forth the hand of friendship to the Germans than we ex-Service men who fought them and have now forgotten all about it in the West.

The Prince's endorsement was praised in the German press, and von Ribbentrop gave his hearty approval in the columns of The Times.[22]

> As experience of meetings of ex-Service men has shown, there is no better way of promoting good feeling than an open and straightforward contact between people who have seen the fighting line. I am certain that the spirit which prevails in most ex-Servicemen's organisations in the various countries will prove a great support to the various Governments in their endeavour definitely to establish peace and cooperation in Europe.

Not everyone in Britain was elated, however. King George V mildly admonished his son for meddling in foreign affairs. Similarly, Vansittart grumbled to his colleagues that the Prince had failed to seek the advice of either the Foreign Office or his own Secretariat before making his remarks. Ralph Wigram, head of the Foreign Office Central Department, was deeply concerned about the implications of the proposed visit.[23]

> From the German side all of this is part and parcel of an attempt to appeal over the heads of such opinion here as is instructed about Germany to an uninstructed and sentimental opinion. The same sort of thing was done before the War with the most conspicuous success. It is difficult for those who do not follow these questions very closely to realize how deliberate and carefully thought out the German action is. It is just as insidious and, in some ways more dangerous, than any Communist propaganda.

Orme Sargent concurred.[24]

> The truth, of course, is – as the representatives of the British Legion will discover for themselves when they visit Germany – that there exists in Germany no non-party organisation of ex-servicemen corresponding to the British Legion. The bodies with which the British Legion will have to cooperate are purely Nazi organisations with the usual strong political bias. It is inevitable, therefore, that they should use any dealings they may have with foreigners as an occasion for Nazi propaganda.

As Sargent and others predicted, the German veteran's organizations had been reshaped and politicized by the Nazis. The oldest of these, the *Kyffhauserbund*, dated from the 1840s, and most nearly resembled the British Legion as a loose confederation of local branches. It claimed a membership of three million, and emphasized pre-war tradition and comradeship. In early 1934 the Nazis became convinced that the *Kyffhauserbund* harbored monarchist sympathizers, and therefore installed a new pro-Nazi head of the organization, Colonel Wilhelm Reinhard. Born in 1869, he began his military career at age 19, served throughout the First World War, and received the highest decoration, the *Pour le Mérite*. The Nazis relished his zeal in combating the Spartacist or Communist menace in the immediate aftermath of the war.

A second organization of veterans, the *Stahlhelm*, emerged as a potent nationalist force during the precarious years of the Weimar Republic. Its relationship to the Nazis was somewhat stormy during the 1920s and early 1930s, although they shared a common goal: undermining the Weimar Republic, and repudiating the Treaty of Versailles. The *Stahlhelm* was initially adopted by the Nazis and given the amended name *National Sozialistische Deutsche Frontkämpferbund* (National Socialist Front Fighters League), but in 1935 it was forced to relinquish its members under the age of 45 so that younger veterans would join the preferred Nazi association, the *NSKOV* (*Kriegsopferversorgung*). This group, known in English as the National Socialist War Victims Service, numbered about one and a half million. Each veteran paid dues of ten shillings, a portion of which went for welfare and insurance benefits. It was clearly intended to be the nucleus of a resurrected German army which, by the spring of 1935, had become a reality due to the introduction of military conscription.

The commander of the *NSKOV* was Hanns Oberlindober. Born on 5 March 1896 in Munich, he received his secondary school education in Berlin and passed the examinations for the *Abitur*. He served in the army throughout the war, eventually commanding a company of Bavarian Pioneers. In August 1918 he was badly wounded, and at the end of the war received the Iron Cross, Second and First class. During the 1920s he started several businesses, but gained the attention of the Nazis because of his early conversion to their cause, joining the Party in 1925, and being elected to the Reichstag in 1930.[25]

In June 1935 the Anglo-German Naval Treaty was signed, which permitted Germany to build capital ships up to 35 percent of British naval tonnage. Whether one was optimistic or pessimistic, the limitation either restricted Germany significantly, or it sanctioned her repudiation of the Versailles Treaty. However, it was clearly a personal triumph for von Ribbentrop who successfully concluded the negotiations, and promptly began promoting a visit to Germany by the British Legion. However, before he could arrange one, an unofficial group of German veterans came to Brighton in order to express their appreciation for the way a local chapter of the Legion had maintained a cemetery where German prisoners of war were buried.[26]

In Britain, Fetherston-Godley approached Vansittart about British legionnaires visiting Germany, and was warned again that the Nazis would use them for propaganda, but in spite of this, a determined delegation including Fetherston-Godley, Crosfield, and Captain Melville Adams Hawes, Naval Attaché in Berlin from April 1929 to July 1933, left for Germany on Saturday 13 July. They reached Berlin the next day, and were met by representatives of the three major veteran's organizations. A printed message of welcome from Hans Oberlindober of the *NSKOV* set the tone for the proceedings: "What lies before us is mutual trust, mutual respect, and the firm belief that out of the comradeship of the front line soldiers there will grow in a not too far off time an honourable comradeship of the people which call these front line soldiers their best citizens."[27]

Also on hand to greet the visitors was von Ribbentrop's personal representative, Heinrich (or Heinz) George Stahmer, whose special position within the Ribbentrop *Dienststelle* was liaison officer with veterans abroad. By recognizing Stahmer in this way, von Ribbentrop showed the importance he attached to this project and signified his intention to formulate his own foreign policy instead of relying on the German Foreign Ministry. Stahmer was born in Hamburg in 1892, and possessed all the requisite credentials for cultivating the acquaintance of other veterans. In 1911 he entered the 13th Regiment of Hussars as an officer cadet, received his lieutenancy in 1913, and served throughout the First World War. In 1916 he joined the General Staff, and later became an aircraft observer. He left the army in 1919 as a Lieutenant Major, and devoted much of the 1920s to a career in business. Well before the Nazis came to power, he joined the *NSDAP* and became a member of the *SS*. Without him, the German veteran's organizations would probably not have been able to make the necessary arrangements for their visit.[28]

Monday, 15 July, the delegation from Britain was treated to a surprise audience with Hitler, whose interpreter, Dr. Paul Schmidt, recalled the occasion.[29]

> On July 15th he received a delegation from the British Legion at the Chancellery, conversing for nearly two hours with Maj. Fetherston-Godley and the five Englishmen accompanying him. He asked each of them to tell him in detail on which sector of the front he had fought, and exchanged war memories with the visitors. But for the difference in language, it might have been a typical meeting of old comrades. At the end, there was a suggestion of politics in Hitler's short speech. After expressing his hearty pleasure at the visit, he emphasized the special value he attached, in the interests of peace, to collaboration between soldiers who had fought in the last war.

Responding, Fetherston-Godley said that the British had fought the Germans only once, and he trusted that this sad necessity would never again arise. Schmidt further reflected on the meeting in his memoirs.[30]

> On leaving the Chancellery these visitors undoubtedly felt much impressed by the manner in which Hitler had received them, but I now noticed something which in the following years was often to strike me. Hitler's effect on his visitors faded out as time went by. During the next few days I accompanied the delegation, showing them round, and I noticed how their attitude to Germany became daily more critical. Things they saw for themselves in National Socialist Germany seemed to confirm what they had heard about Germany in their own country, rather than what Hitler and his colleagues had told them so persuasively.

The British guests were then taken to the nearby cemetery of Stahndorf where interned British prisoners who had died during the war were buried. At lunch, von Ribbentrop returned to the theme of the unique role which veterans could play.[31]

> Great as was the work done by the ex-service organisations in various countries, they were now faced with a more important task, namely, that of bringing about international reconciliation. The spirit of comradeship which had been born in the trenches would be able, more than anything else, to bring the nations of the world closer together. No differences of any kind now existed between Germany

and England, and the Anglo-German Naval Agreement had meant an important step forward in improving relations between the two countries.

Sight-seeing occupied the following day. The Legionaries paid their respects to the grave of the "Red Baron," Manfred von Richthofen, and viewed the *Schorfheide* game preserve, but their main destination was the disabled men's community at Britz, outside of Berlin. It was one of several such settlements which the *NSKOV* administered throughout Germany, providing disabled veterans and their families with cheap and comfortable housing. The one at Britz contained 187 semi-detached, two-storey units, each house situated on a quarter acre of land. The *NSKOV* expected prospective tenants to help in the construction of their houses, or provide a surrogate builder. Future residents paid 3,500 Marks, or 175 Pounds, for the privilege of living in the community, and thereafter owed a modest monthly rent of 13-16 Marks. Units varied in size and number of rooms, depending upon the family's requirements, and a school for the children was nearby. Those who were physically able were expected to take employment in the neighborhood, and by way of trying to make families more self-sufficient, each was provided with one pig, six hens and one rooster. Britz was clearly a project which the Nazis were anxious to showcase.[32]

Not until the weekend of 20–21 July did the bonhomie crack. The British were scheduled to lay a wreath at the Munich war memorial, but as happened once before, they were asked to make a similar gesture toward the Germans who had died during the failed Nazi putsch of November 1923. This time they declined, saying that it was overtly political, and therefore not acceptable. Back in London, the Legion's President, Frederick Maurice, explained to Ambassador von Hoesch why the Nazi martyrs were not honored.[33]

> When Herr Ribbentrop gave me the invitation to the British Legion to come to Germany to visit the chief German ex-Servicemen's organization, I explained to him that the British Legion, as a non-party organization, could only accept the invitation on the understanding that it would not be asked to take part in any form of political demonstration.

British newspapers featured the story, but the Legion wanted to minimize the episode and said that the confusion arose from a misunderstanding about itineraries.

Less publicized when they returned were the observations of Crosfield and Hawes about their guided tour of the Dachau concentration camp. Their favorable impressions contrasted markedly with their expectation of finding a dreary and sinister compound.[34] "In considering the conditions in a German concentration camp it will be necessary not to lose sight of the fact that the country is still in a state of revolution and that the subversive forces are by no means quiescent," they wrote, sensing the resentment still felt by Nazis who had been imprisoned under the Weimar regime. They commented on the camp's pleasing appearance, with trees and shrubs and flowers separating the different "dormitories." On the other hand, they were struck "by the glimpse into the low types of humanity which an inspection of the inmates afforded." The camp authorities explained that Dachau was one of five internment centers throughout Germany, with a total inmate population of about 3,400. The property covered an area of about 45 acres, on the site of a former munitions factory that was torn down under the terms of the Versailles Treaty. In July there were 950 political prisoners, 246 professional criminals, 198 "work-shy" individuals, 26 hardened criminals, 30 "moral perverts," and 85 Jewish immigrants who had returned to Germany, making a total of 1,535 inmates, the largest number in any of the camps under the administration of the SS.

Crosfield and Hawes accepted without skepticism the Nazi contention that one of the camp's main goals was "to reform by healthy exercise, good food, and work at trade," in workshops under the supervision of trained SS foremen. As a result, only seven inmates were on the sick list. Other features highlighted were that warders and prisoners were fed the same food, which was of good quality and abundant, and that inmates could purchase items to supplement their diet, but no alcoholic beverages were permitted. Even solitary confinement was portrayed positively. They were told that this form of internment could only be imposed for a maximum of six weeks, and the cells were well-ventilated and provided with heat in winter.

Crosfield and Hawes judged that the Dachau Commandant, Heinrich Deubel, was an effective administrator. "We thought everyone of the staff, from the Commandant to the humblest warder, was out to help any prisoner make the best of himself and of the situation; and further that just complaints would receive immediate attention."

Had these observations been made in 1933, they might have been plausible, but by 1935 they raise the obvious question whether these men were incredibly naïve, or victims of a clever charade. There is evidence to suggest the latter. Soon after they returned to England, a letter surfaced in London, purporting to be written by a German familiar with internal intelligence matters. It was addressed to a refugee, and posted from Holland. One copy found its way to the former Editor of *The Times*, who forwarded it to the British Foreign Office. Commenting on the recent visit by representatives of the British Legion, the writer said:[35]

> I hear, for instance, from a perfectly trustworthy source, that people here played an incredibly impudent trick upon these worthy Officers when visiting the Dachau Concentration Camp. The real prisoners, with very few exceptions, were driven into a cellar or underground passage and kept there during the visit. The few exceptions were threatened with immediate execution if they should fail to answer the English questions properly. They were mixed up with about 90% specially drilled SS guards, selected by the "Brown House" in Munich and dressed

as prisoners. Among these people were a number with a good knowledge of English so that they could understand what the English visitors said to each other. The selected real prisoners had been properly fed for some days, and were given decent clothing so that they might make a good impression. I wonder whether the Englishmen suspected anything.

This hoax was later confirmed by the official historian of the British Legion: "The Germans, however, ran no risks: most of the Dachau 'prisoners' were SS men in disguise. But the Legion, of course, was, and has remained to this day, unaware of that."[36]

The host and tour guide, de Sager, supplied another perspective of the visit to Dachau.[37]

> The verdict of the two gentlemen [Crosfield and Hawes] find that in contrast with the horror stories that are spread abroad, it is very sensible that such racially and politically inferior elements as we saw in Dachau be kept in such camps. Both gentlemen agreed that their visit to Dachau was much more interesting than all of the previous official functions.

After their guided tour, Crosfield and Hawes drove to Himmler's residence for refreshments. "He gave us the impression of being an unassuming man, anxious to do his best for his country. He had a great sense of humour, as the cartoons of the SS on the walls of his house reveal."[38] Himmler registered great concern about the rise of Communism in Germany, and stated that "The object of the concentration system is to remove and segregate the leaders of subversive movements."[39] De Sager added that "This invitation was very important in influencing these gentlemen, since they got on very well with the Reichsführer."[40] Hawes affirmed this in a note thanking Himmler for his hospitality: "What we saw and heard today will significantly improve the relationship between our two countries. We especially liked the quiet evening in your lovely country house."[41]

It is unclear whether Fetherston-Godley, Crosfield, and Hawes were aware of the disbanding of the *Stahlhelm* in favor of the Nazi *NSKOV* while they were in Germany. All members under the age of 45 had already been forced to resign and join the *NSKOV*, an order involving 900,000 veterans. When Hawes returned, he informed the Foreign Office that von Bary, leader of the *Stahlhelm*, told him that the Government's pretext for eliminating the *Stahlhelm* was its infiltration by Communists. However, von Bary admitted that the rivalry between *Stahlhelm* and the Storm troopers began during the years prior to Hitler's assumption of power. He explained that the *Stahlhelm* had attracted a much better class of men than those who joined the *SA*, and acknowledged that he might soon be sent to a concentration camp for saying these things.

The Cologne branch of the *Stahlhelm* was still active in July 1935, making plans to participate in the reception for the British legionnaires. In fact, a week before the visitors were due, the acting British Consul-General, with the improbable name of Fallow Field, met with members of the Cologne *Stahlhelm* to plan the festivities.[42]

> After the discussion of the programme, proceedings became less formal and the freedom with which all the members of the *Stahlhelm* expressed their feelings with regard to the present regime was extraordinary. The subject arose over the fact that orders had been received from National Socialist Headquarters in Berlin that the *Stahlhelm* was not to have the uniformed guard-of-honour for the guests, nor was the *Stahlhelm* band permitted to play the tattoo (*Zapfenstreich*). This led to a discussion of the various organisations of German ex-Servicemen of whom the *Stahlhelm* disagreed.

Interestingly, Fallow Field sensed that there was an ulterior motive behind the Legion's visit to Germany.

> The British Legion wasn't concerned whether one of the three major German veterans groups was in the process of disintegrating; it was merely determined to have their German counterparts visit England. However, there were other British veterans who resented the Legion's overtures to Germany.

Several weeks after Fetherston-Godley and his colleagues returned to England, another group of four British veterans traveled to the Third Reich: former Lance Corporal P. A. Nichol from Brighton; Private T. Gibbons from Jarro; Private R. J. Spraggins from Norwich; and R. J. Mauker from Wood Green in London. Accounts of their trip appeared in the *News Chronicle*, the *Daily Herald*, and the *Manchester Guardian*,[43] and they called a public meeting in Essex Hall on 20 August in order to present a dissenting report. While readily acknowledging the kind hospitality shown them, they complained of being constantly under the surveillance of officials. Their idea had been to meet other ordinary veterans like themselves and inspect workers' housing, prison conditions, concentration camps, and the remnants of Weimar socialism, but instead were shown only palaces, museums, cathedrals, and parades. Their request to interview political prisoners like Thalmann and Ossietzky had been thwarted, and they were convinced that "The Nazis labour colonies are training grounds for the German army. We saw the pick and shovel men trained up to army pitch."[44]

The Foreign Office concluded that the four who went on this unofficial visit were either Communists, or being manipulated by them. Lance Corporal Nichol was Chairman of his local branch of the Amalgamated Society of Woodworkers, and therefore likely a member of the British Communist Party. At the public meeting, he and Spraggins made statements that clearly demonstrated their pro-Soviet leanings. For example, "All the German people are being taught to look upon the U.S.S.R. as a menace to Germany, and that Russia is under the control of mad Communists and Jews."[45] A member of the Central Committee of the Communist Party of Great Britain, R. W. Robson delivered a vicious attack on the British Legion.[46]

> The British Legion was formed in order to scotch militancy among ex-Servicemen, and also to scotch their cooperation with the ordinary working class movement. We are up against the most cunning and unscrupulous of enemies. The official British Legion visit to Germany was intended to help Hitler in the militarization of Germany. Hitler has turned Germany into a vast training camp prepared for the overthrow of the Soviet Union.

The German Embassy in London sent its own observer to Essex Hall. Dr. Hans Meissner had no doubt about who was behind the meeting, as evidenced by the anti-German leaflets, Communist literature, and Russian newspapers, and added, "According to my careful estimate," at least half of the thousand people there "were Jews."[47] He also commented on the vituperative rhetoric against the British Legion.

> They accused the British Legion in general of having imperialistic goals, and in particular of a tendency toward National Socialism. Most notable was their vehement attack against the Prince of Wales, whom they regarded as already being National Socialist, and who had encouraged the Legion's trip to Germany for propaganda purposes.

Fetherston-Godley and the British Legion took scant notice of this diatribe, assured by the Prince of Wales that he was planning to host a delegation of visiting German veterans in September. Ambassador Hoesch was asked to help choose the delegation so that it wouldn't appear as though it had been hand-picked by Hitler's subordinates.[48] With his customary naïveté regarding the Nazi bureaucracy, he suggested that von Ribbentrop also submit a list of veterans, including the Legion's recent hosts, Oberlindober and Reinhard.

The British Legion then revealed their intention to formally accept German veterans into the existing international organization of allied ex-Servicemen, the *FIDAC*. Their hope was for support from the United States, Yugoslavia, Romania, Portugal, and possibly Poland. However, Belgium, Czechoslovakia, and Greece had already made known their opposition to this motion, and the French delegation was divided. Recognizing that it would be a close vote, Fetherstone-Godley predicted that the British and Americans would break away and form their own organization if the *FIDAC* refused to admit Germans.

A leading article in *The Times* of 17 August threw these plans into considerable disarray. Not generally censorious of Germany, the newspaper introduced a number of troubling issues. Titled "Repression in Germany", an editorial revealed that the *Stahlhelm* was rapidly being disbanded throughout the country, as were Catholic youth organizations. Further, the Confessing Church was being increasingly harassed by the Government, and anti-Semitism was on the rise. More than anything else, this editorial forced the British Legion to reassess, and proceed more cautiously.

The day after the appearance of *The Times* leader, Fetherston-Godley wrote to von Ribbentrop.[49]

> I look on the situation, as regards the friendship between our two countries, as becoming so serious that it is best to write you very frankly. I enclose a cutting of a leader from yesterday's *Times* which very fairly reflects a growing, and rapidly growing, feeling in Great Britain and which I am meeting everywhere, both inside and outside the Legion.
>
> You may say, very rightly and justly, that the internal affairs of Germany are not our business; that is so, but Great Britain has the right to choose her friends as she wishes, and sentiment has a very great deal to do with that choice. It is that very feeling of sentiment that Germany is antagonizing at the present moment, by the various anti-religious agitations.
>
> Your Country has never been able to understand the psychology of England, and it is that deep rooted feeling of *sentimentalism* that has precluded that understanding that is so necessary for our mutual well-being.
>
> If the events in Germany do not very soon become more tranquil as regards the Protestants, the Catholics and the Jews, I am certain that the move for mutual friendship, which started so auspiciously, is doomed to failure and the Legion will have to make a public statement that it is impossible to carry on with the negotiations, and will make public the reasons for such a step.
>
> You can easily imagine the dangerous and far-reaching effects of such a statement, and it will only be made when inevitable, but at the present rate of progress, that time is not very far off.

Von Ribbentrop was sufficiently upset by this letter that he dispatched Graf von Dohna to London to meet with Fetherston-Godley to try and convince him that tranquility would soon return to Germany. Moreover, a delegation of German ex-Servicemen was already scheduled to come to Britain in October. Reluctantly, Fetherston-Godly agreed to this visit, but insisted that it take place at a later date.[50]

The German deputation arrived on Sunday, 19 January 1936, led by von Ribbentrop's personal representative for veteran affairs, Heinrich Georg Stahmer. The eleven-man delegation included Hans Oberlindober of the *NSKOV*, and Wilhelm Reinhard of the *Kyffhauserbund*, both of whom had met with the Legionnaires in July 1935; Baron Kurt von Lersner, head of the now defunct Prisoners of War Association; Major General Ruediger von der Goltz, head of the Officers Association; Air Commandant F. Liebel; and press representative, Dr. Theodor Böttiger.

On Monday, the 20th, a wreath was laid at the Cenotaph, and by contrast with three years before when Alfred Rosenberg performed a similar gesture, the Swastika-beribboned tribute went undisturbed. An elaborate series of luncheons, dinners, reception, and tours were scheduled, including a meeting with the leaders of the Anglo-German Fellowship. However, at the banquet that evening the news of George V's imminent death was announced, and the Germans decided to return home.[51]

A few members of the British Legion had openly objected to this visit. No less a member than the National Honorary Treasurer, Major J. B. Brunel Cohen, expressed his serious misgivings in a letter to *The Times*.[52]

> Nobody deprecated more than he [Cohen] the way in which the German Government was treating minorities, not only Jews. On the other hand, it was a majority of the German people with their own chosen Government who were doing these things, and, seeing that that was so, in the interests of world peace we could not refuse to meet and treat with their representatives.

However, the majority supported the exchanges, and during the months that followed, hundreds of British and German veterans went to each other's meetings. Not until late October 1936 did the next official delegation from Germany come to Britain, headed this time by the Duke of Saxe-Coburg-Gotha. Their itinerary included a meeting with the Anglo-German Fellowship at which Edward VIII received them informally, reminiscent of Hitler's cordiality a year before.

As predicted, the older inter-allied veterans organizations refused to admit Germans, leaving the British to establish a new one, the *Comité International Permanent*. Colonel George R. Crosfield became the Secretary of the *CIP*, and in this capacity attended a mammoth gathering in June 1937 at Kassell where the *Kyffhäuserbund* assembled one hundred thousand members. From a rostrum 30 feet high outfitted with five microphones, Crosfield set the tone of reconciliation between former enemies. Appropriately, Fetherston-Godley was knighted for his services to the Legion and to peace-making that summer.

The largest official group ever to come from Germany, about 88 strong, reached Britain on 22 September 1938. Again, they were led by Queen Victoria's grandson, the Duke of Saxe-Coburg-Gotha. The timing was inauspicious, as the major powers were in the process of deciding the fate of Czechoslovakia. The British Legion was undaunted, however, and seized the opportunity to offer their assistance in resolving the Czech crisis. Sir Frederick Maurice, the Legion's President, had somehow learned the terms that Hitler had proposed in the Godesberg Memorandum: the transfer of Czech territory to Germany; and plebiscites to determine the nationality of the disputed border regions. On behalf of the British Legion, Maurice volunteered a neutral police force to maintain order in the ceded areas of Czechoslovakia during the period of transition to German annexation.[53] In spite of the fact that the British Cabinet had already decided to reject the Godesberg Memorandum, the Foreign Office and Downing Street encouraged the Legion to continue negotiating with the Germans.

After hurried consultations with the German Embassy in London, Maurice flew directly to Berlin and was met by von Ribbentrop who told him that he could see Hitler on the 27th. Hitler explained that there was not enough time to ferry legionnaires from Britain to Czechoslovakia by 1 October, but he liked the idea of their supervising the plebiscites.

Maurice returned to London and issued a hurried call for volunteers. Nearly 17,000 responded, and 12,000 were temporarily mobilized, pending final negotiations among the major

Powers at Munich. The final Agreement of 30 September left open the need for a British Legion police force, and not until 13 October did the Germans formally decline their offer.

The British Legion congratulated its members for their rapid response, and the Duke of Saxe-Coburg-Gotha invited all 12,000 men to visit Germany at the end of October as official guests of the Third Reich. The Foreign Office was told that Hitler would be extremely disappointed if they declined, but the volunteers had already disbanded, and the British Legion turned its attention towards preparations for a possible European war.[54]

The paradox underlying relations between British and German veterans during the 1930s was well summarized by the British Military Attaché in Berlin who wrote in August 1938, "We ex-Servicemen know what war is, and we must do all we can to prevent another one." However, as war clouds inexorably gathered during the following year, a German veteran retorted philosophically, "I quite agree with all this talk of peace, but if there must be another war, we'll all be there again, won't we?"[55]

NOTES

1   PRO, FO 371/17766, C2294, ff. 403–7; and C2462, f. 427.
2   *Ibid.*, C2294, ff. 401–2.
3   Graham Seton Hutchison entry, *Who Was Who?*, IV, 583; also *The Times*, 5 April 1946, p. 7.
4   In 1914, the British Expeditionary Force under Sir John French adopted the name Old Contemptibles after learning that Kaiser Wilhelm II had scorned their small numbers and inadequate fighting power.
5   Scharf was born and educated in Australia, and served the Nazis in Munich as a political cartoonist.
6   H. M. Bateman to the British Foreign Office, 18 April 1934, PRO, FO 371/17766, C2462, f. 423.
7   *Ibid.*, f. 416.
8   D. St. Clair Gainer to E. Phipps, 7 April 1934, *ibid.*, C2392, f. 410.
9   McCarthy to Brown, 12 April 1934, *ibid.*, C2462, f. 429.

10  E. Phipps to J. Simon, 10 April 1934, *ibid.*, C2392, f. 409.
11  Minute by Perowne, 18 April 1934, *ibid.*, C2392, p. 408.
12  Gainer to Phipps, 9 April 1934, *ibid.*, C2463, f. 43.
13  M. Gärtner, *Botschafterin des Guten Willens* (Bonn, 1955), p. 280.
14  R. Griffiths, *Fellow Travelers of the Right* (London, 1980), pp. 101–3.
15  Bismarck to *Auswärtiges Amt*, 14 January 1935, NA microcopy T-120, roll 2707, frames HO31875-77.
16  *Ibid.*
17  Special Branch report, 19 January 1935, PRO, FO 371/19968, C766, ff. 146–50.
18  G. Wootton, *The Official History of the British Legion* (London, 1956), p. 174.
19  Wallace to Eden, 26 February 1935; and Eden to Wallace, 1 March 1935, PRO, FO 371/18878, C1697, ff. 1–5.
20  PRO, FO 371/18882, C4791, f. 292.
21  Wootton, *Official History*, p. 176.
22  *The Times*, 12 June 1935; quoted in *ibid.*, p. 173.
23  Minute by Wigram, 14 June 1935, PRO, FO 371/18882, C4005, ff. 296–301.
24  Minute by Orme Sargent, 17 June 1935, *ibid.*
25  Oberlindober file, BDC, and *Das Deutsche Führerlexikon*, 1934/1935 (Berlin, 1935), p. 336.
26  German Embassy, London to *Auswärtiges Amt*, 27 June 1935, NA microcopy, T-120, roll 2707, frames HO32117-21.
27  *The Times*, 15 July 1935, p. 13.
28  Stahmer file, BDC.
29  Wootton, *Official History*, p. 183.
30  *Ibid.*
31  Norton to Hoare, 24 July 1935, PRO, FO 371/18882, C5639, ff. 364–66.
32  PRO, FO 371/18882. C5845, ff. 391–92.
33  Maurice to Hoesch, 21 July 1935, NA microcopy T-120, roll 2707, frame HO32212.
34  PRO, FO 371/18882, C5845, ff. 386–90.
35  Anonymous letter, PRO, FO 371/18878, C6190, ff. 57–76.
36  Wootton, *Official History*, p. 185, note 1.
37  Report of De Sager, late July or early August 1935, NA microcopy T-175, role 21, frames 2525551-56. We have been unsuccessful in learning more about de Sager, although he was said to be an American by birth. By inference, his wife was American as well. De Sager was also said to have written a book and several articles for the British press which portrayed Germany in a favorable light.
38  PRO, FO 371/18882, C5845, f. 393.
39  *Ibid.*
40  PRO, FO 371/18882, C5845, f. 393.
41  M. A. Hawes to Heinrich Himmler, 21 July 1935, NA microcopy T-175, role 21, frames 2525572–73.
42  British Consulate-General, Cologne, to British Embassy, Berlin, 29 July 1935, PRO, FO 371/18882, C5782, ff. 374–77.
43  9 August 1935.
44  PRO, FO 371/18882, C5845, ff. 429–36.
45  *Ibid.*
46  *Ibid.*

47  Meissner report, 21 August 1935, NA microcopy T-120, roll 2707, frames HO32318-26.

48  Hoesch to German Foreign Ministry, 13 Aug. 1935, NA microcopy T-120, roll 2707, frames HO32304-07.

49  18 August 1935, PRO, FO 371/18882, C6266, ff. 422–23.

50  Graf von Dohna's trip to London is alluded to in Dieckhoff to Bismarck, 27 August 1935, NA microcopy T-120, roll 2707, frame HO32310. An emissary from von Ribbentrop is also mentioned, though not by name, in S. W. L. Ashwandon's confidential report to the Foreign Ministry, PRO, FO 371/18882, C6266, ff. 419–26.

51  *The Times*, 17 January 1936, p. 7; 18 January, p. 11; 20 January, p. 14; 21 January, p. 10; and 22 January, p. 7. See also: Wootton, *Official History*, p. 198.

52  *The Times*, 17 February 1936, p. 9.

53  Wootton, *Official History*, pp. 230–40.

54  PRO, FO 371/21788, C13569, ff. 170–81; FO 371/18791, C12669, ff. 184–85.

55  PRO, FO 371/21711, C8081, f. 811.`

# 13 OTTO KARLOWA AND THE *LANDESGRUPPE GROSS BRITANNIEN*

During the course of 1936 the Nazi *Landesgruppe* in London was somewhat in disarray. Its leader, Otto Bene, was hoping to secure a diplomatic appointment as German Consul-General in London, but unofficially the British intimated that they would not accept him. Pending formal clarification of his situation, Bene maintained a low profile, made periodic trips back to Germany, and delegated much of his authority to Otto Karlowa, his chief lieutenant.[1] Karlowa had been named *Ortsgruppenleiter* in the spring of 1935 when Bene became *Landesgruppenleiter* for Great Britain and Ireland. During Bene's frequent absences, Karlowa managed the *Landesgruppe,* and when it became clear that Bene would not be named Consul-General, but would have to settle for a similar post in Milan, Karlowa was named *Landesgruppenleiter* in May 1937.

Karlowa was born Otto Georg Gustav Karlowa in Heidelberg on 26 July 1883. His family history made it plain that he was destined for a career in the German Navy, serving from 1901 to 1919 and rising to the rank of Captain. In 1919 he met and married Mary Sthamer, daughter of Germany's Ambassador to Great Britain immediately following World War I. In 1923 they took up residence in London where he pursued an import–export business as representative for various German electrical and engineering firms.[2] In the early 1930s, Karlowa was appointmented Consul-General of Batavia in the Dutch East Indies, but his strong pro-Nazi feelings displeased the German Foreign Ministry which retired him in 1933.[3] He then returned to London and settled at 213 Ashley Gardens, SW1, with business premises in Abford House, Wilton Road, SW1. Soon afterwards he applied for membership in the *NSDAP*, and was formally admitted on 1 March 1934. He was increasingly active in the London *Ortsgruppe*, enhanced by his diplomatic experience and independent wealth. By the time he assumed his duties as *Landesgruppenleiter* in the spring of 1937, he was also well known to the British authorities who regarded him as less capable, but rather more secretive, than his predecessor, Otto Bene.

Trends of growth and proliferation begun under Bene came to fruition under Karlowa. By 1936 there were three *Ortsgruppen* in greater London: the original one in Central London, with its headquarters at 5 Cleveland Terrace, W2; a second one in Dalston, East London, with its center at 4 Clifton Grove, E8;[4] and the third in West London, which met at the German Trade School in Ealing, 46 Eaton Rise, W5.

As *Landesgruppenleiter*, Karlowa was responsible for the half-dozen smaller *Stutzpünkten* throughout the British Isles. During the years 1936–39 there were a dozen or so Party members in each of the following areas: Bradford, Birmingham, Liverpool and Manchester, Newport and Cardiff, Hull, Doncaster and Sheffield. Until 1939, Karlowa also had jurisdiction over the *Stutzpünkte* in Dublin.[5]

Although we do not normally include Nazis outside of Greater London in this volume, we mention some of them here because they were under Karlowa's jurisdiction. The actual composition of the provincial *Stutzpüntken* during 1936–38 is not known. However, in most instances the names of the leaders and other office holders have been preserved. One of the most important groups outside London was in Brimingham, with Dr. Enno Becker as *Leiter*. His deputy was Max Funk, while Walter Lehming was concerned with the *Deutsche Arbeitsfront*. Hans Caesar served as the group's treasurer, while Paul Lorch oversaw questions relating to propaganda. Another active *Stützpunkt* served the Liverpool and Manchester area, with Ernst Lahrmann in charge at Liverpool, and his deputy, Karl Rahmann, overseeing Manchester; the treasurer of the combined group was Helmuth Rubarth. In the city of Bradford, the leaders were Adolf Peltzer and Max Kneusels, and the treasurer was Otto Mueller. In Doncaster and Sheffield, the *Leiter* was Dr. Heinz Winkelmann, with Heinrich Kaysser as treasurer. Newport and Cardiff combined under the leadership of Hans Witte, but after 1936 this *Stutzpünkt* ceased to exist. Thriving more successfully was the group in Hull, with Karl Luther as *Ortsgruppenleiter*, and the resident German Consul, Richard Huenecke, as his deputy.

During the latter 1930s, estimates varied as to the total number of Nazi Party Members in the United Kingdom. In February 1937 it was estimated that there were 314 Nazis, and one month later MI5 indicated that it had 220 in its files.[6] Later that same year the *Daily Herald* put the figure at about 500, while two years later MI5 had files for 560 *NSDAP* members.[7]

Some of the discrepancies in these figures can be accounted for by the steady growth of the *Landesgruppen* during the years 1936–39. Since a great many files at the Home Office and MI5 remain closed, one cannot make comparisons with the Nazi Party membership rolls, but, from the data available in the Foreign Office papers and elsewhere, we have tried to reconstruct the composition of the *Ortsgruppen* in London. We can positively identify 405 Party Members for the decade of the 1930s, not all of whom lived in or near London at any one time. Some were there for the better part of a year, while others stayed for nearly the whole decade. The following list shows the progression from the modest beginnings of the first *Orstgruppe* in 1931 to the greatly augmented cadres of 1939.[8]

Members of the London *Ortsgruppen*

| 1931 | 9 |
|------|------|
| 1932 | 31 |
| 1933 | 51 |
| 1934 | 101 |
| 1935 | 137 |
| 1936 | 170 |
| 1937 | 201 |
| 1938 | 235 |
| 1939 | 244 |

The Appendix (p. 257) names the individuals involved, and the approximate years each resided in London and was affiliated with the local Nazi organizations. In a few instances, individuals were not admitted to the Party until after the outbreak of war. However, we have included these because they were in London prior to hostilities and had already applied for membership. Pending their formal admission, they would have been active participants in the *Ortsgruppen*.

The Nazi Party was not known for recruiting women members or acknowledging their participation. One estimate puts their enrollment at less than 5 percent. It is curious, then, to find that there were nearly 70 women among the 405 Party Members living in or close to London.[9] If this figure is accurate, the female contingent in London would have amounted to about 17 percent. The explanation is perhaps obvious: Britain attracted large numbers of women as domestic servants, some of whom were then encouraged to participate in the German community and eventually to seek admission to the Party. Similarly, Party members were recruited among German secretaries, typists, and telephonists.

Somewhat surprising are the number of Germans who joined the Party after they came to Britain, rather than before leaving Germany. There were probably two main reasons for this. First of all, the local Nazi organization abroad did their best to recruit new members, and in the case of London, they were clearly successful. Second, Germans living at home were subject to periodic moratoria on new memberships into the *NSDAP*. Those living abroad were treated differently because the Nazis thought it prestigious to have *Orstgruppen* and *Landesgruppen* throughout the world. This bolstered the idea that Aryan blood transcended national frontiers, and, provided that someone was a German citizen, he or she was eligible for membership. The following list shows the approximate numbers of those who applied for membership and were ultimately admitted from the area of Greater London and the Home Counties during the decade of the thirties.

| | |
|------|----|
| 1931 | 5 |
| 1932 | 13 |
| 1933 | 21 |
| 1934 | 40 |
| 1935 | 15 |
| 1936 | 24 |
| 1937 | 23 |
| 1938 | 39 |
| 1939 | 30 |

The steady increase in newcomers from 1936 onwards may testify to the enhanced reputation and power of Nazi Germany. As it became clearer that Hitler would stay in power, and that as a consequence, opportunities would be open to Party members, there were added pressures to join. The movement fostered a feeling of togetherness which was especially coveted by people living abroad. Only the imminence of war slowed this rise, but the figures confirm that membership peaked in 1939.

On the basis of the information tabulated in the Appendix it is also possible to compile a composite picture of the *Ortsgruppen*. As might be expected, the majority of individuals were in certain age groups, with more than 70 percent being in their twenties or thirties. There were fewer senior officials and elder statesmen, testifying to the youthful idealism of the Nazi movement. However, the age distribution in London may have reflected job opportunities, students living there temporarily, and younger domestic servants. The following table indicates the births per decade of members in the several London *Ortsgruppen*.

| | |
|-------|-----|
| 1850 | 0 |
| 1860s | 9 |
| 1870s | 9 |
| 1880s | 32 |
| 1890s | 165 |
| 1910s | 122 |
| 1920s | 0 |

Here as elsewhere the data for a particular category is occasionally missing from the Party membership cards, so that these figures do not always equal the

405 mentioned earlier. Nevertheless, they provide a reasonably clear picture of the age distribution of the members.

In most cases it has been possible to categorize the London *Ortsgruppen* in terms of occupations. Some defy convenient definition and are listed separately, but the major types of employment emerge clearly. Leading the list are businessmen, with 82 individuals engaged as salesmen, managers, company representatives, and independent entrepreneurs. The next most numerous were clerical workers, including office assistants, typists, clerks, and telephonists, a fair number of whom worked for the German Embassy at one time or another. Journalists numbered 38; however, there were perhaps twice as many from Germany, but half of them were either refugees or non-Party members.

Of the 33 domestic servants, housekeepers and cooks, most were females, while men tended to enter the restaurant and hotel trade as waiters and chefs, and there were 12 of these. Diplomats were well represented with a total of 25, while another 25 were artisans, ranging from pursemakers and locksmiths to hatmakers and mechanics. Engineers and other technical staff came to a total of 21. Students in various disciplines numbered 22, alongside 17 teachers who taught in primary or secondary schools. Other professional careers included law (5), clergymen (5), and medical personnel (8). There were 15 government employees, such as those who worked in the offices of the German railways. And there were at least 11 Party officials who devoted more or less full time to organizing and operating the *Ortsgruppen*. A miscellany of other jobs included unskilled labor (2), housewifery (2), librarianship (1), art (1), economist (1), aircraft pilot (1), social work (1). One person indicated he was unemployed, while the files on others show no indication of what their occupations were.

As to where the Nazis lived, the picture is made complicated by people moving from one lodging to another. This may have resulted in some double counting. A fair number were outside central London. About 20 resided in Surrey, 11 in Middlesex, nine in Hertfordshire, three in Kent, two in Buckinghamshire and one each in Essex and Cambridgeshire. Our standard for including them was whether they could readily commute into London for work and National Socialist gatherings. Within Greater London, about 20 lived in postcode E8, not far from the German Hospital. Otherwise, the East End housed a smattering of Nazis: three in E6; two each in E17, E9, and E5. There was only one each in postcodes E4 and E1. East Central London had four in EC1, and one each in EC3 and EC4. In the South East sector of Forest Hill and Sydenham, there were eight living in SE23, two in SE12, and one each in SE1, SE3, SE10, SE15, SE17, SE21, and SE27.

One of the largest concentrations was in South West London. About 32 resided in SW1, which was also the location of the German Embassy. Another eight were in SW15, seven in SW3, six in SW13, four in SW19, three in SW7, while three each were to be found in SW7, SW10, SW16, and SW18.

Additional pairs were housed in SW5, SW9, SW11, SW17, and SW20, whereas single individuals had addresses in SW2, SW14, and SW23.

The other area where Nazis preferred to congregate was West London. Thirty-four lived in W2, and another 15 in W1. In W5 there were six, in W8 five, and an equal number in W11. Four each were in W3, W13, and W14, two in W9, and one each in W4, W6, and W12. The West Central postcode, including the British Museum and the University of London, accounted for 12 in WC1 and two in WC2. Forty-two lived in North West London, 14 in NW3, followed by eight in NW1, six in NW2, four each in NW7 and NW8, and two each in NW4 and NW11. North London housed the fewest, with five in N6, four each in N3 and N4, and two each in N1, N16, and N22. The other sections had only one each: N5, N7, N10, N13, N14, N15, and N19.

What also complicates the pattern of residencies are the large numbers of unknown addresses. At least 75 Party members came to London and never told the *NSDAP* where they settled. Nevertheless, we have identified nearly 80 percent of their addresses.

During the years 1936–39 the *Landesgruppe Gross Britannien* had its own administrative staff, which changed according to arrivals and departures. While Bene was still *Landesgruppenleiter*, he designated Karl Markau, head of the German Chamber of Commerce, as his Deputy. However, Otto Karlowa chose not to have a deputy, although he kept Edmund Himmelmann as his personal Adjutant. Oskar Vogler remained throughout these years as treasurer, while Bene's secretary, Huberta Hartmann, was replaced by Liselotte Ahlefeldt between 1937 and 1939.

Other *Landesgruppe* officials were Günther Wilmsen who was in charge of the *Hitler Jugend* in 1936, followed by Otto Eichele in 1937. The counterpart for girls, the *Bund Deutscher Mädchen*, was administered by Luise Rieckhoff. Throughout this period, Kurt Frauendorf was leader of the *Deutsche Arbeitsfront*, while Bernard Schreppel oversaw the *Reichsbund Deutscher Beamten* (Federation of State Officials). Karl Markau and his assistant, Reinhold Lassen advised the *Landesgruppen* on commercial matters, while the journalist, Theodor Seibert, did the same regarding foreign policy issues. Whereas Bene appointed Gerhard Meissner to concern himself with Party members who were attorneys, this post seems to have disappeared under Karlowa. However, both Bene and Karlowa made use of a *Schlichter* to settle internal disputes and levy fines. Karl Heinz Kutschke first filled this role, followed by Max Funk.

The press officer for the *Landesgruppe* in 1936 was Günther Tonn, and afterwards, Hans Seligo. Education or more accurately indoctrination leader was R. G. Rösel. As *Kulturwart*, Pastor Gustav Schönberger was supposed to promote membership in the *Landesgruppen* among the broader German community.

Philanthropic efforts were not ignored, and National Socialist Welfare (*NS Volkwohlfahrt*) and the Winter Relief Program (*Winterhilfswerk*) were successively in the hands of Adolf Leipold (1936), Erna Dufour (1937) and Hans R. Dufour (1938). Under Karlowa there was also a group devoted to Veterans affairs (*Kriegsopferversorgung*, or *NSKOV*), which Bruno Anton took over from Ernst Hafels. On the recreational side, Hans Beckhoff coordinated outings into the countryside, showing films, and organizing sports. Gerhard Krause represented the Anglo-German Academic Bureau to visiting scholars, while Captain Adolf Eduard Jäger did the same for German seamen. The Teachers Federation (*Lehrerbund*) had Adolf Wegener as its coordinator.

Although the numbers cannot be precise, it is clear that the Nazi groups grew steadily during the 1930s. Even more rapid was the expansion of the German refugee community in Britain. Before the First World War, it has been estimated that there were 65,300 Germans living in the United Kingdom.[10] That segment of the population dipped dramatically during the war, and only rose gradually thereafter.[11] By 1931 it increased to about 28,000, but many of these had become British citizens during the 1920s, so by 1933 only about 6,000 German citizens remained in London, plus an unspecified number elsewhere in Britain.[12] Some held dual citizenship, but the German population nevertheless grew rapidly from 1933 on, reinforced greatly by political and religious exiles.

The following table lists the number of Germans who entered and departed from Britain for six out of the ten years during the 1930s, together with those who requested to stay for a longer period of time. Many who wished to remain were refugees, hoping to secure indefinite asylum and eventually qualify for British naturalization.[13]

1932: 25,471 entered; 23,645 departed; 1,826 remained.
1933: January–September only: 33,140 entered; 29,768 departed; 3,372 remained.
1934: figures not available.
1935: 59,026 entered; 57,150 departed; 1,876 remained.
1936: 74,870 entered; 71,734 departed; 3,136 remained.
1937: 80,236 entered; 78,255 departed; 1,981 remained.

Presumably, most who arrived and departed in a given year were tourists, short-term students, business trainees, and domestic servants. The steady rise in the number of Germans coming to Britain is extraordinary. Perhaps some felt that they could afford to travel because the German economy was beginning to be responsive to Nazi pump-priming. Among the considerable number of refugees, some arrived only to be told they could not stay beyond a designated number of weeks or months. However, a net increase of 2,000 to 3,000 long-term residents each year resulted in nearly 20,000 German immigrants in Britain by the end of the decade. This figure is consistent with those that the Government gave to Parliament.[14] The following table includes Austrians, since after the *Anschluss* in March 1938, Austrian citizens were reckoned to belong to the Third Reich.

Registered with the British Police

Early 1938: 20,000 Germans, 11,000 women.
14,000 Austrians, 11,000 women.

Early 1939: 22,000 Germans, 12,000 women.
16,000 Austrians, 13,000 women.

October 1939 (soon after outbreak of war):
62,244 Germans. 11,989 Austrians.

The phenomenal influx of exiles from German-held territory between September 1938 and the outbreak of war came about as a direct result of political and military events. During this twelve–month period the Nazis acquired part of Czechoslovakia in the Munich Agreement of September 1938, and the rest the following March. Thus, about 45,000 Germans, Austrians, and Czechs sought refuge in Britain during those fatal months. Among these were Germans who had been granted asylum in Czechoslovakia during the 1930s and who had to flee again once Germany had overrun the Czech nation. As the British absorbed these people, they were aware that some were militant Nazis who might intimidate or harass other refugees.

By 1936 the British press was actively debating these issues. The *News Chronicle* gave many Germans the benefit of the doubt. "Many have labour permits and are pursuing *bona fide* occupations in hotels, restaurants, and domestic service."[15] Other papers, like the *Daily Herald*, were more suspicious.[16]

> In a great new building there [Berlin], operated under the control of the German Foreign Office, there is an index file giving the name, address, occupation, friends, acquaintances, social and political activities of every German resident abroad – whether refugee or Nazi sympathizer. Part of the work of the Nazi network in London and the big cities is to pass on information to Berlin to keep those index files up to date. Scotland Yard men who speak fluent German have been on special duty for months learning of the plans and methods of the Nazi group over here.

This article also suggested that defenseless refugees had been targeted.

> Plans had been formulated which would make it difficult for German-Jewish refugees to live in this country without anxiety. There have been cases of searching by unknown visitors in the homes and flats of refugees. No Germans living in England dare be known to have contact with Jews, whether they be refugees or not.

The British Foreign Office, MI5, and the Home Offic, urged the Cabinet to oust all Nazi organizations and officials from the United Kingdom.[17] The Cabinet procrastinated, but eventually decided to take action. Their prime target was Otto Karlowa, and by early 1939 they felt they had enough evidence to justify expelling him. In Vansittart's note to Lord Halifax, the British Foreign Secretary, he laid out the charge against Karlowa.[18]

> Otto Karlowa, the *Landesgruppenleiter* in London, has been caught out trying to organise espionage and I always said that these German organisations would be used for that and sabotage. I think that he should be got rid of. Indeed I feel that the moment has come when as a matter of national precaution we should get rid of most of the dangerous people here.

Enclosed in this letter was a report jointly signed by Vansittart, Alexander Maxwell of the Home Office, and Vernon Kell of MI5, which provided more details about Karlowa's activities.[19] Karlowa had "instructed a German employee in a London company, which is a subsidiary of a German company, to report to him regularly and bring 'any information of interest' to the German author-ities."

By 22 March 1939 the British Cabinet was prepared to act, and declared that it would authorize the deportation of "a limited number of officials of Nazi organisations in this country who were engaged in undesirable activities."[20] Two days later Vansittart, the Foreign Secretary, and the Home Secretary drew up a short list of expellees and informed the German Government that it had been highly unusual to tolerate foreign organizations like the *Ortsgruppen* and the *Deutsche Arbeitsfront* in Britain. Furthermore, there was "no parallel in regard to British residents in Germany. . . . Certain members of these organisations had already indulged in actions which we would not condone. We were not prepared to give the German Government particulars of these actions, partly because this would compromise our sources. . . . There are in this country some sixty Germans who play the lead in organising, i.e. intimidating, Germans resident in this country."[21] While Vansittart and others wanted to get rid of them all, they admitted that the time was not right to "carry out any such sweeping opera-tion." It was therefore decided to "begin by specifying three Germans, of whom one would be Herr Karlowa, who had rendered their further stay in this country impossible."

Karlowa's Adjutant, Edmund Himmelmann, was an obvious second candi-date for expulsion, being one of the early recruits to the London *Ortsgruppe*, applying for membership in late 1931. In its early days, he was the secretary, then became deputy *Landesgruppenleiter* in 1935, serving as Adjutant to both Bene and Karlowa. He also acted as Steward at the Central London *Ortsgruppe*, living at group headquarters, 5 Cleveland Terrace, W2. In this capacity, some thought that he accrued inordinate personal profits from the sale of beer, sausages and other delicacies. In 1938 Himmelmann was found to be involved in a matter of great concern to the British Foreign Office.[22]

> The English company employed for some ten years as an interpreter a certain Herr Himmelmann. . . . Not long ago the company found it necessary to make certain changes which Himmelmann resented. He accordingly left the company and has since been heard to boast that he would get his own back and would one day be in control. Recently Himmelmann approached an employee of the English company and asked him to put him into touch with a certain other employee (both are English) named L. A. Gale, who is a mechanical engineer, – a man earning perhaps £5 or £6 a week. Gale had been a prisoner-of-war in Germany and his experiences seemed to have left him with a wholesome fear of the Germans.
>
> One evening Himmelmann arrived in a car at this man's house at No. 14, The Triangle, Woking, and asked him to accompany him to the German Embassy to make a statement. Rather frightened, Gale went with Himmelmann to the German Consulate, where he was questioned for four hours and finally signed a statement with which he was apparently assisted by Himmelmann, who was present all the time.

The story proliferated when Gale returned to the German Embassy the next day to ask a Consular official to give him a copy of the previous night's deposition which he took to the London firm of solicitors, Callingham, Ormond & Maddox, who contacted the Foreign Office. Gale's written document revealed that before leaving the English firm he had found some technical plans for new machinery that could prove embarrassing to the parent firm in Heidelberg, and he intended to blackmail the Heidelberg office into severing its connection with the London branch, thus getting revenge upon his former employer.

The Foreign Office reacted immediately. Frank Roberts snarled, "This is just the sort of interference and private spying which we feared might result from the activities of the *Auslandsorganisation*."[23] William Strang went further, "Subject to their report and the opinion of the Home Office, I think that our best course will probably be an intimation to the German Embassy that Himmelmann's presence here is no longer desirable.[24]

Yet Himmelmann was not asked to leave Britain at this time, presumably because his action was deemed primarily internal, and did not directly affect the lives or jobs of British subjects.

Unknown at the time, but revealed 30 years later by Georg Vogel, a Second Secretary at the German Embassy, there were further repercussions from this episode.[25] On the night in question, Vogel was asked to interrogate Gale and take his deposition, but declined because he thought the whole procedure was inappropriate and liable to greatly embarrass Germany if it became known that a British subject was being intimidated. Consequently, another Consular official recorded Gale's testimony. When Gale returned the next day to request a copy of the document he had signed, Vogel happened to be on duty and saw no reason why Gale should not be given a copy. When Karlowa learned what had happened, he was furious, and went to German Ambassador Dirksen to complain about Vogel, who was both a member of the Nazi Party and the *SS*. Vogel was soon transferred from London to Athens, and was never given the pay increases or promotions in rank which he deserved.

The third person designated for expulsion was Anna Johanna Ottilie Wolf, who came to the attention of MI5 and Special Branch during the summer of 1938.[26]

Finally, it was agreed that that Karlowa, Himmelmann, and Wolf must leave Britain by the end of April 1939.[27] As in the summer of 1937, the British hoped that the Germans would withdraw their Party officials rather than forcing the British to expel them. However, by mid-April the news about the deportations had not yet been made public, and the Home Office preferred to release the information to the press itself rather than have it leaked unofficially. Consequently, M.P.s were discussing the activities of Karlowa and Wolf as late as 18 April, not realizing that they were scheduled for imminent departure.[28]

On their side, the Nazis were unsure what to do if they lost their leader in Britain, and as Karlowa said to Bohle, the *Landsgruppe Gross Britannien* would be greatly undermined if it named a successor who was subsequently expelled.[29] They found it hard to accept that their behavior towards other Germans was reprehensible, since it was not only a natural expression of their fervor, but also an internal matter.

During the spring of 1939 the *Landesgruppe Gross Britannien* was outwardly intact and formidable, having commandeered the former Austrian Embassy for its headquarters where it was enjoying all the trappings of diplomatic respectability and immunity. In addition, it had a second office at 28 Cleveland Terrace, W2, that handled the business affairs of the Central London *Ortsgruppe* as well as providing space for the *Deutsche Arbeitsfront*. Membership in the three London *Ortsgruppen* was increasing steadily, and the various instructional and recreational activities of each group thrived.

Yet the British, spearheaded by Kell and Vansittart, had finally made the decision to curtail the operation of these foreign organizations, and if they could not rid themselves of all the Nazi officials at once, they would do it a few at a time.

NOTES

1    See chapter 4.
2    Karlowa file, BDC. See also PRO, FO 371/20741, C7183, f. 268; FO 371/21652, C12607, f. 159; *Völkishcer Beobachter*, 19 April 1940; *Kolnische Zeitung*, 27 April 1940; and Aussendeutscher *Volkenspiegel*, 27 April 1940.
3    E. W. Bohle to Goebbels, 3 October 1934, contained in the F.X. Hasenoehrl file, BDC.

4  This was the home of its *Ortsgruppenleiter*, Kal Schmidt.

5  Information about the various Stutzpünkte may be found in PRO, FO 371/19942, C5497, ff. 166–73; FO 371/20741, C7183, ff. 271–72; FO 371/21652, C7841, ff. 29–30.

6  PRO, FO 371/20741, C7183, f. 269; and PRO, FO 371/20739, C1937, f. 56.

7  *Daily Herald*, 11 August 1937; also PRO, FO 371/23035, C4279, ff. 370–74.

8  *NSDAP* membership files, BDC, supplemented by British Foreign Office files.

9  Claudia Koonz, *Mothers in the Fatherland* (New York, 1987), pp. 57 and 469.

10  *Deutsche Auslandsinstitut Schriften des DAI* (Stuttgart, 1935), I, 96.

11  J. J. Barnes and P. P. Barnes, "London's German Community in the Early 193s," *German Life and Letters*, XLVI (October 1993), 331–45.

12  *European Herald*, 18 July 1936, p. 1.

13  *Parliamentary Debates*, Commons, CCLXXXI (16 November 1933), 1094 and 1131; PRO, FO 371/21651, C3643, ff. 267–68.

14  PRO, FO 371/21651, C3643, ff. 267–68; PRO, FO 371/23035, C4279, ff. 370–74; and PRO, FO 372/3343, T14071, f. 255.

15  *News Chronicle*, 9 August 1937.

16  *Daily Herald*, 11 August 1937.

17  See chapter 14.

18  Vansittart to Halifax, 24 February 1939, PRO, FO 371/23-35, C4279, f. 369.

19  Report of 23 February 1939, *ibid.*, ff. 370–74.

20  Cabinet minute, 22 March 1939, PRO, FO 371/23035, C3890, f. 358.

21  Report of 24 March 1939, *ibid.*, ff. 251–57.

22  Internal FO memo, 14 January 1938, PRO, FO 371/21649, C130, ff. 103–7.

23  *Ibid.*, f. 103.

24  *Ibid.*, f. 105v.

25  Georg Vogel, *Diplomat unter Hitler und Adenauer* (Duesseldorf, 1969), pp. 47–50.

26  See chapter 10.

27  Halifax to G. Ogilvie-Forbes, 3 April 1939, PRO, FO 371/ 23035, C4820, ff. 395–98.

28  *Parliamentary Debates*, Commons, CCCXLVI (18 April 1939), 174.

29  Karlowa to Bohle, 14 April 1939, NA microcopy T-120, roll 49, frame 39432.

# 14

# THE GOVERNMENT'S DILEMMA: WHETHER TO OUTLAW FOREIGN ORGANIZATIONS

As early as May 1935 the British authorities began to think of ways to rid themselves of the Nazi *Landesgruppe*, propelled by Germany's creation of the *Wehrmacht*
and restoration of military conscription two months before. Sir Vernon Kell,
head of MI5, presented the Foreign Office with a preliminary report on the
*Auslandsorganisation*'s activities which pointed out that the *Landesgruppe* now
consisted of two *Ortsgruppen*: one in central London and another in Dalston, plus
several *Stutzpunkten* in Bradford, Birmingham, Hull, the Manchester–Liverpool
area, and the Welsh ports of Newport and Cardiff. Otto Bene, leader of the
*Auslandsorganisation*, was also in charge of a *Stutzpunkt* in Dublin. In all, the
*Landesgruppe* incorporated about 288 *NSDAP* members, of whom 67 were Party
officials. The entire *Landesgruppe Gross Britannien* had in its files upwards of 1,500
British subjects of German extraction who retained their German citizenship
either by being born in the United Kingdom, or of British parents while in
Germany. Kell was troubled about the implications of these figures.[1]

> Since the Nazi machine has unprecedented power over the individual, it can direct
> the energies of every member of the Party in any desired direction. If, as at present,
> the Führer desires English friendship, every man is abjured to act and speak with
> that end in view. We cannot lose sight of the fact that in certain eventualities the
> whole energy of the machine could be directed in the reverse direction. It is, for
> instance, a ready-made instrument for intelligence, espionage, and ultimately for
> sabotage work.

At the Foreign Office, Sir Robert Vansittart reacted swiftly to Kell's concern,
declaring that the Nazi organization in Britain "ought to be broken up now. It
is no good waiting for the trouble to occur. If it comes, we shall have very little
or no warning."[2] He urged MI5 to probe further into all aspects of the

*Landesgruppe* and produce a follow-up report, which was submitted in December 1935 and summarized in a memorandum depicting the clandestine behavior of Nazi Party officials in Britain:[3]

> At present most of these people have some thinly-veiled cover. For example: the head of the *Hitler Jugend* has described himself as a student and has been obtaining free education at the Wandsworth Secondary School; the head of the USCHLA, an *NSDAP* organisation concerned with questions of Party discipline, says that he is doing Canadian constitutional research work; while Otto Bene, the head of the whole organisation for Great Britain and Ireland, who once had a business cover, is now believed to be concerned solely with party matters. But before long we are bound to be faced with a request for an alien to remain here purely on the grounds that he is the representative of some branch of the *NSDAP*.

MI5 thought it pointless to deal with these individuals on a case-by-case basis because as soon as one was asked to leave Britain, another would replace him. What was needed, they maintained, was a policy that provided British authorities with concrete guidelines for specific situations. One suggestion was to allow individual Germans, even Party members, to reside in Britain as long as they did not affiliate with any group or branch of a German organisation while living here. They could retain their membership in a German society they already belonged to, but could not meet as a group. C. W. Baxter of the Foreign Office anticipated inevitable problems with these proposals. "It is possible that the suppression of Nazi organisations in this country would merely drive Nazi activities into underground channels where they would be more difficult to supervise and control."[4]

On 30 January 1936 Kell made a strong plea for concerted action.[5]

> Sir Vernon Kell points out that the information supplied by MI5 showed that while there was no positive evidence that the *Auslands-Organisation* was at present being used to serve purposes detrimental to British interests, it had dangerous potentialities. . . . Sir Vernon Kell said that there was some reason to suppose that pressure is put on British subjects of German extraction employed in important industries to induce them to join the Nazi Party. In such cases there must always be some apprehension lest pressure may be put on such members of the Nazi Party . . . to act in a way detrimental to the interests of this country. For instance, in time of peace they may be employed for purposes of commercial and military espionage. In case of war . . . these British subjects [would form] the nucleus of an organisation for intelligence and sabotage purposes.

He recommended that anyone with dual British–German nationality who joined the Nazi Party should be deprived of his or her British citizenship, and foreign countries be prohibited from establishing branches of their organizations on British soil.

In February, Kell and Vansittart received support for their hardline position from an unexpected quarter. In Switzerland, the Nazi leader, Wilhelm Gustloff, was assassinated, prompting the Swiss government at first to forbid the appointment of another *Landesgruppenleiter*, and then to outlaw the *Auslandsorganisation* altogether. Although the Germans protested, a precedent was established for the British to follow.

In early March, Germany remilitarized the Rhineland, and this growing menace provided Britain with a further reason to heighten security. A full-blown assembly of representatives from selected government departments met at the Home Office on 26 May 1936.[6] Guy Liddell and J. Clenny attended in behalf of MI5, while S. H. H. Mills represented MI6, the Secret Intelligence Service. C. J. W. Torr presented the Foreign Office point of view, while the Public Prosecutor, Sir Russell Scott, spoke for the Home Office. Present also were representatives of the Dominions Office, the Colonial Office, and the India Office.

Uppermost in their minds was the need to define British citizenship. Sir Russell Scott declared that the situation had become extremely complex since refugees from Germany were now seeking asylum in Britain and might well try to become naturalized. He therefore recommended that a Certificate of Naturalisation would no longer be granted to any foreigner belonging to an organisation such as the Nazi or Fascist party. However, once someone was naturalised, the government could not deprive that person of British citizenship and the subsequent right to join the Nazi Party. He worried about driving Nazis in Britain underground if their organization was outlawed, and questioned whether they were actually more of a threat than the Communists.

C. J. W. Torr reacted strongly to this comparison, and asserted that there was indeed an important distinction to be made between the two.[7]

> I pointed out that their aims were very different: the Communists were only dangerous if there was a likelihood of revolution; but the Nazi organisation was a branch of an organism which we had every reason to believe was preparing itself for total war.

Capt. Liddell of MI5 did not like it that there were about 300 Nazi Party Members in the United Kingdom.[8]

> The Nazi dictatorship was extending its control to Germans resident in this country, and not only were the actual Party members in this country at the beck and call of the German Government, but non-Party members could be influenced and controlled in a variety of ways.

Consequently, he submitted the following recommendations:

> (1) that foreigners who are members of branches of a foreign political party iden-

179

tified with the foreign government should be refused naturalisation; (2) that either (a) branches of such political parties established in this country should be banned, or (b) the naturalisation certificates of naturalised British subjects who are members of such parties should be revoked if they refuse to sign some undertaking of disassociation from the party.

He showed little concern that there would be adverse consequences as a result of implementing his proposals.

> If a spoke of some sort were inserted in the wheel, the organisation would operate less efficiently and be so much less a mischief. As far as actual illegal activities were concerned, there was probably as much difficulty in detecting them, if carried on by the present unhampered organisation, as there would be if that organisation were driven underground.

A few days after this meeting, Torr summarized the principal characteristics of the *Landesgruppe Gross Britannien* for the benefit of his Foreign Office colleagues.[9] First, it fostered a "patriotic spirit" among Germans abroad, encouraging members to help each other in business and professional circles, something which Torr regarded as perfectly legitimate, and typical of foreigners living in an alien society. Second, it generated favorable propaganda, just as the British did in a more subdued fashion through the British Council, or the British Library of Information in New York. Third, it supervised "the collection and coordination of information for the foreign affairs section of the Nazi Party headquarters — not necessarily a more obnoxious activity than that of any journalist or British subject resident abroad who gives advice to his own legation or to his office. This activity had potentially disturbing implications in that Party discipline might be used against both members and nonaligned Germans.

> Unless actual spying or preparations of acts of sabotage can be proved, it is not easy to say that the thing itself is contrary to the public good. On the other hand, it is perhaps in its ability to enforce discipline by a form of blackmail that the strength and therefore the potential dangerousness of the organisation lies. . . .

Torr was of mixed minds as to whether it would be possible to bring legal action for blackmail by an overly zealous Nazi against a fellow German, but he found the question of espionage simpler and more straightforward. "Espionage is a crime and can be dealt with as such when proved." Moreover, the spectre of sabotage implied that all 288 Nazi Party members would need additional surveillance, and if war broke out they would have to be jailed.

On 9 June Ralph Wigram, head of the Foreign Office Central Department, wrote to Vansittart concerning the recommendations drawn up at the meeting of 26 May, asking whether he thought that ridding Britain of foreign organisations would display a "manifest hostility" toward Germany, and whether His

Majesty's Government should consult the Dominions before taking unilateral action.[10]

> To take this line, however, would inevitably entail delay, and that may well be dangerous; for the longer we wait the greater prescriptive right these organisations acquire to maintain themselves here; the wider the ramifications they evolve here; and the more delicate become any representations to the governments concerned.

A month of frustrating delay ensued because Sir John Simon, the Home Secretary, did not reply to the several memoranda sent to him by the Foreign Office. On 8 July Wigram gave vent to his exasperation, noting that it was unfair to the other government departments when inaction by the Home Office was causing undue delay. Orme Sargent agreed, and suggested meeting during the following week before Parliament adjourned. On 15 July Vansittart formally requested such a meeting to include MI5, with Wigram representing the Foreign Office. This finally took place on 21 July, with Liddell and Clenny again presenting the views of MI5, and Scott repeating his concern that driving the Nazis underground would make the task of MI5 more difficult. Liddell disagreed.[11]

> Captain Liddell said that even now private meetings took place in private houses; he thought an effective watch could be maintained if the organisation became a secret one. He did not think that communication by couriers could be substituted for postal communications to such a large extent as to render useless the existing methods of supervision. The disorganisation and the ensuing difficulties under which the party organisations would labour if they could no longer be carried on openly would all be to our advantage; the secret activities would perforce be on a smaller scale and confined to certain channels.

Wigram was satisfied with the outcome of the meeting.[12]

> My own view is strongly in favor of the action suggested. *Viz.* a friendly request at least to the German Government . . . to take steps to wind up the organisations in question. MI5 are also strongly in favor of that course. Sir Russell Scott, who was at first inclined to be somewhat lukewarm, was I think very considerably impressed by the force of our arguments and has agreed to the draft.

However, it was now absolutely essential that both Secretaries of State sign the recommendations immediately in order that copies be made and circulated among the Cabinet before its final meeting of the summer session on 29 July. The resulting document bore the formidable title, "Proposed request to German and Italian Governments to secure the liquidation of branches of the National Socialist and Fascist Party Organizations established in the United Kingdom."[13] It covered many of the points in the memoranda from MI5 and the Foreign

Office, and was not expected to anger the Germans since they had not protested the recent refusal to appoint Otto Bene Consul-General in London.

Item 4 in the "Proposed Request" was new, and clearly took account of the fact that some members of the Cabinet regarded the Communists in Britain as an equal or greater threat than the Nazis.[14]

Item 5 suggested that an "informal and friendly" approach to the German and Italian embassies, asking them to dismantle "their party organisations in this country, the presence of which is considered unusual and undesired here." It was considered unwise to provide detailed explanations, but if the Germans and the Italians declined to take the hint, it was agreed that "we should probably be obliged to require the leading organisers and Party officials to leave the country."

Members of the Cabinet were reminded that MI5, the security arm of the nation, heartily supported the joint recommendation, but the possibility of serious repercussions existed, not only in Parliament and the press, but also for Anglo-German and Anglo-Italian relations.

According to the Cabinet minutes of the 29 July meeting:[15]

> In the course of a short discussion on this proposal there was general agreement that the present moment, when His Majesty's Government was trying to promote contacts between the British, Belgian, French, German, and Italian Governments, was inopportune for taking the action proposed. The Prime Minister suggested that it was the kind of point that might be raised towards the end of successful conversations. The Secretary of State for Foreign Affairs said he was only asking [for] authority to deal with the question when the opportune moment arrived. The Home Secretary developed the case in favor of the proposal and the First Lord of the Admiralty reported that MI5 took a serious view of the activities of these Nazi and Fascist organisations. It was suggested that if the question were raised with reference to Nazis and Fascists, there would certainly be a demand for a corresponding action towards the Communists, and much evidence was produced of the activity of the Communist movement in this country, not only among miners and in South Wales, but also in opposition to re-armament.

The following October the Cabinet revisited the topic of foreign organizations, but decided that the time was "inopportune" because Parliament was debating the Public Order bill which sought to regulate street demonstrations, political rallies, and provocative speeches.

January 1937 brought an ominous change of policy from Berlin regarding overseas Germans. Ernst Wilhelm Bohle's *Auslandsorganisation* would no longer be a Party appendage, but would become a part of the German Foreign Ministry. By mid-February MI5 responded with another memorandum to the Home Office and the Foreign Office, hoping they would concur in a further appeal to the Cabinet.[16]

Recent events in connexion with the development of the Party-State in Germany renders this question more acute and suggests that if action is to be taken at all it is desirable that it should be taken at an early date. . . . One effect of these changes is to give a new character to German embassies and consulates abroad and to make their members instruments of the Party as well as diplomatic or consular representatives.

MI5 maintained that there was a serious possibility of espionage or sabotage implicit in the existing circumstances.

Since the matter was last raised, there have been more definite indications of cooperation between the National Socialist Party organisation in London and the German intelligence service. Herr Otto Bene is known to have rendered some assistance to a branch of this service in Hamburg.

With the merging of the *NSDAP*'s *Auslandsorganisation* with the German Foreign Ministry, it was increasingly difficult for Britain to penetrate their ranks behind the cloak of diplomatic immunity. MI5 already had contingency plans to expel at least 100 Nazis belonging to the groups such as the *Deutsche Arbeitsfront*, the Anglo-German Academic Bureau, Hitler Youth, and the *Ortsgruppen* and *Landesgruppe*. The German Chamber of Commerce in London was immune, since it concerned itself more with business than ideology.

The Foreign Office indicated that Vansittart was prepared to support the memorandum if Sir Russell Scott and Sir Vernon Kell would do likewise,[17] but somewhat predictably, each constituency waited for the next to act, engaging in a kind of inter-office minuet. As Eden explained to Simon:[18]

From a purely Foreign Office point of view, moreover, I should naturally be disinclined to see action taken which might be expected to make our relations more difficult with Germany and Italy, but I should be of course very ready to face any disadvantages such action might entail in this respect if the organisations were a proved danger to our internal security.

There things rested for several more months. Meanwhile, Vansittart thought he could buttress the case for outlawing foreign organizations by citing the Union of South Africa mandate governing the former German colony of South-West Africa where the rights of non-British subjects were severely limited. They could not hold office, speak in public, or belong to political parties; and British citizens could not pledge allegiance to any foreign state. On 4 April 1937 Vansittart endorsed this precedent: "I should like to recommend the South African example as a model. I see no reason why we should not follow it. I have been urging action of this nature for at least a year now."[19]

There was another ingredient militating a prompt Cabinet decision: Joachim von Ribbentrop's appointment as German Ambassador to London increased the potential that the German Embassy would become a haven for Nazi intrigue. As a revised memorandum to the Cabinet stated:[20]

> It has also been reported from a reliable source that active steps are being taken by the German Ambassador to perfect the German arrangements for propaganda and espionage in this country and that Germans abroad are either summoned to return to Germany or are subjected to business pressure.

In June 1937 Neville Chamberlain replaced Stanley Baldwin as Prime Minister, and Samuel Hoare succeeded John Simon at the Home Office. Hoare could not ignore the problem posed by foreign organizations because Winston Churchill wrote to him saying that he intended to raise it during Question Time in the House of Commons.[21]

> I propose to ask you some questions about this position on lines which will be apparent from this letter. Before doing so I should like to give the fullest possible notice, and to learn how you feel about it. In my opinion the organisation of foreigners into bodies of this kind ought not to be permitted, and unless redress were given by the governments in question, special measures should be taken against members of the organisation in the sense of inviting them either to report at much more frequent intervals, or to return to their native land.

He added that there were now some 18,000 German males and 20,000 Italians living in Britain, but in times past, "foreigners living in England have lived here as individuals, and not as part of an organised national and political unit."

Hoare told Eden that he was prepared to raise the issue in the Cabinet, but wondered whether it might not be better to use a jointly-signed memorandum which would disguise which ministry was responsible for the action. This approach would merely pose the growing menace of foreign organizations, rather than strongly recommend any one course of action. Eden was agreeable to having the Cabinet grapple with the topic again, yet he cautioned, "My feeling is, as you yourself added in your postscript, that the present moment, with so much tension about, is scarcely an ideal one for any such action."[22] This reluctance on the part of his political superiors greatly frustrated Vansittart.

On 14 July 1937, almost a year later, the Cabinet formally considered the actual and potential risks associated with Nazi and Fascist Party groups in Britain.[23]

> The Cabinet agreed: (a) That the question could not be allowed to drift indefinitely and must be kept under continuous observation; but that, in view of the existing difficulties in securing agreement over questions relating to Spain, no drastic action should be taken at the moment, (b) To draw the attention of the Home Secretary to the need for exercising great care as to granting naturalisation to members or ex-members of the organisation referred to in his Memorandum.

184

Not surprisingly, Vansittart was bitterly disappointed.[24]

Action has hitherto been postponed in pursuit of a Western Agreement: now it
is in pursuit of a Spanish settlement. But both these objects, and reasons for delay,
are likely to prove will o' the wisps. Meanwhile the organisations continue to
strike deeper roots. I suppose this means that all possibility of action will be gone
till towards the end of the year. I am uneasy about this. I suppose there is no
deterrent of intermediate action that the H.O. can devise meanwhile.

In August 1937, a stir was created in London by the expulsion of three Nazi
journalists. This in turn fanned a press campaign against the subversive activities of the *NSDAP* in Britain which became the subject of a conference of
overseas Germans who met in Stuttgart, the Third Reich's center for Germans
abroad. One speech after another by Nazi luminaries such as Bohle, von
Neurath, Hess, Göring, Frank and Goebbels, reiterated that Germans were
peaceful, law-abiding, and non-political when resident in foreign lands; they
were preoccupied with maintaining ties with their homeland, sharing in traditional German festivities, fostering German culture, and assisting one another
in an alien environment.

About a month later, when Bohle came to London for conversations with
Churchill, Eden and others, primarily to reassure the British that they need have
no fear of Germans in their midst, he told the German community assembled
in Porchester Hall on 1 October:[25]

It was no part of the task of these groups to propagate National-Socialist ideas
among citizens of other countries, but their task was to make the life of German
citizens abroad conform to National-Socialist ideas and to the life of Germans
at home. It was therefore nonsense to talk of Nazi members abroad as agitators
or agents of the German Secret police.

On almost every occasion when Bohle was called upon to defend the behavior
of Nazis abroad, including the Nuremberg trials, he referred to an official Nazi
handbook which set forth the following rules.[26]

(i) Obey the laws of the land whose guest you are.
(ii) Leave the politics of the land whose guest you are to its inhabitants. The
internal politics of a foreign country do not concern you. Take no part in them,
even in conversation.
(iii) Avow everywhere and always the fact that you are a member of the Party.
(iv) Always conduct yourself in speech and action in such a way as to honour
the National Socialist movement and therewith the New Germany. Be
honourable, honest, fearless and true.
(v) Regard every German abroad as your fellow citizen, as a man of your blood,
your sort and your nature. Give him your hand without regard to his class. We
are all the "creative workers" of our people.

(vi)   Give heartily, and without waiting to be asked, help to your German fellow citizen when he falls into distress through no fault of his own.

(vii)  Be not merely a member but a first-line soldier. Inform yourself exactly about the nature, substance, and object of our Movement.

(viii) Canvass and fight daily for the entry of every honest German into our Movement. Convince him of the superiority and rightness of our Movement and of the certainty of our victory in order that Germany may live. Fight with spiritual weapons.

(ix)   Read our Party journal and pamphlets and books.

(x)    Unite with your Party comrades in the place where you are living. If a *Stutzpunkt* or an *Ortsgruppe* exists in that place, you must be a disciplined and active member of it. Avoid creating conflicts; struggle instead with all your might to solve any difficulties which may arise.

The *Auslandsorganisation* predictably underplayed the role of Party members abroad, but the Foreign Office continued to be concerned. William Strang, who replaced the deceased Ralph Wigram as head of the Central Department, resurrected the issue in September and reviewed the by-then familiar arguments, concluding that even if His Majesty's Government told the Germans to moderate their Party groups abroad and withdraw some of their more objectionable partisans, there was no way to prevent them from pursuing alternative measures and providing substitutions.[27]

> I am therefore not convinced of the wisdom of embarking on conversations with the German Embassy on this subject, at the present stage at any rate. If the Cabinet will not let us act as we propose (and I fear that with the delay it is becoming more and more difficult to take action: what could have been done in comparative quiet a year ago would now create a first-class storm after all that has been said at Stuttgart), our best course will probably be to continue to watch carefully, and to turn out anybody whom we catch seriously misbehaving.

This judgment was another serious blow to Vansittaart's campaign to move ahead, but there was more to come. Alexander Cadogan, who replaced Vansittart as Permanent Under-Secretary of State when Vansittart became an adviser to the Cabinet, issued his own memorandum after reviewing the situation.[28]

> Perhaps I am not fully documented on this question, but it has always seemed to me – and the draft seems to confirm my doubts, that we have never been entirely clear what our grievance is, or what we want. As it is now admitted that the question may develop into a first-class row, it does seem important to consider the position carefully. . . . It is suggested that we should demand (1) that no British subject should be a member; (2) that no undue pressure should be exercised on German nationals in this country: (3) that no member of the German Embassy should occupy himself with their administration. As regards (1) isn't that for us? Can't we forbid British subjects to join? As for (2), this has always rather puzzled

me. If a non-Nazi German has managed to establish himself in England outside the clutches of the Party, and with no need or intention of returning to Germany, how can the Organisation exercise undue pressure on him more than on a British subject? If he has the need or the intention to return to Germany, of course he is subject to pressure, whatever we may say or do about these organisations. As regards (3), is this a necessary or legitimate demand? What I really want to be sure about is that we aren't having a row about nothing.

The day after Cadogan penned these comments, Vansittart tried his best to repair the damage. He expressed his support for the latest draft memorandum, but emphasized that only MI5 was keeping surveillance of the leading Nazis in Britain. Symptomatic of the confusion that prevailed within the Foreign Office, Vansittart had to instruct the British Ambassador in Berlin, Neville Henderson, not to discuss the question of foreign organisations until the British had formulated a coherent policy.[29]

There was no further approach to the Cabinet. Occasionally the topic surfaced, as it did in April 1938 when Maxwell at the Home Office said that he did not find analogies with Switzerland and South Africa convincing, and suggested that it was up to the Foreign Office, not the Home Office, to pursue the question.[30]

Vansittart found Maxwell's arguments feckless, if not contemptible. To the Foreign Secretary, Lord Halifax, he lamented that Maxwell had entirely missed the point of the repeated Foreign Office memos. "What is suggested is that in the future societies will become not engines of propaganda, but of sabotage and espionage in case of war or the menace of war."[31] As for the Foreign Office taking the initiative, Vansittart was reminded of Sir John Simon, the former Home Secretary and current Chancellor of the Exchequer, who succeeded in delaying things for months on end. "The author of the argument is now apparent," he said resignedly.

Ironically, things looked different to Maxwell a year later. By then not only had Austria disappeared as an independent nation, but so had Czechoslovakia. As he told Vansittart, his views had changed and he was now in favor of expelling some of the local Nazi leaders, even if that meant retaliation by the Germans.[32]

In early 1939 the British Foreign Ministry remained convinced that there was no need to worry about German reaction to stiff measures against some of the members of the *Landesgruppe Gross Britannien* because it was less and less likely that Britain and Germany could settle their differences and negotiate a meaningful peace. Alone, Vansittart continued to repeat his warning: "The real issue is, are we to leave all these agents undisturbed and undiminished here till war actually breaks out? If we do, we shall have sabotage and espionage in plenty. Can we not weed them out in advance?"[33]

NOTES

1   Although this report, dated May 1935, no longer survives in the Foreign Office files, it is summarized in "Memorandum on the question of the possibility of proceeding against the Nazi and Fascist organisations established in the U.K.", 9 June 1936, PRO, FO 371/19942, C4162, ff. 148–52.
2   *Ibid.*
3   Memorandum of 12 December 1935, *Ibid.* C1111, ff. 86–87.
4   *Ibid.*
5   Kell's report is summarized in the FO memorandum mentioned in note 1.
6   PRO, FO 371/19942, C4013, ff. 123–33.
7   Torr memorandum, 2 June 1938, *ibid.*
8   See Note 6 above.
9   *Ibid.*
10  Wigram to Vansittart, 9 June 1936, *ibid.*, C4162, f. 144.
11  21 July 1936, PRO, FO 371/199423, C5519, f. 174.
12  *Ibid.*
13  *Ibid.*, C6013, ff. 179–80.
14  *Ibid.*
15  *Ibid.*, C6014, ff. 182–83.
16  Draft memorandum, PRO, FO 371/20739, C1937, ff. 47–58.
17  Strang to Liddell, 19 Feb. 1937, *ibid.*, f. 52.
18  Home Office to Foreign Office, 2 April, and Eden to Simon, 16 April 1937, *ibid.*, C2911, ff. 135–39.
19  *Ibid.*, C2910, f. 129.
20  For the memorandum jointly agreed upon by Vansittart, Scott and Kell, dated 15 March 1937, and later revised, see: *Ibid.*, C2089 and C2010, ff. 72–77, 127–34.
21  Churchill to Hoare, 21 March 1937, *ibid.*, C5002, f. 200.
22  Hoare to Eden, 25 June 1937; and Eden to Hoare, 29 June 1937, *ibid.*, ff. 199 and 201.
23  *Ibid.*, C5161, ff. 213–15.
24  Vansittart to Eden, 24 July 1937, *ibid.*
25  FO memorandum, 5 October 1937, PRO, FO 371/20740, C6886, f. 135.
26  *Ibid.*, f. 137.
27  Strang's memorandum, 13 September 1937, *ibid.*, C6306, ff. 46–57.
28  Cadogan's memorandum, 21 September 1937, *ibid.*, C6378, f. 60.
29  Vansittart to G. Ogilvie-Forbes, 24 September 1937, *ibid.*, C6378, f. 65.
30  Maxwell to Halifax, 12 April 1938, PRO, FO 371/21652, C8324, ff. 34–38.
31  Vansittart to Halifax, 19 April 1938, *ibid.*, f. 36.
32  Maxwell to Vansittart, 21 March 1939, PRO, FO 371/23035, C4280, ff. 375–77.
33  Vansittart's minute, 24 January 1939, *ibid.*, C4278, f. 362v.

# 15 GERMAN JOURNALISTS: FIRST TARGETS FOR EXPULSION

Since the British Cabinet was reluctant to outlaw Nazi organizations in London, it was up to the Home Office, with the aid of Special Branch and MI5, to identify any undesirable aliens. Ideally it was always preferable to refuse them entry into the country rather than deport them afterwards. The problem was to know in advance which of the thousands of arriving Germans were sinister, and which were tourists or commercial travelers.

On 10 April 1937 it was apparent that Customs at Harwich had been tipped off in advance about Otto Karl Ludwig even before he disembarked, because they immediately subjected him to a rigorous search, and confiscated all his papers, address book, foreign currency, and suspicious-looking blueprints.

On 12 April he was brought before a Police Court near Harwich and formally arraigned. As the *New York Times* reported, Ludwig was "charged with an illegal attempt to enter Britain and with possession of documents calculated to constitute an act preparatory to the commission of an offense under the Official Secrets Act."[1] He was described as tall, slim and middle aged. He spoke little or no English and needed the assistance of an interpreter. For those in the know, the presence in court of Lt. Col. W. E. Hinchley-Cooke of the War Office meant that MI5 was involved as well.

Two weeks later the *New York Times* completed this modest saga of intrigue by recounting how Ludwig had been released on 27 April, and told to leave the country immediately. "It was explained in court today that his arrest was based on his possession of plans for an armor piercing bullet about which he refused to explain but which, officials later learned, he possessed quite properly."[2] *The Times* of London put it slightly differently, suggesting that what was initially thought to be secret turned out not to be, and thus Ludwig could be discharged.[3]

It all seemed to be the proverbial tempest in a teapot, but Ludwig knew otherwise. He knew that in his confiscated papers were the names and addresses of seven Germans resident in Britain with whom he was to make contact, and in some instances, reimburse for services rendered. These seven had been supplying him with various kinds of information, some political, some economic and some National Socialist. What he did with this information is uncertain, although the presumption is that there were several organizations or agencies in Germany who were the recipients. In other words, Ludwig may have been running a private news agency in Germany, supplying his clients with material they could not otherwise secure from the highly censored German press.

Ludwig suspected that he had been betrayed by someone in the confidence of the German authorities, or else how could the British have spotted him even before he went through Customs and Passport Control.[4] In this he was correct, but at the time neither he nor the Germans could figure out who it was. Only after the Second World War did Wolfgang Gans Edler zu Putlitz, head of the Passport section of the German Embassy in London, acknowledge his role.[5] He was, as we have already seen,[6] accustomed to alerting the British Home Office to dubious Nazi travelers, and in the case of Ludwig, a distinctly undesirable alien. While Ludwig was in custody, Putlitz quietly perused the papers which had been seized and helped the British to determine the purpose of Ludwig's mission.

Whoever was behind Ludwig in Germany brought pressure on the German Foreign Ministry to secure his release. Ironically it fell to Putlitz as head of the Consular Section to arrange for Ludwig's legal defense. Somehow Ludwig got the impression from his British lawyers that Putlitz was impugning his loyalty to Germany by implying that he had been released after telling the British inter-rogators too much. He was baffled as to why he had been released so soon, and why the story of armor-piercing bullets had been concocted for his benefit. From MI5's point of view, the explanation was simple: they did not want to reveal to the public what they had learned from Ludwig's papers, nor did they wish to compromise their source, Putlitz. For perhaps the wrong reasons, Ludwig put the blame on Putlitz for spreading unfounded rumors, and contrived to have him summoned to Germany for questioning.

Not surprisingly, Putlitz was filled with apprehension at the prospect of a Gestapo interrogation. On the other hand, if he tried to excuse himself from attending, or hesitated to cooperate with the German investigation, he would implicate himself. His only hope was to tough it out and give the impression that he was anxious to be of assistance, trusting that his bluff would succeed. It did, and he was soon back in London.

Meanwhile, MI5 and Special Branch were interrogating the men and women mentioned in Ludwig's list. By the end of June and beginning of July they were ready to share their results with the Home Office and the Foreign Office. Since most of the seven implicated were nominally journalists, it was natural for the Home Secretary, Samuel Hoare, to ask whether Britain needed to tolerate quite so many as the reputedly eighty German correspondents in London.[7]

It seems highly probable that a large part of their activities is not legitimate journalism but consists in the collection of secret intelligence for the German Government, and this view is strongly confirmed by specific information which came to light in the course of inquiry into the Ludwig case.

Hoare proposed to Foreign Secretary Eden that three or four of the implicated journalists be expelled right away, while the others be sent later in order not to unduly provoke the German Government. Eden acquiesced, and it was the end of July before deportation orders were issued.

Despite their best efforts, the British Foreign Office and MI5 were never quite sure whether Ludwig was who he said he was. Decades later, the German Foreign Office was uncertain as well, believing that Ludwig's real name was Friedl. Complicating the task of identifying him is the fact that Ludwig's membership cards in the Nazi Party and the SS are missing from the vast files of the Berlin Document Center. Were they removed at the time to cover his tracks, or did someone discard them during the postwar period?

Fortunately for our purposes, one partial file was overlooked: a census of Nazi Party members in Berlin in 1939.[8] This verifies that Otto Ludwig was indeed his real name, and that his date of birth was 3 June 1897. In 1939 his Berlin address was Paulbornerstrasse 49, Grunewald. He joined the *NSDAP* on 1 May 1932 with membership number 1197056 which listed his occupation as *Angestallter*, a white-collar employee or clerk.

He may have been a member of the SS, but in 1939 he was described as *Foerderndes Mitglied der SS*, meaning that he was a member of an auxiliary organization which permitted him to wear an SS pin. Whatever Ludwig's mission was in 1937, his arrest certainly had substantial repercussions.

High on the list of those to be expelled was the 40–year-old Werner Bonaventura Crome, representative of the Berlin-based newspaper, the *Lokal-Anzeiger*, published by the Scherlverlag. He arrived in Britain on 12 May 1934, indicating he was affiliated with the *Hessische Landeszeitung*. A report by MI5 noted:[9]

> He is not a member of the Nazi Party but is doing his best to curry favour with them in order to get into the Party. . . . In April 1937, Crome was heard to state that he had found the Japanese Embassy very useful for information on naval matters, and especially on British naval matters. . . . When questioned about this by Hinchley-Cooke on 15 April, Werner Crome admitted knowing Ludwig under the name of Friedl, and that he had been supplying Ludwig with secret intelligence reports, for which he had received up to date RM3,000.

At the exchange rate then current, this amounted to about £240. Crome also told Ernst Woehrmann, Councilor to the German Embassy, that he had willingly turned over to the British authorities copies of some of his reports to Ludwig to prove that they dealt with neither espionage nor other illegal topics.[10]

Also asked to leave Britain at this time was Crome's twenty-seven year old secretary, Maria Louise Edenhofer. Like Crome, she was a German citizen, not a member of the Nazi Party. She had come to Britain in October 1931 to seek employment as a domestic servant for £35 a year, and began working for Crome in August 1935. According to MI5:[11]

> Money for her salary comes from Germany and is paid through Messrs. Scherl News Agency of Berlin. . . . She was well-known to Ludwig, the German recently arrested at Harwich, and was one of the persons he was coming to visit and probably pay when he was arrested.

When Hinchley-Cooke interrogated her on 15 April he learned that she had been the person who introduced Ludwig to Crome. She had known Ludwig since 1930, and was recruited by him in 1936 to send private reports on the British situation for RM900 per month. Like Crome, she only knew Ludwig by the name Friedl.

The third potential deportee was another non-Party member and Crome's assistant at the *Lokal-Anzeiger*, Franz Otto Wrede. Born in 1912, he was a recent arrival to the United Kingdom, entering on 23 January 1937 and declaring himself a journalist. although MI5 eventually learned otherwise.[12]

> It has however been found that he is employed by the Bureau Ribbentrop from Berlin and that he is not a journalist at all. He was issued with a press card by the *Scherlverlag* on instructions from the German Ministry of Propaganda. This was done to provide a cover for his real work over here, which is apparently connected with the Hitler Youth Movement and with the spreading of propaganda.

Undoubtedly it was embarrassing for Ribbentrop, the German Ambassador in London, to have one of his staff detected. On the other hand, the British were pleased to be able to rid themselves of Wrede because his wife was actively organizing a branch of the *Bund Deutscher Mädel* (League for German Girls) in London.

A fourth possible expellee was not so much a journalist as a businessman, one of the founding members of the London *Ortsgruppe*, and another of Ludwig's agents. Baron Fritz Tassilo Krug von Nidda came to Britain in 1927 and married an English woman. He had his own business in London and lived at 45 Etchingham Park Road, N3. He was very active in the Nazi Party until his sudden expulsion in 1934, subsequently explained by MI5:[13]

> He was suspended from membership of the *Organisation* [NSDAP] by Hitler's order when it was found that he was an active Freemason. Since then he has been attempting to curry favour with the Party and we have good reason to suspect him of acting as a Gestapo agent. . . . When questioned by Hinchley-Cooke on 17 April, in connexion with the papers found on Ludwig, Krug von Nidda admitted that he had been writing up political intelligence reports, which had been sent under cover to Berlin, and that he had received a retainer of £20 per

month for doing so. In connexion with an Austrian named Holzer he was involved in arms deals in Germany through Ludwig.

Krug von Nidda's explanation of his activity was that his firm, Nottark Co. Ltd., solicited patents in Britain and on the Continent; and Holzer, an engineer, had developed a process for making amour-piercing shells. Blueprints for this project had been entrusted to Ludwig to convey to potential arms dealers, and these were the documents that Ludwig was carrying back to him. Nevertheless, Krug von Nidda, along with the three other supposed journalists on Ludwig's list, had to leave Britain in August 1937.

Another self-styled journalist, Wolfgang Dietrich von Langen, came to the attention of the British Foreign Office in early February 1937 as the result of an article in the *News Chronicle* which stated that he was among those being considered as a replacement for Otto Bene as *Landesgruppenleiter* in London.[14]

> He has been chosen not because of any special knowledge of English conditions, but because the Italian Government has refused to extend his permit to stay in Italy beyond the middle of February. . . . Herr von Langen has ruled the German colony in Rome, which is very large, with an iron rod. Parents were compelled to send their children to the uniformed Hitler Youth. At the frequent meetings of the Party, attendance was enforced by threats of denunciation and military discipline was kept.

The British Foreign Office was especially interested in von Langen if, in fact, he were to succeed Bene. They made inquiries as to where the information originated, including an appeal to Vernon Bartlett of the *News Chronicle* who put them in touch with Richard Freund, a free-lance journalist of liberal Czech–German background who was also Jewish. Freund told Bartlett that he had learned the information about von Langen while visiting a German friend in Rome.[15]

> His relations with the German Embassy people, who were rather scared of him, were notoriously bad. I was told of a number of cases in which he had used threats of denunciation, and even threats of physical violence, to press Germans into the Nazi group.

Freund did not think von Langen was involved in military espionage, adding, "I can imagine that his offence was nothing worse than tactlessness toward the various prominent Italians."

By about this time it became certain that Otto Bene would accept a diplomatic appointment to Milan, and that Otto Karlowa would assume the position of *Landesgruppenleiter*. No thought was given to von Langen until he appeared in June as working journalist for *Zeitungsdienst Graf Reischach*, the National Socialist Newspaper Service, and was given a "conditional permit" to work in Britain for three months with an optional extension. Attaching himself to the office of the

*Graf Reischach* agency at 15 Carleton Road, SW15, he was oblivious of the maneuvering against him in official British governmental circles.

On 30 July von Langen was handed a letter from the Home Office requesting that he leave the country. Since he thought he had behaved correctly since coming to Britain, he was taken by surprise and immediately sought the assistance of the German Ambassador who asked the Foreign Office to reconsider. Von Langen's expulsion was postponed until 7 August, but in spite of several conferences between German diplomats and British officials as well as a personal phone call from Ribbentrop to Vansittart while the former was on holiday in Scotland, there was no change of British policy. The British would only intimate that von Langen was being asked to leave not because of anything done in England, but because of past actions in Rome.

The Germans were convinced that the British were unduly influenced by the articles of Mme. Geneviève Tabouis in the newspaper *Oeuvre*, in which she claimed that von Langen was in London for Nazi Party, not journalistic purposes. For background on Mme Tabouis, the Foreign Office relied on the annual biographical sketches on "Personalities" compiled by the British Embassy in Paris where she was said to possess "innumerable sources of information, the greater part of which are completely unreliable," and had "no sense of discrimination and tends to exaggerate and over-dramatise what she hears."[16] Despite this assessment, the Foreign Office stood firm, and the Home Office agreed.[17]

> Our information from MI5 is that von Langen is a highly placed Nazi official . . . who, in addition to carrying out the normal duties of the *Landesgruppenleiter*, which included spying on the German Ambassador undercover of journalism, became involved in military espionage and was asked to leave Rome by the Italian authorities. The recommendation of MI5 is that von Langen should be told to leave the United Kingdom forthwith. . . .

After the Foreign Office reviewed the expulsion order, they referred it to Guy Liddell of MI5 who acknowledged that von Langen was the subject of a Secret Intelligence Service (MI6) report.[18]

> He was in some way connected with Göring, and this no doubt explained von Ribbentrop's excitement. . . . The general ground of our objection to his staying here is that if Rome was too hot for him, we certainly don't want him here, particularly in view of his non-journalistic activities. Also, there are far too many German journalists here already.

Vansittart agreed, and discounted the not-so-veiled threats which Ribbentrop and other Germans were making which might bring about a worsening of Anglo-German relations. "If you once give way to threats of this kind, we shall be blackmailed into keeping a host of German undesirables in this country, and there are far too many already."[19]

The German Foreign Ministry's inquiry into von Langen's activities in Rome produced contradictory evidence. According to von Plessen, the German Councilor in Rome, there was nothing of substance to British and French reports. Von Langen's journalistic work had been lengthy and thorough, and the fact that he was one of the journalists who accompanied Mussolini to Tripoli showed clearly that he was not in trouble with the Italians. Finally, his work as *Ortsgruppenleiter* had been perfectly satisfactory.[20]

This paradox is disturbing. Either von Langen acted quite improperly in Rome, or MI5 and MI6 got it wrong, and von Langen was no different than other Nazi journalists and Party leaders abroad. A third alternative is that von Plessen was less than candid in his assessment, since the sharpest criticisms of von Langen originated from the German diplomatic colony in Rome which would not have wanted to initiate controversy over an *Ortsgruppenleiter* and presumed favorite of Göring's.

Another casualty of the von Langen deportation was his assistant Frau Ilse Zinzow. As a spokesperson for the Press Department of the German Foreign Ministry complained to a British diplomat in Berlin, Frau Zinzow was only a "harmless lady typist," and it would be considered an unfriendly act by the British authorities to punish her for whatever they held against von Langen.[21] Zinsow came to London at the beginning of July from Berlin where she had worked as a secretary for the Propaganda Ministry. Her duties with *Graf Reischach* and von Langen commenced on 8 July, and within about three weeks she was asked to leave. Perhaps the Home Office and the Foreign Office knew that she was more involved in National Socialism than she appeared to be. Her membership in the *NSDAP* dated from January 1931, and from 1933–35 she worked in London for, among others, Werner Crome. Had the British known this, it would not have enhanced her case, but what clinched her dismissal was the pretext she used for returning to London in July 1937.[22] She told the Immigration official that she had come to England for only four to five weeks as a journalist, and she planned to attend a conference.[23] By the time her appeals were exhausted, she left London on 19 August. Along with Krug von Nidda, Crome, Wrede, Edenhofer, and von Langen, she was the sixth person asked to leave the country within three weeks.

Inevitably, the Germans retaliated. On 9 August the German Councilor in London, Ernst Woehrmann, told Vansittart that Norman Ebbutt, *The Times* correspondent in Berlin, would have to return to England. The Germans claimed that their decision was not in reprisal for Crome and the others, and in a sense this was true. For years they had wanted an excuse to get rid of the overly-critical Ebbutt, and now they could seize the opportunity and not incur a protest from the British. On the other hand, as Vansittart pointed out, the cases were quite different. Crome, Wrede, and the others were undesirable because of their extra-journalistic activities, whereas Ebbutt was being ousted on account of his reportorial responsibilities. Furthermore, if expulsions escalated, Germany would be the obvious loser. "I must point out to him that there were something like 80 German journalists in this country and only about a dozen British journalists in Germany."[24]

To avoid the appearance of retaliation for Ebbutt's departure from Berlin, the British Home Office and the Foreign Office postponed the expulsion of three other German correspondents who had been implicated in the Ludwig affair. One of these was Karl Friedrich Basedow, who claimed to work for the *New York Times* in Berlin, and who made periodic trips to London, staying at 140 Piccadilly.[25] Since each of his visits lasted only a few weeks, he was not required to register with the police, and therefore they had no photograph of him on file. MI5 commented that "he has been showing an undue interest in naval matters," involving not only British waters but along the Mediterranean as well.[26] He was known to impersonate a British subject when casually chatting with British seamen, and he once tried to board a British warship at Gibraltar in the guise of a curious British tourist.

Since Basedow was not in London at the time of the other deportations, Foreign Office concern was for the future, should he return. This could be solved if the Germans were willing to restrict his travel to London. When the subject was broached to the German press attaché to the Embassy in London, FitzRandolph, in January 1938, he was remarkably agreeable. C. W. Baxter later observed: "Dr. FitzRandolph was by no means sorry that we had acted as we did."[27] FitzRandolph could be accommodating because doing so involved no one currently resident in London, and he knew that the British could refuse Basedow entry whenever they liked.

Two other correspondents on Ludwig's list were not German citizens, but ostensibly worked for German newspapers in London. Erna Fiedelholz held a Lithuanian passport when she came to Britain in July 1933 as the accredited representative of the *Kölnische Illustrierte Zeitung*. Her main interest was the Royal Air Force, and MI5 kept track of her visits to airfields and her other activities focused on flying. In November 1936 she aroused suspicion in and about Rochester, Kent, by asking questions about aircraft which were on the "secret lists."[28]

> Mutilated copies of aeroplane journals were frequently found in her dustbin. . . .
> In March, 1937, she received a letter from Germany asking her in her future letters to refer to sums of money under cover of reference to series of photographs. Her informant stated that he had made contact with a military paper whose editor would take photographs dealing with military matters, and asked her to let him have any military photographs she came across.

MI5 concluded with the observation that she possessed two special cameras.

Early in October 1937, after a suitable delay following previous expulsions,

Fiedelholz was given two weeks to wind up her affairs and leave Britain. In a panic, she consulted Rabinavicius, the Councilor of the Lithuanian Legation in London. He in turn made inquiries of Collier at the British Foreign Office. After satisfying himself that she had not been snooping for a Lithuanian agency, he spoke more frankly to Collier.[29]

> His suspicions were first aroused by the statement that she had been working for, among others, the *Kölnische Illusterierte Zeitung*. He asked her how it was that she, a Jewess, could be employed by a German newspaper. Her reply was unsatisfactory, and he thought it well to question her more closely. In the end she was prevailed upon to show him the file of her correspondence with the Cologne newspaper. M. Rabinavicius read it through, and came to the conclusion, from the terms of some of the letters sent and received, that she was being used to obtain information, particularly of aeroplanes and submarines, going far beyond the requirements even of technical journalism. She admitted that she used a code in her correspondence, although she refused to disclose it to him. He says that she is not very intelligent, and may not be fully aware of the significance of what she has been doing. He thinks – from some expressions used in the letters from Cologne – that those who are working behind the facade of the Cologne newspaper have some kind of hold over her.

The last of those linked to Ludwig was George Konstantinovitch Popoff. Estonian by birth, he resided in London at 15 W. Halkin Street, SW1, and nominally represented three rather obscure German newspapers. Besides his journalistic affiliations, he worked for the Congress of European National Minorities and presented information and memoranda on this topic to the British Foreign Office. As British representative to the Congress, he helped plan a conference in England in mid-July 1937, and probably assumed that this affiliation would add legitimacy to his presence in London both as a journalist and a specialist on minority questions.

Popoff's father was Russian and his mother a German Balt. The family had lived in London since November 1927. As an Estonian he could not join the Nazi Party, so had no obvious ties with them. However, in May 1935 he was known to have contacted the *Landesgruppe* in London, and two years later MI5 confirmed a Nazi connection.[30]

> In February 1937 it was found that Popoff was regularly sending secret reports on the British political situation to Berlin through the medium of the German Embassy. . . . His reports go to four different departments in Berlin, of which one is the Propaganda Ministry.

As we noted in chapter 8, Putlitz described how he noticed that reports by Popoff, alias Petkov, found their way to the desk of Achilles, head of the Chancery in the German Embassy.[31]

**197**

There was yet another dimension to Popoff's work that disturbed MI5. "In March 1937 it was found that Popoff, under the name of Beboutoff and passing himself off as a Jewish sympathizer, was in close touch with the New Zionist organisation in London." It is not entirely clear whether posing as a friend of Zionism or injecting himself into the Palestine question was more of a concern to MI5. In any case, they concluded that his motives were primarily monetary, since he seemed to have little fervor for Germany, a country which was not his own.

In the course of their investigation, Scotland Yard called on Popoff at his residence on Halkin Street. He was so troubled by this intrusion that he lodged a complaint with the Foreign Office, unaware that he was being closely scrutinized at the time.[32]

> On Tuesday, the 22nd of June, soon after luncheon time, an officer from Scotland Yard called at my flat at the above address, and said that, as they had received information in an anonymous letter that the Congress of European National Minorities is "a dangerous and militant organisation," he wanted some information concerning that body. I naturally gave him the desired information. ... The officer seemed to be quite satisfied with the explanations given him, and departed, apologizing for having troubled me.
>
> Now I am writing you regarding this matter for two reasons. First, during the conversation with the Yard official I took the liberty of mentioning that the British Foreign Office was well acquainted with the movement of the European National Minorities and would, no doubt, be willing to confirm the statements above mentioned, made by me. And secondly, to raise the question whether something could not be done to prevent the recurrence of such a happening in the future. I have an idea from whence such an anonymous information might have emanated: certain European countries regard the mere existence of the national minorities as an evil, and it is possible that representatives of these countries would not stop at such an unscrupulous act as writing anonymous letters to the police.

R. M. Makins of the Foreign Office distanced himself from this approach by Scotland Yard: "I am rather surprised at this frontal attack, or rather this daylight reconnaissance."[33]

Months passed, and Popoff probably assumed that he had successfully allayed the suspicions of Scotland Yard, but in December 1937 he was asked to leave the United Kingdom. As Fiedelholz had done before him, he sought aid from his native country. However, in spite of a request by the Estonian Minister to review the decision, Collier, in behalf of the Foreign Office, said it would not.[34]

Thus, during the course of 1937 there were nine expulsions from Britain. The tensions then subsided, and no deportations took place the following year. This was also due in part to an understanding which Neville Henderson, British

Ambassador to Berlin, worked out with Goebbels during a Nazi Party rally in September. According to Willam Strang, head of the Foreign Office Central Department:[35]

> When Sir. N. Henderson was at Nuremburg, Dr. Goebbels said that he hoped if His Majesty's Government wished to get rid of any German press correspondent, he [Goebbels] could be informed beforehand. He would in that case at once remove the offender without making any fuss whatsoever. Sir N. Henderson had only to mention the matter and action would be taken.

Notwithstanding this assurance, it did not prove to be that simple, according to C. J. Norton of the Foreign Office.[36]

> In the first place, it would not be wise merely to ask Dr. Goebbels to secure the removal from this country of a German national living here. This would tend to recognise to a greater degree than would be desirable, the exercise by the German Government of authority over Germans living here.

Instead, the Foreign Office proposed that in the future it would suggest that particular journalists leave the country, and if they did not depart within a reasonable time, the Home Office would issue a formal deportation order. Their expectation was that Germany would try to avoid any confrontation or adverse publicity by making sure that the offending journalist left in good time.

In addition to the gentleman's agreement that Goebbels made with Henderson at Nuremburg, the Germans adopted another strategy to counter the perception that there were inordinate numbers of German correspondents in London. On 11 August, at the height of the expulsions, Theodor Seibert, correspondent for the *Völkischer Beobachter* and local head of the *Verband der Deutschen Presse* (German Press Association), delivered to the Foreign Office a list of formally-recognized German journalists. It identified only twenty-nine members of the *Verband der Deutschen Presse* in Britain who were entitled to carry a *Schriftleiterausweis* (German press card). Eight others were included as secretaries or technical staff.[37]

The Foreign Office had its own list which greatly exceeded Seibert's. In addition to the twenty-nine officially-recognized names, it found at least twenty-three others. Then there were Germans who worked for non-German papers, and *vice versa*. When all these were counted, the total approached eighty.[38] The Foreign Office list included, in most instances, the addresses and newspaper affiliations of each of the correspondents.

What the Foreign Office could do with this information became a subject of protracted internal debate. On 13 August they asked the German Embassy to compile its own list of correspondents, so that it could be compared with the one submitted by Seibert as well as the one generated by the Foreign Office. Because this was a task that von Ribbentrop did not relish, he procrastinated until he ceased being Ambassador. Finally, in May 1938 the Embassy responded with its own list which differed only slightly from those assembled by Seibert and the Foreign Office[39]

On 25 September 1937, Vansittart posed the basic dilemma in a note to Russell Scott.[40]

> The question thus arises, what action we are to take, if any? While we should, of course, be entitled to expel from this country any of the persons whose names appear on any of the lists . . . if we found them misbehaving. We could hardly – and I believe this is the view of the Home Office – order a batch of *soi-disant* press correspondents to leave this country merely because we thought there were too many German press correspondents here, or because their names did not appear on Seibert's list. On the other hand, there might be some advantage in letting the German Ministry for Foreign Affairs know how matters stand . . . that we find it difficult to understand why such a large number of people should be required to serve the needs of the German press, and why in particular certain German newspapers of small circulation would require so many correspondents in this country. . . . The result we should hope for from this action would be that the German Government might of their own accord think it advisable to reduce the number of these people resident in this country; and indeed we might perhaps suggest to them in a friendly way that they should do so.

On 16 November Lord Halifax, the Foreign Secretary, incorporated most of Vansittart's points in a dispatch to the British Ambassador in Berlin, Sir Neville Henderson, but commented on a discrepancy that bothered him:[41]

> While for instance the *Völkischer Beobachter*, with a circulation of (I understand) 470,000, apparently has only two correspondents; the *Frankfurter Zeitung*, with a circulation of about 91,000, and the *Berliner Tageblatt*, with a circulation of 60,000, each appear to have four representatives in London.

That same day William Strang provided further background to Henderson so that he would appreciate why Lord Halifax had alerted the German Foreign Ministry to the problem of too many German correspondents in London.[42]

> As you will see, we are not at present concerned with the shortcomings of individuals, but rather with the difficulties caused by the excessive number of their people resident here. According to our information it appears that no less than ten offices in Berlin are separately supplied with confidential reports from this country. These are: The *Auslands Pressestelle* of the *NSDAP*. The Propaganda Ministry. The *Auslandsorganisation*. The Ribbentrop Bureau. The Ministry of Foreign Affairs. The *Aussenpolitisches Amt* of which is linked the anti-Comintern organisation. The Ministry of Defence. The Air Ministry. The *Wehrpolitisches Amt*.
>
> These reports are provided by certain of the resident "journalists," and as the various organisations work largely, it seems, without reference to each other, there is little doubt that lack of coordination, overlapping and even competition exist

among the various journalists who work in part to meet this demand. We are not, of course, concerned with their troubles, but rather with the additional difficulties caused to the authorities responsible for supervision of aliens here by the unnecessarily large number of German journalists resident in this country, and by the doubt which exists as to the precise character of their functions.

Strang also clarified why he and Lord Halifax wanted the subject raised with the German Foreign Ministry in Berlin rather than directly with Ribbentrop and the Embassy in London. Primarily it was that Ribbentrop's own *Dienststelle* was one of the offices in Berlin that was receiving confidential reports from supposed correspondents in London, causing the British Foreign Office to fear that the German Embassy "might be tempted to pigeonhole our communication, or at any rate not pass it on to the Ministry for Foreign Affairs."[43]

Ambassador Henderson in Berlin eventually explained the reason for his instructions: his Counselor at the British Embassy, George Ogilvie-Forbes, had presented an *aide memoire* on the subject to Aschmann, head of the Press Department at the German Foreign Ministry on 23 November 1937, and nothing had been heard from them since. Henderson was clearly vexed by the approach being taken by the British Foreign Office.[44]

> I am not very happy about this question, as I do not understand what you propose to do. Are the extra twenty-three or so journalists suspected of espionage, of breaches of the ordinary criminal law, or of interfering with their fellow Germans? Unless there are very definite cases to be brought against any individual or individuals, I hope that the possible resultant damage to Anglo-German relations at this particular moment by expulsion from England will be given careful consideration.
>
> What is the exact definition of a journalist where there are, apparently, so many part-time men? I presume a journalist, whatever his credentials, has no immunities. Has he any privileges? If so, what, in your view, is the difference between a regularly, and an irregularly, accredited newspaper correspondent?

Meanwhile, some within the Foreign Office in London were also having second thoughts. On 5 January 1938, Mallet asked his colleagues whether it was all that bad to have numerous Germans reporting on British affairs; perhaps the more that Germans learned about Britain the better, presuming their reports were not intentionally distorted. And as for MI5's keeping track of so many journalists: "I feel that it would be a pity to run the risk of a fresh row and of a fresh anti-British press campaign [in Germany] by expelling a number of German journalists merely for reasons of administrative convenience."[45]

Three weeks later he noted, with reference to Henderson's exasperation, "This question is not quite going according to our plan." Disagreements as to what constituted legitimate journalism made it unlikely that the German Government would withdraw correspondents voluntarily. "It would therefore seem better to be content for the present of having made known our opinion that there are too many German journalists here – (we can go on rubbing this in gently from time to time) – and continue to turn out any individual who misbehaves. . . ."[46] This, therefore, remained the Foreign Office policy for the rest of 1938.

Using all the available lists, we can identify the majority of German journalists in London during the last six months of 1937 and first six of 1938.[47] Their numbers fluctuate from month to month as some reporters returned to Germany and new ones came to take their places, but on average, at any given time, there were about thirty Nazi Party Members among them. In addition, there were about thirty who held the *Schriftleiterausweis*, three-fourths of whom were also Party Members. About thirty more did not belong to the German Press Association.

These numbers do not quite tell the whole story, however. Non-Party members belonging to the *Auslandspressestelle* came under official Nazi supervision. Like other German citizens abroad, they could be deprived of their passport and forced to return home, or in extreme cases, stripped of their nationality if they proved troublesome. Sanctions against their friends and relatives in Germany were also implicit, and guaranteed their good behavior in a foreign country. Since they benefited from the freer atmosphere of London, they did not want to jeopardize their privileged position overseas.

Germans who were neither Party Members nor affiliated with the *Auslandspressestelle* could nevertheless be pressured into attending professional meetings of the *Deutsche Arbeitsfront* since they knew that other Germans who belonged to the *Landesgruppe* were observing them. Furthermore, some of these unaffiliated correspondents tried to maintain a low profile because they were furnishing organizations and agencies back in Germany with confidential reports, and the less attention they drew to themselves, the less likely the British authorities were to pay attention to them.

Complicating the task of identifying *bone fide* journalists is the fact that anti-Nazi reporters were also included on the several lists. The British Foreign Office made no distinction between Nazi followers and refugees from Germany. The latter often did not represent any German newspaper because they were *persona non grata* in Germany, but they nevertheless wrote articles in German for émigré publications. This is why some of these names appeared only on the Foreign Office list, since Seibert and the German Embassy did not acknowledge their status as freelance practitioners.

The most conspicuous anti-Nazi journalists were Fritz Heymann, Alfred Kerr and Alexander Nathan. All three were Jewish, and were forced to seek employment outside of Germany. Fritz Heymann was born in 1897, became a newspaper editor in Düsseldorf, emigrated, and was deprived of his German citizenship in December 1936.[48] In London he worked for the *Berliner Tageblatt*, one of the papers the Foreign Office objected to because it employed too many correspondents.

The 70-year-old Alfred Kerr lived in Berlin before the Nazis came to power and was one of the earliest émigrés to lose his citizenship in August 1933. He, too, wrote for the *Berliner Tageblatt*, and the Nazis labeled him a "gutter" theater critic. In London he was an independent journalist, and in 1939 moved to Paris to join the staff of the anti-Nazi *Pariser Tageszeitung*.[49]

Heinz Alexander Nathan was a Berliner by birth in 1906, and retained his citizenship until May 1939. As a freelance journalist in London, he was exposed by another and more prominent German émigré, Ernst Toller, who told the former Editor of *The Times*, Wickham Steed, in the spring of 1935 that Nathan was a Nazi spy even though he nominally represented the liberal Ullstein Press. Toller insinuated that Nathan was posing as a genuine refugee while betraying other refugees like himself.[50] This was not the only time that a former socialist became a Nazi agent.[51]

Kurt Lubinski was another Jewish journalist who retained his German citizenship while functioning as a freelance reporter during the 1930s in London. Not until 1938 did he apply to be a member of the *Reichsschriftumskammer* (German writers' union) since he came to realize that unless he did, he could never hope to have his books published in Germany. Somewhat predictably, he was denied, since at this late date he was deemed unlikely to serve the cause of the Nazi regime.[52]

To knowledgeable contemporaries, Graf Albrecht von Montgelas was distinctly anti-Nazi. Like others, he tried to be discreet about it in order not to jeopardize his standing with the papers he represented: the *Mitarbeit*, the *Neue Leipziger Zeitung*, and the *Frankfurter General-Anzeiger*. As noted earlier,[53] the Ustinovs often hosted small gatherings of anti-Nazi Germans in London, and Montgelas was a frequent guest.[54]

There were four veteran correspondents who commanded the respect of most Germans: Karl Heinz Abshagen, Wolf von Dewall, Kurt von Stutterheim and Carl Erdmann von Pückler. Only von Pückler joined the *NSDAP*, and not until the war broke out in 1939. In his memoirs, Herbert von Dirksen, German Ambassador to London in 1938–39, singled these four out as journalists whose opinions he most respected because they were able to retain their jobs while adhering to a measure of moderation and independence.[55] In a way, they cooperated with the Nazis, but they also interpreted England to their German readers more responsibly than did their Nazi-oriented colleagues.

By the late 1930s, Karl Heinz Abshagen represented about six German newspapers in London. He made a specialty of internal British affairs, and wrote a book on the balance of power as practiced by the King, the House of Lords and the Commons.[56] He also lectured on this theme at the Anglo-German Academic Bureau.[57] As a German citizen and author residing abroad, he had to clear any proposed book with the *Reichsschriftumkammer*, a censoring body which indicated that they would not oppose his book on England provided his views were "appropriate."[58]

Abshagen was someone the British authorities sometimes trusted and sometimes did not, depending upon the circumstances. In late 1933 Sir Vernon Kell, head of MI5, took a dim view of him when he was the London correspondent for the Hamburger *Fremdenblatt* because he worked "in close contact with Otto Bene and the London Group of the Nazi Party" and consorted with Lt. Col. Graham Seton Hutchison and other pro-Nazis.[59] By contrast, by 1937 Abshagen's reputation at the British Foreign Office stood high, according to William Strang: "He is one of the ablest and most responsible of the German journalists here, and so long as we are content that he should stay here we should I think be wise to worry him as little as possible. . . ."[60] In the spring of 1939 the Foreign Office again expressed its satisfaction with him, particularly as he had occasionally offered them useful advice such as warning against acceptance of the 1938 Munich Agreement. Since he traveled regularly between Britain and Germany in order to maintain his contacts, including close ties with the former finance minister, Dr. Schacht, he expected that if the time ever came when Nazi correspondents were expelled *en masse*, the Foreign Office would make an exception for him.[61]

Wolf von Dewall had an extensive career as a journalist before marrying and coming to London with his wife in 1932. Born in 1882, he spent the decade prior to World War I in China, then returned to Germany and worked for the Frankfurter *Zeitung* as Foreign Editor. Later he published a number of books about the Far East. Together with his wife, he led an active social life in London, helping to organize, for example, the Winter Relief Fund in 1934.[62]

Baron Kurt von Stutterheim served two lengthy tours of duty in Britain as a reporter for the *Berliner Tageblatt*. He was here for ten years, from 1922 to 1932, and on the basis of his experiences he wrote a book on the British press.[63] He then spent a few years in Rome before returning to London and writing another book about England.[64] He was married to a sister-in-law of Anthony Eden, and among his admirers was Geyr von Schweppenburg, the German Military Attaché in London, who wrote of him: "To Baron Stutterheim, who was a man with a first-rate brain and deep understanding of British psychology, I owe a great deal of my knowledge of British affairs."[65]

Graf Carl Erdmann von Pückler represented the *Deutsche Allgemeine Zeitung* in London. Like his other well-regarded colleagues, he also published a book about Britain's strength as a world power.[66] At the outbreak of war in 1939 he returned to Berlin, and became a member of the Nazi Party in July 1940. He died at the age of thirty-five in December 1941.

By way of contrast with those who either never joined the Party or did so after they left London, there were others who applied for membership while in

London. Being abroad and associating with other Nazis was conducive to recruitment, especially in the cases of two journalists affiliated with the official Nazi news agency, the *Deutsches Nachrichtenbüro*. Both Willy Konnertz and Hans Winkler probably found it advantageous to join the Party in order to increase security in their current employment. Konnertz was thirty years old when he reached London in 1938. Already a member of the *Verband der Deutschen Presse*, he applied for membership in the Nazi Party in December, and was finally admitted the following June.[67]

Early on, Hans Winkler demonstrated his sympathy with the Nazis by working for six months in 1934–35 for the infamous anti-Semitic paper in Nuremburg, *Der Stürmer*. In May 1935 he came to London and spent four months volunteering with the *Auslandsorganisation* where Otto Bene asked him to initiate a branch of the *Hitler Jugend*. By the autumn of 1935 Winkler was an editorial assistant for the *Deutshes Nachtrichtenbüro*, and applied for Party Membership. He was accepted in December 1936. Two years later the Home office suggested that he leave London voluntarily as a consequence of his close association with pro-Fascist and anti-Semitic British subjects. When a job consonant with his anti-Semitism was advertised in his home city of Nuremberg, he returned and became an expert on the British and American press for the *Antijudische Weltliga* (Anti-Jewish World League).[68]

The British authorities were of two minds about people like Winkler. If too many German journalists were asked to leave, relations with Germany would be further strained, and the Nazis would retaliate against British reporters in Berlin. On the other hand, MI5 and Special Branch felt responsible for too many foreign journalists, which distinctly hampered their ability to keep track of them.

Getting rid of a few press representatives could have eased the pressure on MI5's limited resources, yet it was difficult for them to know whether Leonhardt Franz Singer should be encouraged to depart, since he had committed no obvious misdemeanors. On 22 December 1937 Sir Russell Scott described Singer as someone "who in addition to acting for the 'Bremer Nachrichten' and for certain Scandinavian papers, submits reports to the *Pressedienst Hansa* which, as you know, is a centre for receipt and collection of political and economic intelligence."[69] At the Foreign Office they were aware that he was sending "reports on this country to some intelligence centre in Germany. We see some of his reports: They are on the whole conscientiously done and do not . . . show access on his part to sources of information which ought not to be open to him."[70] When MI5 investigated him, they found that he had little contact with the Press Department of the Foreign Office or with other journalists, which might imply his preoccupation with activities other than those strictly journalistic, but they had to admit that nothing particularly new could be brought against him except that he had lied about his sources of income when entering Britain.[71] Under these circumstances, the Foreign Office decided not to accede to the recommendation of the Home Office to remove Singer, but rather to wait for a time when he or any other reporter did something that would clearly justify prompt action.

However, there was little reluctance to inform a suspected individual that he or she would not be re-admitted to England, and therefore it would save everyone embarrassment if no such attempt were made. This happened to Ernst Ferdinand Harri Christoph Bauer. At the age of 16 he began a kind of unpaid apprenticeship with a newspaper publishing firm, and in May 1934, having just turned nineteen, he went to London as a representative of several National Socialist papers, including the *Preussiche N.S. Zeitung.* Three years later he returned to Germany as a freelance journalist. There is no evidence suggesting why he left London, but the British authorities were firmly convinced they did not want him to return. One way to ensure this was to send a circular letter to immigration officers indicating that Bauer should be refused re-entry. It was also thought prudent to notify the Propaganda Ministry, so that they might discourage his return.[72]

In the case of Hans Georg von Studnitz the British tried to prevent him coming to London in January 1938 because of his unsavory reputation. He was due to work for *Scherlverlag* and the *Lokal-Anzeiger,* which were both implicated in the Ludwig affair as well as the expulsion of Crome; the French relayed information gleaned from Austria that on the basis of his work in Vienna, Studnitz was probably a Gestapo agent.[73] Despite these liabilities, he was eventually allowed to enter Britain.

Occasionally the Foreign Office or the Home Office were suspicious of a particular journalist, but their fears turned out to be baseless. Johann Freidrich Glas was on Seibert's list of August 1937, appearing as a freelance correspondent, not a member of the *Verband der Deutschen Presse.* Nor was he a Nazi Party member. To resolve their doubts, the Foreign Office wrote the British Ambassador in Berlin: "We are anxious to get some information about Captain Johann F Glas, with whom we understand you were acquainted at Innsbrück. We have reason to believe that he is interested in more than mere political journalism, but have not yet been able to make up our mind in whose interests he is really working. . . ."[74] They also asked about Helmut Rütter, who had fled from Innsbrück to Italy following the German march into Austria, and who seemed to be carrying on an extensive correspondence with Glas. Ambassador Henderson replied that the two of them were "at the head of a small private intelligence organization interested in obtaining political and military information primarily, I would suggest, in their own private interest. The function of Glas has been, I surmise, to keep in touch with official and business circles in London with a view to obtaining saleable information of a confidential character."[75] This explanation satisfied the British, and Glas was no longer under suspicion.

The Foreign Office and the Home Office were at odds with one another as to how best to deal with twenty-five year old Adolf Heinitz who was not only on Seibert's list of *Verband der Deutschen Presse* members but assisted Seibert with the official Nazi newspaper, the *Völkischer Beobachter*. He joined the Nazi Party in May 1933, three years before coming to London. Early in September 1937 the German Embassy lodged a complaint stemming from an encounter at Harwich on 29 August.[76] On his return to Britain from a holiday on the Continent, Customs officials had treated him rudely, and since he was well-known to both the German Embassy and the British Home Office, it had been disconcerting to have his credentials questioned. His luggage was thoroughly searched, and he was asked to wait and undergo additional interrogation by officials who allegedly questioned the need for German newspapers to have reporters like him in London when the Embassy could easily provide adequate news and information. Heinitz was also challenged about having broken the terms stamped in his passport that he would not seek employment or receive a salary while in Britain. He protested that his employers were German, not British, and that his income came directly from Germany. In the end, he was allowed to enter the country for only one month.

This complaint came at an awkward time for the Foreign Office, since they had recently expelled Crome, Wrede, von Langen and the others, and it might look as though it was official British policy to harass German journalists. A part of the episode that was not mentioned by the Germans, but was alluded to by William Strang, injected another dimension that may have been unacknowledged.[77]

> I understand that one of the immigration officers at Harwich who has most to do with the examination of German journalists is a Jew (Mr. Gold) who is reported to be good at his job; but it can't be very pleasant for Nazis to find themselves put through it by a Jew on arrival in this country.

The Home Office looked into this matter and discovered that the first Customs officer who dealt with Heinitz was not D. Gold but E. Ward, an employee for only three months. Later Ward realized that he had erred about Heinitz's employment eligibility, but he insisted that he had been courteous throughout the interview.[78] Further light was thrown on the encounter by the more senior official, D. Gold.[79] On the morning of 29 August 1937, he had been working at the desk next to Ward and overheard his mounting exasperation with Heinitz, and so suggested that Heinitz wait until he could attend to the matter. By this time, "Heinitz was . . . in a bad temper . . . grumbling that we were a very suspicious lot." After Heinitz reopened his bags and produced letters of introduction and other papers proving his *bona fides* as a foreign correspondent, Gold acknowledged that Ward had been mistaken, and that there was no difficulty with Heinitz continuing his work in London for various German newspapers. At the same time, Gold decided that he would probe a bit more deeply into Heinitz's activities.

> I then took the opportunity to see if anything interesting could be gleaned, and speaking conversationally said that, now that everything had been settled, it would be interesting to know why he had accused us of being suspicious. He appeared to respond, and he eventually said that although he had been associated with Crome, Wrede and von Langen, he had done only journalistic work in this country.

As part of his investigation, Gold solicited a letter that the *Deutsche Arbeitsfront* had written to Heinitz in July 1936. "We hear that you are moving your residence to England from 1.10.36, and we hereby commission you to undertake economic, social and political reporting as our English representative. We are especially interested in your making full use of the trade union press."[80]

As a result of Gold's inquiries, Heinitz was sent an apology, stating that no rudeness had been intended, and that he could apply to the Home Office for a permit to stay in Britain on the same basis as before. The Foreign Office and the Home Office also agreed to furnish Customs officials with lists of acknowledged foreign correspondents in the future: "Journalists on this list might then as a general rule be admitted with the minimum of examination, though of course if we had any grounds for suspecting any one of them of undesirable activities, we should be perfectly free to put whatever inquiries we thought necessary."[81]

Effective as British surveillance organizations were, they could not prevent some journalists from slipping through their net. Such a one was Arnold Wilhelm Heinrich Littmann, who represented the *Hamburger Fremdenblatt* from 1936–39, and was a member of the *Verband der Deutschen Presse* as well as the Nazi Party since May 1933.[82] A Berliner by birth in 1901, he was just young enough to avoid military service in the First World War. After earning a doctorate at the University of Berlin and publishing his dissertation in 1926, he became a freelance writer on scientific subjects for the *Jugendpressedienst* (Youth Press Service) and other educational publications. An incident in 1935, however, radically altered his life. He was charged with homosexual activity while under the influence of alcohol. The court, prompted by the Gestapo, gave him the option of avoiding imprisonment if he cooperated with the secret police. As a report later stated: "He was sent by the Gestapo to England for the purpose of gathering information."[83]

What sort of "information" was of interest to the Gestapo can only be imagined. Ordinarily the Gestapo dealt with domestic security and not intelligence-gathering abroad. However, there was one major exception, having to do with German citizens resident abroad, and former citizens turned refugees. In these cases, the Gestapo kept track of those who communicated with anyone in Germany; whether they were involved in illegal transfers of currency; and whether they were leading other Germans astray. One possible clue to Littmann's "cover" while he worked for the Hamburg paper was his job as the representative of a German publishing firm in Britain, possibly *Scherlverlag*.

In July 1939 a court in Berlin reviewed his case and offered him amnesty against further prosecution, noting that he had served his sentence back in 1935 which allowed him to return to Germany. However, the legal stigma of homosexuality did not entirely disappear. In the spring of 1940 the Propaganda Ministry was told that Littmann had a criminal record which resulted in losing his full-time job, yet he remained exempt from military service.

Demonstrably, the most important among the German journalists was Theodor Seibert. Born in Bavaria in 1896, he joined the Second Bavarian Infantry Regiment in 1914. For two years he served in various sectors of the Western Front, then trained as a fighter pilot and saw action over Verdun in 1916, and later at the Second Battle of the Marne.[84] During the war he rose to the rank of First Lieutenant, but with the armistice he lost no time mustering out and enrolling in the University of Munich where he spent much of his time and energy engaging in para-military exploits such as joining the *Freikorps* in order to subdue the Soviet Republic of Bavaria, and assisting Wolfgang Kapp, the right-wing demagogue, in seizing power from the fledgling Weimar Republic. When these adventures failed, he searched for action at the Polish frontier in Upper Silesia.

From 1921 on he carved out a career in journalism as a writer for the *Hamburger Fremdenblatt* from 1923 to 1936, which included a stint in Moscow (1925–29) that enabled him to write and publish a book in 1931 titled *Das Rote Russland*. In 1932 he traveled to London, and after the expulsion of Hans Thost in November 1935, he was named his replacement at the *Völkischer Beobachter*. Then in January 1938 he was recalled to the paper's main office in Berlin to be its foreign editor.

At the time he joined the *VB* in London, he enjoyed a reputation for moderation. As *The Times* pointed out, he was willing to take British opinions at face value, and report them straightforwardly, rather than with irony or contempt.[85] However, when the British press alleged that in the wake of the August 1937 expulsions there were anywhere from 80–100 German press representatives in London, Seibert countered the claim with his list of thirty.[86]

Like Thost, Seibert supplied confidential reports to Rosenberg, who was both Editor-in-Chief of the *VB* and head of the *Aussenpolitisches Amt*. One of these provides a typical example of Nazi "objectivity".[87] Presenting the British view of current international relations, Seibert first described the English reaction to the recent Nazi Party congress at Nuremberg which he said impressed the British with the large demonstrations of public support for the government and the Party in power. He reported further that nowadays one seldom heard that the German people did not uphold their regime with enthusiasm; no longer was

Hitler's Four Year Plan of economic and industrial expansion viewed with skepticism by the British press, but rather was regarded as something which would most likely succeed. As Germany was becoming stronger, many in England shared the views of the "Beaverbrook circle" who felt it imperative to get along with her. For some, this support fostered isolationism and also encouraged the British press to take "a position of neutrality." *The Times* and the *Telegraph* especially gave vent to their fear of growing German power, paralleled by enhanced French timidity. The *Sunday Times* was even advocating that the Czechs be pressured to arrive at a settlement of their differences with Germany.

Seibert saw the British beset by a dilemma which admitted of no easy answer. On the one hand, they favored some kind of Western diplomatic accord which would link together the three major powers: Britain, France and Germany. On the other, should such an understanding be achieved, Germany would feel free to make inroads in the Eastern part of Europe, introducing the dreaded potential of war. Regarding anti-Semitism, he perceived the British as giving the Russians the benefit of the doubt, ignoring the speeches of Goebbels and Rosenberg that linked Bolshevik and Jewish affinities. "Anti-Semitism is growing in England, but it is scarcely beyond the stage of personal feelings," Seibert wrote, adding that the typical Englishman might say: "I detest the Jews but I suppose they must be allowed to live somehow." The systematic and rigorous policy toward the Jews in Germany strikes many in Britain as "somewhat crazy". With respect to Japan, the British had hoped to avoid an intense rivalry in the Far East, but these expectations were dashed when Japan withdrew from the London Naval Conference of January 1936. "The United States is in the best position to keep Japan in line, but the Yankees lack an adequate navy. The Singapore fortifications when completed will prove formidable, especially in providing protection to Malaysia and Australia, but will have little direct impact on the distant Japanese islands. Like everyone else, the British hope that Russia and Japan will act as a check on one another."

Seibert noted that "despite the quieting down of the Abyssinian crisis, the British fear neo-Roman imperialism. They are augmenting their positions in Egypt and Palestine against future Arab expansion, egged on by the Italians. The recent outbreak of the civil war in Spain poses another set of unpalatable choices for England. If the Reds win, it would be a strong stimulus for Communism in England. If France and the Nationalists triumph, they will tend to gravitate toward close ties with Fascist Italy, to the detriment of British naval interests in the Mediterranean." Seibert predicted, therefore, that Britain would try to remain neutral. "As for France, the British generally favor Leon Blum and the Popular Front as the last and best hope for democracy, although there is a risk that this faction might become a left-wing dictatorship, with the further danger of it being Bolshevized. The other alternative is a coup by the Fascists, which would steer France in directions highly uncongenial to Britain."

With confidential reports like Seibert's, it is possible that he told Rosenberg only what he wanted to hear, but except for his formulaic comments on anti-Semitism, Seibert seemed remarkably prescient. It may also have been true that the British were influenced in part by their concerns over Jewish migration to Palestine.

When it came to writing for the German press, as distinct from individuals like Rosenberg, the German correspondents in London were inclined to compete with each other, giving negative portraits of the United Kingdom. They knew what was expected of them by the new regime, and the parameters laid down by the Propaganda Ministry. None wished to forfeit their membership in the *Verband der Deutschen Presse*, and most of them expected to return to Germany eventually, which meant keeping out of trouble while abroad. Yet there were some who put ideology above personal advancement, and these were the ones expelled.

## NOTES

1  *New York Times*, 13 April 1937, p. 7. In 2002 MI5 released the file on the Ludwig case: PRO, KV 2/350 and KV 2/351.
2  *Ibid.*, 28 April 1937, p. 5.
3  *The Times*, 28 April 1937, p. 4.
4  According to the files in the *Auswärtiges Amt* in Bonn, Ludwig's real name was Friedl, as found in the German Embassy's journal for April 1937. However, based on MI5 files, Ludwig seems more likely.
5  Putlitz, *The Putlitz Dossier* (London, 1957), pp. 100–3.
6  See chapter 8.
7  Hoare to Eden, 28 June 1937, PRO, FO 371/20739, C4918, f. 179.
8  BDC, A-3340–PC-roll 063.
9  PRO, FO 371/20739, C4918, f. 182. Crome subsequently joined the *NSDAP* in 1939.
10  These reports were sent to Ludwig in Berlin at 21 Luetzenallee, Charlottenberg. See: Woermann to the German Foreign Ministry, 5 August 1937, NA microcopy T-120, roll 913, frames 384393-97.
11  PRO, FO 371/20439, C4918, f. 183.
12  *Ibid.*, f. 184. For a brief biographical sketch, see E. Stockhorst, *Fünftausand Köpfe: Wer war was im Dritten Reich*. Bruschsal/Baden, 1967), p. 455.
13  *Ibid.*, PRO, f. 181.
14  At the time von Langen was *Ortsgruppenleiter* in Rome. See: *News Chronicle*, 4 February 1937, p. 13.
15  Freund to Bartlett, 9 April 1937, PRO, FO 371/20739, C2479, f. 82.
16  For the 1936 and the 1939 "Personalities", see: PRO, FO 371/20696, C1470, f. 36, and FO 371/22939, C9935, f. 46.
17  Home Office to Foreign Office, 22 July 1937, PRO, FO 371/20739, C5605, ff. 224–28.
18  Memo by W. Strang, 31 July 1937, *ibid.*, C5606, ff. 229–32.
19  Minute from Vansittart, 31 July 1937, *ibid.*
20  Memo of von Plessen, 10 August 1937, NA microcopy T-120, roll 913, 384403.

21 Ogilvie-Forbes to the British Foreign Office, 7 August 1937, PRO, FO 371/20739, C5726, ff. 160–62.

22 Woermann to the German Foreign Ministry, 5 August 1937, NA microcopy T-120, roll 913, frames 384393-97.

23 Memo by C. W. Baxter, 19 August 1937, PRO, FO 371/20740, C6003, f. 2.

24 Vansittart minute, 9 August 1937, *ibid.*, C5766, ff. 267–69.

25 The librarians of the *New York Times* kindly searched their records but could find no connection between the paper and Basedow.

26 PRO, FO 371/20739, C4918, f. 187.

27 Memo, 10 January 1937, PRO, FO 371/21685, C196, ff. 23–27.

28 PRO, FO 371/20739, C4918, f. 185.

29 Memo, 22 October 1937, PRO, FO 371/20741, C7258, f. 324.

30 PRO, FO 371/20739, C4918, f. 186.

31 Putlitz, *Putlitz Dossier*, pp. 134–35.

32 Popoff to R. M. Makins, 24 June 1937, PRO, FO 371/21252, C12376, ff. 51–57.

33 *Ibid.*

34 Memo, 9 December 1937, PRO, FO 371/20741, C8494, ff. 415–16.

35 Strang minute of 22 September 1937, PRO, FO 371/20740, C6427, ff. 77.

36 Norton to Home Office, 19 October 1937, PRO, FO 371/20741, C6944, ff. 193–201.

37 PRO, FO 371/20740, C6304, ff. 41–44.

38 For additional names of journalists on the Foreign Office list, see: PRO, FO 371/20741, C7066, ff. 231–32.

39 PRO, FO 371/21685, C5196, ff. 88–101.

40 Vansittart to Scott, 25 September 1937, PRO, FO 371/20740, C6677, ff. 107–10.

41 Halifax to Henderson, 16 November 1937, PRO, FO 371/20741, C7066, ff. 227–30.

42 Strang to Henderson, 16 November 1937, *ibid.*, ff. 225–26.

43 *Ibid.*

44 Henderson to Sargent, 20 January 1938, PRO, FO 371/21685, C559, ff. 45–52.

45 PRO, FO 371/20742, C8805, ff. 504–7.

46 31 January 1938, PRO, FO 371/21685, C559, f. 45.

47 In July 1938 a further listing of German journalists was made. See: PRO, FO 395/572, P2171, ff. 312–22. This, and the earlier lists referred to, have been supplemented with information from the BDC as well as London street and telephone directories.

48 BDC.

49 *Ibid.*

50 *Ibid.* Toller's view of Nathan was given at the Swiss inquiry into another émigré journalist, Hans Wesemann. See report of 23 March 1935 concerning the Wesemann case, p. 253a, Staatsarchiv, Basel.

51 J. J. Barnes & P. P. Barnes, *Nazi Refugee turned Gestapo Spy* (Praeger, 2001).

52 Reichsschriftumskammer to Propaganda Ministry, 27 August 1938, BDC.

53 See chapter 7.

54 Ustinov to J. J. Barnes, 22 November 1979.

55 H. Dirksen, *Moskau, Tokio, London* (Stuttgart, 1949), p. 225.

56 K. H. Abshagen, *König, Lords und Gentlemen* (Stuttgart, 1938), translated into *King, Lords and Gentlemen* (London, 1939).

57  *Deutsche Zeitung in Gross Britannien*, 25 February 1939, p. 3.

58  Abshagen to *Reichsschriftumskammer*, 2 October 1938, and *Reichsschriftumskammer* to Abshagen, 13 October 1938, in the BDC.

59  Kell report, 4 December 1933, PRO, FO 371/16751, C10679, ff. 72–80.

60  Strang to Holderness, 4 October 1937, PRO, FO 371/20740, C6607, f. 105.

61  Minutes of 27–29 March 1939, PRO, FO 371/20740, C6607, f. 105.

62  *European Herald*, 16 November 1934, p. 2.

63  Stutterheim, *Die Englische Presse* (Berlin, 1933).

64  Stutterheim, *England: Heute und Morgen* (Berlin, 1937).

65  L. Geyr von Schweppenburg, *The Critical Years* (London, 1952), p. 16.

66  C. E. Pückler, *Wie Stark Ist England?* (Leipzig, 1939); translated as *How Strong is Britain?* (London, 1939).

67  Konnertz file, BDC, and PRO, FO 395/572, P2171, f. 314.

68  *Ibid.*, and FO 371/20740, C6304, ff. 43–44.

69  R. Scott to Vansittart, PRO, FO 371/20742, C8805, f. 507.

70  Minute by W. Strang, 6 January 1938, *ibid.*

71  Minute by Mallet, 5 January 1938, *ibid.*, f. 505.

72  BDC and PRO, FO 371/20741, C7015, ff. 208–9. Bauer sometimes went by the name of Christian Harri Bauer.

73  Foreign Office to Home Office, 24 January 1938, PRO, FO 371/21685, C426, ff. 36–40.

74  Mallett to Henderson, 28 June 1938, *ibid.* C6399, ff. 114–16.

75  Henderson to Mallet, 4 July 1938, *ibid.* C6809, f. 199.

76  Heinitz file, BDC. For the German Embassy complaint, see: PRO, FO 371/20740, C6304, ff. 35–44.

77  Minute by Strang, 27 September 1937, *ibid.*, C6607, f. 102.

78  Report by Ward, 23 September 1937, *ibid.*, C6880, f. 125.

79  Report by Gold, 23 September 1937, *ibid.*, f. 126.

80  *Deutsche Arbeitsfront* to Heinitz, 26 July 1936, *ibid.*, C6607, f. 104.

81  Strang to Holderness, 4 October 1937, *ibid.*, f. 105.

82  Littmann file, BDC; see also press lists supplied by the German Embassy to the British Foreign Office.

83  Letter from the *Sicherheitspolizei* und *SD* to the Propaganda Ministry, 10 April 1940, BDC.

84  Seibert file, BDC; see also the biographical sketch in the *Deutsche Zeitung in Gross Britannien*, 9 April 1938, p. 5.

85  *The Times*, 24 December 1936, p. 12.

86  *Ibid.*, 14 August 1937, p. 6.

87  Seibert's report of September 1936 can be found in the *Centre de Documentation Juive Contemporaine*, Paris: CXLIII-313.

# 16 NAZI INTIMIDATION LEADS TO DEPORTATION

As early as December 1933, newspapers like the *Daily Herald* began to report Nazi harassment of German refugees in Britain,[1] alleging that the *Ortsgruppe* kept an extensive card file on their fellow exiles, especially those who spoke against the new regime in Germany. It was further contended that the Gestapo monitored this information and took appropriate action when it deemed necessary. Accordingly, the British public was alerted to the specter of foreign police operatives or their agents terrorizing Germans who had taken refuge in the United Kingdom.

The London press was not alone in exposing the long arm of the Gestapo. In August of 1937 the *New York Times* echoed similar fears.[2]

> The Nazis, when they came to power, took steps to organize the German residents so as to be able to control their activities. A swarm of agents of the Nazi Party, secret police, Ministry of Propaganda and army intelligence men descended upon London. Every German even temporarily resident was indexed and enrolled often in several organisations.

That same month, the *Manchester Guardian* wrote:[3]

> There has, it is known, been a good deal of spying and eavesdropping and gathering of private information by Nazis in this country that might be considered useful by the Nazis in Berlin but might be dangerous to Germans residing here, especially to such as may want to return to their own country some day.

The developing sense that there was inappropriate surveillance taking place was confirmed in February 1938 by the German Government's insistence that all citizens abroad register with the nearest German Consulate. Regardless of the innocuous interpretation the Germans gave to this regulation, it undoubtedly enhanced the Nazi ability to keep track of their nationals outside the Third Reich.

214

The German annexation of Austria in March 1938 greatly augmented the number of émigrés in London who now came under Nazi jurisdiction. We can see the effect of this event in the case of an Austrian woman who was satisfactorily employed by a British family as a domestic servant, but once she came under the aegis of the Third Reich, she could no longer work for anyone who was Jewish, according to the Nuremburg laws. Thus, in spite of her employer's desire that she continue, and the fact that the Home Office had extended her permit, she was forced to leave.[4]

As the decade progressed, more and more incidents were called to the attention of the Home Office or the Foreign Office. In late 1938, an Austrian refugee, Erich Heller, was seeking to arrange matters so that his wife could join him in London. Presented with the proposition that this could be arranged if he were willing to dispose of property he owned in Austria, Heller realized the implied threat that he either sell the property at a nominal figure, or the Gestapo would block Frau Heller's departure.[5]

Pressure of this kind increased as the Germans seized successive countries along with their archives. Following the *Anschluss* of March 1938, the files of the Austrian Embassy were confiscated, and the archives of the Czech Embassy succumbed to Nazi occupation a year later. Suddenly refugees everywhere in Europe felt insecure, uncertain which of their homelands would next be occupied, and they, in turn, would be subject to systematic Nazi scrutiny.

Further contributing to the confusion felt by exiles was the prospect of infiltration by *agents provocateurs*. In May 1939, a Mrs. Davies of the Catholic Refugee Committee expressed forebodings to the British authorities when two suspicious Germans visited Bloomsbury House, claiming to be refugees and asking questions. One of them, Fritz Briess, asserted that he was a British citizen, but inquiries revealed no passport in his name. The other, Vicktor Haefner, indicated that he was a former high-ranking German army officer.[6] Whether these men were genuine refugees was never determined, but London had its share of turncoats who duped their fellow émigrés.

During 1938 the Home Office received many complaints from Jewish employers and Jewish employees of German firms. The Home Office relayed the details of one incident to the Foreign Office.[7]

> A German maid employed by an English Jewish family gave notice that she was leaving. When asked why, she said that she had been warned that she was an Aryan and therefore ought not to work for Jews. She said that she had been told that if she remained "it would go hard with her brother in Berlin."

On 1 June 1938 the *Daily Herald* covered a story on yet another example of discriminatory employment and official Nazi pressure. The article didn't mention any names, but they were known by the Home Office and later told to the Foreign Office.[8] When Mrs. Hetty Cohen tried to employ an Austrian,

Maria Lukaseder, she was turned down because she was Jewish. However, when Mrs. Sattin applied for a helper from the Anglo-German Agency, she succeeded in procuring another Austrian, Karoline Maresch, who promptly resigned when she realized that the family was Jewish. Special Branch of Scotland Yard looked into these cases, but not before both women had returned to Austria.

A similar fate befell Louise Peturnig, an Austrian woman who was told that she must leave her employer, Mrs. Railing, once Austria came under German control.[9]

German companies with offices in Britain also sought ways to get rid of Jewish employees. Early in 1938 Siemens-Schuckert Ltd. of 30 New Bridge Street, EC4, began to make excuses as to why they would have to dismiss certain staff, all of whom were Jewish. One worker, Mabel Wilson, protested, and her case came to the attention of the Home Office. Special Branch looked into her complaint and confirmed that it had become company policy to dismiss Jews, although admitting that "This reason for her dismissal would be to the effect that it was because of reorganisation."[10] Siemens apparently resisted pressure from Berlin for awhile, but had finally yielded. Mabel Wilson was the fourth of six Jewish employees targeted for redundancy, but before the last two were notified, a question was raised in Parliament by Vyvyan Adams on 10 February 1938.[11] This slowed the process, but some months later the remaining two Jews were downgraded, which proved sufficient incentive for them to resign.

When the British firm, Loewy Engineering Company Ltd., proved to be too keen a competitor for the Germans, they tried to gain the upper hand by forcing German nationals crucial to the English company's existence to resign, using the pretext that Aryans should not work for Jews. Ludwig Loewy devoted 25 years of his life managing a plant in Düsseldorf. In April 1936 he emigrated to Britain, bringing his expertise in the manufacture of hydraulic presses and rolling mill machinery with him. According to the Home Office:[12]

> He brought with him from Germany a number of specialists. In January 1938 five of these specialists received letters asking them to call at the German Embassy. They went to the Embassy and were seen by Dr. Weber, the Commercial Attaché. Inducements were made to them to leave the company on the ground that they were working for a competitor to German industry, and it was suggested that they should join German firms or H. A. Brassert and Company Limited, a firm which has just been appointed as consulting engineers to the German Government.

When the men declared their intention to remain with Loewy, they were told by Dr. Weber to declare their reasons in writing so that their explanations could be sent to the authorities back in Germany. They were also advised to join the *Deutsche Arbeitsfront*, pay any back dues, and reconsider their decisions. Other forms of pressure were also applied. One of the five, Eduard Haffner, was visited at his home in Harrow by Günther Lobkowitz, a former employee of Loewy's who had accepted a higher paying job with Brassert's.[13]

> Mr. Lobkowitz repeated the proposal which had been made to Haffner by Dr. Weber and hinted that if Haffner did not relinquish his position with the Loewy Engineering Co., the consequences might be very serious for him and his family. Haffner is not particularly concerned about himself, because he hopes that he may be allowed to establish himself in this country, but his parents are living in Germany and he fears that some serious mischief may befall them if he sticks to his present employer.

When Haffner left town on business, his wife accepted an invitation to the Lobkowitz home where "both he and his wife . . . thoroughly frightened Mrs. Haffner." Coincidentally the President of the Brassert Company was an American from Chicago, Hermann Alexander Brassert, who developed a process for the production of steel from inferior iron ore which he had sold to the Herman Goering Works of Essen. Like many cases documented by the Home Office, it was never clear whether or not Haffner and his associate remained with Loewy. Either way, the British were becoming increasingly alarmed.

Dr. Walter Maria Weber was the Commercial Attaché and Secretary of Legation in the German Embassy in London at the time of the Loewy Company affair. A year later he found himself embroiled in another high profile case. As a career diplomat, he had come to London in 1936, and applied for Nazi party membership in January 1937, presumably at the urging of Ambassador Ribbentrop.[14] He and his wife settled comfortably into Dover Cottage, Highdown Road, Roehampton, SW15. British officials who dealt with him were impressed until an Indian merchant lodged a complaint against him with the India Office. It was alleged that in discussions at the German Embassy concerning the possibility of exporting tobacco from India to Germany without using a British concern as an intermediary, Dr. Weber suddenly changed the subject and tried to elicit anti-British and anti-Colonial sentiments from the man.[15]

> He [Weber] asked him how the Congress ministries were faring. The Indian said that they were carrying on satisfactorily as may be seen from the remarks of the Viceroy and the various governors. Mr. Weber said he knew all about such public statements, and there was no use referring him to such speeches. He may say that he was in touch with Indians and was aware of the real inward trend of events. What he wanted to know was how Indians were feeling toward the British and how long they were going to tolerate them.

When the merchant tried to affirm that relations with the British were quite good,

Mr. Weber said that he had definite information to the contrary, and that Indians were preparing to get an independent status. He further said that Great Britain will very soon not be in a position to help India in times of crisis, and Indians must be prepared to look to allies who will stand by them. . . . The one final and clear impression left on the Indian as a result of this part of the conversation was that, according to Mr. Weber, Indians had the best friends in Germans, and if they wanted to develop economically and politically they should welcome Germans and benefit by their advice.

On 23 January 1939 Frank K. Roberts indicated that the Foreign Office would not tolerate this sort of intimidation.

Dr. Weber's action was most improper, and it seems to me to justify our informing the German Government that he is *persona non grata* anywhere in the British Empire, and requesting his removal from London immediately. The Germans would perhaps take some retaliatory measure with or without some justification, and it is therefore for consideration whether we wish to provoke a quarrel on this issue.

In spite of a possible adverse reaction to his declaration, Roberts was in favor of "taking action." The following day, Ivone Kirkpatrick agreed: "Dr. Weber has not been guilty of a more serious offense than German officials are committing all over the Empire, but I agree with Mr. Roberts that when we get a concrete case we should act."

Taking the opposite view, F. T. A. Ashton-Gwatkin argued against Weber's immediate deportation.

[I] would much rather keep Dr. Weber here — as the account shows he is not a dexterous propagandist — than have someone else who would do the same kind of thing more cleverly. Dr. W. has neither the ability nor the character of his predecessor, Dr. Bielfeld; as this paper shows he is rather conceited and rather stupid. I had both of these impressions of him already; they are now deepened.

Vansittart's retort was acerbic: "Gwatkin's minute misses the point, which is that we must show the Germans that we have teeth in such matters; and that may slow down their whole poisonous propaganda machine."

This case highlighted a problem that seemed to admit of no solution. If the Foreign Office gave the Germans a plausible explanation as to why Weber was being deported, it would necessarily involve mentioning the Indian merchant, and this would ruin any hope of his concluding a commercial arrangement with the Germans. On the other hand, if no explanation was offered, the German Embassy would have every reason to advise their Government to retaliate by expelling a British diplomat from Germany.

Vansittart thought he could resolve this dilemma by telling the Germans that

Weber was being asked to leave "on the ground that we have detected him in improper anti-British propaganda. He has probably indulged in so much of it that he will not know precisely to which incident we refer. . . ." But Kirkpatrick was dubious: "The whole point of having Dr. Weber removed is not to get rid of this particular German agent, since he would presumably be succeeded by a similar man; but rather to make an example and to indicate to the Germans that we were not prepared to tolerate this sort of thing."

The Foreign Office finally decided to proceed against Weber, and in mid-March Lord Halifax outlined the reasons to Ambassador von Dirksen in the vaguest terms. Weber's expulsion order coincided with several others, causing the Foreign Office mild concern as to how many permits they could rescind, especially in the face of the Board of Trade's favorable impression of him, and the assurances by Theo Kordt, second in command at the German Embassy, that Weber was not an orthodox Nazi. Finally it was decided to allow him to stay, on the pretext that it would offset the impending expulsion of other German officials.[16]

Perhaps the most distasteful instance of German harassment involved Helene Schliecher, a nurse who came to Britain in July 1937 and secured employment as a mother's helper. After working faithfully for about a year, she was summoned to the German Embassy and told that her passport would lapse in a few days, even though it had been issued in December 1936 and was supposed to be valid for five years. "Pressing for a reason, she was told that it was for the purpose of a sterilisation operation" to take place in Germany, based on the fact that she had suffered a breakdown in 1927 and was committed to a mental hospital for some months with a diagnosis of *dementia praecox*.[17] In 1932 she married unsuitably, and in 1936 her husband sued for divorce on the grounds of her prior mental instability. Between the time of her divorce and the summer of 1938, the Nazis authorized enforced sterilisation of the mentally ill, so if she refused to comply with this law, she would forfeit her citizenship. The Home Office rather reluctantly decreed that: "the question whether she would return to Germany on or before 27 August 1938 was a matter for her to decide."

As we have seen in chapter 15, the Home Office and the Foreign Office deliberated extensively from January to April 1939 before demanding the removal of three Nazi officials: Otto Karlowa, Edmond Himmelmann, and Johanna Wolf. Although Vansittart and others used the term "espionage" to describe their activities, it was largely spying on individual Germans, some of them Jews, and it was the sort of surveillance which had been responsible in part for the recall of Hans Wilhelm Thost in 1935.

The British anticipated that the Germans might retaliate in response to the enforced departure of Karlowa, Himmelmann, and Wolf, but hoped that they would voluntarily withdraw before it was necessary for the Home Office to issue deportation orders on 30 April. This would result in a minimum of press coverage, and the possibility of saving face all around, and was consistent with the tacit understanding with Goebbels in late 1937 regarding future expulsions of journalists. However, by the spring of 1939 relations between the two countries were sufficiently strained that no such courtesies were observed. On 22 April, even before the British released the names of Karlowa, Himmelmann, and Wolf to the press, the Germans selected three British subjects working in Germany as a *quid pro quo*: Leslie Parkin, director of the Eastern Telegraph Co. in Hamburg; Joseph Cowan Edminson, a merchant also in Hamburg; and John Neill, a partner in the Berlin office of Price Waterhouse.[18]

The British reaction was swift. A previously-prepared list of expellees was submitted to the next meeting of the Cabinet, six of whom were asked to leave: Kurt Frauendorf, Adolf Jäger, Ernst Lahrmann, Rudolph Gottfried Rösel, Gunther Schallies, and Friedrich Scharpf. Rösel was placed in this group mainly because he was an effective propagandist who had run a German information service. However, none of the others were journalists. If they had a common denominator it was their membership in the *Deutsche Arbeitsfront*.

Richard Hans Kurt Frauendorf was born in Leipzig on 13 January 1901. Some 31 years later he came to London as the representative of the Leipzig Fair, and started his German Commercial Information Service. Although this was his principal job, he became increasingly involved with the *NSDAP*, and by 1936 he took charge of the *DAB* for the *Landesgruppe*, and later became head of the Ealing *Ortsgruppe*. He applied for membership in the Nazi Party late in 1933, and was admitted in March 1934. Next to Karlowa, and perhaps Rösel, he was the highest ranking official of the *Landesgruppen Gross Britannien*.[19]

Capt. Adolf Eduard Julius Jäger was born in 1899, the same year as Hitler, but whereas Hitler knew little of the sea, Jäger grew up in the bustling port of Lübeck, and made a career of serving in the merchant marine. He came to Britain in 1929, settled in Ilford, Essex, and worked for the Kirsten shipping concern. He waited until 1937 to seek Nazi Party membership which he secured in February 1938. However, he had a long history of acting as a liaison for the *Arbeitsfront* with the many sailors whose ships entered British ports.[20]

Another Party official actively concerned with maritime affairs was Friedrich Wilhelm Scharpf. Born in Stuttgart in 1908, Scharpf settled in Southampton in 1934 as the representative of the *Reichsbahn* (German Railways) and interacted with the many tourists in Southampton who were boarding ships for the Continent. He was also Honorary Vice-Consul, so he could issue visas to these travelers. He was accepted into the Party in October 1936, and was immediately named *Stutzpünktwalter* for the local group.[21] Although it was never made explicit, Scharpf was deported because he was suspected of espionage. Not realising this allegation, he asked the German Embassy in London to intercede on his behalf and ascertain whether he would be welcome in another part of the British Empire, since having a background in German railways and tourism he wanted to secure a job in an English-speaking country. Predictably, the Foreign Office contended that they could hardly recommend someone to the Dominions whom they had refused permission to stay in Britain.[22]

Most of those who were told leave Britain in the spring of 1939 only joined the *NSDAP* once they had arrived in England, but Gunther Schallies was the exception. He was an "old fighter" whose Party number dated from September 1931. As one of the leaders of the *Deutsche Arbeitsfront* in London, he became the unwitting subject of a question in Parliament: was it true, the Home Secretary was asked, that the premises at Absord House, 15 Wilton Road, Victoria, harbored a Nazi Brown House?[23] Sir Samuel Hoare replied that this was the address of the business premises of a German national (Schallies), and was not a Nazi center. He chose not to elaborate specifically why Schailles was targeted for expulsion.

The sixth of those expected to leave the country by mid-May 1939 was Ernst Lahrmann. Born near Hamburg in 1901, he came to Britain in the early 1930s as a businessman based in the Liverpool and Manchester area. His early membership in the *NSDAP* – June 1933 – gave him seniority over other German émigrés, and he soon became the leader of the local *Stutzpünkt*. By 1939 he had earned a reputation of pressuring other émigrés to join the *Deutsche Arbeitsfront*, which made him the focus of two questions in Parliament on 18 and 20 April 1939. Well before this, however, his name had come to the attention of the Home Office and the Foreign Office. The previous January the German Embassy had asked permission to appoint him Vice-Consul. This was not an honorary title, but rather a formal appointment that necessitated an Exequatur which conferred official recognition of his position by the British. Consequently, as had occurred when Otto Bene's name was put forward in 1936 as Consul-General,[24] and again in 1939 regarding Lahrmann, the Foreign Office rejected combining Party and Consular duties. As F. K. Roberts reiterated:[25]

> In this capacity (*Stutzpünktleiter*) he is already in a position to exercise considerable pressure on the local German community, and his power in this respect would of course be much increased if he were able to combine his party functions with the post of German Vice-Consul. MI5 would also regard such a combination of offices as dangerous from the internal security point of view in the event of a crisis in view of the practical immunity enjoyed by a consular officer, and they are fearful lest such an appointment should establish a precedent.

The German reaction to this round of deportations was immediate. On 3 May they announced that six British subjects, including a reporter for the *Daily Telegraph*, would have to be out of Germany by 24 May.[26]

There was no longer any pretense of diplomatic civility. In an atmosphere of mounting tension, several more expulsions were ordered by Britain, but they were handled more discreetly and did not provoke counter measures by

Germany. One of these was Fraülein Dargel.[27] The German Embassy could not understand why she was now being asked to leave after residing in Bournemouth for 15 years. The Foreign Office was adamant, but gave no details. She was not a member of the Nazi Party, but probably was caught intimidating a fellow national.

Another seemingly harmless German requested to leave in the latest wave of expulsions was Hans Zapf who joined the Nazi Party in May 1933 and soon thereafter worked in France for several years. By 1935 he and his family were in Glasgow where he was employed by the W. and J. Martin Company, manufacturers of leather goods. The following year the *Auslandsorganisation* appointed him leader of the Glasgow Stutzpünkt as well as head of the local *Deutsche Arbeitsfront*. Perhaps it was a consequence of his First World War military service, or the result of the damp atmosphere of Glasgow that Zapf contracted rheumatism and returned to Germany in May of 1939 to take the cure at Bad Mergentheim near Worms. While away from the British Isles he was informed that his return to Glasgow would not be welcome, because, among other things, his fellow employees at the Martin firm objected to his continued employment. Efforts on his behalf by the German Embassy in London and the German Consulate in Glasgow were unavailing, and he was told by the personal secretary to the head of the *Auslandsorganisation*, Robert Fischer, "I am very sorry that you also have become a victim of the senseless English persecution of the Germans. At least your chief has been quite decent about it, and I hope you will soon find a post which will suit your situation and ability."[28]

The British tactic of refusing undesirable Nazis re-entry into the United Kingdom while they were on holiday was employed twice more in the spring of 1939. Normann Günther joined the Nazi Party in April 1933 and was Managing Director of a German firm in London from 1935 to 1939. He lived at the Connaught Club, 75 Seymour Street, W2. The British authorities told him not to return after visiting the Continent for a few months, even though his visa was still valid.[29]

Fritz Peter Krüger seems neither to have held a leadership position in a Nazi organization nor been active in the *Deutsche Arbeitsfront*. A lawyer by training, he and his wife came to London in July 1935, where she acquired a job as a hospitality secretary for the Anglo-German Academic Bureau. This included the use of a flat at the Bureau's headquarters, 45 Russell Square, WC1. Krüger was a relatively early convert to Nazism, joining the Party in May 1932. A year later he entered the ranks of the *SS*. He came to Britain claiming that he wanted to study British legal traditions. In 1937 the German Embassy in London hired him as an adviser and translator for the German delegation that attended periodic meetings of the International Sugar Conference. Krüger was active in newspaper and magazine journalism, and contributed articles to the *Berliner Börsenzeitung*, *Hamburger Tageblatt*, and other provincial outlets as well Nazi-leaning periodicals such as *Europaischen Korrespondenz, Parteipresse Sonderdienst, USSR-Dienst, Juden Frage, Nationalsozialistiche Landpost, Hochschule und Ausland,* and *Koralle.*

In the spring of 1939 he went by himself on holiday, returning on 27 May to Britain via Harwich where he was refused entry, without explanation. Petitioning for reconsideration, his wife, still in England, said she feared that the British had misinterpreted a publishing contract that Krüger was carrying. For some time he had been working on a history of the Jews in England, which the *Nordland Verlag* of Berlin agreed to publish, and which may have suggested that Krüger was anti-Semitic. His wife tried to convince the British that it was a genuine piece of scholarship, and not propaganda.[30] However, whether he wrote in his own name or used the pseudonym Peter Aldag, Krüger had difficulty convincing the Home Office that he was not a propagandist, official or otherwise.[31] It was suspected that he may have been financed by the Propaganda Ministry, for why else would a lawyer stay away from an active practice in Germany.

Understandably, the Germans were convinced that the British had altered course and embarked upon a systematic plan of disruption and expulsion. They could not understand the antipathy toward Nazi organizations abroad, since they saw their foreign groups not as vehicles of espionage but organs of Party discipline and propaganda. Furthermore, they had not objected to British associations like the English Speaking Union or the British Council that were allowed to function in the Third Reich.

The British intention to disrupt Nazi national and local groups in the United Kingdom had serious implications for the future. Two weeks before his departure from London, Karlowa asked his superior, Ernst Wilhelm Bohle, whether the time had come to dispense with a *Landesgruppenleiter,* since it was clear that the British would suspect anyone who replaced him and might well expel the next incumbent. As head of the *Auslandsorganisation,* Bohle agreed, and sent out a memo suggesting that Nazis abroad might have to get used to a lack of structure and clear leadership if the British persisted in their tactics.[32]

During June and early July 1939 Bohle's personal assistant, Robert Fischer, compiled a list of those who had been expelled on the basis of correspondence and conversations with those who had been told not to return. He drew no major conclusions, but merely stated facts. Whether Bohle realized the intent of British policy is not clear. However, a reporter for the *New York Times* certainly did. As early as 7 May 1939 he wrote: "One cause doubtless was the desire to teach the Nazis that they cannot intimidate Germans resident in London and get away with it."[33]

By the time Fischer's report reached Bohle on 8 July, no expulsions had taken place for more than a month, and the Nazis might well have believed that the British had exhausted their list of candidates for expulsion. However, they were wrong, especially regarding Theodor Böttiger, former press secretary for Ribbentrop and the representative in London of the main Nazi papers, the

*Völkischer Beobachter* and *Der Angriff*. Böttiger requested an interview with the Home Secretary, Samuel Hoare, something that neither the Home Office nor the Foreign Office were inclined to grant. Moreover, he was already slated for deportation, according to one Foreign Service officer: "I should add for your secret and confidential information that Dr. Böttiger is one of two German journalists selected for expulsion from this country if we decide to retaliate for the action the German Government are taking against the *News Chronicle* correspondents in Berlin."[34]

Before leaving for his summer holiday, and ignorant of his sullied reputation, Böttiger asked the Home Office to renew his permit to remain in Britain for another year. Within the Foreign Office they thought that this seemed pointless if he were not going to be allowed to return. Charles Peake unhesitatingly reiterated:[35]

> We have on previous occasions considered the question of expelling Dr. Böttiger, and if we were now called upon to prepare a list of names of German journalists to be expelled, so far as the News Department is concerned, we should unhesitatingly put Dr. Böttiger at the head of our list.

On purely journalistic grounds, there was no pretext for taking immediate action against Böttiger, but his close association with Ribbentrop marked him as suspicious. Born in 1903 in La Paz, Bolivia, he came to Germany to attend Hamburg and Heidelberg Universities. He received a doctorate in political science in 1927, and worked for the next five years at the *Deutsche Allegemeine Zeitung*, where he became a foreign political editor. During the 1920s he admired the Nazis, and so after they gained power in 1933 he both joined the Party and began writing for Goebbels's mouthpiece, *Der Angriff*. Two years later the Propaganda Ministry recognized that he would make an effective press adviser to the *Dienststelle Ribbentrop*, and soon he was Ribbentrop's personal assistant, collecting the daily dispatches from the official German news agency, the *Deutsches Nachrichtenbüro*, and delivering them to Ribbentrop at his villa in Dahlem. They would then decide together which items were worthy of comment. Later, Böttiger would attend press conferences sponsored by the Propaganda Ministry and the Ministry of Foreign Affairs to make sure that he and his colleagues at the *Ribbentropbüro* were cognizant of the official Party line. Ribbentrop came to rely upon him heavily, and therefore, when he became Ambassador to Britain in the late summer of 1936, he invited Böttiger to accompany him.

In London, Böttiger combined two positions: personal Press Secretary to Ribbentrop, and Press Attaché at the German Embassy, where he replaced Fritz Hesse.[36] Because Ribbentrop liked his personal entourage to be members of the SS, Böttiger took the necessary steps to join. However, as late as the autumn of 1939 he had not yet convinced the watchdogs of the SS that he was sufficiently Aryan in his origins.[37]

When Ribbentrop returned to Germany in early 1938 as the newly-appointed German Foreign Minister, Böttiger remained in London at 3 Inner Park Road, Wimbledon Common, SW19. He ceased to be Press Attaché at the Embassy, but kept working for the *Völkischer Beobachter* and *Der Angriff*. His letters to the Editor of *The Times* and other papers alleging British mendacity continued to appear regularly.[38] On 19 April 1939 he published an article in *Der Angriff* accusing American Ambassador Joseph Kennedy of being a warmonger trying to push Britain into a conflict with Germany, and in other columns singled out Harold Nicolson and Duff Cooper as having warlike tendencies. These journalistic excesses vexed the Foreign Office. Accordingly, on 8 June 1939, when Böttiger asked the Home Office to extend his permission to remain in Britain, they balked. Hoping to return to London, he left for Germany on 16 June, leaving his wife and children behind. By 18 and 19 July, Vansittart expressed the attitude shared by many in both the Foreign and the Home Office: instead of granting an extension, urge the German Ambassador to advise him to stay away permanently. [39]

> This is polite and unsensational and at the same time rids us of one of the larger snakes. Apart from the damage he does by the venom of his articles in the *Völkischer Beobachter* and by the false impression that he conveys to the Ribbentrop school, he is in very close touch with all the Mosley gang which advocates courses and principles opposed not only to the policy but to the constitution of this country.

## NOTES

1 *Daily Herald*, 6 December 1933, pp. 1–2.
2 *New York Times*, 12 August 1937, p. 12.
3 *Manchester Guardian*, 26 August 1937, p. 8.
4 *Daily Herald*, 1 June 1938, p. 3.
5 E. N. Cooper of the Home Office to William Strang, 24 December 1938, PRO, FO 371/21652, C15995, ff. 252–59.
6 FO 371/23039, C11064, ff. 406–7.
7 FO 371/21652, C12607, f. 124.
8 *Ibid.*, f. 127. See also the *Daily Herald*, 1 June 1938, p. 3.
9 *Ibid.*, f. 129.
10 *Ibid.*, ff. 149–50.
11 *Parliamentary Debates*, Commons, CCCXXXI (10 February 1938), 1235.
12 PRO, FO 371/21652, C12607, ff. 130–35.
13 *Ibid.*
14 Weber file, BDC.
15 PRO, FO 371/23035, C793, ff. 206–17.
16 For further details of the Weber case, see: PRO, FO 371/22988, C3456, ff. 263–68; *ibid.*, C4294, ff. 309–12; *ibid.*, C4471, f. 313; PRO, FO 371/23035, C4820, ff. 395–98.
17 PRO, FO 371/21652, C12607, f. 162.

18  PRO, FO 371/23036, C5761, ff. 72–74.
19  BDC file. See also: Fischer memo of 8 July 1939 in NA microcopy T-120, roll 49, frames 39449-50; PRO, FO 371/19942, C5497, f. 166–73; FO 371/21652, C7841, f. 28.
20  *Ibid.*
21  *Ibid.*
22  PRO, FO 371/23038, C9763, ff. 302–3.
23  *Parliamentary Debates*, Commons, CCCXLVI (18 April 1939), 173. See also: PRO, FO 371/23036, C7016, ff. 266–67, and BDC.
27  See chapter 6.
25  PRO, FO 371/23055, C3569, ff. 339–42. Lahrmann's case is discussed in *ibid.*, C5601, ff. 50–51 and in PRO, FO 371/23036, C5704, ff. 70–71. His *NSDAP* membership card can be found in the BDC.
26  Memo by Woermann, Berlin, 3 May 1939, NA microcopy T-120, roll 49, 39443–44; FO 371/23036, C6531, ff. 153–56.
27  PRO, FO 371/23037, C7195, ff. 321–26.
28  R. Fischer to H. Zapf, 23 May 1939, BDC. See also microcopy NA T-120, roll 49, 39449–50.
29  BDC files and NA microcopy T-120, roll 49, 39449–510.
30  Krüger's book appeared in two volumes: *Juden Beherrschen England* (1939) and *Juden Erobern England* (1940). He subsequently wrote other more obviously propagandistic pamphlets: *Unsere Gegner und Ihr Krief* (1941); *Der Macht der Juden in England* (1940); *Dollar-Imperialismus* (1942). Krüger has a large file in the BDC. See also: PRO, FO 372/3345, T7343, ff. 134–45; *ibid.*, T7863, ff. 130–33.
31  PRO, FO 372/3345. T7300, ff. 119–23.
32  Karlowa to Bohle, 14 April 1939, and Bohle memo of 18 April 1939: NA microcopy T-120, roll 49, 39432–35.
33  *New York Times*, 7 May 1939, p. 5.
34  PRO, FO 371/22989, C4737, ff. 351–57.
35  HO to FO and FO to HO, 6 July 1939, PRO, FO 371/23090, C9515, ff. 275–76.
36  For Hesse's activities in London, see chapter 7.
37  In addition to the Böttiger file at the BDC, there is useful background in H. A. Jacobsen, *Nationalsozialistische Aussenpolitik* (Frankfurt am Main 1968), pp. 272, 293, and 299. See also PRO, KV2/1294.
38  Samples of Böttiger's letters to the Editor may be found in: *The Times*, 3 May 1939, p. 14; 7 March 1939, p. 8; 15 July 1939, p. 8.
39  PRO, FO 371/22990, C10503, pp. 337–43.

# 17 THE QUESTION OF ESPIONAGE

After the First World War and especially during the 1930s it was assumed that in spite of the official end to hostilities Nazis were involved in espionage on a large scale in a number of European countries because they believed that intelligence would be the key component in spreading National Socialism. A corollary to this assumption was that each member of the *NSDAP* living outside Germany might be a potential intelligence agent, loyal to the Third Reich and willing to carry out secret assignments.

Evaluating this perception necessitates focusing on the *Auslandsorganisation* (foreign department) of the National Socialist Party whose job it was to supervise all German citizens outside the Reich, and more particularly, those who belonged to the Party. The persistent question has been: were those in the *Landesgruppen* (national groups), *Ortsgruppen* (local groups), and *Stutzpünkte* (point groups), part of a network of foreign surveillance?

Discovering the answer to this question involves knowing more about Ernst Wilhelm Bohle, head of the *Auslandsorganisation* from 1933 onward. Bohle was born on 28 July 1903 of German parents in Bradford, England, which automatically qualified him as a dual citizen. Later this proved very useful in securing a job with the *Auslandsorganisation*. At some point before the First World War his family moved to Capetown, South Africa, where he attended the English high school and furthered his facility in English. After graduating from secondary school in 1919, he returned to Germany and spent six semesters studying political science and economics at the universities of Cologne and Berlin. These subjects did not interest him, so he enrolled in a commercial academy in Berlin and received a diploma in 1923. From 1924 to 1927 he worked for several British and American export firms in Holland and the Rhineland, and between 1927–30 was a bookkeeper in Hamburg for the American automobile firm, the Chrysler Corporation, before starting his own car accessory business.

On 27 November 1931 he joined the Nazi Party, volunteering his services to Hans Nieland, head of the *Auslandsabteilung* whose headquarters were in Hamburg. From December 1931 to April 1932, he was placed in charge of overseas Nazi groups in South Africa, Britain, and the United States, and by September he was an Inspector for all the activities of the *Auslandsabteilung* as well as assuming the role of Nieland's personal assistant.[1] Bohle was not the only member of his family attraced to subscribe the Nazi cause. His father Hermann, who was a Doctor of Engineering, and his mother, Antonie, also became Party members.

By April 1933 Bohle's automobile business was in danger of failing, like many other companies affected by the Great Depression. As a consequece, he sought paid employment in the Party, and in the course of doing so, talked himself into the leadership of the *Auslandsabteilung* at the expense of his boss, Hans Nieland. His arguments for replacing Nieland were persuasive: Nieland had recently become Police President of Hamburg and therefore could devote less time to Party affairs; and although Nieland had served in the Reichstag, he had virtually no experience living and working abroad. On both counts Bohle contended that he was better qualified to guide the ever-growing section of the Party concerned with Germans outside the Fatherland.[2]

Bohle's appointment as head of the *Auslandsabteilung* was formally announced on 8 May 1933, and he eventually assumed the title of *Gauleiter* and was on a par with leaders who administered different regions of the Third Reich. By early 1934 the *Auslandsabteilung* adopted its official name, *Auslandsorganisation*, and by the mid-1930s moved its headquarters from Hamburg to Berlin.

On 30 January 1937 Bohle was given a joint appointment with the German Foreign Ministry, signifying that his organization would henceforth be sanctioned as both a Government as well as a Party entity. Observers in Britain and elsewhere saw this as extremely sinister. As we have seen elsewhere,[3] the British Foreign Office took a very dim view of Nazi Party officials combining their Party and diplomatic duties, since it meant that German citizens abroad, especially those who were anti-Nazi, were at the mercy of Consular or Embassy personnel with strong ties to the *NSDAP* and its political agenda.

Curiously, the Nazis never implemented the potential of this joint arrangement. Bohle gained little if anything from being added to the German Foreign Ministry, and although from the outside it appeared that the Party was seeking to infiltrate the Ministry, in fact the Foreign Minister, von Neurath, regarded the move as a way to try to exert more control over the Party's activities abroad.[4]

During the Nuremberg trials, Bohle stressed how insignificant his position was both before and after January 1937. He pointed out that the Foreign Ministry allocated him only one office and a modest staff of three, and claimed that his work for the ministry consumed scarcely a couple of hours each morning while the rest of the day was devoted to the work of the *Auslandsorganisation*. Under Neurath and then Ribbentrop, he portrayed his work at the

Wilhelmstrasse as distinctly a "sideline."[5] By way of illustrating his compara-
tive isolation from the rest of the Party leadership, he lamented after the war: "I
was never once, in the 12 years of the National Socialist regime, invited to the
house of one of the German *Gauleiters*. I had my own field of work, my own
collaborators, and was not officially but practically excluded from the Party hierarchy."[6]

In trying to defend his modest role and that of his colleagues at the
*Auslandsorganisation*, Bohle emphasized the narrow scope of his operation, and
reminded the panel that he was responsible solely for German citizens abroad.
This specifically excluded all ethnic Germans or *Volksdeutsche*, who came under a
separate office, the *Volksdeutsche Mittelstelle* or *VoMi*.[7] Nor was the *Auslandsorganisation*
concerned with contacting or administering Nazi Party members abroad, even
when these individuals represented a Party agency, as in the case of Party
members working for the German Labour Front in foreign countries. He
acknowledged that activities such as Hitler Youth and the Winter Relief Fund
were monitored by the *Landesgruppen* leaders in their respective countries.

Bohle stoutly maintained both before and after the war that his operation
had nothing to do with espionage, and that regulations governing the behavior
of Germans abroad specifically forbade any such activity. He admitted that he
had no way of preventing individual Germans from working for the Gestapo or
the *Abwehr* (German Military Intelligence), and he would have had no way of
finding out whether they did or not do so, since any clandestine work would
have taken place without the knowledge of local group leaders.

When questioned at Nuremberg Bohle denied that the *Auslandsorganisation*
employed any kind of cipher or other secret means of communication with
groups abroad. Neither did they have special wireless transmitters to broadcast
holiday messages to Germans throughout the world. The chief means of keeping
in touch with the various branches was through couriers who delivered instructions from Berlin and brought back reports from national group leaders.

In this connection, Detective Sergeant William East of Special Branch
disclosed the normal method employed by Otto Bene and Otto Karlowa when
they were in London in the 1930s. The Germans had two ships, the *Monte Pascoal*
and the *Monte Rosa*, which plied the waters each week between Hamburg and
Greenwich. While moored in the Thames, they were able to maintain their
extraterritoriality and be virtually immune to official British scrutiny. Local
group leaders could board these vessels for conferences and social occasions, and
the ships proved especially convenient for regular transmissions of letters and
reports outside the jurisdiction of the British postal authorities.[8]

Bohle readily admitted that reports from groups abroad could be circulated
among offices or departments other than those of the originating *Landesgruppe*.
Depending upon their contents, dispatches might be sent to the Foreign
Ministry, the German Labour Front, Rosenberg's Foreign Policy Office, or even

to the headquarters of the *SS* or the Gestapo. When pressured by the Nuremberg Prosecutors, Bohle granted that information from abroad could be passed to the *Abwehr*, but he insisted that this "very seldom" happened.[9] He never acknowledged that the *Auslandsorganisation* cooperated in placing *Abwehr* agents abroad or providing them with legitimate cover as members of *Ortsgruppen*, and only agreed to having received hundreds of reports each month, some of them containing information which might be useful to one or another agency of the Third Reich.

The Prosecution did not entirely accept Bohle's disclaimer, and persisted in asking whether or not the *Auslandsorganisation* sustained a liaison with the . Bohle's initial response was: "No, I had only one assistant who maintained an unofficial connection with the *Abwehr*, if the occasion arose."[10] He insisted on making a distinction between "official" and "unofficial," although the Prosecution did not seem to care about this difference and continued pressing him about the issue, asking if "Schmuss" was the assistant in question. Bohle answered, "He did not come from the *Abwehr*; he was chief of personnel of the *Auslandsorganisation*, and his function as liaison was purely unofficial."

The *Auslandsorganisation* and its staff repeatedly stated that their chief focus was internal: to supervise and encourage groups of Germans living abroad in their common goal of serving the Party and the Reich. Far from seeking to subvert foreign governments, they encouraged members to preserve their status as foreign guests and observe the ten rules that governed their conduct abroad.[11] They constantly lamented that they were misunderstood and misjudged, and were often victims of anti-Nazi violence, as in the case of Wilhelm Gustloff who was assassinated in Switzerland in 1936 although he had broken no Swiss laws.[12]

Bohle's position at his own trial at Nuremberg, as distinct from the trials of others where he was only a witness, was not helped by being a member of the *SS*, since it was listed as a criminal organization under the tribunal's guidelines. It didn't help either that he had not sought membership but had been recruited during the Olympics in the late summer of 1936 in Berlin. Within its ranks he received periodic promotions, yet there was no evidence that he ever had anything to do with identifying Jews for the Final Solution.

The Nuremberg Tribunal and other post-war investigations were principally preoccupied with espionage and sabotage, and what came to be known as Fifth Column activity. Coined during the Spanish Civil War, the phrase "Fifth Column" signified bands of disloyal individuals who would betray their homeland in time of war in order to facilitate the victory of an outside enemy. In Britain of the 1930s the term came to mean Germans who sought to persuade other Germans, whether they were refugees, long-term residents, or naturalized British subjects, to betray England and her allies. Contrariwise, Sir Oswald Mosley, a professed British patriot, tried to enlist his own countrymen into the British Fascist movement as Nazi sympathizers.

Evidence suggests that Fifth Columnists were indeed active and successful in countries like Norway, Holland, and Spain during the early years of the Second World War. However, to what extent they collaborated or made contact with local *Ortsgruppen* is moot, although it was widely perceived at the time that they were controlled by the *Auslandsorganisation.*

Almost a war-hysteria reigned in Britain in the spring of 1940 as one nation after another fell to Nazi aggression. Defense Regulation 18-B was employed to round up large numbers of British subjects, including Sir Oswald Mosley. Reflecting this frenzy, Detective Sergeant William East recalled:[13]

> I can tell you that there were many [British] I saw at the [German] Embassy as guests of Ribbentrop who would not like it to be known to-day. Many of them were there on legitimate diplomatic business by which they served this country, but there were many others – I might say hundreds – who were nothing less than what we term to-day, Fifth Columnists. I assembled quite a card index at the Yard of some 600 of those I knew to be the most dangerous. It was made over years of careful investigation of the antecedents of those who called at the Embassy and the Party H.Q., and in addition to names and addresses each card bore a pen picture of the person named and details of his or her connection with the Nazis. Many of these I noted have since been interned or have left these shores for more healthy climes, but there are probably still a considerable number of those Hitler spawned at large ready to damage our cause.

Like many others at the time and since, East did not make a distinction between pro-Nazi British subjects and Germans resident in Britain, whether or not they were naturalized British Subjects. However, to discover the threat posed by Nazis through the tentacles of the *Auslandsorganisation* in London, we need to highlight this difference. The MI5 report on Otto Bene, drawn up in the spring of 1936 following his self-removal from the British scene, embodies this problem. In it we learn that it was unclear whether once Bene left London he would try to return, and if he did, in what capacity. To decide this, the British authorities were challenged to make up their minds as to just how much of a threat Bene really posed. Sir Vernon Kell of MI5 wrote of Bene to Russell Scott of the Home Office: "What I feel is that it is the organisation rather than the individual at the head of it which is definitely dangerous."[14] Everyone concerned with British security acknowledged the place of espionage and sabotage in time of war, but Kell felt that priority ought to be given to framing a policy based on the current state of tenuous peace. Therefore, he minimized Bene's role and that of the Party, saying "that so long as they commit no breach of the law, they and their activities are of no concern to us." However, he did acknowledge that Bene imprinted his personality and style on the membership, and so his actions could not be ignored.

Accordingly, the first complaint that MI5 made against Bene read: "He works in close touch with the *Hafendienstamt* which is in liaison with the Gestapo for the purpose of supervising the activities of German nationals in this country and for maintaining Party discipline." Since the German merchant marine came under the jurisdiction of the *Auslandsorganisation* when outside German waters, any seamen who landed at British ports was subject to the *Landesgruppenleiter*, Otto Karlowa. British authorities always suspected that German seamen might be manipulated while in the United Kingdom, and willingly acknowledged that mariners would probably keep their eyes open and report items of interest to Party superiors; but the same was true of British sailors in German harbors. The chief difference was that the Nazi Party officials could bring more pressure to bear on their nationals.

Kell's second concern involved the "infringement of British sovereignty" by quasi-judicial actions which were taking place on British soil by Nazi magistrates. When the Party felt it necessary to adjudicate intra-Party disputes and impose discipline, they utilized a semi-legal *Schlichter*, or judge, to arbitrate conflicting evidence. He could reside in the foreign country for several years, as Karl-Heinz Kutschke[15] did in London, and he had the power to recommend expulsion from the Party, which he did in the case of Krug von Nidda, one of Bene's chief lieutenants.[16] The British deplored this procedure, but allowed it because it dealt with "internal affairs" of the Nazi Party, and probably had minimal implications for espionage.

The third charge against Bene was more serious: "There is evidence that, in one case only, he has performed counter-espionage duties by reporting to the *Hafendienst* on a British subject visiting Germany in circumstances which appeared suspicious to the *Landesgruppe*." Here, as in the first allegation, it was suggested that such information could be turned over to the Gestapo. Ordinarily, the Gestapo was concerned with domestic security and not with Germans abroad or foreigners generally. However, their long arm sometimes extended beyond frontiers if it meant keeping track of German citizens who were promoting anti-Nazi activities, or foreigners on German soil seeking contacts with anti-Nazi factions. Was Bene's asking the German Harbor Service to look out for a particular Englishman materially different from someone in the British legation or the British Council alerting homeland authorities to the imminent visit of an undesirable Nazi?

The fourth concern of MI5 was not a matter of espionage, but rather the effect of propaganda disseminated by Bene's organization toward ethnic Germans.[17]

> There is evidence that the *Landesgruppe* is used as an instrument of German foreign policy to the extent that Otto Bene has played a prominent part in working for the creation of a pro-German feeling in Great Britain. That is, of course, unexceptionable in itself but it is difficult to resist the inference on general grounds that this is done as part of a policy whose ultimate object is to neutralize Great Britain and separate her from France.

In his final point, Kell raised the very real possibility of Bene establishing a Fifth Column in Britain.

> A special organization, subordinate to the *Landesgruppe*, exists with the sole and express object of Nazifying these "old Germans" [ethnic or *Volksdeutsche*]. . . . The name of this organization is the *Deutsche Vereinigung*. . . . We have recently heard that the British Embassy in Berlin has obtained information that proves conclusively that the Party organization in Berlin and its leaders are particularly pleased with the progress which has been made in the *Landesgruppe* under Otto Bene in London in winning back these "old Germans" to their allegiance to the Swastika. In the event of war between Great Britain and Germany, after all German subjects had been deported, the "old Germans" – British subjects – of the *Deutsche Vereingung* would remain in this country as ready-made machinery for the organisation of sabotage and espionage work.

Throughout the 1930s, the spectre of subversion haunted British authorities despite the fact that there were comparatively few naturalized British subjects of German descent. The dilemma was that such people could not be deprived of their British nationality in time of war, and existing law did not permit them to be interned.

What is strange about the official pronouncements of Kell, Vansittart and others, was their unwillingness to grant that wartime necessity justified new and extensive regulations against unreliable British subjects, whether of German descent or not. Yet, during the First World War governments had gone to some lengths to abridge the civil rights of citizens. Most of Kell's and Vansittart's fears were framed in prospective terms, whereas the simple solution from hindsight would have been to "Collar the Lot."[18] German citizens could have been deported or interned at the outbreak of war if there were any reason to suspect them of pro-Nazi leanings, and British subjects of dubious reliability could also have been detained.

In the same report that detailed Bene's offenses, Kell recognized that increased British security would have to be put in place once war broke out.

> It is possible that the British Empire may find itself at war with either of these powers [Germany or Italy] within the next three or four years. It is certain (insofar as judgments can be based on existing tendencies in all the countries concerned), that any such war will be started without any formal declaration, by a surprise attack launched by a large fleet of air bombers on London, other British industrial centers, and, in the event of war with Italy, on our naval bases in the Mediterranean. . . . Air Forces will be used not only to secure the great advantage of initial surprise, but to destroy the enemy by attack on the civilian population – men, women, and children – in their homes and in the munitions factories as well as on the armed forces.

This turned out to be a fairly accurate forecast of Germany's invasion of Poland in early September 1939, but it was a woefully inadequate projection for Britain. Even Hitler recognized in 1940 that he could not hope to defeat Britain unless he could invade the country, which meant defeating the British navy. Kell's logic was sound if one assumes that a surprise enemy attack would unleash a coordinated orgy of sabotage based on previously accumulated espionage.

Just who would be carrying out this espionage, and how were they going to do it? The British press and some members of Parliament thought they knew, and were eager to provide a variety of answers. Perhaps the favorite targets of suspicion were foreign domestic servants. Thousands of households employed serving girls, nannies, governesses and charwomen from Germany or Austria. We have already seen how the *NSDAP* sought to control these women, but there was the added fear that they would overhear or observe things which were meant to be kept secret, and would transmit the information to the German authorities. In 1938 the *Sunday Express* estimated that 10,000 German and Austrian women had secured work permits as domestic servants.[19] Other newspapers echoed the alarm, and the German language newspaper in England, *Deutsche Zeitung in Gross Britannien,* found these allegations libelous, while Detective Sergeant William East found them plausible.[20] In 1940 he wrote that the German Labour Front "did much to keep the servant girls on their toes in their search for information useful to Hitler. As a result, the girls became highly organized under a woman leader (married to an Englishman) with an employment exchange."[21] East's allusion was to Mrs. Alexander Raven Tomson, head of the Anglo-German Agency, whom we have already witnessed warning newly-arrived domestics against working for Jewish families. However, she was not a leader within the German Labour Front, nor did she have anything to do with promoting domestic espionage.

Undoubtedly some eavesdropping and snooping occurred, but it is reasonable to assume that those with sensitive information, such as military personnel, took precautions when around German or Austrian servants. In the absence of relevant Home Office data, there is little evidence of this kind of domestic espionage, an opinion shared by the historical spy-hunter Ladislas Farago, who estimated that there were at most only a few servants in Britain who were under the supervision of German Military Intelligence.[22]

As in all wars, attractive foreign women were suspected of being spies. The *femme fatale* syndrome was popularized in suggestive pamphlets like *Guilty Women,* published by Richard Baxter in 1941. A certain number of German and Austrian women were portrayed as either lower-class servants hanging about military bases in order to seduce unwitting soldiers and sailors, or upper-class hostesses and aristocratic temptresses. Detective Sergeant William East shadowed Baroness von Trescow and discovered that she was having an affair with a young

234

naval officer on the Admiralty staff; and when she was not with him, she kept company with either a Nazi official or an Air Force officer at Hendon Air Base.[23] According to officer East, the result of his exposé was that the Baroness was eventually asked to leave Britain. Whether Baroness von Trescow was actually an intelligence agent is obscure, but undoubtedly the Nazis did employ alluring women in this way. The wife of a double-agent, William de Ropp earned a reputation for sleeping with a number of German officials in Berlin. However, it is difficult to measure the damage caused by this sort of espionage.

Frank K. Roberts of the Foreign Office, in a minute dated 16 May 1938, recorded a particularly bizarre spy story involving a woman.[24]

A Mr. Bedbroke, director of a firm of travel agents, whose card is attached, called today to communicate the following information which he thought might be of interest to our Intelligence Service. In his spare time Mr. Bedbroke interests himself in psychical research and through this he had come in contact with a Miss Patterson who was in England on a Canadian passport working in England for a Canadian advertising agent called Bennett. This girl was living with an English lady, Miss Hellings, of 10 Colville Road, 11 Bayswater, N11. Miss Hellings had brought Miss Patterson to psychic research meetings and the latter had, according to Mr. Bedbroke, been so moved by spiritualistic experience that she had confessed to Mr. Bedbroke that she was in reality a German national, Baroness von Rohbach of Heidelberg, who had been sent over to Canada when a child where she had acquired Canadian nationality and had been trained in spy activities in which she was now indulging in this country. Mr. Bedbroke understood that she was in touch with several former Austrian nationals in this connection. He claimed to have considerable influence over her through his psychic powers and suggested that he might be able to discover a good deal of information which might be useful to our authorities if the latter suggested to him the lines on which he should work.

Captain Guy Liddell of MI5 was asked to look into this case and rendered his opinion in a communiqué dated 30 May. Unfortunately this is missing from the Foreign Office files, since it was returned to the sender.

There may be a logical explanation as to why the *Abwehr* did relatively little spying in Britain after 1935. It has been suggested that Hitler himself gave orders to the *Abwehr* to cease operations across the channel following the arrest and conviction of a German agent in Britain, Hermann Goertz. It has been exceedingly difficult to pin down an order of this kind by Hitler. Estimates range from its being issued as early as November 1935 to September 1936, and many historians have referred to it, but few have cited it satisfactorily.[25] The fullest explanation of the *Abwehr*'s pre-war intelligence policy is in Paul Leverkuehn's book in which he affirms that during 1935 Admiral Canaris discouraged the activities of agent provocateurs abroad, and quotes an *Abwehr* officer who oversaw naval matters in the Western theater of Europe.[26]

Initially all intelligence work against Great Britain was forbidden, and it was only in 1936 that this ruling was somewhat relaxed and a certain measure of observation activity was permitted; even then, however, the employment of regular agents was denied to us. But in the autumn of 1937 these restrictions were removed, and we were given full liberty of action, not only in the United Kingdom itself, but also for the collation of reports on naval stations and bases overseas.

Ladislas Farago deciphered the code names of many *Abwehr* agents sent to Britain and the United States and claims that there were about 253 operatives in the United Kingdom before the war.[27] Because he fails to offer adequate bibliographical citations, it is difficult to verify his statement, since some of his sources may have been published documents, like maps, service manuals, almanacs and newspapers. On the other hand, judged by arrests, expulsions, and other revelations, there were indeed remarkably few *Abwehr* agents active in Britain.

Another reason why relatively few Nazi agents were detected before September 1939 may be the efficiency of MI5 and the Special Branch of Scotland Yard. It has become fashionable to denigrate the counter-espionage efforts of the British security services, especially in view of the postwar disclosures relating to spies like Philby, Burgess, McLean, and Blunt. However, the evidence would suggest that despite their modest numbers and budgets, both agencies were remarkably successful in discouraging and detecting Nazi espionage of a military or industrial type.

Within MI5 three individuals shared primary responsibility for anti-Nazi espionage: Dick White,[28] Maxwell Knight[29] and Guy Liddell.[30] White had a degree from Christ Church, Oxford, and spent several years at the universities of California and Michigan. He became actively involved with MI5 during the course of 1936, and was later an especially good friend of Fritz Hesse, head of the *Deutsches Nachrichtenburo* (German News Agency) in London.[31] Vernon Kell, head of MI5, asked Knight to set up a special counter-subversion section whose agents could infiltrate not only Communist but right-wing organizations. Knight was quite successful in penetrating the British Right as well as being skillful in recruiting German or Austrian refugees to pose as pro-Nazis. One of his double agents was an Austrian woman, Friedl Gaertner, who became secretary to the novelist Dennis Wheatley. Her code name was "Gelaline," and it was generally unknown at the time that her sister was married to the younger brother of Stewart Menzies, head of MI6.[32]

Captain Guy Liddell was originally active in the ranks of the Special Branch of Scotland Yard, but was co-opted by MI5 in the early 1930s. Since MI5 relied on the Special Branch to make many of its inquiries and to provide surveillance, it was useful to have Liddell as liaison between both services. We have already noted how two Special Branch officers, William East and Hubert Morse, gathered much helpful information regarding German meetings, social occasions, and conversations.

Both spoke and understood German well, but often pretended that they did not.

East learned his German "in the bitter school" of a First World War German prison camp where he was taken captive on the Western Front in October 1914 when serving as a sergeant in the Grenadier Guards.[33] Following his release at the end of the War, he continued corresponding with some of his German acquaintances. In 1933, he was assigned to keep track of Nazi activity, especially on the two German ships, the *Monte Pascoal* and the *Monte Rosa*, he did not conceal his affiliation with the Metropolitan Police, but professed strong admiration for Hitler and the Nazi movement. Over a period of months he managed to persuade Bene, Himmelmann, von Nidda and other *Ortsgruppe* leaders that he was on their side, and since the Nazis accepted that their public meetings would be scrutinized by the police, they asked to have East perform this function. Eventually he admitted that he spoke German fluently.[34]

> I attended meeting after meeting, and at the suggestion of Himmelmann and Bene adopted an alias intended to deceive Nazis coming over from Germany. I became Wilhelm Braun, born of a German father and a Scottish mother in Glasgow. It proved a useful *alias* inasmuch as it covered any defects in my accent and also served to disarm suspicion which might be directed against the Nazi friends who were then helping me.

East's dissimulation may not have deceived the Nazis. Moreover, they may have thought they were fooling him by feeding him only what they wanted the British authorities to know: that the *Ortsgruppen* were peaceful and harmless. However, East was convinced that he had successfully hoodwinked them: "I had the open sesame to all meetings and the members spoke openly with me. I went in and out of the Embassy as I liked and was looked upon as an unofficial liaison between the German colony and the police here." His privileged position with the Nazis ceased, however, once Bene left London in 1936, perhaps because his successor, Otto Karlowa, did not trust East. Thereafter it fell to others in Special Branch as well as a gradually expanding MI5, to monitor the *Landesgruppen*.

Certain events that took place in London in the autumn of 1935 may have signaled the Germans that British tolerance of their activities was at an end. During that year Hans Thost, the correspondent for the *Völkische Beobachter*, was expelled, and Dr. Hermann Goertz, the one clear and bona fide *Abwehr* agent in Britain, was apprehended These setbacks may have prompted Canaris to retreat, at least temporarily.

Goertz was born in Lübeck on 15 November 1890. As his mother, Milly, later wrote of his father: "My husband was the leading lawyer in Lübeck, and for a long period a member of the Reichstag."[35] It was thus natural that

Hermann attended the local *gymnasium* for his secondary education and continued at university. However, before doing so, he spent a year attached to *Garde Regiment zu Fuss*, and remained in the army reserve while studying law in Berlin, Heidelberg, and Kiel. He traveled to Scotland and took several courses at Edinburgh University, but when the war broke out in 1914, his unit was activated.[36] He was wounded, recovered, and became a pilot, which led to working with German air intelligence, interrogating captured allied aviators. In 1916 he married Ellen Aschenborn, daughter of a Vice-Admiral, an affiliation which no doubt helped him in his military career. They eventually had three children. As a budding lawyer, Goertz spent the first five years after the war with the industrial firm of Bergbau A.G. Lothingen in Bochum and Hanover. In 1925–26 he went to New York and renewed his contacts with several formerly captured American airmen, returning in 1927 to practice law in Hamburg.

From 1929 to 1932 he left his family in Germany and took a job in London where his chief client, the Siemens company, was engaged in litigation with the British Government. In 1934, divorced and depressed, he sought employment with the emerging intelligence service of the Luftwaffe. He was told that he was officially turned down because he was more than 40 years old, but in fact he was given a special assignment in Britain. Undoubtedly it helped that he not only had the Aschenborn connection, but his brother-in-law worked for the German defense establishment, and two of his brothers were in military service.

He arrived in Britain for the second time on 18 August 1935, accompanied by his alleged niece, the 19-year-old Marianne Emig.[37] They rented motorcycles and toured East Anglia and Kent for about a month, then rented a cottage at Broadstairs. For six weeks they visited airfields as though they were tourists or, depending on who spotted them, writers gathering material for a novel about flying. When not cultivating Marianne's charms, Goertz used her as a decoy to lure young pilots into conversation in order to elicit information. However, she became worried about what they were doing, and on 23 October persuaded Goertz to take her back to Germany. He made excuses to their landlady, assuring her that he would return soon, and left his trunk as surety for the unpaid rent. The landlady was skeptical, and contacted the police who forced open Goertz's trunk and found maps, sketches of airfields, a notebook of addresses, and some private correspondence. When Goertz returned to England, he was accused of making drawings of the Royal Airforce station at Manston as well as other breaches of the Official Secrets Acts of 1911 and 1920. At his trial the jury deliberated only one hour before finding him guilty, and he was sentenced to four years of imprisonment at Maidstone.

Goertz tried in vain to convince the court that he was merely a writer with an aviation background. One of the most puzzling pieces of evidence found in his trunk was a letter from the German Air Intelligence Service, rejecting his application of 1934. The Prosecution pointed to this in order to show that

Goertz had aspirations to be an intelligence agent. In his defense, Goertz insisted that there was a distinction between gathering intelligence of a public and legal nature, and spying for a secret service. He was willing to admit the former charge, but denied the latter. He presumed that the letter from German Air Intelligence would prove that he was not spying.

Although Goertz joined the Nazi Party in 1929, his membership was suppressed before he went to England in 1935, following the convention that professional spies did not formally belong to the Party, and if anything, avoided contact with the *Landesgruppe*. After the war Goetz mused, "I have never understood the mild charges and mild sentence, as the English knew far more against me than they had disclosed."[38] He made no pretense about his activities in 1935, and proudly acknowledged his abortive mission.

> When the Führer came to power in Germany I was immediately called for military re-training. On this duty I learned the German official view about the Royal Air Force, which did not correspond with my personal view and experience. I offered to prove that England was about to build a great bomber fleet directed exclusively against Germany. My offer was accepted, and thus I became active in the German Military Intelligence and went to England.

Depending upon interpretation, Goertz was either a consummate bungler or a fairly clever but unlucky operative. He clearly hoped to get away with the fiction that he was gathering material for a book, and therefore approached air bases openly instead of clandestinely. Perhaps he might have succeeded had Marianne Emig not panicked and insisted on returning home before the mission was completed. Ironically, his appetite for espionage was not dulled by his four years of imprisonment. Not long after his release in February 1939, he rejoined Luftwaffe Intelligence, and in January 1940 was transferred to the *Abwehr*. Eventually he was sent to the Republic of Ireland for the purpose of organizing against the British, but soon was apprehended and spent the rest of the war in prison. In 1947, when he realized that he might be extradited to Germany to stand trial for war crimes, he committed suicide.

It may seem strange, but Goertz was only one of a very few *Abwehr* agents clearly identified as active in Britain prior to the Second World War. Another was a former German naval captain, who had seen service in the South China Sea, Gustav Simon.[39] On three separate occasions in 1938 he went to Britain as an ordinary tourist, traveling from the Hook of Holland to Harwich. He aroused little interest among British immigration officers, and freely roamed throughout England, concentrating on new airfields and factories in Kent and East Anglia unknown to the Germans. Early in 1939 he was picked up by British authorities who were curious about his movements, especially the notebook he kept in code. He was almost able to cover his tracks with reasonable explanations, but failed and spent six months in a British prison. He was released in

August 1939 on the eve of the war, and returned to Germany along with his coded notes.

Arthur Owens, a Welsh nationalist with ardent anti-English feelings, was another pre-war *Abwehr* agent.[40] Born in 1899, he spent until 1933 in Canada, and then returned to the British Isles. For the next few years he and his wife and child lived in Hampstead. Sometime in 1936 he offered his services to British Naval Intelligence, explaining that his work as an engineer for a British metal company periodically took him to Belgium and Germany. For a modest fee he was prepared to gather information while on the Continent and share it with the British Navy upon his return. However, by the end of the year he felt that he was being underpaid by Naval Intelligence, and offered his expertise to the Germans. Recruited by the *Abwehr*, he came under the control of Captain Nikolaus Ritter during the summer of 1937. Ritter operated from Hamburg, nominally as head of a firm of importers and exporters, although he was actually there gathering information about Britain and America. He used the name "Dr. Rantzau".

Ritter employed Owens as a "sleeper," or dormant agent who could be activated in an emergency. Between the summer of 1937 and 1939, Owens made occasional contact with Ritter, but did little to earn his allegedly high pay. Then, shortly before the outbreak of war, he was summoned to Hamburg where he underwent intensive wireless training. When he returned to London he collected a radio that had been deposited for him in the left luggage office at Paddington railway station, and on 28 August he was authorized to begin transmitting.

Owens was no novice when it came to espionage. Back in 1937 one of his letters to Ritter was intercepted by MI5, and he had to do some fancy talking to persuade the British that he was still working in Naval Intelligence, infiltrating the *Abwehr*. MI5 was skeptical about this, but refrained from prosecuting him because they did not wish his connection with the Navy to be revealed in court. At the end of August 1939 he was due to go into action for the Germans, knowing full well that he was a prime suspect in the eyes of MI5. Consequently, he brazenly approached British intelligence and told them about his wireless set and the instructions from Ritter to begin broadcasting. MI5 decided this warranted his being placed under temporary arrest. He was incarcerated in Wandsworth prison, and his messages to Ritter were monitored. Using the code name "Johnny", he proceeded to broadcast an array of minute details designed to impress the Germans without actually revealing anything vital. One historian summarized his impressive output in the early days of the war.[41]

> JOHNNY transmitted data on ship movements. R.A.F. concentrations in England and France, deliveries of war material from the United States, strengthening of coastal defenses, the use of balloon barrages, and the location and camouflage of oil tank farms which served as reference points for air reconnaissance.

Later in 1939 Owens was set at liberty because the British Secret Service was confident that he really was working for them. They encouraged him to recruit actual or notional subagents in order to convince the *Abwehr* that he controlled a small espionage ring. From time to time he traveled to the low countries where he met with Ritter, but these rendezvous ceased once Holland and Belgium were overrun by the Nazis in May 1940. He contrived to meet Ritter twice more in Lisbon, in June and again in September 1940. For his part, Ritter was beginning to have doubts about Owens' loyalty, and was perplexed as to how he was able to reach Lisbon twice without the connivance of the British. Owens cut back on radio messages in late 1940 and early 1941, and in April sent his last wireless report. Ultimately unmasked, he spent the remainder of the war in Dartmoor Prison.

To this day, historians divide as to Owens' true allegiance.[42] Some believe that Ritter knew that Owens worked for the British, while others contend that Owens never divulged his British controllers. Each time that the *Abwehr* alerted Owens to the arrival of a clandestine German agent, he tipped off the British, who accordingly had few illusions about their double agent whom they dubbed "Snow."

One Gestapo agent, Hans Wesemann, lived in Britain for several years, but carried out assignments mainly on the Continent. Born in 1895 in Nienburg an der Weser, Wesemann attended several German universities after serving in the First World War. Eventually he earned a doctorate at the University of Freiburg in political economy.[43] From the mid-1920s he worked as a journalist for almost all of the left-of-center German newspapers, which sent him to Switzerland and Latin America as well as Germany. Not long after Hitler came to power in 1933, he went into voluntary exile in England, partly because Goebbels threatened him with retribution for writing a specious article about interviewing Hitler.

For about a year Wesemann resided quietly in London, associating mostly with other German emigrés and trying to eke out a living being a free-lance journalist. By the summer of 1934 he ran short of money and initiated contact with the German Embassy, offering to identify German refugees who expressed anti-Nazi sentiments, especially concerning the forthcoming plebiscite in the Saarland. Additionally, Wesemann needed to renew his passport, which necessitated that he return to Berlin. He naturally hesitated to do this, since he was known as a Social Democrat, critical of the Nazis. However, now that the Gestapo showed interest in him as an agent, they were willing to grant him safe-conduct.

From September 1934 to March 1935 Wesemann accepted a variety of assignments from the Gestapo, mainly directed toward refugees in Denmark, Holland, France, and Switzerland.

Ostensibly there was no reason for the British authorities to pay attention to him, since he appeared to be simply a liberal German living in London who

**241**

published occasional articles on German affairs. However, by January 1935, he himself became uncomfortable with his complicated double life. While waiting for the annulment of his marriage, he became engaged to a rich Venezuelan, and was about to emigrate when the Gestapo summoned him to undertake one last assignment: lure the writer, Berthold (Salomon) Jacob, to Switzerland and abduct him to Germany.

Jacob was an outspoken emigré critical of the Nazis for rearming, contrary to the provisions of the Versailles Treaty. Wesemann cultivated his trust for several months by offering to help him place articles in the British press. He also knew from personal experience that a stateless emigré like Jacob would do almost anything to secure a valid passport, so he used this bait to entrap and betray him. Once Jacob found himself back in Germany he was put in a cell by the Gestapo, and when the unsavory story became known, public opinion was outraged. Wesemann tried to cover his involvement in the scheme by remaining quietly in Switzerland, but the Swiss police found and arrested him, and he was sentenced to three years in prison.

Under the conventional meaning of the word, Wesemann was not guilty of espionage, reprehensible as his conduct was. Nor can the journalist Arnold Littmann, another Gestapo agent who worked in Britain in the late 1930s and returned to Germany undetected by the British.[44] As for Otto Karl Ludwig, it is impossible to be sure how involved he was with the *Abwehr*, and how long he had been being supplied with information by the seven journalists listed in his captured papers.[45]

What is striking about the notorious cases of espionage during the 1930s is that they involved mainly British subjects or people who had dual nationality. Those found guilty of contravening the Official Secrets Acts of 1911 and 1920 were accused of consorting with Germans in time of peace, but they did not pose an actual threat to British security, according to Kell, Vansittart and others.

The broad scope of the Official Secrets Acts made it possible to detain almost anyone acting suspiciously. For example, it was not necessary to communicate information to an enemy, only to gather it. Thus, taking notes which might prove "prejudicial to the safety of the state," or which might be "directly or indirectly useful to an enemy"[46] qualified as actionable. Furthermore, as one Prosecutor stated, "It was not necessary for the information to be secret. It was sufficient if it were calculated to be directly or indirectly useful to a potential enemy."[47] This provision covered many things in the public domain which could be learned through perfectly legitimate means. That so few arrests were made in the 1930s may support the conclusion that relatively little contact and cooperation with German security services was taking place.

The case which most shocked the British public was that of Norman Baillie-Stewart. It was hard for most people to believe that a Lieutenant in His Majesty's Seaforth Highlanders would betray his country solely for money. Born in 1909, he was commissioned an officer in 1929, and promoted to First Lieutenant in January 1932. Shortly thereafter he enrolled in a course for Junior Officers where he learned about problems involving military supplies and weapons. While on this course he had access to semi-classified materials, including maps, photographs, and manuals stamped "for official use only." At the end of the course he took a month's holiday in Germany.[48] It is not clear whether he made the acquaintance of a German intelligence officer before reaching Berlin on 1 August 1932, or during his visit there.[49] Most likely it was the latter. Observed as a spendthrift, Baillie-Stewart succumbed to the officer's proposal that he collect "useful" information for a fee. Returning to the United Kingdom, he pretended to remain there until he was due to report for duty at the beginning of September. In fact what he did was make a quick trip to Holland on 28 August, followed by two other forays toward the end of October and beginning of November 1932 to meet with German operatives.

On 12 October 1932, someone using the name "Marie Louise" wrote to him from Berlin, saying how much she missed him, and enclosed ten five Pound banknotes in payment of his loan to her. Using a false name, Baillie-Stewart acknowledged the money, but replied to Otto Waldemar Obst rather than "Marie Louise". In early December, "Marie Louise" sent another 40 Pounds, hoping that Baillie-Stewart could get away sooner than March 1933.

It didn't take MI5 too long to detect this charade. By late 1932 they intercepted the letters, made copies, and were ready to pounce. In January, an Army officer questioned Baillie-Stewart, mentioning that there were some inconvenient facts which had come to light for which he no doubt had a perfectly logical explanation. It took until mid-February to acquire the evidence to arrest him, and his court martial took place in March 1933.

His defense was ingenious, if unconvincing. He could not substantiate the loan to "Marie Louise" because he knew that British Military Intelligence were aware that he lacked sufficient funds to do this. He therefore invented a persona for "Marie Louise": an attractive German woman in her early twenties, whose last name he never discovered. He claimed that the money she had sent him was for sexual "services rendered," but when asked where these had occurred, he avoided mentioning a hotel or automobile, either of which could have been traced.

As the court martial unfolded, speculation was rife as to who the mysterious "Marie Louise" might be. Various names were put forward, but the most plausible was the daughter of Captain Franz von Rintelen,[50] who had an ambivalent relationship with the Nazis. He also had a daughter whose name and age fitted the situation. To his credit, Baillie-Stewart was gentleman enough to publish a disclaimer in the press denying that Fraulein von Rintelen was the mysterious "Marie Louise".

Found guilty, Baillie-Stewart was sentenced to five years imprisonment at

Maidstone. Ironically, when Hermann Goertz was interned there in 1936, the two became friends. After his release Baillie-Stewart went to Austria where he worked for a tourist agency and tried to enlist in the German army. Once hostilities with Britain commenced in 1939, he began broadcasting propaganda for the same service where William Joyce (Lord Ha-Ha) worked. In 1967 he wrote a book justifying his actions and admitted that there had never been a "Marie Louise" or a "Herr Obst", but he named a German Military Intelligence officer, Major Müller.[51]

After thirty-five years, Baillie-Stewart persisted in denying that he had betrayed his country in 1932.[52]

> After much mature consideration it seems highly probable that Major Müller sent the money in order to maintain me as a contact for future use. I admit freely and frankly that I was responsible for getting myself into this highly dangerous position with a Major in the German War Office, for I accepted the money. But I never had any intention of giving the German military information of a nature that could be used against Britain. I had none to give. There was never any truth, direct or indirect, that I ever did so. Any military matters that I discussed with the German were freely available in widely-circulated official books. I was found guilty on suspicion and assumption.

A second British subject who ran afoul of the Official Secrets Acts was Eric Joseph Gardner Camp. He was a thirty-three year-old draftsman living in Kilburn when he was alleged to have made drawings or taken notes on aspects of British military aircraft between December 1935 and August 1936. It was never imputed that he transmitted this information to an enemy, nor was Germany ever mentioned by name, yet under the Official Secrets Acts merely acquiring information that could be used by the enemy was punishable.[53]

Camp's trial at the Central Criminal Court, Old Bailey, took place in late October 1936, and because of the secret nature of the evidence, it was held *in camera*, with the press and the public excluded. He was found not guilty by the jury on two out of three counts since he had clearly not meant to spy, although he had technically breached the law. Under the circumstances, the judge gave him a suspended sentence of two years during which he had to report monthly to the authorities and maintain good behavior. Unlike the other suspects, there was no evidence that Camp had any dealings with Germans.

Mrs. Jessie Wallace Jordan, Scottish by birth and German by marriage, was the third Briton arrested under the Official Secrets Acts. Born in 1887, she ran away from home at the age of 16 and entered domestic service. A few years later when she was twenty, she married a German named Jordan who was living temporarily in Great Britain. Neither his first name, nor where he came from in Germany, appeared in newspaper accounts. She was widowed during the First World War, remarried briefly, and divorced. She resided in Germany until after the Nazis came to power, but was induced to return to Scotland because the name Jordan had Jewish connotations for some Germans.

In March 1938 she was arrested, and stood trial in Edinburgh the following May. Described as a hairdresser working and living in Dundee, the press reported: "She had spent a considerable part of her life in Germany, so long that she at times found it rather difficult to converse in her native tongue."[54] *The Times* summarized the charges against her: "The modified indictment alleged that Mrs. Jordan had been in communication with foreign agents between June 1, 1937, and March 2, 1938, 'for purposes prejudicial to the safety and interest of the state.'" She was also accused of entering a "prohibited" area in Fife in order to make "a sketch or plan thereof . . . calculated to be directly or indirectly useful to an enemy." In addition, she was said to have gathered information about Scottish coastal defenses.

The Prosecution pointed out that she had received money for her espionage work, "but it did not amount to very much." It was also said that nationality "meant nothing to her"; in fact, she professed no "hostility or ill-will to this country." Nonetheless, she was convicted and sentenced to four years imprisonment. She was incarcerated in Perth Prison. Soon after her conviction her name surfaced in an American indictment of eighteen conspirators, four of whom were in custody in the United States, thirteen were sent back to Germany.[55] The spy ring reportedly had three components: Americans and Germans gathered information in the United States; crews on German ships conveyed information to Germany; and intelligence officers in Germany sifted and collated material. "The conspiracy was furthered, it is alleged, by conferences among the defendants in New York, Buffalo, Bremerhaven, Bremen, Berlin, Hamburg, Dundee, and Havana", said *The Times*.[56] Mrs. Jordan unwittingly disclosed the American dimension when she admitted being a "mail-drop" for German agents, receiving letters and forwarding them either to Germany or the United Kingdom.

The FBI in Washington were apparently unaware of the number of individuals working for German military intelligence until MI5 told them about Jessie Jordan's role in forwarding a letter which described a plot against the commanding officer of Governor's Island who was to be lured under false pretenses to give German agents a set of plans detailing harbor defenses. "When the letter marked X was received, it was deemed necessary to impart its contents to the American authorities in order that they might prevent a violent plot to overpower Colonel Henry W. T. Elgin and steal his confidential documents."[57]

Jessie Jordan was not an official *Abwehr* agent, and neither was Joseph Kelly, an Irish bricklayer in Lancashire who was employed by a construction firm erecting the Royal Ordinance Factory at Euxton near Chorley. Toward the end of 1938 Kelly went to the German Consulate in Liverpool and indicated that he might have something interesting to reveal. He was told that his name would be forwarded to the "right quarter" in Germany. Kelly believed that he had been speaking with the German Consul-General, Walther Reinhardt.[58]

Early in 1939 he received a letter from an unsigned correspondent in Holland suggesting that it might be possible to do business with him. A second letter followed, urging him to visit Germany. Kelly replied that he could not afford the fare, whereupon ten American dollars were sent with instructions to use the money for a British passport and a German visa.

On 1 March he broke into the ordinance factory and stole two sets of plans detailing the layout and structure of the facility. The next day he applied for a passport, and with an additional twenty American dollars, bought a one-way ticket. He crossed the German frontier on Friday 17 March, and was met by an unknown German contact who accompanied him to Osnabruck. Over the weekend he visited Cologne and handed over one of two sets of plans, for which he received twenty Pounds sterling. Returning to Lancashire, he lost no time cashing the twenty Pound note, and was promptly arrested. Since the second set of plans was found in his flat, and he could not account for the thirty Pounds in cash, he agreed to plead guilty under the Official Secrets Acts, and received a sentence of ten years. When questioned, he told the police that he had spoken to the German Consulate-General at Liverpool, but he was unable to prove this. In any case, the British Foreign Office and MI5, after some hesitation, decided to ask Reinhardt to leave Britain since he was held accountable for the actions of his staff. According to the Foreign Office Minute: "The view of M.I.5 . . . is that even if his successor might possibly try and do the same sort of thing, the German authorities are more likely to be more cautious. . . ."[59] Kelly's motives were never articulated, but as an Irishman, he may have harbored anti-British feelings. However, his need for money may have been the sole reason for his behavior.

The last instance of a British subject being arrested for espionage before the war involved Donald Owen Reginald Adams, a 56-year-old "racing journalist" who lived in Richmond, Surrey. In addition to being a newspaperman, he was the London representative of a Dresden firm, Feodor Burgman, which manufactured packing materials and asbestos. Following a trip to Germany in November 1938, Adams received several ten Pound notes from P. B. Fricke, a man in the employ of Karl Raedler of Hanover, ostensibly for copies of a sporting paper. He asked Adams to use the money to bet on promising horses. Since the Post Office had the authority to open mail, these letters were photographed and found to contain numerical codes, supposedly encrypting racing tips. Unfortunately for Adams, the key to the code was discovered inside a volume in his flat, enabling the police to read all of the correspondence and to learn that Adams was furnishing the Germans with published materials such as "Infantry Training in War: 1937." This particular pamphlet could have been purchased at His Majesty's Stationery Office, but Adams received multiple payments spread over eight months totaling about one hundred Pounds for other documents.

Like several of the other defendants, Adams initially pleaded not guilty because he had intended no harm to his country, and the material he furnished could have been purchased by anyone. By the time he was sentenced, war had commenced, and the judge sentenced him to seven years in prison, explaining that had his material been more sensitive, he would have ordered a far more severe punishment.[60] Assessing the extent of German espionage that took place in London before the Second World War, it is difficult not to take Bohle and the *Auslandsorganisation* at their word, because in general they did not recruit or train spies, nor were they working for the *Abwehr*. Their prosecutable offenses had to do with assisting the Gestapo in bringing pressure to bear upon expatriots.

At an international conference held in Stuttgart in September 1937, Party Members from all over the world heard Goebbels, Göring, Frank, and Hess strongly deny that the *Ortsgruppen* and the *Landesgruppen* were guilty of spying. Rudolf Hess deflected this insinuation with irony and sarcasm:[61]

> From time to time the Foreign Organization of the National Socialist Party attracts the particularly affectionate interest of certain foreign politicians, who find it useful every now and again for the purposes of some political job to paint upon the wall of international public opinion the bogey called the "German danger." And how graphically they do it! Our youngest Gau of the National Socialist Party becomes a dark mysterious organization. You, my comrades beyond the frontiers, become spiders weaving a mighty web of espionage. It makes one almost shudder to hear how you carry the poison of your deadly doctrines among foreign nations and threaten great Empires. And it is shattering to hear how you, poor wretches, must continually report morning, noon and night to the offices of the National Socialist Party, to give an account of your activities, and, I might almost say, to report whether you have had good or bad dreams of National Socialism to say nothing of all the other sundry matters of which we ourselves know nothing, but which these politicians know, even if they now reveal them for the first time. But all that will happen, you can depend upon it! Seriously though, if all this appears ridiculous, it has method. By means of lies perpetually repeated, drops of poison and of mistrust are allowed to fall over fresh between ourselves and other nations. The wire-pullers wish, however many lies it may cost, to prevent a further growth of confidence in the new Germany, comparable to that which, to their great regret, has taken place in these last few years.
>
> They want the world to know that the good Communists and the harmless Jews desire brotherly love between country and country, friendship among the nations, freedom for the creative individual and peace upon earth. But these cursed Nazis, they are conspiring to wage a new war with their sinister organization. They want to incite the peoples against one another and to carry murder

and arson over the face of the earth. Naturally these wire-pullers only want to divert attention from those who really threaten world peace.

He went on to declare that National Socialism was not for export but was jealously reserved for Germans at home. Furthermore, the German secret services would never be so naïve as to risk espionage within local centers abroad like the *Ortsgruppen* and *Landesgruppen*. "If we really wanted to create a secret service in foreign countries we would be clever enough to make use of the example of . . . the excellently-functioning world-wide secret service" of the Communists, he declared, emphasizing that the sole function of the *Auslandsorganisation* was to strengthen "bonds binding motherland and nationals abroad."

Common sense would indeed suggest that a security service would not plant agents in the local groups where they would become well known and their movements obvious. Normally the expectation governing intelligence agents would include maintaining a low profile, avoiding repeated social gatherings, shunning publicity and propaganda, and adopting an anti-Nazi pose. In this respect, Hans Wesemann, while on British soil at least, operated as a professional, even though he was not an *Abwehr* agent.

Over all, then, the British must be seen as having been very effective as well as very lucky in curbing attempts at espionage on the part of the Third Reich. It is also worth reiterating that most of the cases of espionage prior to the war involved British subjects, not members of the Nazi party in Britain.

NOTES

1 Bohle to Schmeer, 4 April 1933, NA microcopy T-580, Roll 55, File 293.
2 *Ibid.* and Schmeer to Bohle, 6 April; Bohle to Schmeer, 12 April; Schmeer to Nieland, 19 April; Schmeer to Bohle, 19 April; Bohle to Schmeer, 21 April; Schmeer to Bohle, 26 April; and Schmeer to Bohle, 8 May 1933.
3 See chapters 6 and 16.
4 D. M. McKale, *The Swastika Outside Germany* (Kent, Ohio, 1977), p. 108.
5 *Trials of War Criminals Before the Nuremberg Military Tribunals Under Control Council Law Number 10*, XIII (Washington, D.C., 1952), 1200.
6 *Ibid.*, p. 1203.
7 *Ibid.*, p. 1198.
8 William East wrote a series of articles for the Empire News, the first of which appeared 6 October 1940, p. 9.
9 *Trials of the Major War Criminals*, X (Nuremberg, 1946), p. 36.
10 *Ibid.*
11 See chapter 14, pp. 185–6.
12 *Trials of the Major War Criminals*, p. 14.
13 *Empire News*, 27 October 1940, p. 3.
14 Kell to Scott, 24 April 1936, PRO, HO 45/25385, pp. 5–14.
15 For background on Kutschke, see James J. and Patience P. Barnes, *James Vincent Murphy:*

*Translator and Interpreter of Fascist Europe, 1880–1946* (Lanham, MD, 1987), pp. 167, 213, 282. See also chapter 4.

16  Krug von Nidda was expelled from the *NSDAP* on 3 May 1934.

17  See note 14 above.

18  Peter and Leni Gillman, *Collar the Lot* (London, 1980).

19  *Sunday Express*, 10 April 1938, p. 21.

20  7 May 1938, p. 8.

21  *Empire News*, 3 November 1940, p. 3.

22  L. Farago, *The Game of the Foxes* (New York, 1971), p. 137.

23  *Empire News*, 27 October 1940, p. 3.

24  PRO, FO 371/21651, C. 5221, f. 358.

25  For the later date of September 1936, see: N. West, *MI5: British Security Service Operations, 1909–1945* (New York, 1982), p. 98.

26  P. Leverkuehn, *German Military Intelligence* (London, 1954), pp. 89–93.

27  Farago, *Foxes*, p. 135.

28  C. Andrew, *Her Majesty's Secret Service* (New York, 1985, p. 384.

29  A. Masters, *The Man Who Was M: The Man Who was Maxwell Knight* (Oxford, 1984), *passim*.

30  Andrew, *Secret Service*, p. 162.

31  See chapter 14.

32  Masters, *Man Who Was Called M*, p. 71.

33  See especially East's opening two articles in the *Empire News*, 6 October 1940, p. 9 and 13 October 1940, p. 7.

34  *Ibid.*, 13 October 1940.

35  M. Goertz to Viscount Halifax, 23 April 1938, PRO, FO 371/21760, C. 3639, ff. 11–12.

36  Goertz file, BDC. See also: N. West, *MI5*, pp. 92–98.

37  Many of the details about Goertz's activities in England from 18 August to 23 October 1935 were revealed during the course of his arraignment and subsequent trial. See: *Daily Herald*, 20 November 1935, p. 1; *Daily Mail*, 27 November 1935, p. 6; *Daily Sketch*, 27 November 1935, pp. 1–3; *The Times*, 10 January 1936, p. 9; *ibid.*, 5 March 1936, p. 9; *ibid.*, 6 March 1936, p. 19; *ibid.*, 7 March 1936, p. 7; and *ibid.*, 10 March 1936, p. 22.

38  *Irish Times*, 27 August 1947, p. 4.

39  C. Whighton and G. Peis, *They Spied on England* (London, 1958), p. 48.

40  *Ibid.*, p. 101. See also N. Ritter, *Deckname Dr. Cantzali* (Hamburg, 1972), pp. 15, 19–20, 40–42, 44–46, 128–29, 150–54, 167.

41  David Kahn, *Hitler's Spies: German Military Intelligence in World War II* (New York, 1978), p. 305.

42  Farago, *The Game of the Foxes*, p. 173; and Kahn, *ibid.*, p. 367.

43  James J. and Patience P. Barnes, *Nazi Refugee turned Gestapo Spy: the Life of Hans Wesemann, 1895–1971* (Westport, CN, 2001); J. N. Willi, *Der Fall Jakob-Wesemann 1935–1936* (Berlin, 1972); and C. Brinson, *The Strange Case of Dora Fabian and Matilde Wurm* (Bern, 1996).

44  See chapter 15.

45  *Ibid.*

46  *The Times*, 21 September 1936, p. 9.

47  *Ibid.*, 15 July 1939, p. 6.

48  *The Times*, 18 February 1933, p. 10; *ibid.*, 21 March 1933, p. 11.

49  N. Baillie-Stewart, *The Officer in the Tower* (London, 1967).

50  In 1933 Rintelen tried to embarrass the new Hitler government by castigating the behavior of Vice-Chancellor Franz von Papen, for his bungling of secret espionage work in the United States during World War I. This, despite the fact that Rintelen was himself a member of the Nazi Party currently living in London.

51  It has been impossible to identify this person, since the name Müller is so common.

52  Baillie-Stewart, *Officer*, p. 114.

53  *The Times*, 21 September 1936, p. 9; 3 October 1936, p. 6; and 27 October 1936, p. 11.

54  *Ibid.*, 17 May 1938, p. 13.

55  L. Farago, *The Game of the Foxes* (New York, 1971), p. 69.

56  *The Times*, 21 June 1938, p. 16.

57  Vansittart papers, Churchill College, Cambridge: VNST II, 2/21.

58  *News Chronicle*, 20 May 1939. See also: West, *MI5*, p. 102.

59  HO to FO 2 June 1939, in PRO, FO 371/23037, C8055, ff. 405–21. See also: PRO, FO 371/23036, C6433, ff. 131–37; PRO, FO 371/23037, C7624, ff. 369–74.

60  *Ibid.*, 26 September 1939, p. 5.

61  PRO, FO 371/20740, C6210, ff. 16–25.

# EPILOGUE

On 1 and 2 September 1939, the Home Office, in conjunction with MI5, sent out coded telegrams to the police chiefs and chief constables throughout the country, authorizing the arrest of the enemy aliens whose names appeared on a secret list. The list, running to 39 pages and containing approximately 880 names, had been previously distributed, with instructions not to open or act on it until authorized to do so.[1] Those slated for arrest were exclusively of German or Austrian extraction, and no British subjects were included.

Thus, even before war was formally declared on 3 September, some 40 enemy aliens plus about 37 German sailors taken from ships in British harbors, were temporarily incarcerated in the Olympia Exhibition Hall at Hammersmith. During the next few days about 415 Germans and Austrians were similarly confined.[2] Some of the 880 on MI5's list had already returned to Germany, while others were missing. There was also a delay in police action due to the Home Office wanting to make sure that no mistakes were made, as they had been in the case of a refugee professor who had recently become a British citizen only to find his name on MI5's list of enemy aliens.[3]

Despite Home Office efforts to purge inappropriate names, some anti-Nazi German refugees were confined at the Olympia Hall. Bernhard Weiss, born 30 July 1880, had been the former Vice-President, or deputy chief, of the Berlin police during the Weimar Republic. In the late 1920s he became the target of Joseph Goebbels' sarcasm, reminding everyone of his Jewish origins by dubbing him "Isador." For some years leading up to the outbreak of war, Weiss had lived quietly in London conducting a modest business in office supplies.

Another well-known anti-Nazi was Eugen Spier, born 13 January 1892.[4] As a German businessman, he had settled in London in 1922. From about 1934 to 1937 he was involved with a loosely organized group of anti-Nazis calling themselves *Focus in Defence of Freedom and Peace*. One of the more prominent British adherents to this cause was Winston Churchill.

Another unwitting internee was the journalist Graf Albrecht Leo Eduard Montgelas, born 3 September 1887. In the late 1930s he represented several German newspapers in London, the *Neue Leipziger Zeitung* and the *Frankfurter*

*General-Anzeiger.* In 1936–37 Montgelas attended public meetings of the Anglo-German Fellowship, but this could be said of a number of other anti-Nazis who were eager to promote better relations between Germany and Britain. Years later, the actor Peter Ustinov recalled how Montgelas frequented his parents' flat, a quiet haven for those out of sympathy with the Third Reich.[5] As late as 1942, Amt VI of the Reich Security Main Office was anxious to make sure that he was still interned in Great Britain.[6]

Rather more problematic was the situation of Ernst Franz Sedwick Hanfstaengl, born 11 February 1887. In the 1920s he had been one of Hitler's closest confidants, but eventually, especially after the Nazis came to power in 1933, Hanfstaengl found himself sidelined. By the mid-1930s he was convinced that he was targeted for assassination, so sought protection in England. However, at the beginning of the war the British were unwilling to give him the benefit of the doubt, and he was arrested.

There were a handful of notorious supporters of Hitler and the Nazi Party that the British had no qualms interning. One of these was Hans Joachim Schiffer, a former Prussian police officer and an avowed enemy of Bernhard Weiss. Prior to the war Schiffer built up an arms and munitions business in London, and although he seems not to have joined the Nazi Party, he was a conspicuous admirer of the Third Reich.

Another ardent Nazi and long-time resident in London was Constant Pilar von Pilchau, born 14 October 1886. He seems to have come to England in the early 1930s to manage the office of the North German Lloyd shipping company. While in London he applied for membership in the Party, and was admitted in October 1934.

Although we were fortunate in finding a list of those slated for arrest at the outbreak of war, we have not been successful procuring the names of those who were actually interned for longer or shorter periods of time. The dire situation in September 1939 was made more confusing when the British Government decided to examine personally, before special tribunals, every one of the 71,553 enemy aliens of German and Austrian extraction. These hearings took place from October 1939 to January 1940, and it was stipulated that aliens could have no legal representation, but they could be accompanied by a friend who could vouch for them.

The most dangerous or unreliable among them were classified as Category A, and numbered about 572. Under Category B were 6,690 doubtful cases concerning those who posed no immediate threat, but whose background raised questions. The vast majority, some 64,290, were put in Category C, and about 55,000 of these were designated "refugees from Nazi repression."[7] Although Category B individuals were allowed to remain at large and not be confined, they were strictly regulated. They could not travel beyond five miles of their residences, nor could they possess cars, cameras, or large-scale maps.

During September 1939, many of the internees were moved out of London to a temporary facility, a former Butlin's holiday camp or seaside resort, at Clacton in Essex. Later in the autumn many were relocated to another camp on the Devon coast at Seaton. By March 1940 some of the more avowedly pro-Nazis were sent to a mansion in Swanwick, Derbyshire.

An undetermined number of Category A internees went by ship to Canada. One of these was Pastor Fritz Wehrhan, who had joined the Nazi Party in May 1934.[8] He was among those who did not survive the Atlantic crossing. On 1 July 1940 the *Arandora Star* sailed from Liverpool with about 1,600 on board, of whom 478 were Germans or Austrians. Early in the morning on 2 July the ship was torpedoed by a German submarine, and all the British, Italian, and German passengers, plus the crew of about 650, drowned.

It is difficult to know precisely which of the Nazi Party members still resident in Britain in early September 1939 were included among the 572 internees in Category A. However, a perusal of the Appendix provides a fairly detailed indication of those who did not get out of Britain in time, and had to remain there throughout the war.

The Home Office list of 880 names is one measure of those targeted for arrest. The voluminous *NSDAP* membership files housed at the Berlin Document Center provide another clue. If someone left Britain before the war began, he or she would normally notify the Party headquarters, and a notation would be made of the revised address. If no such information appears on the card, the presumption is that the person remained in Britain, whether or not interned. Many Party members left Britain well before the war broke out, and they of course do not figure into the calculation of those interned.

Party membership was enjoyed by a wide variety of people. Elisabeth Ahlenfeld was an early convert to Nazism, having joined the Party in May 1932. At one time she was a secretary for Otto Bene at the *Ortsgruppe's* headquarters, 5 Cleveland Terrace, W2. Her name was on MI5's list of those to be arrested, but she had already returned to Germany. Someone who did not leave Britain in time and was therefore arrested, was the bank official Johannes Beilharz who had come to London in 1935 and applied for Party membership, being admitted in August 1936. Ferdinand Bertram left Britain in early September before he could be apprehended. His job as clerk at the German Embassy may have provided the necessary diplomatic protection, although not all employees or servants were as fortunate. Erna Block, a secretary who had only been a Party member since May 1937 managed to return to Germany in spite of being on the MI5 list.

Being out of favor with the *NSDAP* did not guarantee of protection from the Home Office. Elisabeth Bodenstein worked as a domestic servant in England for much of the 1930s, and was an early follower of Hitler. From London she had applied to join the Party, and was accepted in March 1933. By 1939 she seems to have allowed her Party affiliation to lapse, and so was dropped from membership, but she was arrested in September. Another early adherent of Nazism who applied for membership while he was in England was Hanns Boelitz. He joined in October 1933, and slipped out of Britain shortly before the first wave of arrest warrants were served.

During the first few months after war was declared, the Home Office actively sought to facilitate the exodus of Germans, since it would reduce the numbers needing to be interned. During World War I, many thousands of Germans had to be closely guarded, and it was hoped that far fewer would qualify this time. People who were on MI5's list were not permitted to leave, since some of them possessed knowledge of British installations or production that could be useful to Germany. However, there was one window of opportunity, from 3 to 12 September, when German students, employees, tourists, and others were assisted in their departure.

Once the German diplomatic staff had left London, the question arose as to which neutral state would represent the Third Reich diplomatically. The Swiss agreed to take over the German Embassy and its archives and help clarify a number of issues involving Germans in Britain, but the British Foreign Office doubted that anyone in the Swiss Legation could cope with the German Embassy files. They therefore requested that the former *Kanzler* of the archives, Friedrich Wilhelm Achilles, be permitted to return to London. He was not a Nazi Party member, but rather a diplomat of the old school who had served in the German Embassy in London prior to World War I. As one foreign service officer argued, "poor old Achilles should certainly be as harmless as anybody from our point of view. He is the typical German of the old caricatures and pre-1914 German street bandsman kind. . ."[9] However, the intelligence branch was adamant: "MI5 won't have Achilles at any price and in fact are opposed in principle to anyone remaining from the German Embassy."[10]

The system based on categories A, B, and C, lasted for about six months. In April and May 1940, after Germany invaded Norway, Belgium, the Netherlands, Denmark, and France, the British Cabinet took fright, convinced that Norway and the Low Countries had fallen so quickly due in part to Fifth Column subversion by their own citizens. As France's position worsened, fears grew that there would be a German invasion of the British Isles, and enemy aliens could and would collaborate with the enemy.

Within a matter of days, a second batch of warrants were served on all German and Austrian males between the ages of 16 and 60 who resided in the East or South of England. Not only were enemy aliens to be interned, but also pro-German Fascists like Sir Oswald Mosley. Upwards of 27,000 were initially detained, although many of them were released during the next twelve months.

The Nazi Party members analyzed in this volume, with a few possible exceptions, were interned for the duration of the war. What had undoubtedly seemed to many of them only a few years earlier as an opportunity to live abroad and earn more money than they could at home, turned into a nightmare of wartime imprisonment. Their membership in the *NSDAP* had carried its privileges and prestige, but ultimately there was a high price to pay.

NOTES

1 Home Office War Book (HOWB), IX, 2, Home Office Library.
2 Ronald Stent, *Bespattered Page?* (London, 1980), p. 30.
3 A. Maxwell to V. Kell, 1 Sept. 1939, HOWB, IX, 2.
4 Spier, *The Protecting Power* (London, 1951) See also Spier, *Focus: A footnote to the History of the Thirties* (London, 1963).
5 Peter Ustinov to J. J. Barnes, 22 November 1979.
6 German Foreign Ministry Archives, Bonn, Inland II-G, Band 3, R-101046. The Amt VI report to the German Foreign Ministry is dated 14 July 1942.
7 Statistics about categories A, B, and C vary slightly from one source to another. We are using the numbers in F. A. Hinsley and C. A. G. Simkins, *British Intelligence in the Second World War*, IV (London, 1997), pp. 31–32.
8 See chapter 9.
9 PRO, FO 372/3329, T11793, f. 107.
10 *Ibid.*, T11794, f. 111.

# APPENDIX

Name, Address, City, Born, Occupation, Years in England, Party #, Date joined, Remained in England, On internment list

Adrian, Willy, 36 Rensburg Road, London E17, 1901, artisan, 1934–39, 3452962, May 1934 (from England), yes, no

Ahlefeldt, Elisabeth, 5 Cleveland Terrace (work), London W2, 1906, secretary, 1937–39, 1152487, May 1932, no, yes

Albert, Frida, 30 Frognal Lane, London NW3, 1913, domestic, 1936–38, 3695480, February 1936 (from England), no, no

Amos, Hans Egon, –, –, 1908, lawyer, 1939, 3403363, May 1933, yes, no

Anton, Bruno, 173 Kings Road, London NW1, 1888, restaurant, 1934–38, 3402597, February 1934 (from England), no, no

Auer, Theodor M., 8 Carleton House Terrace, London SW1, 1899, diplomat, 1931–34, 3398113, January 1934 (from England), no, no

Bachmann, Peter, 5 Cleveland Terrace, London W2, 1913, party official, 1934–36, 3658001, June 1935 (from England), no, no

Baier, Georg, –, Surrey, 1904, business, 1937–39, 4456848, October 1937 (from England), yes, yes

Bartels, Hermann, –, –, 1909, unknown, 1934–39, 1882894, May 1933, yes, no

Beckert, Charlie, London Hotel, Piccadilly, London W1, 1918, unknown, 1937–39, 4768350, September 1937, no, no

Beckhoff, Hans, Porchester Square, London W2, 12 Chepstow Crescent, London W11, 39 Linden Gardens, London W2, 1906, government, 1931–37, 669794, December 1931 (from England), no, no

Behlau, Herbert, 306 Kings Road, London SW10, 1906, diplomat, 1937–39, 6087608, July 1938 (from England), no, no

Behnke, Luise, 10 Aldford House, Park Lane, London W1, 1899, domestic, 1937–39, 3914234, July 1937 (from England), no, no

Behr, Ludwiga, 2 Birch Grove, London SE12, 1900, party official, 1937, 709715, October 1931, no, no

Beilharz, Johannes, Endsleigh Gardens, London WC1, 86 Woodside Road, London N22, 1913, business, 1936–39, 3733659, August 1936, yes, no

Beinhoff, Gerhard, –, –, 1909, business, 1932–39, 1170465, July 1932 (from England), yes, no

Beissner, Hans, 65 Combemartin Road, London SW18, 1903, engineer, 1938–39, 6096144, August 1938 (from England), yes, no

Bene, Otto, 39 Great Tower Street, London EC3, 46 Cleveland Square, London W2, 1884, 5 Cleveland Terrace, London W2, business and party official, 1930–36, 839863, December 1931 (from England), no, no

Benemann, Joachim, 27 Mecklenburgh Square, London WCI, 1911, party official, 1934–39, 5518162, April 1938 (from England), no, yes

Berger, Carl Sylvester, 30 Grandison Road, London SW11, 1882, science, 1930–39, 7332433, December 1939 (from England), no, no

Berger, Otto, 55 High Street, Walthamstone, London E17, 1880, artisan, 1935–39, 2513605, August 1935 (from England), yes, no

Bertram, Ferdinand, 46 Honor Oak Road, London SE23, 1902, clerk, 1938–39, 3604830, March 1935, no, yes

Bethmann-Hollweg, Joachim von, 21 Campden Hill Gate, London W8, 1911, student, 1934–39, 1722448, May 1933, yes, no

Betz, Richard, 56 Aberdeen Road, London SW 19, 1904, artisan, 1938–39, 6997095, December 1938 (from England), yes, no

Beuchler, Johannes, –, London SW 1, 1911, unknown, 1938–39, 3877466, March 1937, yes, no

Bielfeld, Harald, Parkmead, London SW15, 1895, diplomat, 1934–38, 3752094, October 1936 (from England), no, no

Bischoff, Wilhelm, Holland Park Gardens, London W14, 1889, business, 1933–39, 1584557, May 1933 (from England), yes, yes

Bismarck, Otto von, 9 Stanhope St., London W2, 1897, diplomat, 1930–36, 2700155, May 1933 (from England), no, no

Blasberg, Aenne, –, Epsom, Surrey, 1886, domestic, 1933–39, 1584480, May 1933 (from England), yes, yes

Blaul, Friedel, 10 Devonshire Terrace, London W2, 1914, clerk, 1939, 5498609, May 1937, yes, yes

Blessing, Kurt, –, Middlesex, 1905, party official, 1936–39, 2613871, August 1935, no, yes

Block, Erna, –, Claygate, Surrey, 1909, secretary, 1938–39, 3802068, March 1937, no, yes

Böckheler, Paul Martin, 23 Manor Mount, London SE23, 1904, clergy, 1936–39, 3452953, May 1934, yes, yes

Bode, Otto Bernhard, 149 Manchester Square, London W1, 1899, doctor, 1934–39, 3398084, January 1934 (from England), yes, no

Bodenstein, Elisabeth, 36 Harley House, Regent's Park, London NW1, 14 City Road, London EC1, 1902, domestic, 1933–39, 1369365, March 1933 (from England), yes, yes

Boeckmann, Harald, 30 Kensington Gardens Square, London W2, 1910, journalist, 1938–39, 4604637, May 1937, no, no

Boelitz, Hanns, –, –, 1886, business, 1933–39, 3285730, October 1933 (from England), no, yes

Boeszoermeny, Udo, Finsbury Park Road, London N4, 1917, clerk, 1938–39, 7906205, January 1940 (from England), yes, no

Böhm, Reinhold, –, –, 1909, party official, 1932–34, 771372, December 1931, no, no

Böhmer, Hans, 28–29 Bedford Place, London WC1, Gray's Inn Road, London WC1, 1909, librarian, 1936–39, 3480991, May 1933, no, no

Boitin, Helmut, 29 Manor Road, London SE23, 1892, clerk, 1935–39, 1489572, April 1933, no, yes

Borchardt, Franz, Brunswick Court, Ealing, London W5, 1909, domestic, 1938–39, 7050572, May 1939 (from England), no, no

Borcke, Ilse von, –, –, 1907, secretary, 1937–39, 2226147, May 1933, yes, no

Böttiger, Theodor, 3 Inner Park Road, London SW19, 1903, journalist, 1936–39, 2672847, May 1933, no, yes

Brass, Richard, 9 Fortis Green Ave., London N2, 1888, domestic, 1934–39, 3591238, December 1934 (from England), no, no

Braun, Fritz, 15 Carleton Road, London SW15, 1904, journalist, 1937–38, 3427353, May 1933, no, no

Bresan, Johann, 3 Upper park Road, London NW3, 9 Carleton House Terrace, London SW1, 1907, diplomat, 1936–37, 3744980, August 1936 (from England), no, no

Brill, Richard Julius, 35 Forest Dale, London N14, 1887, business, 1935–39, 3280744, July 1933, no, yes

Brücklmeier, Eduard, 48 Elm Park Road, London SW19, 1903, diplomat, 1936–38, 4789475, December 1937 (from England), no, no

Bunke, Waltraut, 170 Warwick Way, London SW1, 1914, secretary, 1939, 5756423, May 1938, no, no

Bürger, Hans, 24 Beeches Road, London SW17, 1899, science and technology, 1936–39, 3762754, December 1936 (from England), yes, no

Busse, Adolf, –, –, 1887, journalist, 1937, 3173927, May 1933, no, no

Clausen, Hans, –, –, 1900, restaurant, 1938–39, 783739, January 1932, yes, no

Cords, Carl, 44 Tavistock Square, London WC1, 1887, engineer, 1935–39, 3918598, May 1937 (from England), yes, no

Cramer, Heinz, 65 Hazlewell Road, London SW15, 1901, journalist, 1937–39, 5518161, April 1938 (from England), no, yes

Cramer, Willi, 56 Cleveland Road, London, 1908, business, 1932–39, 1078958, July 1932 (from England), yes, no

Cutberlett, Heinz, 22 Courtfield Gardens, London W13, 1903, business, 1935–39, 3610063, April 1935 (from England), yes, no

Czechanowski, Kurt Dietrich, Cleveland Terrace, London W2, 1916, artisan, 1935–37, 3592838, December 1934, no, no

Daerr, Eberhard, German Hospital, Dalston E8, 1912, student, 1938–39, 5423722, May 1937, yes, no

Dahm, Diana Mary, 23 Madrid Road, London SW13, 1912, journalist, 1932–39, 1302719, September 1932 (from England), yes, no

Dahm, Wilhelm, 23 Madrid Road, London SW13, Ramsgate, Kent, 1907, student, business, 1932–39, 117691, April 1930, yes, yes

Dannehl, Martin, –, –, 1902, pharmacist, 1937–39, 3783184, March 1937 (from England), yes, yes

Daufeldt, Hans, 15 Loveday Road, London W13, 1908, student, 1935–37, 753151, September 1931, no, no

Decke, Hanns, 15 Carleton Road, London SW14, 1878, engineer, 1936–37, 3946782, July 1937 (from England), no, no

Deters, Robert, White House Motel, –, 1903, business, 1934–39, 3001925, May 1933, no, yes

Dettmann, Hermann, Connaught Motel, –, 1896, chauffeur, 1938–39, 2666475, October 1935, no, yes

Dickhöfer, Rudolf, 72 Ballards Road, London NW2, 1900, business, 1938–39, 6096146, August 1938 (from England), no, no

Dietsche, Albert Otto, 11 Bloomfield Court, London N6, 1902, business, 1937–39, 3946785, July 1937, no, no

Dietzsch, Theodor, –, –, 1868, pharmacist, 1930–39, 2513881, August 1935 (from England), yes, yes

Dillenburg, Wilhelmina, 29 Hyde Park Gate, London SW7, 1902, domestic, 1936–39, 5505608, January 1938 (from England), no, no

Dinse, Erich, –, –, 1907, business, 1933, 560553, June 1931, no, no

Dirksen, Herbert von, 9 Carleton House Terrace, London SW1, 1882, diplomat, 1938–39, 3811159, March 1937, no, no

Dörnberg, Alexander von, –, –, 1901, diplomat, 1937–38, 3398362, January 1934, no, no

Dufour, Hans Rudolf, 17 Skeena Hill, London SW18, 1899, business, 1934–39, 3399085, January 1934 (from England), yes, yes

Duhr, Helmut, 23 St. Mary's Road, London N1, 1911, artisan, 1937–38, 3946786, July 1937 (from England), no, no

Ebe, Herbert, 52 Castleton Road, –, 1912, business, 1935–39, 2720975, May 1933, yes, no

Ebel, Max, 9 Broomfield Road, London N6, 1908, business, 1937–39, 3918599, May 1937 (from England), no, yes

Eckardt, Otto, 10 Tyson Road, London SE23, 1891, clerk, 1938–39, 1489443, April 1933, no, no

Eckert, Helmut, 9 Carleton House Terrace, London SW1, 1911, domestic, 1938–39, 7262050, November 1939 (from England), no, no

Eckes, Lorenz, –, –, 1912, artisan, 1932–37, 397806, May 1932 (from England), no, no

Egg, Fritz, –, –, 1909, student, 1932, 660691, October 1931, no, no

Eggemann, Johannes M., Fairmead Road, London N19, 1863, –, 1936–39, 3710199, May 1936 (from England), no, yes

Ehrhardt, Hans, 5 Cleveland Terrace, London W2, 1907, business, –, 3936559, June 1937, yes, no

Eichele, Otto, 106 Norfolk Road, London E8, 1909, teacher, 1934–37, 3710198, May 1936 (from England), no, no

Elis, Karl, –, –, 1915, restaurant, 1938–39, 5505575, January 1938 (from England), yes, no

Engelen, Gerhard, 3 Upper Park Road, London NW3, 1906, clerk, 1937–38, 2715887, October 1934, no, no

Engert, Willi Herbert, 85 Gordon Road, London W5, 1908, party official, 1934–39, 3401230, March 1934 (from England), no, yes

Erlachner, Berta, –, Stanmore, Middlesex, 1903, domestic, 1935–39, 1306711, November 1932, yes, no

Evermann, Lillian, 66 Onslow Gardens, London SW7, 1915, domestic, 1933, 1369168, March 1933 (from England), no, no

Fastenbauer, Fritz, –, –, 1907, government official, 1938–39, 6096160, August 1938, no, no

Feist, Wolfgang, 162 Elsenham St., London SW18, 1911, teacher, 1938–39, 4379811, May 1937, no, yes

Felleckner, Marianna, 10 Bedford Place, London WC1, 1905, clerk, 1935–37, 2587131, May 1933, no, no

FitzRandolph, Sigismund-Sizzo, 13 Enbankment Gardens, London SW3, 1902, journalist and diplomat, 1933–39, 2593962, April 1934 (from England), no, no

Frauendorf, Kurt, –, Harrow, Middlesex, 1901, business and party official, 1932–39, 3401210, March 1934 (from England), no, no

Frei, Martin, –, Greenfield, Middlesex, 1897, artisan, 1936–39, 3733512, May 1936 (from England), yes, yes

Friedl, Franziska, 37 Ormonde Gate, London SW3, 1901, domestic, 1939, 7010940, June 1939 (from England), yes, yes

Furth, Hermann, 41 Fellows Road, London NW3, 1912, journalist, 1936–39, 3733513, August 1936 (from England), no, yes

Gaab, Dr. Erich, German Hospital, London E8, 1910, student, 1938–39, 715733, November 1931, yes, no

Garcke, Hermann, 25 Langdale Road, London SE10, 1897, pastor, 1935–39, 1987306, May 1933, yes, yes

Gaupp, Walter, Downs Park Road, London E5, 1905, teacher, 1935–37, 4121581, May 1937 (from England), no, no

Geyer, Egbert J., 18 Belgrave Square, London SW1, 1909, diplomat, 1938–39, 1137190, May 1932, no, no

Gläser, Erich, –, Baldock, Hertfordshire, 1903, artisan, 1938–39, 5505706, January 1938 (from England, yes, yes

Glück, Willy Walter, 49 Hillier Road, London SW11, 1907, clerk, 1938–39, 5505745, February 1938 (from England), yes, no

Gossler, Bernd R. von, 9 Queen's Gardens, London W2, 1904, government official, 1934–36, 2014704, May 1933, no, yes

Graefner, Konrad, Lambeth Road, London SE1, 1911, restaurant, 1938–39, 5505605, January 1938 (from England), yes, no

Graf, Ludwig, 25 Lothair Road, London N4, 1881, restaurant, 1935–37, 1745257, June 1933, no, yes

Grill, Antonie, Hillington Village, London E11, 1905, business, 1939, 7050580, May 1939 (from England), yes, no

Günther, Leonhard, 131 Cresset Road, London E9, 1913, electrician, 1938–39, 1352773, November 1932, yes, no

Günther, Normann, Connaught Club, 75 Seymour St., London W2, 1894, business, 1935–39, 1667399, April 1933, no, yes

Haase, Horst Ewald, 10 Gresham St., London EC2, 1904, business, 1938–39, 6087361, July 1938 (from England), yes, no

Haenel, Erica, St. John's Road, Wimbledon, 1901, clerk, 1938–39, 1331060, September 1932, yes, no

Hansen, Wilhelm, 53 Horton Road, London E8, 1899, pastor, 1934–36, 2759666, October 1934 (from England), yes, no

Hantken, Heinrich, 49 Dalmeny Road, London N7, 1913, clerk, 1937–39, 4865108, May 1937, no, no

Härtel, Herbert, –, –, 1910, business, 1938–39, 1130810, May 1932, no, no

Häussner, Elsbeth, 5 Cleveland Terrace, London W2, 1914, clerk, 1933–37, 3783186, March 1937 (from England), no, no

Heckler, Franziska, 17–19 Ritson Road, London E8, 1905, student, 1934–36, 3402583, February 1934 (from England), no, no

Heinitz, Adolf, 19 Freeland Road, London W5, 1911, journalist, 1936–38, 3037403, May 1933, no, no

Heinemann, Bernhard, –, Stanmore, Middlesex, 1906, business, 1935–39, 2513761, August 1935 (from England), yes, no

Heinen, Paula, 74 Wigmore St., London W1, 1913, domestic, 1931–32, 879370, January 1931 (from England), no, no

Heinze, Eduard, Dorchester Hotel, Park Lane, London W1, 1916, student, 1939, 6085934, October 1937, yes, no

Heising, Kurt von, 20 Maria Drive, London NW7, 1906, engineer, 1935–39, 2613850, August 1935 (from England), no, yes

Heitfeld, Heinrich, New College Court, London NW4, 1892, –, 1938–39, 6990969, October 1938 (from England), yes, no

Heller, Karl Friedrich, Ritson Road, London E8, 1905, business, 1932–39, 568941, June 1931, yes, yes

Hellwig, Helga, 30 Ashburn Place, London SW7, 1911, secretary, 1938–39, 7218147, October 1939 (from England), no, no

Henkel, Albert Anton, 69 Holland Park, London W11, 1904, business, 1934–39, 3399079, January 1934 (from England), yes, no

Herbster, Karl, 8 Carleton House Terrace, London SW1, 1878, domestic, 1934–39, 3591211, December 1934 (from England), no, no

Herm, Heinrich, 33 St. Mark's Rise, London E8, 1888, artisan, 1934–35, 2758326, October 1934 (from England), no, no

Herrmann, Albert, 20 Weymouth Ave., London W5, 1906, business, 1937–39, 4009324, August 1937 (from England), no, no

Hesse, Friedrich, 10 Phillimore Gardens, London W8, 1898, journalist and government official, 1935–39, 2655914, May 1933, no, yes

Hessen, Prinz Ludwig von, 8 Carleton House Terrace, London SW1, 1908, diplomat, 1937–38, 5900506, May 1937, no, no

Hildebrandt, Lydia, 27 The Vale, London SW3, 1906, domestic, 1935–39, 3610064, April 1935 (from England), no, no

Himmelmann, Edmund, 13 Porchester Square, London W2, 1 Westbourne Terrace, London W2, 1906, business, 1930–39, 879368, January 1932 (from England), no, no

Hinze, Reinhard, 35 Bolingbroke Road, London W14, 1912, business, 1933, 1584558, May 1933 (from England), no, no

Hippenstiel, Hans, 106 Norfolk Road, London E8, 1912, teacher, 1935–36, 2792600, May 1933, no, no

Hirth, Antonia, –, –, 1914, clerk, 1939, 7421472, February 1940 (from England), yes, no

Hoff, Walter, 112 Camden St., London NW1, 1913, artisan, 1934–37, 2760396, October 1934 (from England), no, no

Hoffsommer, Günther, 47 Warrington Crescent, London W9, 1910, student, 1938–39, 570213, July 1931, yes, no

Höfling, Alfred, 19 London Road, London SE23, 1902, clerk, 1938–39, 2875392, October 1934, no, no

Hofmann, Otto, 26 Kelso Place, London W8, 1905, business, 1939, 7262093, November 1939 (from England), yes, no

Hohmuth, Gerda, Montpelier Road, London W5, 1912, domestic, 1939, 1832967, April 1933, no, no

Holasek, Hans, –, –, 1903, business, 1934–35, 2999117, November 1934, no, no

Holland, Erich Arno, 32 Southill St., London E14, 1907, business, 1934–39, 3455488, June 1934 (from England), no, yes

Holtermann, Henry, –, Welwyn Garden City, Hertfordshire, 1869, business, 1938–39, 2727262, May 1933, yes, no

Horn, Wilhelm, 45 Hale Drive, London NW7, 1895, artist, 1930–39, 6997091, December 1938 (from England), no, yes

Horst, Joachim von der, –, –, 1907, business, 1933–39, 1143773, January 1932, no, yes

Huber, Helmut, German Hospital, London E8, 1911, doctor, 1938–39, 5251561, May 1937, no, no

Hübner, Johannes, 139 Golders Green Road, London NW1, 1907, engineer, 1937, 2445640, May 1933, no, no

Ising, Albert, 24 Elsworthy Road, London NW3, 1913, clerk, 1939, 7050575, May 1939 (from England), yes, yes

Jaeckh, Manfred, 15 Gloucester Road, London W5, 1912, student, –, 3398109, January 1934 (from England), no, no

Jäger, Eduard, –, Ilford, Essex, 1889, business, 1930–39, 5505749, February 1938 (from England), no, no

Jansen, Maria, 6 Laverton Place, London SW5, 1905, clerk, 1934–39, 3398100, January 1934 (from England), yes, yes

Jasper, Wolfgang, 18 Belgrave Square, London SW1, 1913, diplomat, 1938–39, 3339995, June 1933, no, no

Jenniches, Richard, 4 Orme Court, London W2, 1895, teacher, 1939, 2719812, May 1933, yes, no

Jockelmann, Otto, 40A Belsize Park Gardens, London NW3, 1894, business, 1937–39, 1866839, May 1933, yes, no

Joost, Wilhelm, –, Surbiton, Surrey, 1899, journalist, 1938–39, 2026685, May 1933, no, yes

Juchelka, Hans, –, –, 1906, lawyer, 1935–39, 2097875, May 1933, no, yes

Juettner, Heinz, –, –, 1911, engineer, 1936–38, 246062, May 1930, no, no

Jung, Heinrich Peter, 139 Sherbrooke Road, London W6, 107 Beverley Road, London SW13, 1907, domestic, 1935–39, 3604533, March 1935 (from England), yes, no

Jungkenn, Helmut, 5 Hurstwood Road, London NW11, 1915, clerk, 1939, 7055028, August 1939 (from England), yes, no

Jüttner, Siegfried, 17 Carleton House Terrace, London SW1, 1915, domestic, 1937–38, 3918600, May 1937 (from England), no, no

Kaiser, Karl, 182 Albion Road, London N16, 1910, artisan, 1935–39, 2554818, August 1935 (from England), yes, no

Kaja, Martha, 47 Portman Square, London W1, 1908, domestic, 1936–37, 1672620, April 1933, no, no

Käppler, Fritz, –, Purley, Surrey, 1902, business, 1938–39, 7054038, June 1939 (from England), yes, yes

Karlowa, Otto, 213 Ashley Gardens, London SW1, 1883, business, 1930–39, 3401220, March 1934 (from England), no, no

Katz, Martha, 33 Ridgeway, London NW11, 1885, domestic, 1934–39, 3550397, 1934 (from England), yes, yes

Kircher, Georg, –, –, 1914, restaurant, 1935–37, 2559469, May 1933, no, no

Kircherer, Wilhelm, 31–32 Pembridge Square, London W2, 1907, journalist, 1938, 4268334, May 1937, no, no

Kistler, Gerd, 12 Birchwood Ave., London N10, 1909, student, 1932, 1170339, August 1932 (from England), no, no

Klähn, Ernst, 11 Nightingale Road, London E5, 1903, artisan, 1934–39, 3399073, January 1934 (from England), yes, no

Kloss, Gertrud, –, –, 1912, secretary, 1937–38, 6997140, 1937 (from England), no, no

Klüger, Johann, 9 Carleton House Terrace, London SW1, 1888, domestic, 1937–39, 5505576, January 1938 (from England), no, no

Knatz, Thomas, 29 Hilda Road, London E6, 5 St. Alban's Ave., London E6, 1906, lawyer, 1937–39, 4456854, October 1937 (from England), yes, yes

Knoll, Hans, –, Twickenham, Middlesex, 1914, business, 1935–37, 3024430, May 1933, no, no

Koch, Lore, –, –, 1908, doctor, 1934–37, 3222929, May 1933, no, no

Kölle, Fritz, –, –, 1889, business, 1937–39, 1693610, April 1933, yes, no

Köllmann, Konrad, –, –, 1901, lawyer, 1934–35, 2209073, May 1933, no, yes

Konnertz, Willy, 41 Fellows Road, London NW3, 1907, journalist, 1938–39, 7054040, June 1939 (from England), yes, yes

Kordt, Erich, 11 Palace Gate, London W8, 1903, diplomat, 1936–38, 4679244, November 1937 (from England), no, no

Kordt, Theodor, 7 Cadogan Place, London SW1, 1893, diplomat, 1938–39, 7054874, August 1939 (from England), no, no

Kotthoff, Heinrich, –, Weybridge, Surrey, 1892, business, 1934–39, 7054049, June 1939 (from England), yes, yes

Kraetzer, Helmut, 85 Edith Road, London W14, 1912, clerk, 1938–39, 1408320, May 1933, no, no

Krajewicz, Helmut, 22 Boveney Road, London SE23, 1906, clerk, 1936–39, 3604796, March 1935, yes, no

Kramer, Franz, –, –, 1900, journalist, 1939, 5943421, May 1938, yes, no

Krämer, Karl-Heinz, –, –, 1914, clerk, 1937, 4175743, May 1937, no, no

Krause, Gerhard, 69 Fordington Road, London N6, 1908, government official, 1936–39, 2636053, May 1933, no, yes

Krebs, Karl, 47 Gower St., London WC1, 1910, teacher, 1935–37, 3144456, May 1933, no, no

Krebs, Walter, –, Letchworth, Hertfordshire, 1898, business, 1937–39, 5505709, January 1938 (from England), yes, yes

Krieglstein, Heinrich, 73 Huntly Drive, London N3, 1907, business, 1939, 7262083, November 1939 (from England), yes, yes

Kries, Wilhelm von, 1 Fernshaw Close, London SW1, 1886, journalist, 1930–39, 7050565, May 1939 (from England), no, yes

Krogulski, Adelbert, 11 Clifton Road, London E8, 1912, clerk, 1932–39, 936632, February 1932, yes, no

Krohn, Lieselotte, 9 Carleton House Terrace, London SW1, 1908, secretary, 1935–36, 711811, November 1931, no, no

Krug von Nidda, Tassilo, 45B Linden Gardens, London W2, 1894, business, 1931–34, 1166274, August 1932 (from England), no, no

Krüger, Edith, 5-A Pall Mall, London SW1, 1912, secretary, 1936–38, 5505748, February 1938 (from England), no, no

Krüger, Friedrich Wilhelm, 35 Netherhall Gardens, London NW3, 1902, engineer, 1931–32, 670657, November 1931 (from England), no, no

Krüger, Fritz Peter, –, –, 1906, lawyer, 1935–39, 1178758, May 1932, no, yes

Küfmann, Raymond, 59 Mount Park Road, London N5, 1914, business, 1938–39, 1570016, April 1933, yes, no

Kügele, Karl, German Hospital, London E8, 1903, clerk, 1936–39, 3783188, March 1937 (from England), yes, no

Kügelgen, Wilhelm, 11 Lower Regent St., London SW1, 1914, clerk, 1939, 7015148, November 1938, yes, no

Kuhlmann, Alfred, –, Twickenham, Middlesex, 1897, chemist, 1937–38, 3946783, July 1937 (from England), no, no

Kuhlmann, Herbert, –, Cambridge, 1908, student, 1932–33, 998124, January 1932, no, no

Kuhlmann, Wilhelm, 28 Douglas Road, London N1, 1884, business, 1936–39, 3710196, May 1936 (from England), yes, no

Kutschke, Karl-Heinz, 5 Cleveland Terrace, London W2, 26 Marloes Road, London W8, 1901, party official, 1934–35, 1814546, May 1933, no, no

Lang, Eugen, 37 Aylmer Road, London W12, 1906, engineer, 1936–39, 3733514, August 1936 (from England), yes, yes

Lang, Friedel, 17 Clanricard Gardens, London W2, 1912, teacher, 1931–32, 996563, May 1932 (from England), no, no

Langen, Wolfgang von, –, –, 1906, journalist, 1937, 297948, September 1930, no, no

Langheld, Heinz Hermann, 10 Eastmearn Road, London SE21, 1 Lavengro Road, London SE27, 1907, business, 1934–39, 3401216, March 1934 (from England), no, yes

Lassen, Reinhold, 12 Shepstone St., London E6, 1911, business, 1936–39, 3452974, May 1934, no, yes

Lauterbach, Johanna, 10 Norfolk Square, London W2, 1898, secretary, 1936–39, 3771591, December 1936 (from England), no, yes

Lemke, Gerda, 91 Eaton Terrace, London SW1, 1908, secretary, 1938, 3956544, May 1937, no, no

Leon, Alfred, Hermitage Lane, London NW2, 1910, restaurant, 1932–35, 1241264, August 1932, no, no

Lescher, Alfred, German Hospital, Ritson Road, London E8, 1905, hospital attendant, 1933–39, 3398111, January 1934 (from England), yes, no

Leverenz, Erich, 9 Queen's Gardens, London W2, 1905, government official, 1931–32, 839847, December 1931 (from England), no, no

Limper, Erich, 106 Norfolk Road, London E8, 1906, teacher, 1934–35, 3285736, September 1933, no, no

Lindemann, Helmut, Ravenna Road, London SW15, 1912, journalist, 1938–39, 7054041, June 1939 (from England), yes, no

Lipinsky, Agathe, Regent's Park Road, London NW1, 1898, secretary, 1933–37, 3285759, November 1933 (from England), no, no

Lipperer, Hans, –, –, 1896, business, 1933–34, 3402586, February 1934 (from England), no, no

Littmann, Arnold W. H., –, –, 1901, journalist, 1936–39, 1846292, May 1933, no, no

Loesch, Artur Heinrich, 102 Gower St., London WC1, 8 Upper Westbourne Terrace, London W2, 1908, student, 1931–39, 433363, January 1931, no, yes

Lorenz, Walter, 48 Ladbroke Grove, London W11, 1913, government official, 1938–39, 4456428, October 1937, yes, yes

Lückenhaus, Alfred, 28 Charlbert St., London NW8, 1902, journalist, 1934–37, 2594518, May 1933, no, no

Lührs, Georg, 9 Carleton House Terrace, London SW1, 1879, cipher clerk, 1938, 1331819, September 1932, no, no

Lünzner, Hilde, 114 Sutherland Ave., London W9, 1912, secretary, 1936–39, 2178434, 1934, no, no

Lust, Herbert, 12 Ardwick Road, London NW2, 1909, business, 1936–39, 3762755, December 1936 (from England), no, no

Mahnck, Hans, –, –, 1911, clerk, 1939, 5581957, December 1937, yes, no

Maier, Franz Adam, 182 Albion Road, London N16, 1909, artisan, 1935–39, 2554811, August 1935 (from England), yes, no

Maier, Hans, –, Hitchin, Hertfordshire, 1891, artisan, 1934–39, 3489943, January 1938 (from England), yes, yes

Markau, Karl E., 7 Washinton Road, London SW 13, East Croydon, 1875, business, 1932–39, 1547693, May 1933 (from England), yes, yes

Marschall von Bieberstein, Adolf, –, –, 1893, diplomat, 1934–37, 2233897, May 1933, no, no

Massmann, Gunther, –, Pinner, Middlesex, 1914, apprentice, 1935–39, 3480167, May 1933, yes, no

Massmann, Heinrich Ernst, 64 St. John's Wood Road, London NW8, 1882, engineer, 1935–39, 618785, August 1931, yes, yes

Matthes, Ernst Georg W., 71B Bartholomew Close, London EC1, 1900, engineer, 1937–39, 3452976, May 1934, yes, yes

Meissner, Gerhard, 45 Russell Square, London WC1, 1913, student, 1936–39, 1067890, April 1932, no, yes

Meissner, Hans Otto, 18 Belgrave Square, London SW1, 1909, diplomat, 1936–39, 3762629, December 1936 (from England), no, no

Metzer, Albin Max, –, Baldock, Hertfordshire, 1894, mechanic, 1933–39, 3285739, October 1933 (from England), yes, yes

Michel, Erich, Goring Hotel, Ebury St., London SW1, 1912, hotel employee, 1939, 3657917, June 1935, yes, no

Mierswa, Hans, –, Beckenham, Kent, 1889, business, 1935–39, 3056861, May 1933, yes, yes

Morgenroth, Alfred, 44 Kingsland High St., London E8, 1904, business, 1939, 7262085, November 1939 (from England), yes, no

Mühlhoff, Walter, –, –, 1908, business, 1939, 7421514, February 1940 (from England), yes, no

Müller, Elise, –, Surbiten, Surrey, 1914, domestic, 1936, 3733664, March 1936 (from England), no, no

Musslick, Charles, 65 Brunswick Road, London W5, 1895, domestic, 1934–39, 2867277, October 1934 (from England), no, no

Neumann, Gerhard, –, Hertford, 1908, teacher, 1935–38, 6087357, July 1938 (from England), no, no

Niepmann, Carl Hubert, –, Richmond, Surrey, 1896, business, 1937–39, 3946784, July 1937 (from England), no, no

Otto, Ernst Emil, Ashley Court, London SW19, 1894, engineer, 1936–39, 2753559, October 1934, no, yes

Pape, Günther, 22 Howitt Close, London NW3, 34 Denning Road, London NW3, 1898, business, 1934–39, 3399072, January 1934 (from England), yes, no

Pfüller, Charles, Cranworth Gardens, London SW9, 1910, hotel employee, 1934–36, 3453518, May 1934 (from England), no, no

Piepenstock, Walter, 217 Dollis Hill Lane, London NW2, 1900, business, 1939, 7050568, May 1939 (from England), yes, no

Pilar von Pilchau, Constantin, 35 Clifton Hill, London NW8, 1886, business, 1934–39, 2759215, October 1934, yes, yes

Plütte, Wolfgang, –, –, 1914, official, 1938–39, 3595804, January 1934, yes, no

Pohl, Hilde, 13 Cromwell Place, London, 61 Harley St., London W1, 1905, cook, 1933–37, 3285755, October 1933 (from England), no, no

Porath, Fritz, 29 Albert St., London NW1, 1901, teacher, 1930–35, 2513384, August 1935 (from England), no, no

Portz, Peter, 7 Brewer St., London W1, 1879, artisan, 1934, 1504716, March 1933, no, no

Pöttgen, Hans, –, –, 1915, official, 1938–39, 5518219, April 1938 (from England), yes, no

Prayon, Carl Werner, 40 Birch Grove, London W3, 1913, clerk, 1938–39, 7685402, July 1940 (from England), no, no

Priedemann, Carl August, 86 Langford Court, London NW8, 1880, business, 1938–39, 7050567, May 1939 (from England), no, yes

Puth, Georg T., 49 Chingford Mount Road, London E4, 89 The Crescent, London N15, 1887, artisan, 1933–39, 3285745, November 1933 (from England), yes, yes

Rahmann, Karl, –, Manchester, 1905, teacher, 1936–39, 2928120, May 1933, no, yes

Rangs, Hildegard, 21 Regent's Park Road, London NW1, 1914, secretary, 1937–39, 7054043, June 1939 (from England), yes, no

Recke, Adelbert von, 46 Cleveland Square, London W2, 1907, student, 1931–32, 359744, November 1930, no, no

Reger, Karl Friedrich, –, –, 1910, student, 1934–35, 1665348, April 1933, no, no

Reichardt, Charlotte, 64 Compayne Gardens, London NW6, 1903, –, 1933–35, 1584463, May 1933 (from England), no, no

Renz, Paul Otto, 29 Leinster Gardens, London W2, 1914, clerk, 1935–39, 3709021, April 1936 (from England), no, yes

Reupke, Wilhelm, 59 Coleridge Road, London E17, 1901, teacher, 1934–39, 2760417, October 1934 (from England), yes, no

Ribbentrop, Joachim von, 9 Carleton House Terrace, London SW1, 1893, diplomat, 1936–38, 1199927, May 1932, no, no

Richter, Bruno, 1 Lyndhurst Road, London NW3, 1897, journalist, 1937–39, 7054047, June 1939 (from England), yes, no

Richter, Reinhold, 9 Nevern Square, London SW5, 1911, clerk, 1937–38, 5518157, April 1938 (from England), no, no

Richthofen, Wilhelm von, Westbourne Terrace, London W2, 1888, unemployed, 1933–34, 738662, 1930, no, no

Rieckenberg, Theodor, 29 Elvendon Road, London N13, 1910, salesman, 1938–39, 6095774, August 1938 (from England), yes, no

Rieckhoff, Luise, 20 Beauchamp Place, London SW3, 1913, nanny, 1937–39, 5505753, February 1938 (from England), no, yes

Riede, Carl, 12 Claigmar Gardens, London N3, 1878, secretary, 1935–39, 3733661, August 1936 (from England), no, yes

Rintelen, Franz, –, –, 1878, navy (retired), 1932–39, 1347406, October 1932, yes, no

Rippe, Fritz, 5 Cleveland Terrace, London W2, 1891, teacher, 1934–35, 3280908, July 1933, no, no

Ritzel, Jean, 75 Cadogen Terrace, London E9, 1900, artisan, 1934–39, 2760585, October 1934 (from England, yes, no

Roder, Josephine, –, Hemel Hempstead, Hertfordshire, 1911, domestic, 1938–39, 6087356, July 1938 (from England), yes, no

Röhreke, Gustav, Cedars Road, London SW13, 1911, student, 1938–39, 7055029, August 1939 (from England), yes, no

Romahn, Emil, –, Kew, Surrey, 1916, laborer, 1939, 5384668, May 1937, yes, no

Rösel, Rudolf Gottfried, 17 Coville Terrace, London W11, 316 Coombe Lane, London SW20, 1900, journalist, 1930–39, 3398114, October 1933 (from England), no, no

Rudolph, Karl, –, Slough, Buckinghamshire, 1895, artisan, 1937–39, 5505764, February 1938 (from England), no, yes

Rudorff, Dagobert, Grafton St., London W1, Shewte Farm, London N1, 1898, engineer, 1933–39, 3285728, October 1933 (from England), yes, no

Rüssell, Anni, 8 Blockhed, London SE3, 1912, sales, 1936–39, 501457, May 1931, yes, no

Sack, Elfriede, –, –, 1913, nursery school teacher, 1933–35, 715616, November 1931, no, no

Sauer, Bruno, –, Wembley, Middlesex, 1879, artisan, 1936–38, 3733658, August 1936 (from England), no, yes

Sauerwein, August, 26 Eaton Rise, London W5, 1905, official, 1934–39, 267316, June 1930, no, no

Sauk, Bruno, 38 South Hill Park, London NW3, 1901, party official, 1934–39, 2759527, October 1934 (from England), no, yes

Schallies, Günther, 15 Wilton Road, London SW1, 1908, official, 1938–39, 630106, September 1931, no, no

Schatte, Ernst, 41 Portland St., London E1, 1911, cook, 1934–39, 3455490, June 1934 (from England), no, no

Scheck, Otto, 19 Finsbury Road, London N22, 179 Hendon Way, London NW2, 1910, artisan, 1934–39, 2760656, October 1934 (from England), yes, no

Schenke, Wolfgang E., –, –, 1914, journalist, 1937–39, 1328745, September 1932, yes, no

Schicht, Franz, –, Weybridge, Surrey, 1891, business, 1939, 7421471, February 1940 (from England), no, yes

Schild, Alexander, 9 Carleton House Terrace, London SW1, 1901, clerk, 1933–34, 1411408, April 1933, no, no

Schlattau, Hildegard, 7 Jacksons Lane, London N6, 23 Highpoint, North Hill, London N6, 1898, journalist, 1937, 5505755, February 1938 (from England), no, no

Schlick, Bruno, 11 Exeter Road, London E16, 1910, business, 1937–39, 5518168, April 1938 (from England), yes, no

Schlitter, Oskar, 25 The Grove, London SW10, 1904, diplomat, 1937–39, 3591227, December 1934, no, no

Schmidt, Barbara, –, –, 1908, domestic, 1937–39, 1473006, October 1933, no, no

Schmidt, Edgar, 168 Valley Road, London SW16, 1909, journalist, 1937–39, 5505756, February 1938 (from England), yes, no

Schmidt, Franz, –, –, 1911, artisan, 1935–39, 2054404, May 1933, yes, no

Schmidt, Karl Friedrich, 4 Clifton Grove, London E8, 1901, business, 1935–39, 3280743, July 1933, no, yes

Schmidt, Siebert, –, –, 1909, laborer, 1933–36, 622726, September 1931, no, no

Schmidt, Wilhelm, 138 Aldergate St., London EC1, 1884, business, 1934–39, 875692, April 1932, yes, no

Schmidt-Rex, Erich Walter, –, Carshalton, Surrey, 1892, pilot, 1935–39, 2592574, May 1933, no, yes

Schmitz, Josef, –, –, 1906, business, 1938–39, 2642153, May 1933, yes, no

Schmoll, Heinrich, –, Iver, Buckinghamshire, 1905, business, 1932–39, 5505757, February 1938 (from England), no, no

Schnadt, Friedrich Julius, 32 Pembridge Square, London W2, 1900, journalist, 1938, 2998504, May 1933, no, no

Scholtz, Martin, German Hospital, Ritson Road, London E8, 1902, doctor, 1939, 3483920, May 1933, yes, no

Schön, Kreszenta, Bickenhall St., London W1, 1911, domestic, 1936–39, 3709025, April 1936 (from England), yes, no

Schönberger, Gustav, 19 Graham Road, London E8, 1898, pastor, 1933–39, 3285731, October 1933 (from England), yes, yes

Schott, Anton, 5 Mercer St., London W2, 1912, cook, 1939, 7077232, September 1939 (from England), yes, no

Schramm, Walter, –, Letchworth, Hertfordshire, 1895, photo chemist, 1937–38, 5505707, January 1938 (from England), no, yes

Schreppel, Bernhard, 60 Alexandra Crescent, Bromley, Kent, 1898, diplomat, 1926–37, 3398096, 1934, no, no

Schreyer, Walter, 34 St. George's Road, London SW1, 1880, business, 1933–39, 1745560, June 1933, yes, no

Schröder, Claus, –, –, 1911, clerk, 1934–37, 3228260, May 1933, no, no

Schröder, Franz Gerhard, 41 Redesdale St., London SW3, 1901, engineer, 1937–39, 5518674, March 1938 (from England), yes, no

Schröder, Hans, 11 Girdlers Road, London W14, 1912, party official, 1937–39, 3031230, May 1933, no, no

Schröder, Manfred von, –, –, 1914, student and business, 1934–36, 3391488, November 1933, no, no

Schuster, Theresia, –, Stanmore, Middlesex, 1911, domestic, 1935–39, 3657169, May 1935 (from England), yes, yes

Schwab, Agnes, Upwood Road, London SW16, 1912, domestic, 1936–39, 3445481, April 1934, yes, no

Schwarz, Arthur, 44 Birch Grove, London W3, 1912, business, 1936–39, 3733515, August 1936 (from England), no, yes

Seib, Walter, 19 York St., London W1, 1910, salesman, 1935–39, 2513868, August 1935 (from England), no, yes

Seibert, Theodor, 90 Twyford Ave., London W3, 1896, journalist, 1932–37, 3285932, October 1933 (from England), no, yes

Seligo, Hans, –, Abinger, Surrey, 1898, journalist, 1937–39, 3550125, February 1936, no, yes

Seligo, Irene, –, Abinger, Surrey, 1904, journalist, 1937–39, 7050571, May 1939 (from England), no, yes

Seydel, Hans, 75 Penshurst Gardens, London NW9, 1903, government official, 1934–37, 1547358, May 1933, no, yes

Sieker, Fritz, 9 Carleton House Terrace, London SW1, 1902, domestic, 1937–38, 989260, May 1932, no, no

Sommer, Ernst, 106 Norfolk Road, London E8, 1902, teacher, 1935–36, 3037812, May 1933, no, no

Staden, Otto von, 25 The Chase, London SW16, 1918, clerk, 1938–39, 4183926, May 1937, no, no

Stadler, Otto, 76 Deodar Road, London SW15, 1908, journalist, 1937–39, 6096152, August 1938 (from England), no, yes

Stamm, Wilhelm, 36 Claremont Road, London W13, 1914, business, 1932–33, 1276440, November 1932 (from England), no, no

Stein, Bruno, 104 Leander Road, London SW2, 1909, domestic, 1937–39, 7421524, February 1940 (from England), yes, no

Steinbrücker, Gerhard, 21–23 Churchfield Road, London W13, 1914, –, 1934–35, 3452971, May 1934 (from England), no, no

Steinmetz, Ludwig Max, 34 Castlebar Road, London W5, 1910, business, 1937–39, 3452963, May 1934, yes, yes

Stelmach, Eduard, Savoy Hotel, Strand, London WC2, 1913, hotel management, 1937–38, 5505758, February 1938 (from England), no, no

Stocky, Julius, –, –, 1913, business, 1938–39, 6096155, August 1938 (from England), yes, no

Stoldt, Adelbert, 17 Manville Road, London SE17, 1910, teacher, 1939, 4802169, May 1937, no, yes

Straede, Wolfgang, 132 Charing Cross Road, London WC2, 1906, journalist, 1937–39, 6087353, July 1938 (from England), no, yes

Studnitz, Hans Georg, 52 Ebury Mews, London SW1, 1907, journalist, 1938–39, 2849897, May 1933, no, no

Sturm, Emil, 167 Queen's Road, London N4, Nunhead Lane, London SE15, 1905, business, 1933–39, 1751582, July 1933 (from England), yes, yes

Sziefuss, Kurt, 71 Westmere Drive, London NW7, 1902, artisan, 1937–39, 4789378, December 1937 (from England), yes, yes

Tancré, Hans, 11A Ewelme Road, London SE23, 1911, clerk, 1938–39, 6087601, July 1938 (from England), no, no

Templin, Heinz, –, –, 1910, clerk, 1936–38, 2645233, May 1933, no, no

Thiemann, Ulrich, –, –, 1912, –, 1938–39, 533133, April 1931, yes, no

Thorner, Heinz, 9 Carleton House Terrace, London SW1, 1912, diplomat, 1937–38, 562124, June 1931, no, no

Thost, Hans Wilhelm, 73 Vineyard Hill Road, London SW19, 316 Coombe Lane, London SW20, 1899, journalist, 1930–35, 140611, July 1929, no, no

Toggenburg, Paul von, 18 Aubrey Walk, London W8, 1904, journalist, 1938–39, 3592614, December 1934, no, yes

Tonn, Eva, 7 Museum Mansion, Great Russell St., London WC1, 1908, journalist, 1936–39, 3657173, May 1935, no, no

Tonn, Günther, 7 Museum Mansion, Great Russell St., London WC1, 1893, journalist, 1936–39, 3285748, November 1933, no, yes

Tonnies, Norbert, 6 Lawrence St., London SW3, 1914, journalist, 1936–38, 5311554, May 1937 (from England), no, yes

Treger, Adolf, 11 Honor Oak Road, London SE23, 35B London Road, London SE23, 1887, clerk, 1933–39, 3398116, January 1934 (from England), no, no

Uhlemann, Joachim, –, –, 1909, clerk, 1938–39, 2554517, August 1935, yes, no

Vaupel, Walter, 7 Culmington Road, W13, 1913, clerk, 1934–39, 3398079, January 1934, yes, no

Velhagen, Adolf, 9 Carleton House Terrace, London SW1, 1906, diplomat, 1938–39, 5598237, April 1938, no, no

Villinger, R. H., 26 Eton Ave., London NW3, 1906, domestic, 1933, 1746727, June 1933 (from England), no, no

Vincenz, Rudolf, 9 Carleton House Terrace, London SW1, 1904, domestic, 1937, 5505578, January 1938 (from England), no, no

Vogel, Emil, Basil Street Hotel, London SW3, 1908, student, 1936–37, 3106500, May 1933, no, no

Vogel, Georg, Dover Hill Road, London SW15, 1903, diplomat, 1937–39, 3773811, January 1937, no, no

Vogler, Emma, 4 All Souls Place, London W1, 1908, housewife, 1932–39, 1201045, August 1932 (from England), yes, yes

Vogler, Oskar, 4 All Souls Place, London W1, 1907, business, 1932–39, 1201245, August 1932 (from England), yes, yes

Vogt, Werner, –, Isleworth, Surrey, 1900, business, 1938–39, 7077235, September 1939, yes, no

Vorlaufer, Adele, 65 Thistle Grove, London SW10, 1905, social worker, 1935–39, 3510914, January 1936 (from England), yes, no

Voss, Edgar, 9 Carleton House Terrace, London SW1, 1914, clerk, 1939, 7906314, July 1939 (from England), no, no

Vossmeyer, Johann, –, Richmond, Surrey, 1888, business, 1935–39, 3551564, February 1936 (from England), yes, no

Wagner, Wilhelm, –, –, 1896, business, 1937, 3752042, October 1936, no, no

Wallfeld, Karl W., 9 Carleton House Terrace, London SW1, 1901, diplomat, 1939, 82138, March 1928, no, no

Walter, Julie, 6 Holly Park Gardens, London N3, 1911, domestic, 1934–39, 2801181, October 1934 (from England), no, no

Wappler, Hiltrud, 92 Maida Vale, London W9, 1915, –, 1936–37, 3783189, March 1937 (from England), no, no

Wassermann, Johannes, 37 Frederick St., London WC1, 1909, student, 1932, 669935, November 1931, no, no

Weber, Brunhilde, 18 Cheviot Gardens, London NW2, 1912, –, 1932–33, 1117565, June 1932 (from England), no, no

Weber, Edith, –, –, 1912, –, 1938–39, 3709497, April 1936, yes, no

Weber, Georg, –, –, 1913, baker, 1933, 1125184, May 1932, no, no

Weber, Walter Maria, Highdown Road, London SW15, 1899, diplomat, 1934–39, 4009188, August 1937 (from England), no, no

Wegener, Alfons, –, Welwyn Garden City, Hertfordshire, 1905, teacher, 1933–39, 3285738, October 1933 (from England), yes, yes

Weger, Eduard, 111 Wilberforce Road, London N4, 1913, cook, 1934–39, 3401223, March 1934 (from England), yes, no

Wehrhan, Fritz, 19 Beverley Road, London SW13, 1872, pastor, 1933–39, 3453529, May 1934 (from England), yes, no

Weidemann, Herbert, –, Sidcup, 1911, cook, 1933–39, 2760565, October 1934 (from England), no, no

Weinert, Joachim, German Hospital, Ritson Road, London E8, 1910, doctor, 1939, 4579959, May 1937, no, no

Weissenborn, Dora, 71B DuCane Court, London SW17, 1893, secretary, 1938–39, 3591210, December 1934 (from England), no, no

Weitbrecht, Wolfgang, 40 Dorchester St., London N1, 1909, engineer, 1935–39, 3231811, May 1933, yes, yes

Welck, Wolfgang, 10 Lowndes Square, London SW1, 1901, diplomat, 1938–39, 2549805, August 1935, no, no

Wels, Galli, 54 Kensington Gardens Square, London W2, 1913, student, 1934–36, 3657171, May 1935 (from England), no, no

Wendt, Lothar, German Hospital, Ritson Road, London E8, 1907, doctor, 1936–38, 3762753, December 1936 (from England), no, no

Wenk, Hermann, –, –, 1905, clerk, 1937–39, 3452456, May 1934, yes, no

Westfehling, Ilse, 10 Avenue Crescent, London W3, 1912, teacher, 1934–37, 2759017, October 1934 (from England), no, no

Wetzel, Erich, 6 Nicoll Road, London NW10, 1890, engineer, 1938–39, 5505761, February 1938 (from England), no, no

Widenmann, Helene, 30 Ashburn Place, London SW7, 1907, secretary, 1937–39, 5518164, April 1938 (from England), no, no

Wiebeck, Theodor, 25 Cancell Road, London SW9, 1906, journalist, 1938–39, 712288, November 1931, no, no

Wihl, Barbara, 124 Tulse Hill, London SW2, 219 Knightsbridge, London SW1, 1907, cook, 1933–39, 3285758, November 1933 (from England), yes, yes

Willnow, Erich, 48 Argyle Road, London W13, 1895, consular official, 1935–39, 3709277, April 1936 (from England), no, no

Wilmsen, Günther, –, Bromley, Kent, 1908, teacher, 1936–39, 3402579, February 1934, yes, yes

Wiltschi, Juliana, 45 Hyde Park, London W2, 1903, domestic, 1938–39, 7054045, June 1939 (from England), yes, no

Winkler, Hans, 44 Powls Square, London W11, 1915, journalist, 1935–38, 3771543, December 1936 (from England), no, no

Winter, Ellen-Ursula, –, Staines, Middlesex, 1908, secretary, 1934–39, 867631, November 1931, no, no

Winter, Kurt, –, Kew, Surrey, 1912, student, 1936–37, 3783340, March 1937 (from England), no, no

Wittmann, Gertrude, –, –, 1913, student, 1934–37, 1789046, July 1933, no, no

Woehrmann, Ernst, 9 Carleton House Terrace, London SW1, 1888, diplomat, 1936–38, 4789453, December 1937 (from England), no, no

Wogram, Eberhard, 60 Woodstock Road, London W4, 1911, railway inspector, 1936–39, 3751896, October 1936 (from England), no, no

Wolf, Johanna, 1 Linden Gardens, London W2, 1896, domestic, 1934–39, 4789376, December 1937 (from England), no, no

Wolff, Lotte, Highwood Hill, London N7, 51 Queen's Gardens, London W2, 1910, –, 1934–38, 3401215, March 1934 (from England), no, no

Wolff-Metternich, Peter von, –, –, 1915, student, 1939, 5839909, May 1937, yes, no

Woltmann, Gerhard, 46 Abbey Road, London NW8, 1913, business, 1939, 2864504, May 1933, yes, no

Wriedt, Rose-Maria, –, –, 1905, housewife, 1937–39, 921457, February 1932, yes, no

Wunderer, Rolf, 46 Cleveland Square, London W2, 1910, business, 1931–32, 174340, December 1929, no, no

Wurm, Margot, –, Stanmore, Middlesex, 1903, domestic, 1935–39, 3657170, May 1935 (from England), yes, no

Zech, Theodor, 7 Holly Park Gardens, London N3, 67 Hatton Garden, London EC1, 20 Colville Terrace, London W2, 1897, business, 1935–39, 2518260, August 1935 (from England), yes, no

Zinzow, Ilse, 55 Haverstock Hill, London NW3, 15 Carleton Road, London SW15, 1903, secretary, 1933–37, 429623, January 1931, no, no

Zitzewitz, Ernst Bodo von, 2 Mansfield St., London W1, 1910, economist, 1932–39, 1232063, September 1932 (from England), yes, yes

Zwanzig, Walter, 4 Vaughan Ave., London NW4, 1897, engineer, 1931–38, 3452964, May 1934 (from England), no, yes

# INDEX

273